Boom!

How Jürgen Klopp's Explosive
Liverpool Thrilled Europe

Paul Tomkins, Chris Rowland, Daniel Rhodes,
Andrew Beasley (and more).

A Tomkins Times' Book
www.tomkinstimes.com

For Isabella and Jacob

Contents

ACKNOWLEDGMENTS

First of all, a massive thank-you to Chris and Daniel for their hard work on this book, and to Andrew, who became a weekly columnist for the site this season.

In addition, a big thank-you to all of *The Tomkins Times'* subscribers who contributed to the book, and to Anthony Stanley and Mick Thomas for checking over the final draft. Thank you to all the TTT subscribers and benefactors in general, who help keep the site afloat and allow us to produce quality content free of advertising, clickbait and advertorials, and who create a friendly and intelligent community on the site.

Paul Tomkins, May 31st 2018

Introduction

So, it all came apart in the final half of the final game of the season; although for the underdogs in red it had already become an even bigger mountain to climb when, in the first half, Sergio Ramos performed a move – one that has been described by mixed martial arts and judo experts as deliberate and illegal (because of its potential to seriously injure) – on Mo Salah to remove Liverpool's most potent threat from the game (and, for good measure, then elbowed Loris Karius in the face, off the ball, just minutes before the keeper made his first blunder). Liverpool's young and inexperienced team had looked more than a match for Real Madrid's football, easily out-shooting them (9:2) when Salah was on the pitch – but were not a match for the underhand tactics; nor their insanely big squad, whose wages are funded by a bank loan, as if even with their humungous turnover they still choose to shop on credit. At 1-1 Madrid brought on a player who cost a world-record fee. Welcome to modern football, ladies and gentleman.

For Madrid to be the favourites – the monied, bankrolled team club whose squad costs and wage bill absolutely dwarfs Liverpool's three-to-one – and still have to resort to taking out the Reds' best player (and trying to injure the Reds' goalkeeper) makes for, I feel, a pyrrhic victory that will be remembered as a point where the modern game reached a new low; just as the great Zinedine Zidane is partially remembered for his infamous headbutt in a World Cup final, his team sullied their reputation on the world stage, winning with what in boxing would be several low blows. Spanish football wowed the world a decade ago, but with its glorious Catalan heartbeat. Ramos was part of that success, too – its steely core – but here, as he has on many occasions in the past, he just played dirty.

With all their advantages of money and experience, it was as if Goliath, as he watched David swing his little sling of rocks, wheeled out the three giant trebuchets and launched a torrent of unholy missiles. When the underdog plays dirty (not that Liverpool ever do under Jürgen Klopp) you might not like it but you might understand it; when the bloated giant does so, it seems nothing but distasteful. (The fact that Graeme Souness kicked a few people 40 years ago seems to be a recurring theme from some neutrals, but that was 40 years ago. And in fairness, most neutrals seemed to think that Ramos' actions ruined the Reds' chances.)

Gareth Bale's stunning overhead kick was worthy of winning any game, but it was achieved only after Salah was sent to hospital.

It proved a bitterly disappointing way to lose the final, with Karius' errors so costly, albeit arriving at a point where he'd been having a good game (before Ramos' assault). In line with team orders – orders that had taken

Liverpool to the final in the first place – Karius was trying to keep the tempo up, and in the process, was not as careful as he should have been; but a goalkeeper who takes his time only slows the game down. Liverpool needed it to be super-fast to succeed.

Sadio Mané's equaliser proved short-lived – a brief moment of hope – but it's worth remembering that Liverpool had been the better side when he was joined on the other flank by Salah, as the main reason the Reds made the final – the balance of the attacking trident – was partially blunted. Ramos not only removed Liverpool's main goal threat – Europe's 2nd top-scorer after the best player in the world, Lionel Messi – but he halved the searing pace he and his Real Madrid teammates were clearly so scared of, and killed the Reds' counter-attacking verve. With Alex Oxlade-Chamberlain also out injured – coincidentally, also by an opponent falling on him (albeit that time a clear accident) – only one of the club's three quickest attackers was on the pitch after the 32nd minute. Liverpool players' belief clearly faded, and why wouldn't it? There would have been no comeback in Istanbul without Steven Gerrard, and here, what could have been the Mo Salah Final was pulled from underneath us all, as Ramos fell on top of him with that illicit grip.

But hell, *what a ride to get there in the first place.*

So, let's go back to the start ….

Step This Way…

A time machine awaits; enter, if you will, and head back to the summer of 2017. Liverpool's transfer plans are in tatters, up in smoke and wafting signals of concern: Virgil van Dijk, the commanding centre-back the club clearly needs, is being held against his will – or rather, *to his contract* (those old-fashioned notions) – by Southampton, and the main midfield target, Naby Keita, is equally keen to join the Reds – but his club are hanging onto him too, tooth and nail.

Philippe Coutinho, mirroring those players in the football food chain, hands in a transfer request, and, having apparently gone on strike in August (or at least, had one of those wonderfully timed tactical injuries; the bad back is usually hard to detect on scans) will do so again in the winter, and will be gone in January; no one replacing him when he jets off to Catalonia. So far, all pretty concerning.

Elsewhere, Adam Lallana and Nathaniel Clyne will essentially miss the whole season – although Danny Ings will at least return for a fair chunk of the run-in, after over two years out with back-to-back cruciate ligament injuries. Into the club will come Chelsea and Arsenal rejects, Mo Salah and Alex Oxlade-Chamberlain respectively, for fees that some observers find too steep. To many, things are falling apart.

Joining them, a bargain buy from relegated Hull City, who appeases very few of the social media warriors who make so much noise. Daniel Sturridge – virtually the club's sole source of goals when Klopp took charge in October

2015 – will barely feature, and be loaned to West Bromwich Albion, where he will barely feature. Promising but as-yet-unremarkable striker Divock Origi – one of the few Liverpool players to reach double-figures in goals (twice) in recent seasons – will spend the campaign on loan in Germany, while Emre Can's season will prematurely end as his contract dissolves to dust. Last season's club player of the year, and the Reds' top scorer, Sadio Mané, will be very bright in the first few games, but then get the entire Premier League season's *one and only* sending off for a high boot, and after suspension return with his confidence shot to pieces.

Meanwhile, Jürgen Klopp will vacillate between two unpopular goalkeepers – Simon Mignolet's impressive form at the end of the previous season a distant memory as he loses his confidence, and Loris Karius a fellow lightning rod for criticism. Stationed in front of Mignolet or Karius will be the much-maligned Dejan Lovren (whom Klopp will stick by, through thick and thin), and, with a severe injury crisis in midfield, the Reds will end the season relying on James Milner and Jordan Henderson in the heart of the team. The goals will have to come from Roberto Firmino, a centre-forward who is "not a centre-forward", and who "doesn't score enough goals"; as well as from Mo Salah, who seems to remain typecast – by some – as the player he was at Chelsea four years earlier, where he scored just twice. Alberto Moreno – a player who perhaps draws more angst from fans than any other – will start the season by retaining his old left-back slot, while a teenager – along with a player just a few months older – will vie for the role of right-back; as, up front, the young striker, Dominic Solanke, will fail to score a goal in his first 25 appearances for the Reds. To make matters worse, Liverpool face a top-four German side in the Champions League qualifier, as if the start to the season – with four Big Six encounters in the first nine fixtures – couldn't be more daunting.

Klopp's men will overcome Hoffenheim – I'll allow you that much information – but will draw the opening Premier League game away to Watford, and also conjure disappointing stalemates in the first two Champions League games, at home to Sevilla and away at Spartak Moscow, to make qualification from the group look difficult. Early in the league campaign the Reds will lose 5-0 at Man City and 4-1 at Spurs. The last time Liverpool lost by a five-goal margin in the league the manager only lasted eight more games.

With regard to getting decisions from referees, Liverpool will have its worst season in its entire history, eclipsing 1904 for the season when, when balanced out together, the club wins its fewest number of league penalties compared against the number of goals scored, and concedes the most in relation to the number of goals conceded. Liverpool will concede twice as many league penalties as they win, and the only sendings off in games involving them will be theirs. Spurs will win more league penalties in a ten-minute spell at Anfield than Liverpool manage all season long. And what penalties they do win they will mostly miss. Penalties for clearly accidental handball will become almost obsolete (only six were awarded across all teams in the Premier League all season, which includes *deliberate* handballs too), yet Liverpool will concede two within a week in Europe. Crystal Palace and Everton will win three times as many penalties as Liverpool in the league.

Liverpool's excellent league record against the other members of the Big Six (and against Everton) – the foundations of Klopp's two league seasons to date – will crumble. In the four league games against the two most hated rivals – the blues from Merseyside and the reds from Manchester – Liverpool will end up winless. Late leads against Arsenal, Chelsea, Everton and Spurs will be thrown away. Liverpool will also fail to beat West Brom across three games, even though West Brom are the worst side in the league.

Then, just as the season is approaching its climax, Željko Buvač – the man Klopp calls the best coach in the world, and (very modestly on his own part) the brains behind the operation for their 17 years together – will depart the club under a cloud; cited as personal reasons, with the club claiming that he will return in due course, but talk spreads to a bust-up between the admittedly combustible pair (as has happened in the past, albeit with swift reconciliation). And this comes after the highly-rated Pepijn Lijnders – seen by many as a future star of coaching – leaves to take a managerial job in his native Holland.

With all this admittedly *selective* information, you'd probably be putting your money on Klopp receiving his P45 and heading back to Germany; or at the very least, you may see a mountain for the (mountainous) man to climb. With all these details then you would not be surprised if it was an utter disaster of a season. It has all the hallmarks: "best" player departing; key transfer targets missed; senior coaching staff departures; and absolutely no favours from referees. Liverpool will concede five goals against Sevilla over two legs, and six against Roma.

Okay, now fast forward to late April, and try to comprehend that Liverpool – unbeaten in the Champions League all season – will be 5-0 up after 63 minutes of the first leg of the semi-final, having just knocked out a rampantly brilliant and incredibly expensive Man City (who are breaking all domestic records) 5-1 on aggregate; won 5-0 in the first-leg of the last 16 at Porto; and put seven with no reply past both Maribor and Spartak Moscow in the group stages. Liverpool will utterly smash the English record for most goals scored in a Champions League season, and go on to break the *entire* Champions League record; and it's front three will edge towards 100 goals between them. With games to spare – and having played ten fewer than in 2001 – the Reds will break their post-millennial record of 127 goals in a season, set when the Reds played all those cup games under Gérard Houllier.

Yeah, I know; it's a work of fiction. Right?

Bobby Firmino will be a goal away from equalling Michael Owen's best-ever season, and Mo Salah will be four away from matching Ian Rush's club record of 47 in a season; both Firmino and Salah scoring just a single penalty each.

Severely lacking match fitness, Virgil van Dijk will belatedly arrive, in January – for a staggering £75m (although this is only roughly half of what Man United paid for Rio Ferdinand in 2002, once football inflation is applied), and the giant Dutchman will certainly make his presence known. James Milner will be in the team, in part, because of injuries, but then he'll enjoy a grand renaissance; nothing remotely *boring* about his season. Alex Oxlade-Chamberlain – in an Arsenal side thumped 4-0 by the Reds in August – will swap allegiances days later and after a tentative start, become a real favourite at Liverpool, until his knee ligaments give out in the Champions League semi-final. Andy Robertson is another who struggles for game-time early on, but then becomes a massive cult hero. Loris Karius has a spell of form so good that the fans' talk of the necessity to sign a new goalkeeper is put on hold.

Context is everything. Now, as I've been noting for over a decade, Liverpool are not part of the elite rich clubs in England; rich in heritage, undoubtedly, but not money, ever since multi-multi-billionaires were allowed to 'financially dope' the game. So expectations have to be lower than in the halcyon days – whilst, at the same time, not lowered to the point of accepting genuine mediocrity (Roy Hodgson's mission statement, if you go back and listen to his pre- and-post-game comments, such as not wanting to get thrashed by Middle-Eastern minnows in preseason and hoping not to lose 6-0 away at Man City, and talking about how formidable bottom-tier Northampton Town would be ahead of losing to bottom-tier Northampton Town).

Despite being the 9th-richest club in the world, the Reds only have the 5th-biggest budget in England. And with Spurs leapfrogging Liverpool in terms of on-pitch performance during the fading days of Brendan Rodgers' tenure, there are essentially six clubs contesting those crucial top four places each year. Each season two have to miss out, and this limits the European experience most clubs can rack up; as well as meaning destinations like Real Madrid, Barcelona, PSG and Bayern Munich are more attractive to top players, because as well as the financial might, there's the virtual guarantee of participation in Europe's ultimate competition, which could one day morph into a Super League at the rate so many domestic leagues outside of England are being hogged by one team. The more cash these clubs rake in from Europe, the more they can pay for players, and so a virtuous cycle just gets reinforced by UEFA's Financial Fair Play rules, albeit the alternative was clubs being bankrolled by billions from oil barons. Liverpool's place within this hierarchy is slightly unstable, although it somehow manages to punch above its weight in Europe, with five finals in the past 17 seasons; this current season perhaps the biggest surprise since Rafa Benítez took half a team to

Istanbul and had to rely on the likes of Djimi Traore, Milan Baros and Djibril Cissé.

Indeed, as I said throughout Benitez's tenure, in various books and online articles – the aim for Liverpool, in this new financial landscape, has to be to be competitive in May; to have the season not be over when evening games in the spring kick off not with floodlights but with the sun still in the sky; to reach cup finals in Europe, whilst nestled within the top four.

And this last part is no mean feat, either. My research shows that in the Premier League era, cup runs tend to, on average, lower a club's league position by several points and *at least* one place; unless the clubs were Manchester United and Chelsea during their periods of peak wealth, 2004-2010. One of the Rich Three (the two Manchester clubs and Chelsea) having a domestic cup run (which might be just four or five games) doesn't do much damage, but having two cup runs can; especially if one is in Europe. The smaller the club, the more a cup run can take out of a season, when compared against league performance the year before and the year after, and also when compared against expectations based on their financial ranking. You only have to look at how teams end up resting players for the cups when the season get serious.

Juggling everything – like Manchester United did in 1999, and Liverpool did in 1984 – is just not possible anymore. Chelsea finished 6th when winning the Champions League in 2012, to show that competing on two major fronts is very difficult indeed, at a time when FFP rules started to make the first dents in their spending. And when they won the title in 2017 *it was without any European competition whatsoever*, just as Leicester had experienced a year earlier (as unexplainable as that success was in almost every other sense). Liverpool's only title challenge since 2009 came in 2014, when there was also no European football; indeed, no cup football at all, in reality. All of which puts 2009 into even sharper focus, when the Reds finished 2nd with 86 points, with a small squad compared to the richer clubs, and played both Real Madrid and Chelsea twice in the knockout phases of the Champions League.

What marked out Jürgen Klopp's success at Dortmund was how he took a team reeling from near-bankruptcy, and brought in cheap, obscure players like Robert Lewandowski, Ilkay Gündogan, Mats Hummels, Neven Subotic, Marco Reus and Shinji Kagawa – as well as homegrown talents including Mario Götze and Nuri Şahin– and elevated them to back-to-back German championships and a Champions League final. With clever scouting and elite coaching – and a couple of years to configure everything – he was able to smash the living daylights out of Bayern Munich's financial advantage ... until Bayern started simply poaching their best players. No team cycle lasts forever, but Klopp did something truly remarkable in Germany, and in England already averages a cup final per season, along with significant league improvements.

About This Book

This book is a contemporaneous account of the unfolding of the season – of the multifaceted aspects of this thrilling campaign, written in near real-time. It centres around a series of 'diaries' from Liverpool supporters – from those hailing from the city, and from much further afield (around the UK, with others jetting in from Scandinavia, America and Australia) – as they travel to watch the team all over Europe; some seeing their first-ever game, whilst at the other end of the scale, the reflections of two fans who first went to Anfield 57 and 59 years ago respectively. All this is interspersed with my observations on the football, along with input from *The Tomkins Times'* key contributors, as events played out. In addition, we have written some detailed reflections on the season specifically for *Boom!*, penned as the campaign drew to its dramatic conclusion.

This book also includes some below-the-line comments taken from the site, given that these can often be better than a lot of articles you might read elsewhere. We hope this all adds up to a unique and varied look at Liverpool's return to the top table of European football, even if it's impossible to tell the *full* story of such an eventful 12 months.

As a very brief history to the uninitiated, *The Tomkins Times* (TTT) evolved from my own personal semi-paywalled blog in 2009 – hence the site's eponymous title – to a small, niche business that favours quality over quantity. (That said, in-depth reads are quite common, so the *word count* certainly isn't tailored to the short attention span. But this book has a lot to cover, and as well as wanting to be as concise as possible, we don't want too many trees to be hacked down for its printing.)

Although initially my own small site, TTT soon went onto employ writers and editors in the form of Chris Rowland, Daniel Rhodes and Andrew Beasley, plus tactical guru Mihail Vladimirov, until he was poached for a role within professional football (at least three of our writers have gone on to work within the game), as well as technical and support staff.

Aside from the contributions of our paid staff, many match-going subscribers voluntarily shared their experiences at games home and away, all of which was initially taking place before we realised how exciting this season could eventually become; after all, the Reds' start to the league campaign wasn't the best – Liverpool were 9th in October – and the first two Champions League games ended in disappointing draws.

However, by the turn of the year it looked as if something exciting might be afoot. So we thought it was worth pulling all these accounts together, along with excerpts from all areas of the site that would make for an interesting cohesive narrative of a remarkable season as it played out before our eyes. As with my very first book in 2005, the idea – commenced in the winter – was to capture a season, without really believing that a Champions League final was on the horizon.

These submissions have been tidied up a little, with typos and grammatical slips (hopefully) removed. And a few clarifications have been made, in instances where a reference would have been fresh in the readers' minds at the time but less obvious many months later. However, none of the meanings have been changed, and all conclusions are from the time in question. We think it gives a flavour of what *The Tomkins Times* is all about, and hopefully captures a very exciting time in the club's history.

I also think it's fair to say that we take a holistic approach to football writing; mixing the passion of the game, and what we see with our own eyes – and feel in our hearts, and in the churn of our stomachs – with the kind of insight that only statistics and analytics can provide (in the way that anything counterintuitive is only usually highlighted by data; such as, "The big clubs get all the decisions" – an oft-cited complaint by the followers of smaller clubs – being countered by the fact that Big Six were awarded 50% fewer Premier League penalties this season than the mighty sextet of Crystal Palace, Everton, Brighton, Watford, Leicester and West Ham).

We know that while statistics can be used to mislead, the key is to interpret them properly and honestly. Of course, no statistic can capture the joy of Salah scoring a crucial goal, or Firmino smashing in another no-look finish. Which is why we don't write dryly about stats, and instead, try to paint the whole picture.

Thank you for joining us on this journey. Buckle up – it's gonna be a wild one ...

Summer 2017

Daniel Rhodes, June 21st, 2017

What happens when you spend all season looking at and analysing Liverpool's transfer targets, mining video clips, compiling stats, even selecting a full XI based on transfer targets only to be fooled when the club decides to sign an old flame? You look stupid, that's what. Alongside Firmino, this one has been more under-the-radar than most of the Reds' recent transfers.

He dribbles, he creates, he gets into the box, he shoots, he scores.

The fee is believed to be around the current record for the Reds when they signed Andy Carroll; however, Paul (and Graeme Riley) adjusted Carroll's fee for football inflation and found, in today's money, that Big Andy 'cost' in excess £90m instead. Which makes the Salah deal look like a bargain, even if it does exceed our current non-inflated record. The negotiations may have taken too long for the fans whose attention span barely reaches beyond that of a gnat. But it always looked like getting done, without any other clubs even in the running.

It may have taken three years longer than we initially thought, yet he has undoubtedly improved as a player in the intervening years so the wait was worth it: Mohamed Salah, welcome to Liverpool.

Paul Tomkins , July 13th, 2017

Now, all new signings can only be discussed *in theory*. They don't necessarily or automatically bring their best traits – sometimes they fail. But we must assume that they can offer the very things that brought them to the club in the first place.

First of all, Mohamed Salah offers exactly what Sadio Mané does – goals (up to 20 a season), and perhaps more importantly, searing pace – and so that not only doubles that particular kind of threat, it also clearly improves the likelihood of Liverpool never having to field a team devoid of pace in wide attacking areas.

Salah is not cover for Mané, but Liverpool should be massively improved by having more quick options. To have just one of Mané or Salah fit would be a big improvement on what happened at times last season. Of course, both could end up injured, but then all 25 players could end up injured if an asteroid strikes Melwood.

Also, will Mané now get even more room if Salah is in the team? Teams certainly can't switch their quickest full-back onto Mané's flank now.

… This Liverpool team is a year older and a year wiser. Perhaps they can be like Spurs last season. The London club made four first-team additions, but three were all but wasted (although they could yet come good). Only Victor Wanyama added anything to their campaign. But the rest of the team were a year older, a year smarter, and the manager's methods were a year further into being understood and drilled to perfection. Without really changing much, other than ageing by a year, they went from just over 70 points to 86.

Daniel Rhodes, July 20th, 2017
For a snip, Andy Robertson immediately solves one of Liverpool's biggest weaknesses last season. We need to be patient with him. The article by Roy Henderson on *The Anfield Wrap* website gives me confidence though, because he used "to run games" from left-back, at such a young age. That just screams character and maybe even something a bit special. The proof, as ever with so many of our left-backs for decades, is in the pudding on the pitch.

The Season Begins

Paul Tomkins, August 14th, 2017

I give opinions, such as saying – last summer – that Sadio Mané looked a great addition (people disagreed and said we'd never improve buying from a lowly club like Southampton), while 70 points, and finishing 3rd-5th, was my prediction for how things would pan out, assuming there were no unforeseen disasters. I was actually below on the points tally – my estimate proved pessimistic by almost 10%, even with an unforeseen winter injury crisis. But I got abuse last summer, and was told Liverpool would do well to finish mid-table with the signings made and the terrible state of the squad, and that I'm a horrible fucking "sunshiner" whose optimism is utterly unrealistic, and whose excuses allow FSG to buy cheap, crap players. After the defeat at Burnley a year ago there was an outrage as if the season was over. I got abuse for saying it wasn't over. I got abuse late last season for saying the club could still finish in the top four.

But now it's over after a draw on day one, away at Watford. Before that, it was over weeks ago, because of the transfer business.

I genuinely think that backing Jürgen Klopp with time and whatever money there is, gradually bringing through the exciting youngsters and keeping his overall vision – hard work, unity, fast football – is the best route to success. That doesn't mean success will therefore follow, because you can only plan for it, never guarantee it. And it's a hugely competitive league at the top right now.

The dread I felt when Watford equalised at the death was not for the lost two points, because you will drop points a third of the time even if you're champions (although it obviously stung to concede so late on), but more the dread of the uproar, the "FSG-out", the "Klopp doesn't know what he's doing", and so on. The must-win, *must-win* madness. It's the dread of the tumult; of being put in the endless repeat of a spin cycle. It's *Day Fucking One!* Just like it was *Minute Fucking One* (or two) in Istanbul when AC Milan took the lead. Which doesn't mean comebacks like that always happen (although they frequently do when it's 1-0, less so when it's 3-0); nor does it mean they cannot. Nothing is ever decided by less than three percent of the league season. While it's obviously better to win, opening days decide nothing.

Crystal Palace (H), August 19th, 2017
REDM

It's the first home match of the season and we leave the house at just after 06:30 to get the train to London Waterloo. Just over eight hours until kick off in one of those retro style 3pm Saturday fixtures. We are leaving even earlier than normal due to major renovation works at Waterloo. In the coming weeks, we will face closures at Euston and Liverpool Lime Street stations.

The planning for the trip starts with waiting for the announcements of which games are on TV. As soon as these are released, it's a rush to book train tickets before all seat reservations are gone and/or prices go through the roof.

Three o'clock kick-offs are pretty convenient for travelling up and down by train. Earlier kick-offs also work for the train but the atmosphere tends to be flat. Later kick-offs require a long drive by car, which is much less enjoyable.

I'm with my eight-year-old daughter. She is showing much more interest in Liverpool than her older brothers. However, her track record of going to games is mixed. Her first ever game was against a West Ham team that hadn't won at Anfield since the days of Bobby Moore. That all changed with a 3-0 win to the Hammers, and a few weeks later Brendan Rodgers was gone.

She then saw a relegation-bound Newcastle come from 2-0 down to draw before finally witnessing a Liverpool win last season in a stodgy 2-0 over the hapless combination of Sunderland and David Moyes. We were due to go to the last game of last season (vs Middlesbrough) but a tyre blow out on the M6 meant we spent the afternoon in a recovery truck and a Kwik-Fit waiting room. I'm a Richard Dawkins reading rationalist in everyday life – however, I can't help wondering whether her run of bad luck will continue.

We arrive in London and get the underground across to Euston. It starts to feel like going to a football match as we see Liverpool and Palace supporters in the concourse. We get on the train, stopping to explain to a naïve foreigner that his expensive train ticket didn't necessarily mean that he would get a seat but would entitle him to spend at least two hours squeezed into a corridor.

We get to our reserved seat. The carriage is very full, with a small group of Aussie Reds standing in the corridor by our seats. Glad as I am to have a reserved seat, I find the proximity of an Australian arse about six inches from my nose a bit off-putting. Luckily, the arse is perfectly behaved for the whole journey.

While my trip to the match is a long one, there are usually plenty of people on the train with much more involved trips. On previous trips, I've met many Norwegians in particular who travel to Anfield a few times every season.

The train arrives on time at around 11:20 at Lime Street. A quick trip to the Gents is enlivened by a drunken Red who thinks he has offended me with a comment on the way in. As he sways in the urinal next to me, I assure him there is no problem and silently hope he focuses more on the matter in hand. Fortunately, there is no splash back and I escape unscathed.

After killing some time in the city centre, we catch a bus to the ground where we grab some food and drink. The first match of the season allows us to get our first glimpse of new players in the flesh. We see Andy Robertson up close in the first half and he looks very impressive. Apart from his positive attacking contribution, he is generally where you would want him to be when Palace are attacking – which is often not the case with Alberto Moreno or indeed sometimes James Milner when they play left-back.

Consistent with the retro kick-off time, it's a fairly uneventful home win. After taking the lead, we are waiting for the clichéd "I reckon Palace will have one more big opportunity, Brian" moment but it never comes. A reasonably comfortable 1-0 at Anfield is a rarity these days and we leave happy, curse hopefully broken for good.

We do the journey in reverse and it all goes pretty smoothly. Some Palace fans decide to sing various charming ditties as we get off the train at Euston, inevitably including "You'll never get a job" to the tune of *You'll Never Walk Alone*. While I would hate some hippy-style brotherhood of football fans, I can never understand the attraction of taunting opponents about unemployment and deprivation. When I went to matches in the 1980s, I seem to remember it was from the likes of Chelsea primarily (getting £10 notes out their wallet and waving it at Liverpool fans as their supporters coach left Anfield). These days it seems to be anyone, including supporters from "proper" clubs like Palace and Newcastle, based in areas that aren't exactly without their own challenges.

Anyway, we are home before 11pm, just in time to catch some of Match of the Day. However, even in the absence of Alan Shearer on the panel, I fight a losing battle to stay awake until the Liverpool match is on.

Chris Rowland

Another season, another day out courtesy of Northern Rail. But there's something unusual about this first home league game – it kicks off at 3pm on a Saturday! Something we only managed twice in the league at home last season.

It means no anxiety about early trains or late trains. I can get there fine, and get back fine. Stress-free bliss. It means I catch the 10.06 to Manchester Victoria, and have 35 minutes to kill before the train to Lime Street. Just time for a coffee at the splendid Java Bar at the far end of the concourse. Beats Starbucks hands down for me. But it's hard to be in this part of Manchester, with the steps leading up to the still-closed Arena, steps I've been up and down many a time seeing Elbow, Rush, Muse and others, without thinking of that atrocity of human hate inflicted upon concert goers to see Ariana Grande that night of May 22nd 2017. Flowers, cards and bouquets offer a poignant reminder of the horror that occurred one night, right here.

The journey is as incident-free as I've ever had. Everything on time, and I arrive at Lime Street at 12.06.

The appointed meeting place is The Shakespeare in Williamson Square. Bob, the normal match day coordinator, is on holiday 'on a cruise' – we reckon he's on a narrowboat on the Rochdale canal! – so in his absence the selection of a decent pub has fallen into the wrong hands. Suffice it to say I wouldn't have chosen the Shakey – no cask beer and not much else. Modern, bright, utterly bland and featureless.

The preseason mood matches the surroundings – low key and downbeat. There is no seething hotbed of excitement here. It seems our failings in the transfer business and the Coutinho situation, allied to our match at Watford, have sucked away any optimism. There seems a widespread acceptance that we'll be worse than and finish lower than last season.

And as we move onto the Richmond and the Victoria Cross, we see Man Utd getting their second 4-0 win of the season and universally agree that it doesn't help us when they're doing well, it only adds to the pressure, and has a bearing on our own degree of feelgood.

Taxis to the match, and our driver has a blinder, getting us the closest to Anfield anyone has ever got, given all the pre-match side road closures.

The official site had dark warnings about new improved security measures, metal detectors in use etc so get there no later than 45 minutes before kick off. We approach our Kop turnstile at 14.40 and there is a queue of three in front of us. Straight in, before our circuitous route up the stairs to the top tier than back down one. We're not usually in this early!

The first half is tame, illuminated only by a series of fine crosses in from our new Scottish left-back. We wonder how Matip managed not to score from one of them, heading weirdly leftwards with miles of empty goal net in front of him. Nobody ever misses chances like that against us, notes a neighbour.

The first shout of "crab!" of the season from the other neighbour to my right greets Henderson's first sideways pass. There will be many more.

The crowd seems to have the same downbeat mood as was prevalent in our group. I also note how the Kop no longer responds to away fans and slap them down instantly as they used to. Palace fans sang "You're just a shit Steven Gerrard" to Henderson without retort. A guy behind shouted sullenly that they've never had a player as good as Steven Gerrard in their entire history, but they're not going to hear that 150 yards away.

I remember during last season's home game against Burnley, the Clarets' fans singing "you're not Danny Ings" to any Liverpool player who missed a chance. Then right at the end a Burnley player missed a good chance to equalise. The old Kop would have instantly sung "You're not Danny Ings" to them. But it didn't, and doesn't anymore, and I wonder what happened. The old 'it's nice to know you're here' when the away fans were finally heard after about an hour, that sort of thing. There was interplay between the fans, point and counterpoint, and it was better for it. It felt connected. Now it doesn't.

Afterwards we all trot out the clichés – "1-0 or 10-0, it's only three points", "a win's a win" etc etc. Back in town at the Grapes we bump into any number of the old boys we knew from the '70s, half a dozen or more that I haven't seen for years. We all agree the atmosphere these days is mostly shit.

14

Back to Lime Street clutching kebab – honestly, talk about behavioural remission! – and I'm on the 19:12 Transpennine Express to Newcastle – the one that doesn't stop 13 times between Liverpool and Manchester. In fact it doesn't stop at all until Manchester Victoria, where I get off and grab a quick half of Thornbridge Jaipur at the station bar before my connection back home – and that was on time too. By 21.11 I'm ready for my lift back home and ready to watch Match of the Day, and see BBC have made us the very last game – i.e. the least interesting of today's seven games. Less interesting than Bournemouth v Watford and Burnley v WBA. I marvel again at Joël Matip's miss, see how lucky we got with the goal, wonder just how many chances we had late on that they failed to show.

Not an epic day out, but a win's a win ….

Comment by "Divilmint", August 18th, 2017
I've been missing LFC all summer. Friendlies are like methadone. They're only acceptable when you can't get the real thing. When we miss the football over the summer we are missing the highs, the elation, those jump out of the chair, beer spilling, dog scaring, sudden, guttural, gleeful roar of victory moments. The electric buzz, the empowerment, the man hugs, the validation of a Red identity, the mano et mano, the mainlining adrenaline, seat of the pants, Mach-2 thrill ride of the thing. Football is a drug and if you care enough about it to pay someone to have a place to talk about it then you, I and all of us are junkies. We junkies were promised a fix. Well no we weren't actually promised a fix but with use of twisted junkie logic skewed by three months of cold turkey and acute performance anxiety it sure as hell felt like we'd been promised a fix. I was expecting ecstasy and instead it felt like I was force fed a bad acid trip with flashbacks of the team's least proud moments from the last year.

The problem wasn't with the team. It wasn't down to Klopp or Philgate, it was down to me and my unrealistic expectations of what being a football fan is. If mid-season we had come from behind away from home only to drop two points to an offside goal of course it would have stung. Not exactly the same I know but Man United away last season is my recent benchmark for that feeling. Sure I was angry and disappointed after that match but I never considered taking a season off football then even though it was a much bigger game. Saturday evening I wasn't sure I could be bothered with football anymore. I was seriously asking myself if a season long break would improve my quality of life. It had promised so much and delivered so little. I had worked myself into such a state of expectation that when I was brought down to earth with a bump, my arse was sore and I was deeply, deeply unhappy about it. Had I not been at work I'd have bitched and moaned to anyone who would have listened. Like any addict my arguments would not have been logical. They would be self serving, blaming of other people, disingenuous and possibly spiteful undertones.

Had I seen Shakespeare's ghost in my bad trip he no doubt would have chided me that the fault dear Divilmint is not in our stars but in ourselves. I'm human so I make mistakes. The fault in myself was to expect something divine from a bunch of people who are also human. I respectfully suggest that on Saturday I may not have been alone in this.

No one spends the summer pining for bad refereeing decisions, being out muscled and off the pace or looking forward to groaning at misplaced passes. We all know negatives will happen yet somehow we allow them to be whitewashed in a wave of our own optimistic expectation. When it comes to supporting LFC I have the emotional maturity of a 13 year old boy. Again I suspect I may not be the only one! I admire the work of Paul and others on here who have learned to temper their considerable passion with a streak of rationalism and can think through the emotional roller coaster whilst still enjoying the ride. I can't. I, like many others, have to get off the ride before I can sensibly reflect on it. That in my view is why Saturday was an emotional outlier and why it produced so much negativity from across the fanbase.

Paul Tomkins, August 22nd, 2017

All the negativity surrounding the Reds these past couple of weeks, and yet in eight unbeaten days the team scored three goals away in one game (and only drew due to a clear technical error when the officials got the rules wrong), became the first team to beat Hoffenheim at their place for 15 months, and deservedly (and finally) beat the biggest bogey team – the Double Bogey (*damn-you* Palace) – at Anfield; all achieved without Philippe Coutinho, Adam Lallana and Nathaniel Clyne, and in the case of the some of the games, Daniel Sturridge and Emre Can.

While one game doesn't define a season, the injuries – and the resting of five players – for the first home league fixture of the season was indicative of how much the squad has improved; especially without the best lock-picker, and arguably the second-most creative midfielder at the club, too. The XI didn't look *amazingly* strong, but it obviously wouldn't with so many missing. But it looked pretty good all the same.

Granted, it hasn't always been the Reds at their full-flowing best across these early matches, so maybe it's a good sign that so many chances have been created in the process.

It backs up my assertion, made a couple of weeks ago, that things were improving even without the new signings (which is not to say that new signings were not desirable, and still *aren't* desirable – merely that the club won't collapse if it cannot seal deals in what has become a complex market). And Liverpool "deserved" at least three goals in all three games, based on quality of chances and expected goals (xG) analysis.

I presented Trent Alexander-Arnold as one example of this 'development without purchasing', and lo and behold, he's now shining in the first team, whereas last season he was just making up the numbers, dipping his toe in the water to experience the harsh lessons that all young players need to endure. At 18, he not only played well in Germany, but did something hugely rare for an 18-year-old: he took, and scored, a vital free-kick, and did so not by luck, but with inch-perfect placement (as seen in the U23s last season – so it was no fluke).

And he's probably not even at 50% of what he can become with experience and with further physical strengthening (and maybe growing an inch or two before he hits 21). He will probably experience a dip this season, like all young players, but his best is now good enough to actually elevate the Reds' first team, not just desperately fill in during an injury crisis and hope for the best (which is how a lot of youngsters obviously get their first tastes of senior football). And if he has a dip, there are plenty of other options. Liverpool are not reliant on him.

Hoffenheim (H), August 23rd, 2017
Andrew Beasley
I have always held a strong affinity with the number 23. It's my day of birth, and then Robbie Fowler and Jamie Carragher both wore it with aplomb in my formative football years. Hell, I even once transferred out of a bad job into a better one on the 23rd floor. It just resonates with me, you know?

It's 1pm on the day of the match, and I'm about to get on a train. But not to Liverpool, that would be far too obvious. No, I am bound for Market Harborough.

Where? Oh yeah, Market Harborough. It's the kind of small town that you'll have been to once, but once only. You'll have a Market Harborough of your own, even if it's not this one.

The train journey passes pleasantly enough, thanks to good music (a playlist of my favourite Beatles songs) and a bad book (a trashy Daniel Craig biography I picked up at the library). As the train zooms through my home town of Kettering at 2pm, I ponder if it'll be another 12 hours until I'm back to stay at my parents' house. Spoiler alert: it was.

Anyway, Market Harborough is the current home of one Andrew Fanko (author of the site's perennial *Should They Stay or Should They Go* series). He meets me outside of the railway station, and thus begins an epic road trip. Our first stop is made to collect a certain Paul Tomkins. You may have heard of him. He's a strapping 6′ 2″ hunk (or so he told me to put here) and he has the tickets, so unfortunately we had to take him with us. Ah well.

We pick up Paul in another small Leicestershire town, Enderby. As our journey begins, he asks Andrew and I if we know what important criminal first is related to the town. We draw a blank, so he reveals that Colin Pitchfork, the first person *in the entire world* convicted of a crime based on DNA fingerprinting evidence, raped and murdered two girls in Enderby. It's a cheery start to proceedings, and I'm naturally delighted to learn that Pitchfork shares my birthday of 23rd March.

Andrew and I have travelled to matches together in the past, and our standard stupid conversations get an airing, but with added input from PT. What's the best Liverpool team goal you've seen in person, who was that flop Arsenal striker in '98, and whatever happened to Leyton Maxwell? Pretty textbook football chat, basically.

We also discuss how many Liverpool games we've been to. I'm very much the junior party here; Hoffenheim is my 23rd match (and it's the 23rd of August). Meanwhile, Andrew is at Nelson (111) prior to this match, and Paul is at 200+. Andrew and I may have been to Anfield more recently than Paul, but he put his hard yards in back in the 1990s. It was all back threes and ecru away kits in these parts then, lad.

Thanks to heavy traffic on the M6 (who would've guessed?), Andrew's sat-nav takes us around the houses. Literally, as we pass his mother-in-law's house on the journey. I wonder if this is why Andrew describes this as "his worst ever journey to a game"? Paul and I decide not to take offence, what with him giving us a lift and all.

It was pretty wretched, though; an endless stream of weird roundabout layouts and traffic cones disappearing into the distance. It was enough to outfox even the most elaborate of satellite navigation systems. Paul seems keen to argue with its suggestions at times; I think he misses Twitter.

We roll up towards Anfield with less than an hour until kick-off, so Andrew drops us off near the ground and goes to park the car. Paul and I take a nosey at the new club shop (from outside; we're not total tourists you know, la) and then we go to find our seats.

We're in the Lower Centenary stand, level with the goal line at the Kop end. Two thoughts occur to me: 1) I'd have seen from here if Garcia's goal was in (though of course I saw it was over the line from a pub in London), and 2) bloody hell, the Main Stand really is massive these days.

You'll Never Walk Alone causes goosebumps, as does Zadok The Priest, with its reworking as the Champions League theme tune. I realise then that I'm ticking off another minor personal aim, as I'm at my first Champions League match. Sure, it's only a qualifier, but it's actually more important than most individual group games are, as it's do or die.

Thankfully, this is very much *do*. A red blur sweeps across the pitch for 20 minutes and puts the tie firmly beyond Hoffenheim. Liverpool's number 23 scores his first brace for the club, sandwiching a goal from Salah that looked unbelievably offside from where we were. Remember how we'd discussed the best team goal we'd ever seen on our journey? There's a new #1 in town.

Liverpool are so far ahead of the opposition that "ole"s break out around the stands as the clock shows that a mere 23 minutes have elapsed. Hoffenheim then got a goal back though, and you could feel the anxiety coursing through Anfield for the rest of the half. And I'm certainly not immune from it, don't get me wrong. But when my rational brain kicks in at half-time and I realise the visitors need a 3-0 win in the second half, I calm down. A lot. Nobody does that in the second half of a Champions League match, right?

The Voice of Anfield, George Sephton, keeps the day's Beatles theme ticking over by playing *Komm Gib Mir Deine Hand* in the interval. Presumably it's an olive branch to our visitors from Hoffenheim? I suppose they might want to hold hands for comfort after their first half mauling.

The second half isn't anywhere near as much fun as the first, though it was great that Firmino got a deserved goal. Hoffenheim's second is greeted with a chorus of 'fuck's sake, Reds' around us, but it's very much job done at that point. The full time whistle goes, the away side keeper looks devastated, Jordan Henderson consoles him and Jürgen salutes the fans. With that, we're off into the night.

The journey home is much the same as the journey up. Bizarre diversions ensure it takes far longer than it should, but at least we won; that always cures any travel ills to some extent. As we reach Kettering, Andrew remarks that he's only been there once.

Ah, I see. It's his Market Harborough.

Paul Tomkins, August 28th, 2017

Improvement is never guaranteed in football, but this summer it felt to me – as I stated, over and over – that the club was building steadily and sensibly, with a clear vision.

Instead, the usual tiresome transfer panic overshadowed what Jürgen Klopp actually does: improve players, and improve teams.

The word 'infinite' is perhaps not ideal in this context; and even being 'twice as good' does not get you twice as many points. There's a law of diminishing returns towards the top of the table, but the Reds look capable of beating anyone; and crucially, taking apart deep, packed defences as well as those who leave themselves open. Even the opening day draw against Watford should have been a win, given the late, clearly offside equaliser (the goalscorer standing on the goal-line, a yard offside, and impeding Simon Mignolet) that came with no time left to overhaul the injustice of officials not understanding the rules.

Already, Liverpool have scored several of the best team goals I've seen the Reds score in a long time. Sadio Mané's goal at Watford was from wonderful interplay against a deep defence, whilst Emre Can's side-footed volley against Hoffenheim came at the end of one of the best counter-attacks you'll ever see. The Reds followed this against Arsenal with three more lightning breaks, two of which were once again beautiful team goals.

Klopp has never been a chequebook manager, but when he has bought, he has – along with those who work with him – targeted very specific players. They go into the side with a very defined role. As such, the transfer hit-rate of the Reds since last summer seems beyond all the usual hit-and-miss ratios I so often talk about. New signings slip in as if at the club for years.

As more time passes, and more new buys effortlessly fit in, I can't believe that this is an accident. Obviously some of the buys are young players for the squad more than the XI (Marko Grujić last season, who got injured anyway, and Dominic Solanke this season), and cannot be judged as successes or failures yet, but already Mo Salah has joined Mané, Joël Matip and Gini Wijnaldum from last season in making a real impact, as a first-teamer, in his debut season. Not only has Klopp improved a perceived flop like Roberto Firmino to the point where he's one of the great unsung players in Europe, but those brought in are having a similar impact.

At times, people think Klopp and co. should be more open-minded in the transfer market: have back-up plans, alternative targets. And maybe that's true (and maybe they do, anyway). But anyone targeted is done so for a very clear reason. Good players who don't do what Klopp wants will not be considered. There simply will be no fudging on that.

And so, with no Philippe Coutinho, no Adam Lallana, and no "recognised" right-back – and apparently about 15 signings too few – the club have kept back-to-back clean sheets in the league, and scored four goals against both Hoffenheim and Arsenal. Four wins and a draw from the first five games, given the transfer request of Coutinho less than 24 hours before the start of the campaign and the squeeze that the Champions League qualifiers puts you under, is fairly remarkable. Both teams this week were despatched with ease, with the score-lines flattering to the visitors to Anfield; whilst just over a week ago, the biggest bogey was buggered, as Palace were finally bested at home (the pesky bastards). Suddenly the impressive preseason form seems like a legitimate predictor of the season.

I was lucky enough to be in my old season ticket seat on Wednesday, and the Reds were scintillating. Hoffenheim were arguably naïve, just as Arsenal were half-arsed, but they needed despatching. And it's no coincidence that Liverpool's front three not only do great stuff going forward – with skill, vision and pace – but they harry and win the ball back too. Klopp doesn't compromise on this. He refuses to buy and/or use lazy players. This means that everyone knows where they stand (while Arsenal players seem to know where they stroll).

Post-Match Analysis and Subscriber Comments – Arsenal (H)

Russel Lunt, August 28th, 2017
Thanks for the banker home victory, Arsène. See you next season – or maybe not!

Think it was Alan Shearer, bless him for having a lucid moment, who said, "This looks like a Champions League team playing against a Europa

League side." Personally, I thought he gave Arsenal too much credit there – they looked like a newly promoted side come to Anfield for the "game of their lives in front of the Kop" and they all had stage fright. Cech the only reason we didn't score seven.

One thing that no one on commentary picked up, when Salah is through on goal, Mané runs absolutely flat out across the pitch and gets himself between the recovering defenders and Salah, obstructing them and giving him time to pick his spot. Sheer class, that guy.

Firmino, scored one, assisted one, that turn and footwork leading to the fourth. Salah, scored one, assisted one. Mané, scored one, and ripped the Arsenal defence a new arsehole. Sturridge, scored one. Can, immense throughout – he and Henderson had an excellent understanding today, and he marauded through midfield like Arsenal didn't have any players there. I mean, the only time I realised Ramsey was playing was when he was substituted, and Granit Xhaka's only telling action was to get booked during the move where Mané scored. Moreno, best performance in a red shirt? Brilliant all day. Karius, might be a good keeper if he learns to not dally on the ball. Hard to tell if he's a good shot stopper because he didn't need to save anything. Coutinho, what the hell are you thinking, mate? Wenger? Back three? Seriously? What the hell were *you* thinking, mate?

Oh. I'll just leave this here: seven clean sheets in the last nine Premier League fixtures. What dodgy defence?

Terry Dolan
I'm still buzzing, what a masterclass. I did warn Arsenal that their defence should be afraid, very afraid. That's now 14 goals in the last four games against the Gunners.

We have: the best attack since 2013/14, the best midfield since 2008/09

We need: the best defence since 1985/86. Or at least one as good as 2008/09.

We have a special team that is way beyond the sum of its parts! Can we get better? You bet, Salah is just warming up; and Coutinho hasn't started. If only – there is always an 'if only' – if only Klopp can strengthen the centre of defence with a quality recruit. What a boost if we sign van Dijk! But even if it doesn't happen that quality in the centre could yet come from Gomez. We live in exciting times.

Daniel Rhodes
A little note here: Mo Salah is the off the charts in terms of xG (expected goals) and xA (expected assists) per 90 this season. Tiny, tiny sample of 208 minutes (Premier League only), but as it stands, he's performing to Messi-esque levels.

A staggering 1.5 expected goals and assists per 90 minutes. Nobody in the history of football (data) has performed to that level over a season. Even with just a small regression it could end up close to a goal a game.

Jens aka Joe Bloggs

I honestly thought, since watching Salah and Mané, that Salah still has another gear to get to in terms of his performances, which makes what he's done so far (especially bedding in quickly again, which I'll put down to Klopp at this stage, as we've seen it with almost all our new transfers) exceptionally impressive. I feel Mané and Firmino have kicked it up a level, and from the winger perspective, I feel Mané has reached another level in terms of his attacking runs, his movement and positioning. His finishing has always been good, but to me it now looks like his confidence has reached a tier that is allowing him to really express itself which so far has only been positive! I think the backheels that he's been executing perfectly so far are just one indicator of this.

Salah I've found to be more like how Mané started with us (but still not the same player) and seems more reliant on specifically blistering pace, but less ability to beat a man from standstill and maybe a bit less tricky.

At first when Salah came in, given his goalscoring/assisting rates in Italy, I thought he may be our most productive player this season, but that was before I had really seen Mané play again in the league (especially after coming back from injury), and I have to say that a lot of our players look visibly and shockingly better than last year to my eyes, so I think it's going to be really interesting between those three if any one is the standout player, but all of them look like they're gearing up for one of the best seasons (at least offensively!) in the club's recent history.

August's Results

12.08.2017 – (A) Watford 3 – 3
15.08.2017 – (A) TSG 1899 Hoffenheim 2 – 1
19.08.2017 – (H) Crystal Palace 1 – 0
23.08.2017 – (H) TSG 1899 Hoffenheim 4 – 2
27.08.2017 – (H) Arsenal 4 – 0

Manchester City (A), September 9th, 2017
Chris Rowland

I broke my 'never in Manchester' rule on Saturday by going to a match there. Let me qualify that – it's not that I *never* go to Manchester. I go there to the proper Old Trafford to watch a Test Match. I go there for cask beer because it's got shed-loads of it and lots of great places to drink it in. I go and see bands there.

I even go *through* it, on the way to every home match. But only as a staging post, never a football destination. I've been to the Etihad once, before it was called the Etihad. I've not been to the other Old Trafford since 1999 except to see Liverpool beat Chelsea in the FA Cup semi-final.

But this time … well I could say it was because I was so excited by our attacking against Hoffenheim and Arsenal. But the real reason is – I got a ticket! A £20 pensioner's ticket!

"Do you think I'll get away with it?" I joke.

"Oh I should think so," they all reply.

I can't say Manchester isn't handy for me, about 35 minutes away on the train, and as it's about halfway between home and Liverpool, more like a home game than a home game is, distance-wise.

But it is, at least for us, undeniably Bandit Country! Not a comfortable environment, although our rivalry with City is not quite of the all-consuming intensity as with the other shower.

Of course, it wouldn't be a match day without the kick-off time being an issue. Even this close, it's an early start – the 09:42 arriving at Victoria at 10:17.

Then it's a 20 minute walk across town towards Piccadilly for our designated meeting place – Mother Mac's pub in Back Piccadilly. There's only time for a couple of quick beers before the eight of us catch a bus with 'Etihad Campus' on the front. It would honestly have been quicker to walk – it crawls through traffic at an average of 5 mph, like a double decker narrowboat.

As we walk towards our section, it starts to rain. Then it *really* starts to rain. Drenched in three seconds kind of rain. And we were. I learn my trainers are absorbent. We have wet socks, sodden jeans, and we have to queue to get in.

You know the rest. Until the sending off, there wasn't much in it, and City didn't look all that. There is concern about why Sergio Agüero is left alone for the opening goal. The keeper's save from Mo Salah doesn't disguise the tame finish. And then – *that* incident. On seeing it live, I honestly thought Mané might just get to the ball before the keeper does – a touch either side and he's through on an open goal. And I'm sure that's exactly where Mané's mind was. I'm so unclear as to what happened – and it happened at our end – I even wonder whether the keeper's going to be sent off for impeding a forward who would have been through on goal. But the City fans' reaction and the prone goalkeeper tell a different story. I'm sickened that some of our fans boo the keeper, even when he's stretchered off – though many more applauded.

Paul Tomkins, September 9th, 2017

I had a bit of bad feeling about this beforehand, in terms of anxiety about Liverpool being given a hammering – stating on the site before the game that while it has never happened under Jürgen Klopp, the worry is that if anyone could do that to you, it would be City. Indeed, Liverpool have hammered a few big clubs under Klopp, and never had one in return. It kinda felt due, in a weird and irrational way.

But I still think Jon Moss cost the Reds any chance of getting anything out of the game.

Feet are raised high all the time in English football without even bookings being handed out, and for me, the key issue was that Sadio Mané *didn't even know the keeper was there*. Yes, it looks bad in certain still images – he did catch the keeper in the face – but for me, the circumstances dictate dangerous play. If you don't think someone is there, then you usually don't get punished.

Mané had his foot up to cushion the ball, and his eyes were only focussed on that task. Not once did he glance across at the keeper, because he probably expected him to still be in his box at such a distance from goal; certainly not right on top of him.

Vitally, Mané was also running at an angle, almost at 45-degrees, that was taking him towards the corner flag (in the same way a striker takes the ball round a keeper), as the ball span in that direction, and not directly at goal, where the keeper would naturally be directly in front. As such, when he lifts his foot it's not towards a *player* – unless a right-back miraculously appears out of nowhere. Mané knows he's in behind the defence but he doesn't know where the keeper is; and he has to keep his eye on the ball.

If you look at the still images, you can see that it's Mané's ball. At no point is it ever the "keeper's ball". It's Mané's to try and control. And look how far out of his goal the keeper is.

I still think Klopp's side is much better balanced this season – but that balance died with the loss of Mané, and then the withdrawal of Salah, as ten men could not handle City's pace and movement, allied to their pinpoint passing. Pep Guardiola's sides are very adept at finding space anyway. Any advantage that Liverpool may have had late-on with five or six of the City side being in South America this week (and the continued laughable defending of Nicolas Otamendi in the absence of Vincent Kompany) was lost well before the game even reached half-time.

Trent Alexander-Arnold picked a bad day to have a legitimate "rookie" display (it's all part of the education), and Joël Matip had one of those occasional nervy performances when, instead of his usual cool self, he looks edgy and not in control of his own feet. Ragnar Klavan has a good record in these types of games, and he and Joël Matip have had good games together, but here it didn't work, even from early on – although it was Alexander-Arnold and Matip with the early nerves.

And all of Liverpool's good attacking play broke down with the final pass or attempt. But hey, before the sending off it looked like a strong away performance against a team who spent several gazillion pounds this summer, half of which went on full-backs.

The worry is what it does for the confidence of the team. It was a proper hammering, albeit with 10 men. Even so, losing "4-0" in the part of the game with ten men (after being behind 1-0 with eleven) in the manner that they did is not good enough, and takes the goal difference back to zero after 1-0 and 4-0 wins. At least Klopp can lift the player's spirits by focusing on how even the game was with a full complement of players, but it feels like some wind has been taken from everyone's sails.

And it's horrible to get thrashed 5-0. I can take defeats but as Leroy Sané lined up that fifth it just felt like he'd curl it in, such was the despondency in the Liverpool side as everything City hit fizzed towards the goal.

Such defeats so rarely happen (to Liverpool, at least), and it's the first real thumping under Klopp. That it came on the back of four wins and a draw, and with a really good defensive record going back to the spring, makes it sting like aftershave poured onto an open wound. (Incredibly, I once saw someone do that *voluntarily*, after crashing into a glass patio door at a party and cutting his face open. We were young, and he was drunk. But it seemed to staunch the bleeding.)

This week I've been reading a lot about how mental and emotional pain is every bit as real as physical pain. Because it has to manifest in the body. It isn't just mulled over by the mind – for it to mean anything it has to hurt us in actual ways. I felt real anguish, helplessness and anger in this game. I think I was more angry than usual as the referee had essentially kneecapped us. So much hinged on such a little thing, and in turn, I was duly unhinged.

But it's a busy month ahead, and at least Mané misses a League Cup game in amongst two Premier League matches, and is available for Europe. Three other players were spared the hard-running against ten men by being subbed early. Time to dust ourselves off, and pour a little Old Spice into our wounds.

Burnley (H), September 15th, 2017
Matthew Beardmore

The day starts bright and early with my two organic alarm clocks (a four year old daughter and seven month old boy) affording me the luxury of a lie-in until just before 7am.

Before I leave, I ask my daughter what she would like me to bring back from the game for her; this being the bribe for both a) abandoning her for the day and b) not taking her with me.

She asks for a monkey.

Okay....

My seven-month old smiles beatifically at me. I'll play it by ear as to what I get him.

I head out of the door at about 10:30. From Stone in Staffordshire, between Stafford and Stoke-on-Trent, to Liverpool is about one and a half to two hours' drive, so I naturally set out four and a half hours early in case of an M6 apocalypse.

Funnily enough, the traffic is fine with no sign of Armageddon, and I park up on Townsend Lane at around 12:30, and then have a 15 minute walk up to the ground.

My first task of course is to go into the new megastore. What's the first thing I see as I walk in? A toy monkey wearing an LFC top. My daughter obviously knows more about these things than I do.

As for the boy, I am under strict instructions from my wife not to buy him a kit that he will grow out of within months. This leaves the field rather empty to be honest. I buy him a Jürgen Klopp rubber duck. When I give it to him later, he will smile and start biting it furiously. I have chosen to take this as confirmation that he is now a Red.

I've got a ticket in the Anfield Road lower today. After watching the second half of the Palace-Southampton game on the concourse, I go up to my seat to find a pretty much perfect view. Just to the left of the goal, about half-way up.

The game itself is enjoyable, if frustrating. It feels like we are getting better at breaking down teams that come to just defend, but the final decision is still lacking at times. Either an over-ambitious shot is tried, or the final ball ends up forced and hurried.

The crowd around me seem quite an antsy bunch. No singing, but what they lack in that, they more than make up for in moaning and whingeing. The lad next to me was so unhappy from the first whistle, it did make me wonder why he came in the first place. When Mo Salah equalised, his reaction was to leave his seat. Presumably to go and scream into a cushion.

It was an interesting contrast to the Palace game, when I was in the same stand but right at the back. The atmosphere was so much different – lots of singing, cheering and – here's a crazy notion – supporting.

Today, everyone seemed so tense, as if just waiting for things to go wrong. Which – to be fair – they did when Burnley scored. But I thought we showed a lot of character to equalise within a couple of minutes, and overall, I felt we played pretty well, and on another day would have won two or three-one.

My overall impression was that most Reds players came out of the game with some credit. I was especially pleased for Trent Alexander-Arnold as I felt that Burnley targeted his side for a lot of the match, which I thought he handled well (with a few awkward moments) and it is another valuable lesson learned. He will be some player in the future.

Mo Salah continues to impress me. I was slightly disappointed he didn't see as much of the ball in the second half, as I felt he always looked capable of making something happen. Daniel Sturridge also looked lively and in-tune with the team and the game, more so than the Crystal Palace game.

Although Ragnar Klavan was a target for a lot of the moaning (and was one of those culpable for the Burnley goal), I felt he responded well, and made an important interception late on to prevent one of the Burnley players going through on goal.

As the game goes on, I sense that this probably isn't going to be our day and actually, considering how well Burnley have already done at Chelsea and Spurs, that a draw – while frustrating – isn't the end of the world, and that there were enough positives for me personally to call it an enjoyable match.

At the end of the game, it's a dash back to the car, with a quick call home on the way to make sure the day has gone well. Apparently my daughter has been to a fete and won a slinky on a hook-a-duck had a lovely bounce around on a bouncy castle and got bought a toy Dumbo.

All well and good, but just wait until she sees the LFC monkey….

Comment by Andrew Beasley, September 15th, 2017
Right, now I'm home … This whole thing is paraphrased.

I saw a few tweets saying "why the hell doesn't Klopp sort out the defence?". I subtweeted one saying "clearly there's issues, but a week ago we had seven clean sheets in the last nine in the league. It's not irreparably bad"

First reply (subtweeting mine): This is the worst tweet in eight years of LFC Twitter.

Me (internally): No it isn't. *Mutes account*

Second reply: The defence hasn't improved since Hodgson

Me (internally): WTF has that got to do with anything?

Me (subtweeting): Maybe it hasn't, but I'll take the attack now thanks.

And I gave up after that! Don't know how you lasted on Twitter as long as you did, Paul!

As an aside to all that nonsense, just as our fans underestimated Hoffenheim, I think they've done it again with Sevilla. They're above us in the Euro Club Index table, and have far more European experience than we do. Last night's result was disappointing and a missed opportunity, but we were unlikely to hammer them, and it's not as if we're out. As ever, up the Reds!

Jens, September 20th, 2017
While the result was disappointing and against the run of play, the thing that I simply can't abide anymore is Liverpool fans. I used to be able to give and take a bit of banter from rival fans, which is what this tribal game is about, in some ways. Putting a meaning to the result of one group of men trying to put a leather ball into a net more than the other. The manner in which they do it, and the group of men to which they do it or have done to them creates a narrative for the entire process, which can be anything from genuinely compelling to an overused trope, or stereotype.

But now the one group of people who I should be able to see eye to eye with, that group of millions of individuals who are interested along with myself to see the same group of eleven men placing that ball in a net, are seemingly the ones I can relate to least. And of course a lot of that is due to amount of exposure. If I was a Man United fan in the post-Alex Ferguson era, up until recently I would have probably grown tired of the negativity by now, or if I was an Arsenal fan, seeing people to my left and right chanting for the manager to be sacked after a record of consecutive top four finishes I would probably be exhausted. But all I can say is *what I know*, and that is that I'm tired of our fanbase. I'm tired of the snap judgements. I'm tired of seeing people go from being on top of the world to being livid in the space of a week after some unfortunate results. I'm already tired of seeing the best manager this club has had in *decades* be told he doesn't know what he's doing, and the constant stream of fans who believe that they know best, and more poignantly, 'better' than the manager.

If the job was so easy that you consider yourself more knowledgeable in the running of a football club than a man who has won two league titles (against a titan in world football so successful in its league that it almost coasts to victory, year in, year out), then my god, you should drop everything, your nine to five, the mortgage can wait, the wife and kids will understand, because you are a visionary who can claim to stand shoulder to shoulder with some of the greatest minds in the modern age of football.

When I read people telling Klopp that he can 'Piss off' after stating there aren't five better options at centre-back than what we have available it genuinely shocks me. To take this at face value, without taking the Occam's Razor approach of assuming Klopp is obviously protecting his players and deflecting attention away from the players and towards himself is absolutely preposterous. I suppose with this we can consider nuance dead, both in written and spoken language alike. The fields of literature and language can pack their bags and go home. Both rhyme and reason are a thing of the past. Poetry and fable are a collection of words with a single meaning. Politicians only tell the truth, and everybody says exactly what they mean, always, and in any and all contexts.

I love this site, and the community that it is comprised of. We all self-regulate one another, and even provide insight and genuine, thoughtful responses to those we disagree with. We do it because it's the right way to act, the only way, to remain open-minded. To allow for self-improvement and internal reflection on the reasons behind our opinions, what underpins them, and what biases we are prone to. For all the love I have for this community, I have lately begun to feel that I shouldn't limit myself to this site as my only way to interact with the Liverpool community. Our fanbase is more than a selection of intellectual, moderate individuals, and I felt that I was not truly engaging with the fanbase if I were to limit myself to that bubble. I still agree with this mentality, and will, I hope, until the day I die, as I feel it is the only way to fully appreciate a situation from every perspective. Throwing yourself out of your comfort zone and in among the crowds that simply think differently.

However, despite all my best intentions, I feel this experience has only served to tarnish the sport, and our aforementioned fanbase as a whole, for me. It would be one thing if what I was experiencing was a small, but vocal minority, but this is not the case. At least in terms of internet presence (and these days it is even breaching into radio/traditional media), I've realised that this community (or sanctuary, as it is sometimes known) on TTT is a rather peculiar outlier that sits on the edge of the supporters of this storied club. It is honestly almost a miracle that it has survived this long, given how few in the fanbase seem to value the virtues of patience, modesty and understanding. I know many here have come from the world of Twitter/forums/Reddit or at least observed it from a distance and I must ask how it makes you feel. As a fan of football, our club and even as a human being? To me it feels incredibly isolating, and it is now clearer than ever to me why you shut off social media, Paul. The bad simply seems to outweigh the good.

Of course I can distil down my experience of supporting Liverpool as a whole. From taking it all in, back to only TTT. In the most extreme case I could simply watch the games, maybe a few player/manager interviews etc, and leave it at that, but at the same time I feel a certain guilt, because football is inextricably linked to the people who make it possible, and the interactions between those fans, our club, and the clubs and fans of other clubs. I feel a fanbase, especially for something that should be unifying, such as a football club, should be welcoming and a place for like-minded individuals to share opinion under a common appreciation for the sport, and the players that wear our crest. It is clear to me now that this is not the case, and I'd be interested what the opinions are of the posters here. I could honestly extend this to a concern about society and the way we interact with one another (primarily through the internet), and how it seems to be shifting with time, seemingly not always in what I would consider a good direction. But this is a football site, and a discussion about the fans is already entering that first degree of separation.

I think to preserve my sanity, my only option would be to use TTT as a one stop shop, both as a news source and a way to interact with the community. But at the same time I feel the need, at least this once, to address my feelings about the community as a whole. I am citing a single instance based off a quote by Klopp, but of course there are hundreds, if not thousands of varied opinions about why X should be sold, Y should be sacked, and Z should not only pass the ball horizontally or back to the keeper.

Do you dabble in it and simply allow the garbage to pass through, like a sieve. Do you completely remove it from your daily routine, or is your approach entirely different?

Here's the thing about football, a truth that you must accept or you will boil in the juices of your own angst: you won't like all of the manager's decisions. It's a delusion to expect that you will. It's a delusion to expect that it'll even be close.

Given that results can rely on the decisions of the officials and the randomness of finishing at both ends (and the decisions the players make for themselves that no boss can influence, especially if they are of the acute brain-fart variety), even an elite manager probably only gets 60% of all his decisions right, if that. Football is not chess, where every move has a set of rules as to what will occur.

And to me, when the team does enough to clearly deserve to win (as measured by xG as just one example) but doesn't – like Liverpool this past weekend against Burnley – then finding fault is mostly nitpicking. When you have 35 shots, the keeper makes some great saves (and the spills fall to safety), the referee denies a clear late penalty and you hit the woodwork, you have to accept that, though there are still imperfections in the performance, it was good enough to win, and maybe better than on occasions when you do *actually* win (but maybe spawn a lucky deflected goal and it shows that "you're a great side as you won without playing well", etc.).

To please everyone, a manager has to do everything right – perfect every formation, improve every player, have Plans A-Z, and maybe even a Plan AA, AB, AC, etc. He must always give youth a chance, as "what's to lose?", but he must never play a young player before he is ready, and never lose a game when fielding a young player. He must focus on the defence, but fans of a team that can defend really well without creating much will say that he must focus on the attack – and to do both sides of the game really well is fairly rare. His teams must score from all corners, even though only 2-3% are actually ever scored from, and his team must never concede from set-pieces – especially, for some bizarre reason, if marking zonally – even though set-pieces account for c.30% of all goals.

Here are some examples from "down the road". Man United fans are loving Jose Mourinho. But many hate Marouane "sharp elbows, soft head" Fellaini. And yet the manager adores him to the point where he may name any future children or grandchildren after him, and force them to grow their hair into big bouffant balls.

Would United fans therefore want rid of Mourinho, who may bring them success overall, for something that is just one small aspect of his managerial make-up? Should Mourinho give a fuck what they think if the team he picks is getting results? If you want Mourinho, then you have to accept a Fellaini (or players like him).

To me, it's like going to a concert to see someone whose music you like and then being angry with them for playing the songs *they* want to play, which may not be your personal favourites; even though their aim is to produce a top-class performance. It's not all about you. Or getting pissed off because you didn't laugh at every joke a comedian told. *It's not all about you.* Except, those performers don't have to compete with an opposition trying to stop them (just a few hecklers), nor do they face a referee who may derail the show halfway through by sending off the lead guitarist. These performances can all be rehearsed to perfection, without the constant interference of others. (Try listening to a string quartet in a symphony hall as, also on the same stage, Metallica thrash away through gigantic amplifiers.)

Remember – you, the fan, the observer, are not the one in control of all this, and you shouldn't have the slightest illusion that you are. The greater the illusion that you are in some way in control – via the tweets that get sent, the phone-in time given, the modern mantra that we are all unique and that all our voices matter – the greater the sense of disconnect and rage when the manager, or the board, aren't actually listening. This is not the X-Factor. You don't get to vote players in or out of the team. If you have a top-class manager you enter into a pact to take him, warts and all; just as, if you enter into a marriage, you accept that your spouse will not go around doing everything to your liking 100% of the time.

This is a culture of ever-increasing perfectionism. But real life is imperfect: it has no flattering filters, no special effects. And it's a more entitled, "I deserve" culture; a culture that says we can have what we want, when we want it (what do we want? and when do we want it? what do we want? and when do we want it? etc.). If you think the manager should be paying attention to your wants, your desires, then that's very self-centred. It's almost narcissistic. (Will Storr's outstanding book "Selfie" is a must-read on all this; and thanks to someone on TTT for introducing me to its wisdom.)

And whenever a team is struggling, the manager becomes a "fraud", despite remarkable past achievements. It's been said about Jose Mourinho, Pep Guardiola, Antonio Conte, Jürgen Klopp and just about everyone else who has proven themselves as a top coach. Why do people confuse human imperfections with fraudulence? Why is the lack of a magic wand to cure all ills and remove all setbacks some kind of falseness?

A manager has a thousand things to juggle, and can't rely on half-baked theories spouted on the internet or a phone-in show, which are then completely forgotten when it turns out to be wrong (one basic example: *Luis Suárez will never be a goalscorer.* Hands up if you said that? Hands up if you go around pointing it out all the time, or hands up if you like to pretend you never said it).

In a squad of 25+, there will be some very good players left out. You might not rate them all, but you probably rate some of them. You may want to see them in the team, and be pissed off when those you don't like get games. But you won't see training, you won't have fitness updates, you won't see the chemistry between the players. When you get angry that the manager isn't picking someone, you don't know that the player had a slight hamstring twinge, or perhaps handed in a transfer request 36 minutes earlier. You cannot gauge potential as clearly as a manager.

Now, if he's a 'shit' (aka mediocre or underperforming) manager who only ever gets things wrong, and doesn't fit in at all, that's different. You'd struggle to find anything positive Roy Hodgson did or said during a hellish six months at Liverpool: his style of football was crap, his buys were crap, and his soundbites made crap look like sirloin steak.

However, Jürgen Klopp arrived with fresh, modern ideas about football, and Liverpool have improved, overall, since his arrival: his one full-season being better, on average, than those of his predecessors since 2009; while in his part-season (arriving in mid-October 2015) he took the Reds to a domestic and a European final. Even this season, the Reds have already played a top German team twice, a top Spanish team, and two top Premier League teams, and only lost in the game where they spent 60 minutes with ten men.

Paul Tomkins, September 21st, 2017
Why Liverpool Must Give Klopp The Sack.
Yes, you read that right. Maybe you've even been looking out for such a headline.

Now that I have your attention, I can of course explain that it's a big sack of *time* that I'm referring to. A huge fucking sack, with time, patience and understanding. And maybe a big sack of money too, although Liverpool FC doesn't have the same kind of resources that some other clubs clearly do. (Sacks of money were available this summer and attempts to spend it were made too.)

Yesterday someone said to me that "Bill Shankly said Liverpool Football Club exists to win trophies". Yes, but he also went seven years without winning a single thing, including some pretty dire seasons (low goals scored, lots of draws, not many wins) as he sought to phase out his great double-title-winning side – which, now ageing, had passed its peak – and fashion an entirely new one. Which is not a dig at Shankly, merely a fact. He had seven years without a trophy. Which is not to say managers can now expect to have seven fallow years; just an example of how someone would have been written off by today's standards as a has-been, yet came back to win the league title again in 1973.

Then there's the slimy logic-turd that the fans who travelled to Leicester in what turned out to be a League Cup defeat "deserved to see a strong XI", which ignores that many of those fans (plus other fans) will also be travelling to Leicester (again) on Saturday, Moscow on Tuesday and Newcastle a few days later. You don't pay for the right to see *only the best players*, because the manager has to balance his squad across all kinds of games, because this isn't 1965 (and even then, Shankly rested his whole team in the league just days before the FA Cup Final. *Because he wasn't fucking stupid*).

If the best players play every single game in all competitions, then by February there won't be a fit team to choose from. And people paying to go *then* will see hugely weakened sides. People will be turning up at Anfield to see the U15 team in the Premier League. Then, of course, people will piping up about injuries and Klopp's training methods, and why didn't he rest players before – when they don't have to name any specific times it would have been appropriate to rest players because, back then, any time he rested players they would have been saying "why's he such a douche for resting players when I've gone to the match?".

A main issue right now amongst Liverpool fans – as just one of many differences – is that there are those fans who want to win the league at all costs, as the 'Holy Grailers' (which I understand), and those who want to win even low-value trophies (which I also get) ... such as the League Cup that, ironically, Bill Shankly wasn't even that bothered about in its early days, and whose meaning has diminished in the past decade or two.

But these two aims are almost certainly mutually exclusive, unless you have an über-squad. You can't have a full tilt at the title whilst having a full tilt at the cups, unless you have a massive squad and a huge dose of luck. You occasionally get doubles and trebles, but these are usually teams with a lot of league-winning experience already, and huge squad depth.

This summer Liverpool went for what I call full-blanket players (based on the football managers' mantra that if they pull the blanket one way it exposes the toes, but if they push the blanket down your shoulders get cold. Usually, the blanket is never big enough to cover the whole area.) Mo Salah has the electrifying pace to get in behind defences, but also has great stamina, so he can help stretch the blanket and also help pull it back again to cover the toes. He's not a headless-chicken runner, but a clever wideman who runs into central areas to lose his marker. The same is true of Sadio Mané, who arrived last summer. His pace stretches the blanket with that searing pace. Both in the team together – especially with the best supply line – could be lethal. We know that.

Naby Keita is a full-blanket midfielder. Aerial challenges aside, he does *everything* a midfielder can do, with the stamina and pace to not only score, assist, tackle and intercept in theory but in practice too. Some wise judges feel he can become the best all-round midfielder in world football. It's an amazing coup to get him. But we have to wait. Which, in the grand scheme of things, is okay. Better to get an elite player late than never.

And Virgil van Dijk is a full-blanket defender. He has the supreme pace to defend a high line, the skill to play on the ball, and the height to defend a packed area when forced deep. There aren't many like him. That deal got screwed up, and that sucks. (Just like when I wanted something for Christmas as a child but the store had sold out. So instead of Stretch Armstrong I got My Little Pony. Not that I'm bitter ...)

Paul Tomkins, September 25th, 2017

First, a quick explanation about my article from the end of last week, "Why Liverpool Must Give Klopp The Sack". The über-heavy irony ("the expression of one's meaning by using language that normally signifies the opposite") of the title was explained within the opening paragraph, and the article – 5,000 words of analysis – certainly wasn't "clickbait", as, to me, clickbait has nothing of substance when you click on it. It's empty, hollow.

Also, my clear aim was break out of the echo chamber and get people who wanted Jürgen Klopp out to read a rational defence, as they were unlikely to read "Why Klopp Must Be Given Tons of Time and Patience". I found it hilarious that an Anti-FSG group, which frequently attacks me because I try to be fair to the owners, posted it on their Facebook page (which I only saw as I got an alert about it).

Of course, the trouble with an ironic headline is that reactionary people don't read the articles. They get wound up by the concept, not the truth. And I do understand that we don't all have time to read the deluge of articles that come our way. Still, people comment without having read them, which seems like dismissing a song you haven't heard because you don't like the title. (Although if the title of the song is, say, "I Want To Sodomise Dead Dogs Whilst Eating Cats Alive", then you may be wise.)

As such, I'm slightly uncomfortable with the idea that people were seeing the headline pop up on social media timelines and concluding that a growing number of Liverpool fans want Klopp out – because they weren't going to actually bother to investigate the words. I want the *opposite* of the circus at Arsenal, where it's hard to tell if the team is struggling because of the constant negativity about the manager, or if the constant negativity is because the team is struggling. It's probably a bit of both, although the rumblings whenever Arsenal drop points – certainly when they did so a few years ago – becomes a kind of self-fulfilling prophecy. The players are under more pressure in every single game, and that's not conducive to good football. As soon as fans reach that stage with Klopp then both the fans and the players are edgy, awaiting the first mistake before the vitriol pours down.

Outrunning stupidity is hard, as stupidity runs fast. The good news is that victory at Leicester in the league – after the cup exit there just days earlier – eased some of the ludicrous pressure Klopp has been under. As someone noted on here during the match, Jordan Henderson's goal was a full *five fist-pumper* for the manager.

It was a horrible game, with what I felt was horrible refereeing, played on the "must-win" knife-edge, with the cosh to the head of the home team's tactics. At times it turned into an ugly game of head-tennis, with Leicester launching it in the air and giving Liverpool players no time to bring it down, so all they could do was head it back. But after two undeserved results – both Burnley and Leicester in midweek should have been victories (certainly by the xG models) – it was rewarding to get over the finish line with the three points, by hook or by crook. I can't recall many games I've been as glad to see end, nor as many expletives aimed at one opposition player as those I spewed at Jamie Vardy.

Comment by "ab248", September 28th, 2017

Narratives are something I use in my academic life. Narratives are useful – even essential – to help us make sense of things like climate change which might otherwise might be too complex or detailed for the non-expert. They're also unhelpful and naturally encourage laziness, as is complained about on TTT. They can be astonishingly impervious to the reality outside the narrative frame. Consider the power of the anti-nuclear 'tampering with nature' narrative, for example. It meant the whole focus of the Japanese tsunami that killed some 20,000 back in 2011 was on damage to the (resilient, if misplaced) nuclear reactor – that led to precisely zero direct human harm. Further back, we continue to assume even the world's worst nuclear accident at Chernobyl led to untold deaths stretching into the future, when there were actually less than 50 fatalities. Narratives have consequences, like the cancellation of nuclear reactors that followed the tsunami, which means burning more fossil fuels. (I'm not some kind of nuclear nut, by the way – just an example).

I think the narrative perspective is an important addition to the site that I hope can become as central an idea as using good data. As Paul briefly observed, they get us away from the idea that it's all an anti-Liverpool FC thing. That is simply not credible in any case. It seems to me that probably a majority of both influential pundits and journalists have direct associations with or are sympathetic to the club. Witness David Maddock, Dominic King and Jonathan Northcroft on the reasonably good *LFCtv Press Watch*, for example. Then there's Dominic Fifield at the *Guardian* and, until recently, even the *Times* had a club sympathiser as a main correspondent. It can be also off-puttingly cliquey. And it can run close to conspiratorial thinking – itself a very lazy and blind mindset which is unsurprisingly a key component of contemporary 'selfie' culture; Donald Trump and all. Even for the well intentioned, such bunker mentality 'they're all against us' might cohere but also create a sense of siege which isn't good either for mental health or attracting new custom, and makes the isolation of staying sensible in a sea of madness even more difficult.

Returning to the Liverpool connections, former players as pundits are everywhere, from the moronic to the reasonably intelligent. This is no conspiracy either, of course, and mainly down to generational factors with senior journalists all in their late 40s and 50s, shaped by the glory days, and the former players being partly also the product of this – and the products of intelligent coaching, high profile and self-confidence (likewise witness the success also of Alex Ferguson's former players as pundits). But the narrative is more powerful than any positivity from residual loyalties, particularly for the lazier and less intelligent (and there are other factors, such as how former

Liverpool players demonstrate their 'media maturity' by being more negative than positive about their former team – see Danny Murphy and Jamie Carragher, for example).

On *BT Sport* we have to listen to Steve McManaman (until I turned it off, despite my kids protestations). His tone was relentlessly negative in the Moscow game with not even the appreciation of the attack genuinely shown by Rio Ferdinand, and more falsely acknowledged by Gary Lineker. Everything was what Liverpool 'should' be doing but are apparently miles from realising: winning 'games like this', 'getting the basics right' and the final pass (where he was clearly wrong, as bad luck and snatching at finishing was the issue). All of which we presumably never failed to do in the good old days of McManaman, of course.

Where we get to the real nonsense of the narrative is squeezing a midfielder losing the ball and giving away a free-kick, and the goalie then not saving the resulting shot, into the 'same old' defensive frailties. That not only the defence but the team as a whole defended well, not giving the proverbial 'sniff' to the opposing attack didn't figure. (As an aside, it was interesting that in the half time analysis even boring old Michael Owen became bored of the same old narrative and changed the conceded goal discussion to a reasonably interesting point about how defensive walls have too many players in them, obscuring the goalie's view). The following day's media remarkably continued the 'same old story' of defensive frailties, because of Loris Karius failing to save the free-kick!

Maybe some research would need to be done on the relative strengths of different club narratives but it certainly appears that ours is the strongest and thereby most impervious to reality. We're the biggest casualties for a number of reasons, none of which bears much relation to a host of objective factors like global support and financial health – despite lacking a sugar daddy. We might say we have a 'meta' narrative behind the more specific 'Champions League attack, Championship defence', which is that of the 'fallen giant' with no title for 25+ years.

This is a weighty fact; almost an immutable law of nature that no mere mortal will be able to defy. Importantly, this maintains winning the Premier League as the baseline from which only disappointment can follow and the reference point for McManaman's many 'should's. In the context of the meta-narrative there's a subtext of rather desperately hiring a glamorous, quick-fix manager who we all know just doesn't have the solidity that's required to 'grind out' the Premier League title which is, after all, the only reason to play, watch and commentate on football.

In the same spirit, I don't really go along with the conspiratorial tones of 'BBC Salford'. It's a bit daft to attribute significance to the BBC's physical location in Manchester, and I'm not sure you could argue things would be better if they relocated to Merseyside. You could also argue that TTTers should be obliged to back this up with some systematic evidence given how we see the need for objective data measures elsewhere. It's not an anti-LFC, or pro-Manc thing.

This isn't to say that there aren't some individuals out there who more systematically promote the narratives more than others, perhaps fed by an actual dislike of the club and what it represents. Confirmation bias maybe – but the BBC's online head guy, Phil McNulty, never seems to miss an opportunity to trot out the narrative in its least mediated form. I even noticed them putting a 'Klopp out' nutter's bile on to their site last week.

Where am I going with all of this? Well I'm not sure really. But I do think we should keep this focus on narratives and continue to take opportunities to flag up their glaring disparity with reality – regardless of the individuals and club loyalties. We could also take a step further to focus in on the quality – or lack of it – in football punditry.

'Rate the pundit' would be fun but would also actually be something that could make a bit of a media impact should anyone fancy doing so, getting a bit out of the current bunker. Come up with a (pseudo) metric; perhaps a combination of the extent to which pundits draw upon useful data and also provide insight – precisely by not relying upon the narrative.

Finally, a more personal note against the pundits who trade on their past rather than insight. Given the sleight of hand from former players who were mostly themselves part of the 'fallen giant' years – but by heavily criticising today's version exempt and elevate themselves – wouldn't you love it if a fellow commentator turned around to McManaman (and their ilk) and asked, 'So, Steve, given your own history with the club we'd love to hear your insights into why it's so difficult to overcome inconsistency/blend attacking verve with defensive solidity and win the title?'

September's Results

09.09.2017 – (A) Manchester City 0 – 5
13.09.2017 – (H) Sevilla 2 – 2
16.09.2017 – (H) Burnley 1 – 1
19.09.2017 – (A) Leicester City 0 – 2
23.09.2017 – (A) Leicester City 3 – 2
26.09.2017 – (A) Spartak Moscow 1 – 1

Paul Tomkins, October 3rd, 2017
Football is a loser's game. Or rather, too many fans feel like there's no joy to be taken from almost all possible permutations with a result.

On a basic level, winning obviously should make us happy and losing obviously should make us unhappy, but it's so much more complicated than that. I'll get onto specific combinations of results and performances that leave fans satisfied (or not), but first, something on our mental calibrations.

Positivity bias

People with a positivity bias think that, long term, everything will be okay. And most of us are like this on the really long-term picture, unless in a state of despair and depression (when everything feels doomed). It's a fact that most of us think that in ten years' time everything will have changed less than it actually ends up changing. We don't foresee the illness, death, redundancy and relationship meltdowns that often end up arising within such a timespan. We tend to think things will be mostly as they are now.

On a personal note, while I'm labelled and derided as "too positive", I'd like to point out that last season I predicted 3rd-5th for the Reds, with c.70 points – and the club finished 4th with 76 points. On a TTT poll at the start of this season I predicted 11 points from the first six games, and Liverpool got 11 points. So I don't think I'm overly positive in predictions. (I used to be when I was much younger; this was always going to be Liverpool's year, including 1992, when new expensive buy Paul Stewart was gonna boss the midfield. But that was before all the research I undertook and all the experience and insight I have gained.) I spend most of my time trying to hone my sense of what to expect, although I often get stuff wrong. However, my aim is to have realistic *calibrations*.

I'd actually argue that those with an overly strong positivity bias are the people who get most angry, because they expect great seasons and great results, and so are the most disappointed at any deviation from that idealistic outcome.

I cringe when I see people say "we'll batter these 5-0" before a game, because it's usually fairly unlikely. And that's before factoring in all the performance-related anger, that can often override even a good result.

Negativity Bias

The problem is that, when things occur, we view them through a negative filter. As I've pointed out many times, bad things in our lives can kill us, whereas good things in our lives (food, water, sex, friendship, shelter) are not usually *immediate* life-or-death situations – we can last three days without water, or three weeks without food, but our ancestors wouldn't last three seconds in the mouth of a lion. This meant we evolved to be hyper-aware of predators, fire, falling from mountains, etc. The good things were important, but they could often *wait*.

It's said that we need five positive interactions with a partner to undo one negative one. And we've all seen it with footballers we don't rate – we ignore five good passes and then scream blue murder "look, I told you he was shit!" when one goes astray (which is negativity bias allied to confirmation bias, i.e. noticing only what we want to focus on – such as seeing bad defending in the game away in Moscow when, at worst, it was one instance of bad goalkeeping). The bad stings us more deeply than the good rewards us. It's to tell us not to put our hand in the fire again.

If you don't hone your antennae, and calibrate expectations realistically, you will be more susceptible to angry outbursts. Remember, even the champions usually drop a quarter of all points (and sometimes almost a third), and in the Premier League era, Liverpool have won only half of their games. (It stings right now because the Manchester clubs have only dropped points in one game *apiece*, but they won't keep up that rate, even if they do have great seasons.)

Liverpool at their very best have won two-thirds of all league games in a season, but again, within those fine seasons have been good periods and fallow periods. I worry that we are less able to deal with *form* these days.

Chris Rowland, October 14th, 2017
Anyone who's read my My Day At The Match articles will know that the pincer movement of the uncertainties of rail travel and revised kick-off times tend to loom large in my day.

Well this game set a new low. A 12:30 kick-off and Lime Street being beset by building work as they add two new platforms were problematic enough. The fact that we were playing *them* and I have to travel via Manchester added immeasurably to my sense of unease. A whole lot could go wrong before my day was done, and the prospect of sharing a train with that lot and having to endure their unfunny songs and endless anti-Liverpool agenda did nothing to soften my sense of anxiety. There's only so much Gerrard slippage and 'you nearly won the league' anyone can stand.

Contrary to what the official site seemed to suggest ("the station will be closed to passengers until October 22nd, 2017"), and what my mate in Liverpool said when he phoned the night before ('you do know Limey's closed don't you?'), the website I used to book my tickets on allowed me to book through to Lime Street.

So it was an early start – for me, anyway – leaving home at 7:45 to catch the 8:06 to Manchester Victoria. There I have all of 12 minutes to cross platforms and catch the Liverpool-bound train, due into Lime Street at 10am.

When I leave home it's still dark as night, and it's raining. On the way to the station I stop at the newsagents but the papers aren't in yet. At the station the café isn't open yet. It all adds to a sense of dislocation, of out of the ordinariness. It feels and looks more like the early hours, only I'm not going to the airport for a flight somewhere sunny – the only other time I'm up at such times! – but a football match 66 miles away!

At Rochdale, about 20 or so people get on wearing blue football colours, all together, all knowing each other and talking to each other. I remember Utd playing in blue at Anfield before and wonder whether this is their coordinated theme for the day. Bloody typical of them, I think, there always has to be an agenda. Inevitably they settle upon the carriage that I'm in. Then I overhear them talking about meeting up in a pub in Fleetwood.

So fixated am I on the nightmare prospect of sharing my journey with Utd supporters, I assume, incredulously, that they're going for a pint in Fleetwood before heading for Anfield – which makes no sense whatsoever. This forces me to reconsider and cease overlooking the obvious – fans in blue colours getting on at Rochdale – is it inconceivable they could be Rochdale fans? I check my phone – Fixtures, League Two – sure enough, Rochdale are away to Fleetwood!

At Victoria, bang on time, I walk across a couple of platforms to the waiting Lime Street train, and walk along its entire length on a scouting mission to see whether there are any obvious groups of Man Utd fans to avoid, even though they almost certainly won't be wearing colours. All I see is a couple of Liverpool fans. I decide that if they're brave enough to wear colours in Manchester on a train to Liverpool when we're playing Man Utd, I'm going to sit near them! But then another thought occurs – what if they're very occasional day trippers or Liverpool fans from another country, and unaware of the risk they are placing themselves in? I revise my plan, and settle myself unobtrusively in the corner of a carriage.

We arrive at Lime Street on time. Only platforms one and two are in use, the rest seem to be in the process of being dug up. Drills hammer and squeal, echoing around the cavernous roof. Much of the station concourse is fenced off and boarded up. I make a sharp exit, and head for Williamson Square, where we've arranged to meet in the Shakespeare. Not my sort of place, and no cask beer, but we haven't got long and there are taxis right outside. I spend a few minutes in the club store, where I see a hooded sweatshirt with the slogan 'Walk on Through the Storm' on its front, and find myself irritated by the fact that this is actually not a direct quote from our club anthem but an amalgam of two different parts of it. I feel the club itself, of all things, should be mindful of accuracy with such a central strand of our DNA, should be the guardians and protectors of it. If the club itself can't get it right, who can? I decide it should say 'Walk on Through the Wind, Walk on Through the Rain.' Even if it does require more space and the designer or art director pulls a face because it's messed up the artistic balance. To me, the authenticity matters more. Then they play 'Boys Don't Cry' by The Cure, and I hope that's not an omen. Time for me to leave!

Two pints of nasty keg beer and we're on our way. The day has turned into an unseasonably warm sunny one. Inside the ground I immediately detect a heightened atmosphere – there's even singing inside the toilets! "Bring on your Manchester United, bring on your cockneys by the score ...." The *You'll Never Walk Alone* is passionate, loud and extended, and seems to be sung in every part of the ground but one. The Kenny Dalglish Stand and Kop mosaics are followed by a rousing 'Fields of Anfield Road'. You just hear a snatch of the Cantona song from their lot in response – you're going to sing about your hero, we're going to sing about ours.

So to the game. The Jordan Henderson and Emre Can haters near me are soon in full flow. If either doesn't do something which would be remarkable even for Lionel Messi, it's taken as confirmation of their point that the player is crap. There's some bemoaning at half-time the absence of a 'striker', no end product etc. Jose Mourinho parking the bus as usual, Utd fans ought to be outraged that their very expensive team seems so afraid of losing at Anfield. We think it's Mourinho who's terrified of losing at Anfield though.

At the end, we think we played okay against a team that was joint top of the league – though goodness knows how, on that evidence. It's taken as evidence that we can compete at the top level – at least till we see City's score! [A 7-2 victory against Stoke.] As Jürgen said afterwards:

"For me today, one team who can become champion this year was in our stadium and is not a world apart from us. It's not that we are playing different planets and they are really good and we do not find the entrance to the stadium."

Lately it seems we keep watching the same game – have the better of it, but fail to win it. Watford, Burnley, Newcastle, Sevilla, Spartak Moscow, now this. It's maddening. It was a match where we needed a scrambled goal, a deflection, a goalmouth mess following a corner or free kick with the ball ending up in their net, just find a goal from somewhere. There was always the worry that they might get one such chance, and end up stealing the three points, and that it would seem almost stereotypical if they did. But they didn't. They barely had enough men forward to make it possible.

Afterwards, a good few beers outside in the unseasonably warm sunshine, the Dale Street run: the Ship and Mitre, the Excelsior and the Vernon Arms. Just to demonstrate how some will always find something, anything, to criticise the club or its owners for, I overhear one person say the new Main Stand should have been the Kenny Dalglish Stand, palming him off with the Centenary is a disgrace, FSG have got to go etc. I guess anyone who wants to start a fight can.

I walk back to Lime Street for the 18:00 back to Manchester Victoria, then the 19:16 from there back home. The latter is the Bradford/Leeds train, which is home to a noisy group of young Bradford City fans (they'd been at Bury) who spend the entire journey chanting and clapping their inane songs on an endless loop ("Championship, we're on our way"). As a group of older lads observed when they got on at Rochdale, 'good to see the future is in good hands!' And so, on a day which began with me so concerned about sharing trains with Man Utd fans there and back, instead it's the fans of Rochdale and Bradford City that I encounter in transit.

The travelling part has gone like clockwork all day, and we didn't lose, so not a bad day. But if we could just have just found that one goal ….

Paul Tomkins, October 14th, 2017

There was an amazing moment in this match, that will be talked about for years to come – grandchildren will be sat on knees and have it recounted by trembling voices – where Manchester United had a shot at goal. (Lukaku will presumably be docked a week's wages.) Oh, the joy. Be still my beating heart.

Mourinho, aka The Genius, is now, without doubt, the best football manager the game has ever seen; he captures the imagination, makes children want go over the park and kick a tree. He takes the game to new levels, like a steamroller that cost £500m and is used to run over Ferraris and Porsches, so that no one can be left with any nice things. He did it away at Southampton, too, just to show that he's happy to crush mid-ranking teams with his destructive powers.

In fairness, Alex Ferguson came to Liverpool a couple of times and did the same, with Rooney out wide in a five-man midfield, but that was when Liverpool were one of the best teams in Europe. And generally, his United teams *crossed the halfway line.*

But hey, Mourinho is a genius, isn't he? A right ruddy genius! He has taught the world to sing, and sing it does: a Sigue Sigue Sputnik B-side, off tune and out of key. Right now tears of joy are in the eyes of little boys and girls in Brazil, who will rush out onto the beaches to practice booting the ball 70-yards into the ocean. What a time to be alive. It says something when Burnley come to Anfield with more ambition.

But thank you, Jose, for expanding my mind, and giving us back The Beautiful Game. Tossers like Pep Guardiola and Jürgen Klopp are busy trying to ruin it with fast-paced play, creativity, invention, movement, while you turn one of the most expensive sides the world has ever seen into a bunch of hoofers, clearing the ball 60 yards every time (including Phil Jones' first-touch). It's just a shame that neutrals didn't get to see Marouane Scissor-Elbows Fellaini, as the game could have been taken to new heights – literally. (Is that enough depressed sarcasm yet?)

Maybe Liverpool were indeed wasteful with their chances – again – but at least the Reds are creating them. The team is playing well, and the luck has to turn soon – an opposition goalkeeper who doesn't have a worldie (although de Gea is at least genuinely world-class and not just having a one-off); a referee who gives legitimate penalties; the forwards all fit and in form at the same time; and maybe even a mishit shot that deflects in. At the very least, the fixture list gets much easier after Spurs become the 4th of the other five of the 'big six' the Reds will have faced in just nine league games.

Paul Tomkins, October 18th, 2017

I want to put the Reds' difficult start into context. Which isn't to say some performances or results couldn't have been better, but unlike when Brendan Rodgers' tenure was winding down (which itself came after a fairly poor season, and with growing internal unrest over transfer policy), this is not a clear and fatal downturn in the team's belief. This is a team playing well, and not taking its chances.

Remember, the Reds played better this season when drawing with Burnley at Anfield than they did last season when beating them. This is a team that played better against Man United than last year. The expected goals (xG) difference in both games showed a clear victory to Liverpool on the quality and number of chances created and conceded in these two games, as did the draw at Newcastle, and away at Spartak Moscow. All four draws were clear "points" victories to the Reds in boxing terms, but all ended equal. That's the shitty-stick of football – you don't always get what you deserve, and at the end it doesn't go to a panel of judges if there's no knockout.

The Reds aren't taking their chances, and that's a worry, but the team is actually creating more than last season, and therefore "playing" well. Adding a poacher – the standard response to a goal drought – will likely only make the movement less impressive and end up with less being created. (And even the best strikers have barren spells. For example, as of October 25th 2015, Harry Kane had just one league goal that season.)

In Mo Salah, Roberto Firmino, Sadio Mané and Philippe Coutinho, the Reds have the potential to get 60 goals from their front four. So far, we've rarely seen them together, and at times they've all missed good chances that they'd otherwise take. But striking often goes like that. Hence, Luis Suárez being labelled a wasteful attacker who'll never score 20 league goals in a season for Liverpool, and so on.

On Saturday, Jürgen Klopp got the better of Jose Mourinho, whose plan would not have been to let Liverpool get into great positions, and then rely on the Reds missing the target or his goalkeeper pulling off an utterly unlikely save, even for de Gea. Mourinho got the draw he was after, but in this case, by luck rather than judgement. Coming to Anfield with Liverpool missing Mané and Adam Lallana, and with Joe Gomez making just the 11th top flight appearance of his career, as well as Coutinho – insanely – having played 86 minutes for Brazil on Wednesday, United were still outplayed. They were never going to be torn apart when getting so many men behind the ball, but this was not a Mourinho defensive masterclass. Either United weren't playing well, or Liverpool stopped them having an easy time of it.

The latest stat, which I asked if TTT and LFCHistory.com stalwart Graeme Riley knew the answer to (knowing he would!) is that Liverpool are in a run of six away games from seven fixtures. On just eleven occasions since 1903 (*nineteen hundred and three!*) has such a run occurred. It has happened in just ten different seasons since the club was formed in 1892. Therefore, this is a once-in-ten-to-fifteen-years anomaly. Once Liverpool have gone to Spurs next week, it will signal an end to an ultra-rare level of fixture difficulty; and, as I will come onto, that includes factors other than just the games being away.

Spurs (A), October 27th, 2017
Comment by David Fitzgerald (aka MadchenKliopp)

I just think we've got a lot of the emphasis wrong in our reactions to this game. It's interesting listening to Klopp describe in his post match presser where he felt we went wrong for the four goals conceded. The main fault for the first was that Kieran Trippier got to play the through ball at all – and if you look at it, then he's right that Jordan Henderson and then Emre Can were too casual in not getting their bodies in the way and making tackles too late. For the second goal he seems to be wondering if Alberto Moreno should still have been up there rather than covering. (That one seems a bit harsh considering Moreno's involvement in the chance previously but it's still interesting that he thought there should have been cover for Dejan Lovren.) For the third goal once again it's Can who is too casual – it's even him that is the nearest to Dele Alli and failing to react to the 2nd ball off Joël Matip's lousy header. Klopp doesn't really say much about the 4th, although if he did I feel certain he would mention that Matip shouldn't have conceded the free kick out wide.

So all in all – according to Klopp – the players he considered responsible for the 'school boy' errors in this game are not the list of names coming up regularly throughout this thread, but more so Can, Henderson and Matip when defending out wide. I don't think he's dismissing the errors made by Lovren and Simon Mignolet or turning a blind eye to the need for better quality in that department, but what he's saying is that the way forward is to prevent the service to the goalscorers in the first place. To be fair this is what he's always said and we've seen many a performance to back it up. Like the weekend before against Manchester United for instance.

I think there's a strong case to say that our principal match loser at Spurs was Can, not Lovren, and there's also a case to say that, judging by that performance, his commitment to the club is questionable. I'm not trying to protect Lovren here, but rather say that maybe it would have been much easier for Can to have prevented two goal scoring opportunities than Lovren.

However, the way I look at it, this just highlights the difficulty Klopp has in trying to keep the team on track. Trying to keep players like Can with his contract situation and Philippe Coutinho on board and fully motivated is not straightforward and he doesn't necessarily have all the cards in his hand. There is no point in us the fans trying to pin blame on individual players and start demanding replacements because it's almost bound to be counterproductive. We simply don't know what is involved behind the scenes and what it takes to get the team to perform or acquire and integrate new players. What we do know is that things can spiral out of control when a player goes rogue like Raheem Sterling did, and Brendan Rodgers allowed other players to be scapegoated and cold shouldered. It's been a bruising summer for Klopp with the terrible timing of the Coutinho business and the struggles trying to get Naby Keita and Virgil van Dijk. And surely those sagas

44

have affected Can and Lovren too. I think Klopp's done an absolutely incredible job of holding things together.

The issue for me is team unity. That's what's going to improve our defending and elevate us to the level that Klopp can deliver. We know what a fully functioning Klopp side looks like because we've seen it, and they can defend. The main character trait of his best teams has been total commitment. That means discipline too.

And this is the other thing that I think many people are getting seriously wrong about the performance at Spurs. It wasn't just about 'individual errors'. It was about our team succumbing to the pressure applied by some seriously good tactics executed by a very good, in form Tottenham team who managed to knock us off our balance early on at home. Mauricio Pochettino is a great manager and he's probably been planning revenge on Klopp for a good long while. He beat us with his tactical setup. We lost our discipline. But what is so terrible about that in a match at this level? We are acting like there was no pressure and we just let them in. Even Klopp seems appalled by what happened; but it's not true.

Look at it through Spurs' eyes – just as you would for the tonne of famous steals we have made against top sides in recent years – and you can see that Harry Kane, Dele Alli, Son Heung-min, Hugo Lloris and Kieran Trippier had to perform at the top of their game to force those errors. Yes – we should have been more alert, but we should know better than most that sometimes you can get on top with brilliant players.

And one other thing that I've not heard mentioned much is that, added to all this, is that for one of the first times ever for Spurs, they managed to mobilise the Wembley crowd. I heard they'd already gone to considerable lengths to minimise the amount of LFC fans and when that first goal went in the atmosphere became a real factor in their favour, and dare I say it, it spurred them on. Now where have I heard talk of the home crowd lifting the level of their team's performance recently? Mmm ... let me think ...!

Huddersfield Town (H), October 28th, 2017
Chris Rowland

After last Sunday's horror show, there's one bit of good news. Lime Street station is open again, and it's a Saturday 3pm kick-off! At least there'll be no need to set the alarm. Nice and leisurely for the 10:06 from Hebden Bridge to Manchester Victoria. There are likely to be a few Huddersfield fans on it. I'm expecting a good many more at Manchester when I get on board the Lime Street train. I'm also expecting them to be mighty excitable – and not just because they beat Jose Mourinho's bus-parking crew last weekend. They're playing at Anfield – for the first time in the league since October 23rd, 1971. It's their physical confirmation that they're back in the big time. Cue "where's your famous atmosphere?", "is this a library?", "your support is fuckin' shit",

45

the whole repertoire. Sure enough, we get the full set later, and a few more besides.

All goes smoothly for once on the two train journeys, and I'm into the almost fully functioning Limey just after midday. We are meeting at The Globe in Cases Street near Central Station and St John's. The talk is of which of the four goals at Spurs was the worst to concede. One, two and three are all contenders. One of our bunch, normally a mild-mannered affable laid-back individual, is almost apoplectic about Klopp's failure to do anything about our goalkeeper, our left-back and our centre-back, who everybody knows are not good enough, and have never been good enough, and what has Andy Robertson done wrong to be overlooked and for Alberto Moreno to be preferred? And Emre Can-love is in short supply too.

Amongst the many fractions of conversations bouncing around the packed pub (The Globe doesn't take much packing, mind), I hear someone say "Well I wouldn't accept that if Shanks or Paisley said it so I'm not accepting it from Klopp now either". But I don't know what it is! Before I can butt in, they've downed their pints and left. Fill in your own version if you want … there's definitely a sense of honeymoon over for Klopp though, no more free passes for the man in glasses.

Taxis to the ground, and inside the atmosphere in the Kop is flat, not dead but inert, like an inactive volcano, but one I know can explode back into life. Just not today.

There's a sharp contrast in the away section, which predictably is frothing and bubbling, like an over-excited kid on Christmas Eve. After all, they've got Liverpool at Anfield for the first time in 46 years, we've only got Huddersfield at home – the old saying. We don't even respond when they're goading us about our lack of support. Not even a desultory "who the fuckin' 'ell are you?" Even when they're 3-0 down, with some of the home support leaving they sing "is this a fire drill?" Seems they had the stereotypical great day out spoilt only by the match.

There was a time when being in the Kop meant you were actively involved in the match and with the team, actually affecting the outcome, a participant rather than a mute sullen passive observer and critic like now. It detracts considerably from the matchgoing experience, in my opinion. The old sense of the Kop being able to change the course of a match if you didn't like the way it was heading was very empowering and exciting. Just watching is not the same. We used to be part of the cast, not the audience.

At half-time there's virtually no conversation because there's just nothing to say about the first half. There's a bit of criticism for Klopp over Mo Salah taking the penalty, and why didn't James Milner? I say maybe because Milner missed his last one against Southampton and isn't likely to feature regularly, and so you'd need someone who does play regularly to be your penalty taker – so why not somebody who just recently scored a crucial pressure penalty to qualify his country for the World Cup?

"But he missed" seems to be the answer. "As did Milner with his last one, you're ready to forgive Milner and make him your saviour so why not forgive Salah too?" I ask heatedly. It's the sort of revisionist argument that really riles me. I point out that Roberto Firmino was becoming our penalty taker at one point but then he missed against Sevilla.

What we do agree on is that nobody knew why the penalty was given, the gasp of delighted surprise around the ground as people realised the ref had awarded a penalty was something to behold.

The second half we get a deflection that falls our way for once, and after that it's plain sailing.

Back in town afterwards for a couple of pints and the train back, with plenty of Huddersfield fans around, still singing. At Manchester Victoria the noticeboard announces the Leeds train – the one I want – will consist of two carriages. There's a collective groan of exasperation from the waiting hordes. There's going to be mayhem trying to fight your way onto this train. I somehow manage to get a seat – they're all gone within 15 seconds – and at least 100 at Manchester cannot even get on the train. The previous time I came on this train at this time, there were five carriages all only 2/3 full.

I spend the journey talking to a Huddersfield fan from Tadcaster, who's had a good day regardless and thinks losing to Liverpool is expected, beating Man Utd a bonus (we agree!), and winning your home games against the likes of Stoke and WBA is the key, whilst all around the standing masses sway and surge like coral in a current.

I will watch *Match of the Day* tonight.

Roger Lester
Going to be late tomorrow boss, going to try to get tickets for Liverpool.
So at 6:30am I am up and turning computers on. I log on four times in the next half an hour (a tip I picked up from TTT), different browsers and wait until 8:30. Time comes and I get "you have less than an hour" once and "you have at least an hour" on the other three. Sugarlumps. Not again – don't Liverpool Football Club realise that not everyone has superfast internet? Still 45 mins later I am nearly there, I expect I will manage my usual one game at the back in the Main Stand, worse since the new stand as it's so far away. Then I'm in, I am going for Huddersfield as I know there is a Champions League game in the week so it won't get moved. I look for tickets and can sit ... *anywhere?* What is going on here? So I pick the Kenny Dalglish Stand, midway up row three. Brilliant, best seat I've ever got.

So on a bright morning I am up normal time and think about what time to leave. I am on my own again, same as last time against Burnley. Usually my partner comes with me and goes shopping in Liverpool. That makes life easier as if I'm early I can walk round town with her and then make my way to the ground about 2pm. When I went to the Burnley match I left about 9am and was in Liverpool by 11:45. Easy run up, it's 150 miles from Oxfordshire, no problems through roadworks and had three hours to kill. I decide not to leave much later, all it needs is an accident and I shall be fuming if I'm late. I can always stop somewhere out of town now I have an idea about parking. I parked at the back of an old people's home which was fine, but took me an age to get out. I think I will try the car park at Everton, looks as if I will be able to get out easier. It will be a bit further to walk but should be better.

My journey is straightforward until Junction 16 on M6. A couple of miles before, the queues start. I move along slowly – why do the other lanes always seem to move quicker than the one I'm in? After about 45 minutes it clears and we are off. I go up the M57 and into Liverpool that way, and soon find myself near Everton's ground. I decide to try to park my car – wow, £15, £5 more than last time at the old people's home. Still if it means getting out quicker it may be worth it. A short walk across Stanley park and I'm there. I spoke to a Huddersfield supporter on the way and he said he hadn't been to Anfield since 1971. I didn't realise that was the last time Huddersfield played there, doesn't time fly?

I reach the ground around one o'clock and after getting something to eat, visiting the shop and buying a programme I go into the stadium just after two o'clock. I watched a bit of the Mancs' match but gave up after they scored, bloody Spurs why couldn't they play like that last week?

I thought about whether I would meet anybody, last time it was a lady who travelled up from London every Saturday home game. Her boyfriend was a Chelsea supporter, bet that relationship was fun at times. I sat next to a local chap who was fine except he hated Jordan Henderson, which was a bit unfair as he doesn't usually play the way he did in the first half. Chap the other side didn't speak, even to reply to a comment. Expect he thought "bloody southerners!"

As for the match it was your classic game of two halves. In the first we looked nervous and were obviously intent on not letting Huddersfield score as Alberto Moreno and Joe Gomez hardly got forward at all. Henderson mostly stayed in front of or between the centre-halves. In fairness to Huddersfield they gave us no space at all and seemed to have more players on the field than we did. They "parked the bus" and obviously nicked Man United's bus last week and brought that along as well. Admittedly we were very slow and lacking in confidence to play many forward passes and seemed to be scared to lose possession. After last week I suppose it was understandable but there just seemed a lack of inspiration. Nobody around me could tell why we had a penalty, this is probably the only drawback to being so close. You just can't see the action properly when there was a crowded penalty area. I overheard the comment "Worst first half I have ever seen Liverpool play". Was it that bad? Dull, yes, but we didn't concede – so surely that has to be better than most. I think it was better than last week but perhaps he didn't see that.

Second half was totally different. Not sure if Jürgen gave them a pep talk or rollicking but you tell from start they were up for it. I said to the chap next to me "I think Jürgen changed their batteries at half-time" and he laughed and agreed. Then we scored; it took a bit of luck but that is all you need sometimes, and it was like a weight lifted. Suddenly it was back to normal and it was obvious that it was only a matter of time before we scored again. So we did it, got a result, kept a clean sheet, no doubt got a bit of confidence back and hopefully gave them the thoughts to forget about last week.

The game ended and the long trek home begins. Quick walk across the park and wait to get out of the car park. This happened reasonably quickly and I tried to avoid the main road from there as I queued all the way to the motorway last time. Managed to find my way to the M57 – not the best way but did it fairly quickly and did it half an hour quicker than last time. Worth the extra fiver I think! I swear blind if I win the lottery I will make councillors use their road signs and see if they can get out of places. Directions until a fork and then nothing. And it is not just Liverpool, my lad lives in Reading and that is worse and I am not the only one who thinks it. Journey home was straightforward, no hold ups and I walked through the door at 8:35.

So after eleven and a half hours, 320 miles and £15 parking was it worth it? Yes of course it was, if only to see Daniel Sturridge's smile as he scored. Hopefully it will restore his confidence and push him on. I watched him run, chasing the ball down the left hand side in the second half and he looks as if he was really going for it. Fingers crossed we will get the 2013 Sturridge back one day. It wasn't a classic but it was an important game we couldn't really afford to lose or even draw.

A couple of observations about the Kenny Dalglish Stand: it is such a different atmosphere from the Main Stand. Nobody sings and that is an observation from three games. There are also many disgruntled people, last time against Burnley I sat in front of a lady who moaned the whole match. She moaned at Emre Can for lofting a ball that resulted in a goal. Didn't learn from that and kept it up the whole game. Luckily she wasn't there yesterday but there was plenty to take her place. What was bizarre was that the chap behind me was obviously moaning but in Russian or some similar language. Still it doesn't spoil my day but I must try to get a ticket in the Kop and see what that is like.

So roll on November and I can start the ticket buying process again. Hopefully I shall get my fourth ticket so I can be eligible for better access next season.

Paul Tomkins, October 28th, 2017

The English Premier League table does not lie (too much) at the end of the season. But earlier in the season the table does not tell the whole truth, even after 10+ games. Some teams will have had more difficult starts, having played many of the stronger teams. And other teams will have had easier starts, having played many of the weaker teams. So how do you produce a table that takes account of the quality of the opposition? *The Tomkins Times'* subscriber Tim O'Brien proposed use of the Ratings Percentage Index (RPI).

Here's what Tim said last October (2016):

"… I have been thinking about a way to quantify the strength of our start, and I attempted to do so using something from American sports called the Ratings Percentage Index (RPI).

In basketball at the University level in the U.S. there are 351 teams who play in Division 1, the highest level. These teams play roughly 30 games per season (it is not a set amount) against varying levels of competition. As a result, there can be vast differences in the quality of two teams who both had 17 wins and 13 losses.

There is a committee tasked with deciding which 68 teams are given entry to the tournament at the end of the season to determine the champions. This tournament is probably the closest thing we have in the States to the FA Cup. This committee uses the RPI as one tool to help them make their decisions. It is not perfect by any means, but by and large it does a good job of defining the true quality of the various teams. A given team is usually within a few places of where a poll of coaches ranks them.

The formula for the RPI is simple. It assigns a 25% weight to the team's winning percentage, a 50% weight to the average of all of that team's opponents' winning percentages, and a 25% weight to that team's opponents opponents' winning percentage.

I made a slight adjustment as, unlike football, there are no draws in basketball. Instead of using winning percentage, I used % of points gained versus those available. For example [remember, this explanation was written a year ago], Liverpool have gained 20 out of a possible 27 for 74.1%. I could not think of a way to weight home and away matches, so I ignored that factor.

All kinds of things can happen in the remainder of a season. Teams lose form and others find form. Places shift. Teams get injuries; others spend big in January or change their managers. There is no crystal ball; you can assess probabilities, but fate will often intervene.

However, using Tim's system, I thought it was worth comparing the positions of teams in both his RPI standings from twelve months ago, and the league table from the same time (after game nine: hereafter called PL9), against the final league positions. What was closer to the *eventual* truth? The league table after a quarter of a season in 2016/17 or the RPI table from the same time?

Well, there's a fairly big difference. The final league table had eight clubs within two places of where they were after PL9; so eight teams stayed roughly where they were at a quarter of the season in. However, the RPI had ten, so it was 25% more accurate.

More tellingly, the final league table had eleven clubs within three places of where they were in PL9, but a whopping seventeen of the RPI table were within three places. Ergo, last season, after game nine, you were better off trusting the RPI table than the league table in terms of what would *later* transpire. Only three clubs ended up more than three league positions away from where they sat in the quarter-season RPI.

I don't know if this is a regular occurrence, nor do I know how statistically significant it is. However, it's an interesting finding.

What's true is that Liverpool have never played so many top four English, Spanish and German sides, as well as last season's Champions League quarter-finalists, by the same stage of a season. (And the same applies if including Italian teams in previous seasons too, as the fourth of the big four European leagues.) My theory for some of the Reds' struggles this season – the Reds currently sit 9th – has not just been playing the extra games that the Champions League brings, but the difficulty of the first three fixtures in particular (two of which were in the qualifying round, meaning two additional games), plus the bruising League Cup tie at recent champions Leicester (contrast that to playing a third-tier team at home in the first cup game of the season). The first really easy fixture the Reds have had this season was Maribor away.

In the RPI table after the 9th league game, the Reds sit 2nd, behind Manchester City; suggesting that Klopp's men are far better than the mid-table position suggests.

This is something to revisit later in the season, to see how it all pans out.

Paul Tomkins, October 28th, 2017

No brand new Liverpool signing in the entire Premier League era has ever scored nine goals in all competitions by league game nine. Last week I asked TTT and LFCHistory guru Graeme Riley to run a search, and no new player can touch Salah in 25 years' worth of data. As a debut, it is *unprecedented*. A couple started on fire over the first two or three games – Nigel Clough and El Hadji Diouf – but Salah has maintained a superbly strong start. In the past there were a few easy League Cup games before the autumn, but Liverpool didn't have such luck this season.

Indeed, it's a rare achievement for an established Liverpool player to have nine in *all competitions* by the same stage; Ian Rush did it a few times in the 1980s, and in the Premier League era – i.e. a time when the Reds have not been the league's dominant force – it has only happened in five previous seasons, or roughly 20% of the time. But again, those goalscorers didn't have it as tough as Salah has in terms of the quality of opposition faced, and they've also taken penalties.

The standouts are Robbie Fowler, at his imperious best, with 10, in 1994/95, and again the next season, with nine; Michael Owen with 10 in 2001/02, when he was voted European Player of the Year; Steven Gerrard and Djibril Cissé with nine each in 2005/06; and Daniel Sturridge, with 10, in 2013/14, when watching him sprint onto a ball was a thing of great joy.

But we can discount Gerrard and Cissé from this list, given that the Reds played three qualifying rounds of the Champions League, with four more games than the Reds have faced this season, all against opposition far weaker than even Maribor. Gerrard scored five against TNS of Wales and two against FBK Kaunas; Cissé scored one against TNS, and like Gerrard, also got two against FBK Kaunas. They were already towards half a dozen goals each when the season "proper" started. So that puts Salah's nine goals into context.

Also, Gerrard and Cissé each scored a penalty in their nine goals. Salah has scored no penalties, and non-penalty goals (NPG) are always a better indication of a natural goalscorer. (Of course, Salah has gone and missed a penalty since I drafted this part of the article yesterday.)

Owen's 10 in 2001/02 is down to nine when you take out his penalty against Everton. So Fowler stands ahead, with his 10 non-penalty goals in 1995, along with Daniel Sturridge, with the same tally, when at his brilliant best four years ago. (Sturridge has showed that while he seems to struggle to run, he remains a world-class finisher, although he had been missing a few when stuck on the niggling 99 career goals.)

For a team that apparently "needs someone who can score goals like Fowler or Owen", Salah seems to be doing a remarkably good job. Before he arrived, the average number of all-comps goals registered by Liverpool's top scorer after a quarter of the season (1992-2016) was just six. That is the average for *all* players, not just new ones.

Six just happens to be the number notched by Roberto Firmino going into the Huddersfield game, where he bagged his seventh. Not bad for someone who "can't score goals". The Brazilian is in keeping with the average for a club that has had some outstanding finishers in the last 25 years, and to have a one-in-two ratio. And he's not even a last-shoulder striker, just as Mo Salah isn't even a centre-forward.

Fernando Torres had bagged seven by this stage in his debut season, five the season after, and eight in his final full season with the Reds.

But the more recent averages have been far lower. Before Salah, the Reds' top all-comps scorer after nine league games had five last season (Coutinho), and three before that (Ings), and three before that (Sterling). For such a free-scoring team in 2013/14, the wheels really did come off when Luis Suárez left.

It's totally confusing to some people that Liverpool's goal-poacher right now is not the centre-forward, but the *wide-man* who takes up central positions when the centre-forward drops deep or wide. Today it was Firmino who got the goal, not Salah.

October's Results

01.10.2017 – (A) Newcastle United 1 – 1
14.10.2017 – (H) Manchester United 0 – 0

17.10.2017 – (A) NK Maribor 7 – 0
22.10.2017 – (A) Tottenham Hotspur 1 – 4
28.10.2017 – (H) Huddersfield Town 3 – 0

Paul Tomkins, Comment, November 3rd, 2017
I agree with others on Emre Can. He's an excellent player, who offers some bite and some height. He scores a few goals. And he should get better.

But he's not *integral*. It's a blow losing one of the best younger players at the club, especially for nothing. But if he's not committed, fine – we move on. Keita is younger, and better, although smaller.

The bigger issue is losing him, aged 24, *and* Coutinho, 26 (as they'll be next summer). If we don't sell Coutinho then we'll have the same old shenanigans. These are players not quite in their peak yet, and ideally you want to hold onto those. And losing two first-teamers at once would be a disruption. I guess the good news is that Coutinho's value has risen, at a time when Can's has run down to £0. Liverpool also got Keita for about £30m less than Leipzig wanted this past summer, due to his contract situation. It's swings and roundabouts.

West Ham United (A), November 4th, 2017
Andrew Beasley
When I first met Jim, Roy Evans was Liverpool manager. But so was Gérard Houllier. That partnership didn't last long, but Jim and I have been mates since our first year at university.

Yet despite this being the 20th season of our friendship, and both being keen Liverpool fans, we've only ever managed to go to a couple of matches together. Both were away wins; a 2-0 at Fulham, and a 3-0 at Southampton.

The first was late in the 2007/08 season, when Rafa rotated ahead of a Champions League semi-final, and we were sitting with the home fans for the latter. The West Ham match promised to be a bit more meaningful and lively than the previous two were.

Truth be told, there simply haven't been many chances for us to go to a match together. I've only been to 23 matches, after all, and Jim hasn't been too often in recent times either. I did once sell him a League Cup ticket for a match at Spurs when I couldn't make it. It didn't end well.

So this was always going to be a good day out. But there are two reasons in particular as to why:

Jim got the tickets off a Scouser who works with his wife, so we are in with the Liverpool fans.

The London Stadium is 30 minutes' walk from my flat.

The proximity is a definite plus, as it means we can meet for beers near my house before taking a stroll to the ground. My local knowledge, and prior experience of the stadium (if for athletics and para-athletics, rather than football) proves invaluable. Simply put, there is nowhere decent to drink anywhere near the ground. Praise be for my local pub, and the Foundation bitter on tap.

Jim mentioned he'd placed some bets on the 3pm kick-offs, so I decide to do likewise. I predicted results in the four top flight matches, and got them all wrong. I cursed the likes of Tony Pulis and Sean Dyche (not for the first time), finished my pint, and we're off to the match.

The London Stadium may not have a lot to recommend it for as a football venue, but we got straight in and bought a beer within about a minute, so it's not all bad. The bar staff were wearing red tops with 'Kop A Load Of The Action' emblazoned across them. A nice touch, or trying too hard? You decide. Jim and I chat for a bit over our overpriced lagers, before going to find our seats/standing positions.

We were in row seven, so we were at least close to the pitch even if the view wasn't great. The atmosphere around us was good, with plenty of chanting, though some of our fans are more concerned with flicking "Vs" at the West Ham supporters closest to our section, which seems weird to me.

The first half was defined by its first two corners. My heart was in my mouth as Liverpool lined up to defend one, yet within about ten seconds of it being taken, they've taken the lead. As the Reds (Oranges?) broke away up field, I'm torn between watching it live or on the big screen behind the West Ham goal. The screen offers a better view, but is delayed from what's actually happening. By the time I decide, it's 1-0, so who cares?

Two minutes later, Liverpool lined up a corner of their own. "We never do anything with corners", says Jim, and it's hard to argue with the sentiment. Especially once it appears to have been scuffed along the ground, but fortunately West Ham can't defend and Liverpool are two up.

I mentioned Jim doesn't go to many games, but he was at Palace last season when Liverpool won 4-2. He's now been to two games since the start of last season, and Matip has scored in both of them. Maybe Joël should buy Jim a season ticket?

The game then died down for a spell, and I was struck by how their fans seemed to get loud at weird times. But then I realise as football fans, you've seen it all before from your own team. I see Mark Noble playing a short backwards pass to retain possession, which seems reasonable enough. Hammers fans are fed up of repeatedly being two goals down and then seeing slow play, so a pass like that winds them up.

It's part of the fabric of being a fan. You're destined to be frustrated by the same things for years at a time. When Ragnar Klavan missed a relatively simple defensive header at 0-0, the Tottenham debacle flashed before my eyes.

But I digress. Liverpool reached the break two up, and Jim spent the interval queueing for another beer. We then had to down it so as not to miss much of the second half action. It's a hard life.

Klopp's boys then conceded a goal, as they tend to on the road, and the giant bubble machine in front of our stand sparked into life in celebration. This made it all the sweeter about a minute later when Alex Oxlade-Chamberlain restored our two goal advantage, and was able to celebrate in the bubbles before they faded and died.

As Liverpool fans rushed down the steps to greet their heroes at the front of the stand, one kid by me fell to the ground and another burst into tears at the mayhem. It certainly takes you out of the moment when you see that happen, but thankfully no harm was done.

The rest of the match passed off in straight-forward fashion, with Liverpool scoring one and missing a few other decent opportunities. Most of the home fans cleared off early, whilst we still had plenty of songs to sing. At the end, Klopp headed towards us and gave the travelling Kop a salute. The whole evening was a job well done by the manager, the players, and the fans alike.

I strolled home and within an hour of full-time I was sat on my sofa enjoying sausage and chips from the local takeaway. Talk about your dream away days. To cap it off, I watched *Match Of The Day* for a decent view of the action, and I spotted Jim and myself going mad in the crowd following the third goal. Pretty perfect, wouldn't you say?

Paul Tomkins, November 4th, 2017

Liverpool just ran in four largely lovely goals against West Ham, and it could have been more. The Reds' defending wasn't perfect, but even the chaos of Andy Carroll only caused a few flutters, and a couple of bruises to Emre Can's head.

The goals are flowing. And there are two reasons why I've felt this would be the case. First, the early fixture list was very tough, but has eased off; and second, the creativity had been there, but the finishing – by good finishers – was off, and supposed flops (like Alex Oxlade-Chamberlain) are now adding goals too.

The previous nine games (excluding the League Cup) had seen Liverpool's "form" – or, actually, the *results* – change from stagnant to productive. But we can actually see the value of expected goals (xG) as an analysis tool over this period. The tenth, today, further confirmed that this is a team dominating games, with just one really bad day at the office at Wembley the other week. It is a team that can defend systematically, but which makes individual errors. Remove those errors, and things look far more sensible.

Liverpool's shot-map today shows a team that is working chances in the box, not just banging the ball from distance. (Pot-shots are often a waste of possession, but I'm all for them now and then, to mix things up.) The Reds are even scoring set-piece goals, although today it appeared to be from *West Ham*'s set-pieces. The improved results are simply following the trend of that creativity.

While ten games remains a small sample, it's far better than one game, where xG can still tell a story (just like the scoreline can) but can also be unpredictable. While these aren't all league games, ten games is more than a quarter of a league season. So it's a decent sample size. (And the ten games includes Champions League games as well, so not easy cup matches.)

In the five games from Burnley to Manchester United, Liverpool won just once, drawing the other four. But this is where the value of xG comes in. While I'm not an xG expert (an xPert?), I know enough to say that, if you keep winning on xG, the wins will likely follow. I said this back at the time of those draws. (Using football statistician Michael Caley's xG figures.)

It didn't feel like the usual slump that some teams have, when they aren't creating anything. But these days, any kind of problem for a team or a player leads to mass hysteria.

Four of those five opponents created between 0.1 and 0.6 xG against the Reds. In other words, add all of their efforts together in each of those games, and the likelihood was they didn't merit even a single goal. For a variety of reasons, in real terms they averaged a goal per game.

But Liverpool's expected goals at the other end remained consistent: from 1.6 away at Newcastle to 2.2 away in Moscow, with the other three games ranging in between. Be it away in Russia, Newcastle, Leicester, or at home to Burnley and Man United, the Reds were "worth" two goals a game. But in actuality they averaged just one.

Now, patterns can flip. But logically, it was clear that if the Reds kept creating two-goals' worth of chances, and kept it below one goal xG at the back, they should have started winning games. Hence, four wins from the last five, and eighteen goals scored. Corner duly turned.

Daniel Rhodes, November 15th, 2017

Sixty-plus shots with less than a one in three chance of going in. My general perception – and clearly those of fellow Reds and fans of other clubs – was that he'd had a bigger proportion of 'big chances'.

What is a big chance? According to Opta:

"A situation where a player should reasonably be expected to score, usually in a one-on-one scenario or from very close range."

Thanks to TTT stalwart Dan Kennett, who has tracked clear cut chances (the old brand name) over the past seven seasons, we know:

"… the percentage of all shots that are non-penalty big chances has stayed very similar across the seven years; min of 10.9%, max of 12.4% with an average of 11.5%. So we could reasonably define that the top decile of non-penalty shots are definitely "big chances. The seven season average conversion rate is 37.6%. But it has gradually increased year on year from 33.3% at the start to 46.2% last season."

One way to remove the Opta 'subjectivity' is to assign an expected goal value, with everything over that being classed a big chance. Dan suggested if we assign 0.35 (or 35%) then we are referring to the 85th percentile and above. According to this cut-off:

- Salah has had 12 big chances in total, and ten non-penalty big chances.
- He has converted eight out of 12, for a 66% conversion rate.
- Taking penalties out, it rises slightly to 70% or seven out of ten.
- The proportion of all these big chances is slightly above the norm at 16%, but nothing significant.
- Even if you use all 15 shots, the conversion rate is still above 50%.
- 14 out of the 15 shots above were with his left foot!

To describe a player as wasteful means they are missing chances they are expected to score. All footballers, including the very best (Lionel Messi, Cristiano Ronaldo, Harry Kane, Sergio Agüero) miss chances they are expected to convert. In fact, Agüero's record on big chances is worse than 35%!

At first I thought Salah must have missed easy chances that cost Liverpool points? The Huddersfield penalty at 0-0? The save from Petr Cech early in the Arsenal game? The 'open goal' against Leicester at 0-0? Liverpool won all of those games. There was a big chance he missed against Newcastle at 1-1 (which was on TV in the UK), and also the attempt that was saved at Manchester City, at 0-1, just before the Sadio Mané sending off. Surely fans (or experts) would not base their view of a player on just two chances that – at a very big push – cost the Reds points? And at the same time ignore all the goals he's scored!?

Only one conclusion can made from all evidence presented:

Liverpool fans are woefully wasteful with their opinions and perceptions of finishing ability.

Mohamed Salah is a world class finisher.

Dan Kennett, Comment, November 17th, 2017
The self-promoting cabal of ageing British managers are a hindrance to the game in this country, not a benefit. The root cause of the problem is that British managers aren't good enough to establish teams in the top half of the Premier League and what club challenging for honours is going to give a job to someone with nothing on their CV other than the correct nationality? At best, most British managers are specialists in avoiding relegation, which will never be enough for a club challenging for honours or aiming to establish itself in the top half of the Premier League. In recent Premier League history, only Eddie Howe and Brendan Rodgers have tried to do otherwise. Maybe Garry Monk at Swansea as well but his results were crap and he paid the price.

Until the English/British system produces coaches that can actually coach, improve players and show a tactical awareness of the modern game, they will not get these jobs or be headhunted by overseas clubs. Right now, flavour of the month is Sean Dyche and, in my opinion, he's clearly earned a promotion to a club with more resources than Burnley. He's shown that he can make Burnley far more than the sum of their parts, is relatively young (46) and is very innovative in the sports science field (if not wider analytics). At his next job, the onus will be on Dyche to show he can build on what he did at Burnley and adapt his style accordingly. His gameplan of insane hard work, supremely organised deep defence and direct play wouldn't be accepted for long at a club like Everton for example.

You ask West Brom fans how they feel about Tony Pulis now, the novelty of finishing 9th has already worn off for most of them. Most of the top foreign coaches given the top jobs in this country have already come through their own domestic structure and many have had success in other countries on top of that. Other than Dyche/Howe/Rodgers, how many are coming through the British structure? How many British managers have even tried to broaden their experience? Steve McLaren did with FC Twente but his career has nosedived in the last five years. David Moyes at least took the job in Spain but was a complete failure. Despite his historic success at Celtic, Rodgers remains a joke figure for most of the British media. (I don't count the Neville brothers at Valencia because they only got the job because Peter Lim is a huge Man United fan.)

The advocates of British managers need to recognise our shortcomings and accept that it's not a race to the bottom, it's about improving standards and creating a meritocracy. One positive is that at least the English FA seem to have capable people in place below the board and executive team, perhaps learning from the outrageous success of Sport England and Team GB. Other than the Aidy Boothroyd association, I believe Dan Ashworth is well respected and doing a good job as Technical Director. The head of performance is Dave Reddin who was involved with Clive Woodward in his most successful period. The heads of science and medical are also industry experts and widely respected. Maybe in 10 years time we'll be actually producing the coaches that are being headhunted for the top jobs at home and abroad?

Southampton (H), November 18th, 2017
Hemal Shah
I normally manage to go to about five matches a season, with my mate who I have grown up with. Both of us started supporting the Reds while growing up in Kenya. We both now live in London so it is easier to go together. In this instance, I managed to secure four more tickets from a mate, and so four other mates who we grew up with in Kenya but now live in London came with us.

We met up at Euston and jumped on the very busy 10:07 train to Lime Street. Three Saints fans were already sitting at our table of four seats, and only got up when we showed them our reserved seat tickets, and then they sat on the next table down, where we also had two of the seats reserved; they looked very pissed off having to get up again. Because of their dickish attitude, muttering about Liverpool fans in London etc., I couldn't be happier with our start of the day as they ended up standing the whole way through.

We started drinking early on the otherwise uneventful journey and reached Lime Street at 12:15. We made our way down to the Ship and Mitre for a few ales before getting to the ground at 2:30, where we made a quick stop at the club shop for some Christmas shopping and bade farewell to the four mates whose seats were in the Main Stand. We had Kop block 305, towards the back.

The game seemed to take a while to get going, and not much happened in the first 20 minutes. Although the stand near us never stopped singing, it felt quite flat and not many were joining in. Mo Salah then scored a beauty, the Kop found its voice and everyone relaxed a little when the second went in.

The big issue in the Kop was which Salah song to sing, with the part near the Main Stand going with Mo Mo Mo Mo Mo Mo (Toure brothers version) and the rest of the Kop going with Salalalah song. Needless to say, I prefer the Salalalah one. Dejan Lovren's hack on Virgil van Dijk with their free kick seemed like the only moment of concern, with Simon Mignolet nowhere near covering it if it was on target. Saints were a little better at the start of the second half but the third goal put paid to the match and the subs made sure the match fizzled out. Highlight of the second half was a 10 min rendition of the Gary Macca song sung over and over again around the 70 min mark.

We met our mates outside and made our way back to Lime Street where we had a couple more drinks at the Wetherspoons in the station before getting on the very busy train. Back to Euston and we decided to go for a late night curry and drinks. We got home at 1am.

It was a great day out but it has now caught up with me and my Sunday has been spent recovering!

Paul Tomkins, November 19th, 2017

Jürgen Klopp's Liverpool are a brilliantly bonkers back-to-front side, with nothing quite where you expect it. How do you mark a team that doesn't fit into conventional patterns?

Against Southampton it was a near-perfect attacking display, backed by a faultless defensive performance. As with the earlier draws in the season, when the stats were more flattering than the results (which suggested those results were deceiving), it was yet another 2-0 victory on expected goals; creating chances and giving nothing away at the back. It's been going on for over ten games now, the Wembley horror aside (a worse xG) and the away thumping of Maribor (a better xG). Liverpool are getting games won and bringing off key players to cruise the final twenty minutes.

The movement, the interchanges, the reverse passes – it's too much for teams to handle; and that's mostly been the case even without Philippe Coutinho and Sadio Mané, whose previous absences made this the first time the first-choice front four has started a home game together. And it's more evident, too, now that Liverpool have broken through the ludicrously tough early-season schedule (although this coming week will be about as testing as it gets for a few months).

Yet this is a side with few "traditional" performers in their respective positions. To put it into the parlance of past players, essentially, the current version of Javier Mascherano – the best ball-winner – plays as a centre-forward, while Ian Rush – the pacy goal glutton – starts on the wing. Peter Beardsley plays in midfield. In the past Liverpool have had fluid formations and versatile players, but this is a little different.

Indeed, whereas Mascherano won the ball deep to give it to Xabi Alonso and Steven Gerrard to start attacks – a perfectly logical approach – Roberto Firmino wins the ball on the edge of the opposition area in order to give it, quickly, to Mo Salah, Philippe Coutinho and Sadio Mané. A shot on goal arrives seconds later.

You can talk about the need for holding midfielders, commanding centre-backs, and so on, but if you can regularly win the ball that high up the pitch it lowers the likelihood of it ever reaching your defence. And if you can turn those high-field possession turnovers into goals, that saps the opposition's morale. Once they're 3-0 down they won't come at your defence as hard, either.

I haven't seen the stats but during the game I counted at least four times that Firmino won the ball in dangerous areas, and that becomes the equivalent of making four ultra-incisive final-third passes – even if he finds a red shirt in space just by rolling the ball one yard. If you can get the ball to the feet of players like Salah, or take a shot yourself, from harrying the opposition, it becomes your creative outlet, as Klopp has noted many times.

Like Pep Guardiola's Manchester City, Klopp has a team full of midfielders. And it's a good thing. Perhaps more accurately, as I noted early last season, it's that everyone is shifted back one row in the team. Against Southampton, Liverpool started with three up front – none of whom are traditional, bog-standard strikers; but also fielded two more semi-strikers – no.10s – in midfield. Plus, attacking full-backs. And the holding midfielder was previously a box-to-box midfielder. Yet it feels beautifully balanced right now. Liverpool aren't getting stretched in games, the Spurs debacle aside – and even that was largely self-inflicted by one player (who, in fairness, came back strongly yesterday against his old club).

We wondered last season what it would be like if Coutinho moved from the left-side of a front three to a no.8 role, and although he nearly moved to Barcelona instead, he is now creating chances and scoring goals from that deeper position. (Thankfully, for now at least, he's no deeper in terms of global latitude.)

Sevilla (A), Champions League group stage, November 21st, 2017
Paddy Smith

As soon as the draw was made my oldest son begged and begged to 'do' Sevilla away. I finally agreed on condition we got tickets in the ballot; of course, we didn't.

A few weeks before the game I bumped into someone of influence at the club who owed me a favour and managed to bag two tickets. Of course by this time any flights to Malaga or Madrid were £200 each way if available at all. It's amazing the creative travel plans you can come up with when you really need to! After discounting Stansted (where the fuck is it?), London, trains from Manchester £130 each, Leeds, East Midlands, etc., someone mentioned the word Dublin ... two return flights, Manchester to Dublin £46, airport hotel £50, Dublin to Malaga £200 all in, and we're all booked.

So, Monday night sat in Terminal 3 with my oldest boy who is skipping college for two days for a different kind of education; that's what I tell his Mum anyway! 10pm take-off delayed by an hour, and we check into the hotel at midnight. Getting ready for bed when the lights go out without a switch being touched – power-cut, so a quick change of room; 1am by the time we're in bed. Before you can say 'top of the morning' our 5:30 alarm is going off. We're up, out and checked out of the hotel and checked in at the airport, a quick bite to eat and then off we go.

We meet up with two mates in Malaga who've been out for a few days and sorted a car; next time we really need something bigger than a Fiat Panda with no AC! A very hot and sweaty two hours later and we're checking into our hotel, showered and ready for what Sevilla has to offer.

Sevilla is cool, the people are really friendly – a place with history that's a living, breathing city, a place where you know people love to live. Small streets, ace tapas bars, character without the cliché or Disney-fied version you see in some cities. We meet up in a place called Bodaga Santa Cruz near the beautiful cathedral, a stand up bar, small, ice cold beer and a few tapas sets us up for the day. A great chat at the bar with locals coming in for a bite and a beer, mixing with Reds ... lots of Reds! There must have been at least double the amount here without tickets; everyone we bump into asks the same question: 'any spares lad?'

A zig-zagging walk towards the ground with a few refreshment stops on the way and we get to the ground around 8pm; it's ace to do that, walk through the city, a couple of beers and then there you are, no soulless bowl in the middle of nowhere. We were in Munich in the summer for the preseason friendlies, and as great as the Allianz Arena is it's a real schlepp to get there, with no bars apart from official club ones.

There is a heavy police presence there and it's only after we hear of the trouble the police caused. Hand on heart I can say all day there wasn't an ounce of trouble, not even the threat of trouble hanging in the air, everyone was there for a laugh and a good time, maybe the police were on guard because of Leicester last year, but it seemed they must have been looking for confrontation.

Anyway we got in in plenty of time, said 'see you later' to my mates and agreed to meet up outside the ground at full-time. Get to our seats only to find my mate sat right next to us! Funny sometimes, life, isn't it! I've got to say on TV the ground doesn't look all that, but inside is impressive, a proper football ground and some atmosphere, even after the first minute goal, although at 0-3 it did go very quiet with a lot of whistles at half-time. In our end it's fucking mayhem! Fantastic football, all the goals scored in front of us. At half-time all the talk was 'even we can't fuck this up, can we?'

You know what's coming, they're going to come at us hard, just like in Basel in the Europa Cup final; stay strong, see out the first 15, and they'll blow themselves out and we can cruise to an easy win, qualification and top the group to boot. In my mind I can still see that happening now! I've not seen the goals back yet – don't know if it was a penalty, not really been on social media either, but you could see, you could *feel* the lack of game management. In my eyes only Joe Gomez comes out with any credit. At 2-3 with 75 mins gone though I did think we had the game won.

Final whistle, and to end 3-3 feels like a defeat. Trying to work out if we've qualified anyway. Kept behind for 15 mins. Trudge back into town for one last beer and a bit of a moan but you can't be too down, as we've had a brilliant time, real father/son time that he will always remember and we can laugh about in years to come, and he can bore his kids with daring tales of old.

In bed for 1am with alarm set for 5:45 and train back to Malaga, flight back into Dublin, pint of Guinness (*pint of Guinness in Dublin*, one more of my bucket list ticked off) and then all being well, home for 9pm. Sitting on the train typing this now, the sun just coming up over the plains of southern Spain, lad asleep next to me, we've had fun. Go to Sevilla, it's great, take the wife, husband, girlfriend, boyfriend, partner or mates, the people are nice people which counts, it really does. Food's great, so is the beer, and it's cheap ... just don't go to watch Liverpool play footy there!

Paul Tomkins, November 22nd, 2017

The best thing about a draw that feels like a defeat is the reminder that it was still, after all, a draw. Unlike a defeat, you get to take something from it. It's a bit like thinking you've won £10m on the lottery, only to find out you instead won £1m. Life sucks, eh?

And to come away with a point from Spain, against a team who were 25 games unbeaten at home, is still a good result, even if it sucks the biggest suckable fucking eggs to go from 3-0 to 3-3 in one half of football; 60 seconds from winning a Champions League group to having to go again on the final day. A bummer, but not the end of the world. Or the group. Or the season. Or, anything.

Equally, although it's not the toughest of groups, to get through for the first time since 2009 – as a draw at home to Spartak Moscow would ensure – would represent progress. That's firmly in Liverpool's hands going into the final match, at Anfield, against beatable opposition.

The hardest half-time team-talk is probably when the game feels won, but even at 3-0, no game between two good teams can be said to be over. (And as much as I loved Roberto Firmino's no-look goal, it now feels like needless showboating; next time, save it for the seventh goal!)

It just takes one goal to make it interesting. Good Liverpool sides have squandered 3-0 leads against teams like Newcastle*, Southampton and Crystal Palace over the past 20 years, and we all know the feeling when 3-1 becomes 3-2; was saw it in the eyes of AC Milan's players (a team that had recently won the Champions League, and would soon again win the Champions League). We've seen Liverpool need three second half goals against Olympiakos, and grab that vital third late in the day. (* In that case, a last-minute equaliser was overturned by an even later Robbie Fowler header.)

And of course, it's now also clear that the Sevilla manager told his players at half-time that he has cancer. You saw their superhuman reaction to it. They had nothing left to lose, and everything to gain – for themselves, and for him.

I also think it fair to point out that Jürgen Klopp, labelled naïve by the knee-jerkers, replaced three players with more defensive-minded substitutes, which helped the Reds regain more of a foothold in the game, and almost saw the lead stretched to 4-2 when Emre Can failed to find Sadio Mané with an open goal, and James Milner also rolled the ball across an empty goal-line.

Maybe Klopp could have done this at 3-1, or even at half-time, but that was the XI that had been making Sevilla suffer. And as soon as you go more defensive, you invite on pressure. Sometimes it works, sometimes it doesn't. I often point out the hypocrisy of the post hoc analysis, as sometimes attacking remains the best form of defence. Sometimes it doesn't. Every game is a unique set of circumstances, that can never be repeated. If it goes wrong, you should always have done the *opposite* thing, even if the opposite thing cost you last time.

However, the nerves of a 93rd-minute corner can plague a plenty of teams, especially when a lot is riding on it. Just as Liverpool gained from Sevilla's bad set-piece defending in the first half, the Spaniards saw the ball fall to them in the box. Liverpool were set up nicely in a zone, but no one reacted quickly enough when the ball ran loose.

I've seen it said in a few places that Liverpool need to re-learn how to play in Europe. But this season it's four wins and three draws in Europe, no defeats. (Maribor are substandard, but Hoffenheim certainly aren't.) Liverpool have already played 20 European games under Klopp, won 10 and lost just two. (And two more games have been played away from Anfield than at Anfield, with just eight of the 12 at home.)

These 20 games include six games against German sides, five against Spanish sides and two against Manchester United (where the opposition was English but the two-leg situation distinctly European). The only defeat outside of the Europa League final was a last-minute goal away at Villarreal, but the second-leg was duly won 3-0. And Borussia Dortmund were hardly "naïve" in Europe when they ran into the second-half thunderstorm of the Kop after taking an early 2-0 lead, and the same thing happened to Liverpool last night in Spain – Dortmund weren't necessarily weak, just blown over in a gale.

Chelsea (H), November 25th, 2017
Andrew Potter

I don't want this to sound boastful but due to unbelievably good luck I was at the game yesterday, in the Directors' Box (now known as the Boardroom).

Before I describe what it was like, I want to establish some credibility. I am a Scouser, went to a secondary modern school and university in Liverpool, my first trip to Anfield was in 1970 (T-Rex was played on the loudspeakers). I had a Kop then Main Stand season ticket from 1989-2005, when I moved to Oz and stupidly gave it up – now I'm back in the South East of the UK and rarely get to go anymore.

But boy I struck lucky yesterday.

The ticket came as a result of my boss being unavailable, so it was all a bit last minute. But luckily I sorted a train from East Grinstead to Lime Street – 07:07 departure via Euston on Saturday morning – even getting a reserved seat.

Curiously, people talk to each other more on commuter trains at the weekend but there was some disbelief at East Grinstead: "To Liverpool? For Football? It's on BT Sport!"

No football fans visible until Euston at 08:30 – and then the majority seemed to be Brighton fans heading to Manchester ... I did have the (wrong) thought of lambs to the slaughter.

A smooth journey up to the reopened Lime Street – even though it's under construction again – and then a taxi to my sister's to change into my suit. First nerves start. What do you wear?

Okay, so this was the first time I had ever been to Anfield for hospitality (and when wearing a tie) – mental note: what are 'tailored trousers' when they are at home? (...described as part of the dress code!)

She dropped me off at the Arkles and I made my way in at 2:45pm. At reception I was greeted by a really friendly receptionist.

Her: "You know where you are going?"

Me: "Of Course" (thank goodness there was a massive 'Boardroom' sign so I couldn't fail to swagger toward a second reception desk. There I got my lanyard (subsequently used over my pyjamas) and into a quiet boardroom. Champagne offered from a gloved hand.

I was early so it was quiet. I took in the view of the pitch from the dining room and I spotted a few supporters in the distance taking selfies in the Main Stand. What struck me was how fast a steward was over to take their photo for them (moving them so they had the Kop in the background). That small gesture would have meant they had a great photo.

As I looked around the empty stadium my mind flashed back. There's where I was for my first ever game (by the corner flag at the very front of the Anny Road – now the away area). There's where I stood when Ruddock made it 3-3 against United, there when Collymore scored the fourth against Newcastle. I counted up the years – 47 years I've been coming and look at the place now.

I then spotted Mr and Mrs Dalglish arrive and took a trip to the Gents (odd it said that on the door of such a posh place, I thought). As I recall it, a trip to a loo at Anfield generally involved a long queue with water in the sink optional – yesterday it was no such thing. White flannels rolled up next to a beautiful array of handwashes.

I won't go into the details of the subsequent experience but it was truly fantastic. For what it's worth though, here are my reflections:

I was expecting to leave last night having applied some inverted snobbery, reflecting miserably that "it's now an industry" and coming away somewhat sad at the demise of the people's game.

Actually, I was blown away and I truly think the club is in really great hands. Here's what I found:

The sheer professionalism of everyone who works behind the scenes – incredible attention to detail; the investment in the Main Stand itself – many have commented on this; Peter Moore, CEO, who addressed the room – a truly competent, impressive individual who was credible, engaging and passionate about the club. He was ably supported by the ambassadors who create a very professional impression (of course they would though).

I find it unfathomable that the attention to detail prevalent at the 'top' of the club has not been rolled out right the way down to affairs on the training ground and onto the pitch.

The mood music I picked up (for what it's worth) was that a) 'the squad is carrying quite a few minor injuries at the moment, hence the rotation'; b) that Klopp really *is* the man – even though the defence is not fixed as fast as wanted, he's sorted a lot of other stuff out. Priorities are clear and he is extremely highly regarded ('lucky to have him')

So I am now super optimistic for the medium-term. The strong impression I got is that the owners are right in there, nobody is asleep at the wheel 5,000 miles away – they are living and breathing this.

Regarding the crowd. Nothing succeeds like success. A bit of a run and that will sort itself out. I think we just need a reason to believe, which will come. Remember what it was like under Brendan Rodgers … imagine what that will be like when Klopp gets us close.

So there you go. In the end it was a super positive day.

That said — I would still have enjoyed fish, chips and curry sauce from the Chung Ku more than the 'dining experience' — so I am an inverted snob really!

But what a view ….

Paul Tomkins, November 26th, 2017

Yes, Liverpool threw away a three-goal lead in the week. And yes, the final moments in Seville were as scary as Cher in a high-crotch leotard.

But it was away, in the Champions League, to Sevilla; not at home to some promoted Premier League dross.

Yes, Liverpool ended up drawing with Chelsea, but Chelsea are the reigning champions, with a far more expensive squad than the Reds, and who had a nice midweek stroll for over 70 minutes against 10-man Qarabag (Qarabag, Qarabag, they don't do the fandango?), not a game against one of the top 20 sides in Europe. Liverpool had an extra day to prepare, but Chelsea essentially had a training session in Azerbaijan. Sevilla are 15th in the Euro Club Index, and unbeaten at home in 25 games; Qarabag are 161st. If they played every game with 10 men, Qarabag would be 710th.

Liverpool have now played the rest of the top six, within just 13 games. That's half of the Big Six head-to-heads in just a third of the season. So, five such fixtures in 13 games, then five in the remaining 25 games. Now tell me that doesn't skew the picture? How is that representative of a full season? I believe that Manchester United have played just three so far. United are racking up points against beatable opposition, but so too are Liverpool lately. The swings and roundabouts is that Liverpool aren't as dominant against the other Big Six sides.

There is also a clear top eight in the Premier League so far this season — eight teams with 21 or more points, compared to the 16 points of Brighton in 9th. Liverpool have played everyone in the top eight. The Reds also just need a draw in the final game to reach the knockout stages of the Champions League. And yet Jürgen Klopp is apparently "taking Liverpool backwards", according to idiots like Joey Barton and other rent-a-gobs. It's nine years since the Reds were in the knockout stages, and only once in the previous eight seasons had the club finished in the top four.

This is not making excuses, it's context. It's using *brain cells*.

Go back just over two years, to just before Jürgen Klopp pitched up, and we were thankful for beating Aston *Fucking* Villa. Anfield sounded as low-key yesterday as it did back then, when West Ham were winning 3-0 on the ground, or when Sion were grabbing a draw; just a few months after Crystal Palace won 3-1 on the ground, and just a few months after Stoke beat the Reds 6-1. Yeah, Klopp — why are you giving us results as bad as that, you *loser!*

The final 15 months of Brendan Rodgers' reign were largely poor, and that's what we are moving forwards from. Equally, his overall win percentage is boosted by one incredible season, for which he deserves more credit than he sometimes gets, even if Luis Suárez was like a man possessed. But he was the manager, he deserves praise for it. It's possible to praise Rodgers for what went right and to blame him for his clear role the decline thereafter, although I think part of the problem was that the improvement in 2013/14 was too swift – Liverpool weren't ready for the Champions League.

Another problem was that Rodgers was very poor in the transfer market, and we can now see for certain that he actually held back the transfer committee, rather than vice versa. Finishing 2nd allowed him to have more influence on transfers and it took the club in the wrong direction.

Look back at the squad from the start of 2015/16 and compare it to now. This vintage is much better, in part because of the improvement of existing players under Klopp (such as Roberto Firmino, Emre Can and Adam Lallana), but also because the transfer process is picking up players like Sadio Mané and Mo Salah. (According to someone I spoke to at the club, the committee also spent over a year trying to get Rodgers to agree on signing Joe Gomez, but he wouldn't until Sean O'Driscoll, England's U19s manager, tipped the scale.) Klopp and co are revitalising the whole club, with the U23s – many of whom train with the senior team – walking their division right now, with very few senior players making up the numbers to skew things.

Paul Tomkins, November 27th, 2017

Okay, this is getting a little insane. I'm hearing more of people thinking that *Jürgen Klopp has to go*, that Liverpool are going backwards. This is lunacy.

Comparing Klopp's tenure with the whole of Brendan Rodgers' doesn't look so great for the German; there's not much between them, at 50% vs 51% win rate.

But Klopp didn't inherit the swashbuckling side of 2013/14; he inherited the side of 2015/16, a team that had just shat out a measly 11 goals in 11 games, winning just three; and which, in the two games beforehand (at the end of 2014/15), had shipped nine (*nine!*) goals to Crystal Palace and Stoke City. That's six conceded at Stoke, and three at home to Crystal Palace and three more at home to West Ham in a short space of time, all of which were lost. Suddenly, shipping three away to one of the best sides in Spain, and getting what at the outset would have been a creditable draw, equated to this kind of garbage?

Klopp inherited a side that wasn't *scoring*, as well as not defending well. The Reds average almost two goals a game under the German, massively up on what he inherited, even if not as mental as the Suárez-era Rodgers' side. (But that was once-in-a-blue-moon football.)

Liverpool scored 78 last season in the league alone, and are on course for 73 in the league this season, and have already scored 22 in seven European games.

Had Klopp inherited Raheem Sterling, Luis Suárez and a fit, super-speedy Daniel Sturridge, then this might be different. But he didn't, did he?

Had Rodgers been able to retain those, then things might have been better for him, too; but he replaced those with his choices of Rickie Lambert, Mario Balotelli, Danny Ings, Adam Lallana (who has improved under Klopp but still isn't a big goalscorer), and Christian Benteke.

To look at what Rodgers left behind – and *not what he had in 2013/14* – we just need to look at his final season-and-a-third (when the wheels came off), and compare it to Klopp's two seasons to date. Yes, this doesn't include Rodgers' best season, but as stated, that wasn't the situation he was bequeathed (and it also doesn't include his difficult first six months, when his win percentage was also poor).

We can take Klopp's tenure as a whole, as it's still fairly short in itself, but let's compare it to how Liverpool were performing for the (pretty significant) sum of 69 games – dating back to the start of 2014/15 – before the German took charge.

– 50% win rate in Klopp's tenure to date, 120 games; 20% of games lost, or exactly one-fifth

– 42% win rate in Rodgers' final season-and-a-third, 69 games; 29% of games lost, or almost a third. (*A third!*)

So, Klopp has performed 19% better in terms of wins, and 33% better in terms of avoiding defeat, in the 69-game vs 120-game samples.

Then, a specific focus on the period that cost Rodgers his job; which was essentially his final 18 games, but we'll extend it to 21, to be kind to him, as the Reds have played 21 this season.

– 48% win rate in Klopp's most recent 21 games (i.e. this season); 14% of 21 games lost (three), or exactly one-seventh.

– 29% win rate in Rodgers' final 21 games; 33% of final 21 games lost, or exactly a third. (A *third!*)

Klopp has performed 66% – *sixty-six percent* – better in terms of wins in his most recent 21 games (which were far tougher on paper) than Rodgers did during his final 21 games. (His final eighteen games, starting with the horrible FA Cup semi-final performance versus Aston Villa, saw a meagre 22% win rate, which is more than twice as bad as the current run. That's one win every five games.)

Klopp has performed 42% – *forty-two percent* – better in terms of number of defeats in his most recent 21 games, including seven in the Champions League, than Rodgers did during his final 21 games, which contained no tough European games.

The club is in much better hands. Believe me.

Stoke City (A), November 29th, 2017
Kris Patterson

A bit of background on me before I go onto the Stoke game. Thirty-three years old, son to an avid Everton-supporting dad with a season ticket for +30 years! Happily for me, I was taken to my first ever live game by my granddad on my mum's side, a huge Liverpool fan. I have little memory of the event/game/day, but do remember that I loved the colour of the kit: the Blues never stood a chance against the mighty Reds!

I've been going to Anfield for more than 15 years but have never had the privilege of a season ticket. I have about 10 good friends who all have access to tickets so usually get offered a ticket for every other home game, and make about 8-10 a season. One huge note on this though is that they're always at home – I've not been to an away game, in the away end before. So when I was offered the chance to go to the Stoke game, I jumped at the chance …. Forget that it's at the end of November, 8pm KO – wrap up warm and get behind the lads!

I live in Chester, so worked as normal, got changed in work and got in the car. A nice, easy drive to Crewe station to pick up my ticket-giving mate (he'd come from London) and on to the Bet 365 (a horribly named stadium). We got to within a quarter of a mile of the ground by 6:45 but didn't get parked up until 7:20 – traffic was horrendous. Ended up at the back of an industrial park, literally the last space in the car park. More on that later (although I'm sure you'll already see where that's going).

Got into the ground by 7:30, good atmosphere with our fans with a bit of singing and lots of chat about the starting lineup – how will Dejan Lovren/Alberto Moreno cope with Xherdan Shaqiri (who's been playing some good stuff this season)? Dominic Solanke up front, does that push Roberto Firmino out wide? And what does Danny Ings need to do to get into the side?! A swift pint of Pedigree and a meat and potato pie (not bad!) later and we were up to the seats – right in the middle, perfect seats! Now get the gloves, hats and scarves on – an absolute must, as the temperature dropped to 2-degrees.

The game starts and we look comfortable on the ball, but with not a lot of penetration. Build up is a bit slow and there's a bit of a lack of pace to the game. The ball is given to Sadio Mané a lot but he looks a bit nervous/unwilling to take the man on. Gini Wijnaldum is everywhere though, winning the ball back and starting the attacks. Seventeen minutes in, the first goal – such good play from Solanke to get hold of the ball in the box, control it and find Mané with the pass. Definitely onside and a lovely dinked finish over the keeper. Delayed celebration as we all thought it was offside, but correct decision given. Good, unselfish play from Bobby to shadow it into the goal to make sure it couldn't be cleared … there would've been cross words if he'd have nicked it though!

Nerves settled in the stands, but we still look like we need a 2nd; whilst Stoke are offering very little going forward, there's always a chance of a Peter Crouch knock-down and strike. In the 26th minute a half chance for Alex Oxlade-Chamberlain on his left foot from a knocked-down throw in, but a good save from Lee Grant. Then, 39th minute, a great chance for Solanke to get one for himself, played through on a back-heel by Bobby onto Dom's right foot. Time to pick his spot … but rushes his shot, far too close to the keeper, simple save. Gutted he missed, would've loved to have seen him score.

Almost straight after, ball through for Mame Biram Diouf and Simon Mignolet takes him out! He's off, *gotta be* … no! A yellow only, and free kick. *Wow.* Huge decision, home fans are absolutely up in arms, and rightly so, it looked like a stonewall red card to the away fans. Hushed silence and a huge sigh of relief to see it yellow. Nothing comes from the free kick. Lucky to get away with that one.

Just before half-time, Mané is put through by the very impressive Solanke for a one-on-one. This could finish it off before half time, but no! Hits the post. Groans of frustration, we need to take these chances. Half-time, head inside to try and thaw out. Signs everywhere stating that no alcohol will be served, but the taps are flowing so we get another pint each. Worried for the 2nd half that they'll come out of their shells and threaten more. Just worried that we've missed a couple of big chances.

Second half starts with a huge chance for Joe Allen to level it up. Just as we feared, big ball into the box, knocked down by Diouf and deflected wide! Far too close for comfort … a bit of concern around us, they're coming back into this. A bit of niggly stuff, not a lot of good football or chances before the two substitutions – James Milner on for Ox, Mo Salah on for Solanke. Both players coming off played really well.

Sixty-ninth minute, another typical Stoke chance – ball into Crouch, headed down to Allen again but he can't control his half volley and it flies over the bar. Phew. Then, the settler – 77th minute. Mané with a brilliant feinted turn to get away from his man, dinks the ball to the back post and Mo is there to slam home the volley! Crowd goes wild, singing both of his chants (any other players you can think of with two chants?). What a player, game over, now we can celebrate! Eighty-third minute, brilliant from Mo for the 3rd – harries the last defender, takes it off his toe for a one-on-one. Never in doubt, 3-0, perfect … aside from a late free kick from Gini hit straight at the keeper, and a farcical miss for Stoke in 91st minute, nice and easy – job done, great three points, never in doubt! Could've been seriously different if Mignolet had been sent off though ….

Man of the match for me was Gomez, without a doubt. What a player we've got there … he's self-assured, strong, good on the ball, reads the play well. Just outstanding.

Fantastic game and experience throughout. One part I enjoyed was standing and singing! I usually sit in the paddock at Anfield, and it's quiet down there – it's not often a song gets to us. I hate the fact that I feel like I have to keep that part of me inside, but felt nothing of the sort as part of the away crowd. I came away happy and hoarse, if a little cold!

Walked back to the car, got into the queue and didn't move for an hour – sat and warmed up and listened the Radio 5 fawn over Wayne Rooney's hat-trick (including a missed/deflected pen and a goal into an empty net), but everything else was pretty good – fair play to Stoke. Got home at 12.30, straight to bed, floating on a cloud of happiness!

Paul Tomkins, November 30th, 2017
If defeat hurts, that's good. Scream in pain if you have to, but then wake up to the reality.

Klopp has got us out of our protective shells – our foreboding joy (defined by Brené Brown as, and here I paraphrase: not even feeling hope – backing away from joy – because it's all going to go wrong, we just know it, etc.). And Klopp has us *feeling* again. Feeling is good. Let the *feel* in. Feel that fucker! Even the pain means we're alive, and not in some zombie-like trance.

Taking teams to cup finals and then losing is miles better than the disinterest at going out in the third round to lower league opposition, even if losing a final hurts more. Is that not a 100% logical statement? What's better? Losing in a final, by miles. It hurts more, but it's proof of being better.

And while the joys of being a fan are not built on logic, our mental health should always be predicated on reality, not dreams. If our mental health is based on dreams, we're not on solid ground. Equally, if our mental health is based on perfection – not conceding a late goal in Seville, say – then that's dangerous too. Life isn't perfect. Sport isn't perfect. Defenders are not perfect. And no one can perfectly control any situation; just try to *influence* it.

November's Results

01.11.2017 – (H) NK Maribor 3 – 0
04.11.2017 – (A) West Ham United 4 – 1
18.11.2017 – (H) Southampton 3 – 0
21.11.2017 – (A) Sevilla 3 – 3
25.11.2017 – (H) Chelsea 1 – 1
29.11.2017 – (A) Stoke City 3 – 0

Andrew Beasley, December 1st, 2017
Mohamed Salah has made an incredible start to his Liverpool career, and is already the Reds' top scorer for any of the four seasons since Luis Suárez left the club. With twelve league goals under his belt, he is also currently the Premier League's top scorer. Can he end the season with the most goals and

claim the Golden Boot? The bookies aren't yet convinced, and currently have him as joint-second favourite.

For those of you who are not gambling-minded, the odds here mean they think Salah has about a 14 percent chance of topping the scoring charts in May. Harry Kane is clearly the red-hot favourite though. His price here implies he has around a 31 percent chance of claiming his third Golden Boot in a row.

Yet as it stands, only two of the past five Golden Boot winners had more goals than Liverpool's electric Egyptian at this point of the season, and one of those had to score four goals in match 14 to overtake him. With apologies to John Ruddy, you can probably guess who that was.

Sergio Agüero may have had 14 goals at this point in 2014/15, but he 'only' scored another 12 across the rest of the campaign (in part due to injury). Three of the last five Golden Boot winners didn't rack up 3,000 minutes, so on this front Mohamed Salah should be okay. He may also have an advantage over some of his rivals too.

In the last three seasons, Kane has only played over 2,600 minutes once, and Aguero hasn't at all. Neither has Alvaro Morata, though that has been down to not being a first choice striker; will his body hold up to a whole season of 'muck and bullets' Premier League football? Gabriel Jesus is also quite new to the league and suffered a bad injury last term. Only Romelu Lukaku has consistently played around 3,000 minutes per league campaign in recent times.

Competitions inevitably get prioritised as seasons develop though, and the former Roma man will surely be utilised in whichever one offers Liverpool the best chance of success. If that happens to be the Champions League, then Salah might miss some of the lesser league matches.

At present, Agüero is the only Golden Boot rival who has scored a penalty this season, and nobody has a direct free-kick goal to their name. Much like Salah, Lukaku has taken a spot kick and missed, and Kane will take Spurs' first penalty of the season when it inevitably arrives. It seems Manchester City's record scorer is the main man to be wary of in this category though.

Brighton (A), Paul Tomkins, December 1st, 2017

Liverpool's Brazilians ran rampant, as Mo Salah gave his shooting boots a rest. But it felt like the game could have hinged on that moment of refereeing insanity. At 3-0 up, the referee gave what I have on good authority is the worst penalty decision since the late 19th century, when Bertie Bothleswait gave a spot-kick against a player who had died the previous year.

If a player falls in the box when no one is around, does he exist? It was slapstick, stagecraft. Fall over and look like you've been taken out, but the other angles show no one near you. Even so, the referee should have seen it. It turned a stroll into a stress. Blind men locked in unlit basements have seen more clearly. Drunk men in comas have seen more clearly. Albino moles who have no eyes, and who were sadly stillborn and then eaten by badgers, have seen more clearly. A chance to rest players ahead of two massive games was taken away, the scoreline suddenly slightly perilous again, until those late goals wrapped it up. Thanks, ref!

With Joël Matip injured, Ragnar Klavan recovering from flu and Joe Gomez out with a virus, the obvious answer was Gini Wijnaldum and Emre Can in a back three. *Obviously.* Yeah, that old one. I've noted before how both Jürgen Klopp and Pep Guardiola love their midfielders in all positions, but today was taking it to a new level. Wijnaldum in defence? And yet it worked.

Every single one of Liverpool's outfield team today, bar Dejan Lovren, is either a midfielder/winger by trade, or an ex-midfielder.

The best of the bunch was Bobby Firmino – bought two and a half years ago as an attacking midfielder – who now has 11 goals this season, with just one of them a penalty. He's racking up the assists as well, on top of the work-rate of a long-distance runner.

His fellow Brazilian, Phil 'The Phil' Coutinho wasn't far behind, netting another one of those under-the-wall free-kicks. And Simon Mignolet had a stormer, when called upon; a couple of huge saves, when Brighton finally broke through. No one played badly. After a tight first 20 minutes, Liverpool were almost unstoppable, until the ref intervened. And then, later on, the Reds were unstoppable again, running out 5-1 winners.

One pundit (Danny Higginbottom, I think) noted in the week that he thought Liverpool counterattacked even better than Manchester City, and I was a little sceptical. But I don't think I've seen any team counterattack better than the Reds did today. It really was that good on a couple of the goals. City have a greater number of elite technical players, but even without Sadio Mané, Liverpool broke like lightning. The Reds moved so fast that some Brighton players may as well have been at the Withdean Stadium.

Spartak Moscow (H), December 6th, 2017
David Perkins

When my dad died in 1988, he was a member of the Executive Club at Anfield. His mate bought his membership from my mum for £1,250 – a hell of a lot of money back then. Her comment was: "bloody hell, I never begrudged him his football, but I never realised it cost us so much!" Why am I telling you this? Because on Monday I saw that there were still some hospitality tickets available for last night's game in, you guessed it, the Executive Suite. The only problem was that they cost £707!

Even if I could convince myself, there is no way that I could convince Mrs Stevenson88 that this would be a shrewd investment. With no BT, I was resigned to following it on BBC Sport updates and via the comments on *The Tomkins Times*. Then, out of the blue, a call from my brother who had somehow managed to procure two tickets for the Main Stand, block L7, so between the halfway line and the penalty area at the Kop end. Our first chance to sample the new stand and for a crucial Champions League match – don't you just love younger brothers? Ok, maybe not, but the boy done good.

I left home at 4:15pm, to pick him up *en route*, for the 60 mile journey to Anfield. We were to follow the tried and tested plan: get across early, park at Goodison, grab a takeaway from the nearby Chinese chippy, eat it in the car, then stroll through Stanley Park to have a good look at the new stand, get in early and soak up the atmosphere (if only). There was a four-car smash on the M6 near Leyland (thankfully nobody appeared to have been hurt) with the motorway down to one lane – otherwise known as a car park. Finally it cleared, leaving a straight run through into Aintree; and just over two miles from the ground, traffic grinds to a halt and cars ahead start to turn round. A warehouse fire and road closed, so we join the huge queue going back on itself to try again. I finally abandoned the car about a mile from the ground at the back of a derelict pub (£10 to some Scouse Poles) on the corner of Utting Avenue, and we ran towards the ground. My first sight of the new stand in all its match-day glory: for those who are used to it by now, you might have forgotten, but it takes your breath away, it is truly awesome. We join the queue to get in, quick trip to you-know-where whilst brother grabs a couple of pies and we're in. It's taken three hours and 30 minutes door to door to cover 60 miles, but we're in!

Two minutes later and I nearly lose my pie: 1-0, Coutinho. I'm not sure how many in the crowd could bear to watch – when was the last time we actually converted a penalty (question of the day?). A stuttering run up (I hate those), then waits for the keeper to dive and strokes it the other way. If that was a good moment, the second goal was sensational, with Coutinho again side-footing home. I won't go through all the goals because it will take too long, but Mané's volley was a thing of beauty (as was Milner's cross with his left peg, on the run). Coutinho's hat-trick goal was a slightly fortunate finish to some unbelievable play by him. I heard that some guy called Johan Cruyff once did a fancy turn – that has nothing on little Phil's turn by the far touchline. The defender ended up at Goodison, he was thrown so far off the scent as Phil headed towards the box. It was the football of a brilliant player, full of confidence at the top of his game – in fact the same could be said of all of them. The front four have rightly garnered the plaudits this morning, but Wijnaldum and Can provided the control in midfield that allowed them to dance away in front of them. Good luck to Sam Allardyce when he reviews those tapes ahead of Sunday!

I have been lucky enough to watch great Liverpool teams from the early '70s onwards. I never thought any team could beat some of the play of the Alan Hansen, Graeme Souness, Ian Rush and Kenny Dalglish team. Then we had John Barnes, Peter Beardsley, John Aldridge and Rush again. We had Luis Suárez, Daniel Sturridge and Raheem Sterling. But this lot? I have never seen football quite like it. They seriously looked as though they would score every time they got the ball, and the sheer joy that they show is magnificent. Mo Salah was delighted to end his goal drought – of one game. He must have the quickest feet of any player I have seen. The number of times the defender thought he had the ball, only for it to have been spirited away as he set off on another run. As seems to happen with this Liverpool team, the goals came in little bursts, three in the first 15 minutes or so then two braces in the second half. It could easily have been more with two very good penalty shouts waved away and Sturridge missing from close range – plus Mané blazing over when put through. It could have been double figures and it would have been deserved. I thought the atmosphere was great, although obviously things occasionally went a bit quiet because, well, because it had been at least five minutes since the last goal ….

I don't know how badly Alberto Moreno was injured, but it didn't look great; I would think ankle ligament damage, but Milner was excellent when he came on. There was also an interesting change with about 20 minutes to go. Dejan Lovren off, with Joe Gomez to centre-back and Trent Alexander-Arnold at full-back. Okay, we were 5-0 up at the time, but Klopp was clearly having a bit of a look at how we could cope with the two youngsters on the right hand side of the defence – I think he will have been pleased, with Alexander-Arnold looking to get forward as much as he could and Gomez pretty much as solid in the middle as he'd been at full-back – in fact the more I watch him, the better I think he can become. There was one point in the second half when the ball was played over the top towards the corner of our penalty area. He gave the attacker a couple of yards start, overhauled him the get to the ball first and played a brilliant 40 yard pass down the line to a teammate. He's also not afraid to bring the ball out from the back and it might just be that we have the next Alan Hansen on our hands – I think he could be that good.

We stayed to the last to applaud them off and were able to exit surprisingly easily to make our way back to the car and head out. We got home in 75 minutes! It was an absolutely brilliant night despite the travel problems on the way there. The new stand is stunning, the Anfield atmosphere for a Champions League night match was as good as ever and the football was from a different planet. It will have been a long flight back to Moscow for their players suffering from twisted blood syndrome – the poor buggers didn't know what was happening to them. If I never see Liverpool play live again, I have the most amazing memories stored away from a truly great night at Anfield.

Anthony Stanley

Curiously, I think it's much easier being at the game than watching at home or in the pub.

Living in Ireland obviously makes it tough to get to a game but I've given up watching matches in a pub unless I really have to. And even then, if I have to resort to a pub, I try to take a seat as far away from the crowds of lads as I can.

It's not just the haters. It's the clowns wearing Liverpool shirts, the buffoons who shout 'shoot' every five minutes or sagely tell each other that Alberto Moreno is 'shite' or that Jordan Henderson 'isn't captain material'. I can't bear it. I once got called a 'know it all' in a pub and was told that it was impossible to talk about football with me because I pointed out that any person who has made it to the absolute pinnacle of their profession is in no way 'shite'.

That was the end of that.

Paul Tomkins, December 7th, 2017

While using war terminology outside of a conflict can seem fatuous – especially about a German (don't mention the war) – Liverpool's wonderfully modern, cosmopolitan side can be described using two key words from WWII: "bombing" (as in, bombing on, bombing forward); and *blitzkrieg*, the German term meaning "Lightning war", often shortened to blitz in English. These terrible events become innocuous metaphors, used in everyday language.

(In this case, last night, there were also a lot of shellshocked Russians, and a red army, although here the German came out on top. Of course, back then the Russians were famed for digging in during winter, although if I torture this analogy any further I may be tried for crimes against metaphors.)

Like warfare, football is a tactical battle of attack and defence; advance and retreat. You can hunker down, or go gung-ho. Football isn't about life or death, but the tactics of where to focus your resources within an arena has clear parallels. (Although there was that infamous match at Anfield under Roy Hodgson against Utrecht where both teams hunkered down, the midfield a depressing no-man's land.)

Jürgen Klopp's brand of football is distinctly in the latter bracket of gung-hoism, although I feel that is a team that attacks and defends (mostly) with a great shape; unlike the exciting 2013/14 vintage, this is a *swarming* side, rather than exceptional individuals often picked out with clever long passes from deep during Steven Gerrard's last hurrah (one of Brendan Rodgers' best decisions). At times, Luis Suárez would do a lot of it on his own, albeit enabled by the structure put in place.

Sometimes this side swarms too far upfield, and that can make it hard for its own central defenders when it breaks down, but this vintage – while still prone to the individual errors seen in Rodgers' great campaign – doesn't actually give up a lot of chances. The swarm mostly keeps the ball away, at the other end. Sometimes that high-press is beaten, but even then, the energy of players like Emre Can, Jordan Henderson, Alberto Moreno and Gini Wijnaldum means that a lot of the time numbers can get back, too; but mostly the Reds keep the opposition encamped in its own half.

As the late 20th-Century philosopher and army corporal Orville Richard Burrell* said – and which could be used today to sum up Liverpool's own General – "I'm Mr. Boombastic, say me fantastic, touch me in my back she says Boom! Boom! Boom!" (* Better known to most as reggae-rapper Shaggy.)

And, as the noted World War One poet said so eloquently, "Boom boom boom! Boom. Boom! …"

Twelve goals in four days, with teams who were supposed to be pretty good at defending absolutely wiped off the map. With 23 in six games it was the most goals ever scored by an English team in the group stages of the Champions League, and this came after six goals had already been put past a top German side over two legs. That's 29 in eight European matches, with 19 of them coming in the six games against top German and Spanish sides, and the Russian champions.

This, when some serious numpties are saying English football is at a low ebb, when four teams top their Champions League groups and a fifth, the reigning English champions, qualify; making for five teams in the final 16 for the first time in the competition's history.

It's all further proof, to me, that Klopp has massively improved Liverpool; but the issue is that, since his appointment, Manchester United have appointed Jose Mourinho, Manchester City have appointed Pep Guardiola and Chelsea have appointed Antonio Conte. The Manchester clubs then spent well over £200m each; United spending that, almost, on just two of their many signings. Liverpool raised the bar when getting Klopp, and everyone else had to raise the bar too. So Liverpool's progress looks muted by contrast, especially with City's form, but make no mistakes, this is a wonderful Liverpool side.

Everton (H), December 10th, 2017
Chris Rowland

It's been a few years since I've been to the Anfield derby, one reason or another. It always gets me tingling, in a way quite different to the Man Utd match – less negative, less dominated by the utter fear of losing, more excited by the occasion. A 2:15pm kick-off isn't the worst either, for a Sunday, it could easily have been much earlier or much later. It means I can get the 09:05 off my local station and be in Manchester Victoria in time for the 10:35 to Lime Street. Better still, the Manchester-Liverpool train is the Transpennine Express from Newcastle, which doesn't stop anywhere (unlike the Northern stopper, which stops at everyone's house on the way from Victoria to Liverpool). I'll be in Lime Street for 11:08, which is about right.

However, even when you don't have trains and kick-off times to worry about, there's always the weather. With a forecast for heavy snow across the North and the prospect of cross-Pennine travel, actually getting to my local station down a one-mile steep hill to catch that early train seems tricky enough, never mind the four trains there and back that I have to get (incidentally, why do we need 11 separate tickets to cover four journeys? At home I've got a tiny old British Rail ticket from the 1977 European Cup Final saying 'Rome and back'. One ticket covering a 2,000 mile return journey! How have we improved life by now needing 11 for a total journey of 132 miles?) That last one back from Manchester across the Pennines after a day's snowfall seems particularly susceptible to delay or cancellation.

So I get up in darkness and peer out, expecting a blizzard and a snowdrift to battle through just to get to the station. Instead it's not snowing, and it hasn't overnight, since last late afternoon. It's fine. And all goes to plan. Just before Victoria, I get a call from one of the Liverpool lot, saying he assumes I won't be coming. because all the Midlands and London contingent cannot get through, apparently. He has reallocated their tickets, no shortage of demand in the city on derby day! I reply *au contraire mon brave*, I have battled across the frozen tundra of the Pennines and am just coming into Manchester!

At Victoria I see on the noticeboard that the train through from Newcastle to Lime Street is on time. Just time for a coffee in the lovely cosy inviting atmosphere of the Java Bar at Manchester Victoria – if you're ever there, it beats Starbucks in every way, both physically and philosophically! It's too early for any signs of the Manchester derby, which given the transport problems because of the weather I predict will have an attendance of just over 40,000 at Old Trafford!

By just after 11 I'm in the city – on derby day! But there's no discernible extra tingle as yet, as there used to be. We're meeting at Mackenzie's in Rodney Street at midday, and I get there at 11.30. It's not open yet. So I try the famous Roscoe Head round the corner, but that's not open yet either. Then to the cask beer mecca The Dispensary back on Renshaw Street but neither is that. The quickest and cheapest pub crawl you've ever had! I have a quick half of Guinness in the Liffey, it being open, and back to Mackenzie's, now gone midday and still not open – nor the other two. Doesn't feel much like a derby day so far, nowhere near urgent enough, more a sleepy Sunday.

And it has started snowing.

Then I see it. Round the corner comes something I can barely conceive of. An utter abomination. Something I cannot for the life of me understand the manufacturer of. How do they imagine there to be a market for the product before they incur the costs of manufacturing – a half-and-half Liverpool/Everton scarf? They must know something I don't. A category of person, maybe?

I gaze open-mouthed at the wearer, like forest tribesman staring at a flying aeroplane in blank wonder. It simply cannot be. It cannot exist. It cannot work. Sometimes you can't proclaim to be two things. Jew *and* Arab. Serb *and* Croat. Protestant *and* Catholic. The divide is deep, absolute.

If you really must have a half-and-half scarf as a souvenir, because it's your birthday or special day or a once-in-a-lifetime trip to Anfield, and you feel you need a reminder bearing the antichrist's name and colours, then either tuck it away out of sight or just have the red part showing. Just don't wear it openly in its full twin-named bi-coloured horror as though it's okay and normal, thus demonstrating beyond debate that you simply *don't get it*, in which case what are you doing with a precious derby ticket when thousands of locals can't get one – it really antagonises, on this day more than any. Assuming he was going to the match, that is. If not, it's even worse, wearing that on derby day. "What's up la, can't make yer fuckin' mind up?"

Ahead of their derby, Man Utd fans had asked Greater Manchester Police to reassure them they'd arrest any Utd fan wearing a half-and-half scarf, and I wholeheartedly sympathise! With *Utd* fans ….

Our normal group has been reduced to five by the weather, just me and four locals. Later we do go to the Roscoe Head, and Bob asks me how things are going on the website. And as part of my answer I mention xG – and get an unXpected reaction. I have stepped on a landmine. Suddenly my friends who I've known and been to the match since the early 1970s turn into a hissing multi-headed hydra.

I run into a brick wall of xG cynicism.

"Seen this shite has started appearing on Match of the Day, means fuck all".

"So where do these figures come from, a panel of so called experts deciding what constitutes a chance, how fucking patronising, I don't need any cod scientist telling me what was a chance and what wasn't."

"How should you have scored 0.87 of a goal, fucking ridiculous, laughable."

xG is summarily dismissed and ridiculed.

"Bloody hell, a four-headed monster" I laugh. "It's just a way of measuring who actually deserved to win a match."

"For unsighted fans only then is it?"

The exchange is brought short by the need to get a taxi – just one will do us this week, we normally need two.

Looking at their phone, someone announces the team line-up. It raises a few eyebrows. The other four are proponents of "always play your strongest team, and definitely in the derby", and here are two of the Fab Four on the bench, including someone who is presumably buzzing after a hat-trick in his last outing. I suggest it may be because Klopp has the midweek game in the back of his mind, but that thought is instantly lambasted just as xG was – "we need three points today, never mind Wednesday, it's fuckin' Everton, win the game you're in, he shouldn't even be giving Wednesday a thought. Beat these blue bastards first before you start thinking about Wednesday".

"Merely offering it up as a possible explanation chaps" I say. "Seems like having finally come to terms with rotation, Klopp has suddenly developed a taste for it."

But we are all pleased to see Danny Ings on the bench.

As for the game, within minutes the man to my left launches into his usual Pavlov's Dogs tirade at Henderson. "Crab. Fucking crab. Sideways, sideways. Crab! Crab! Fuck off Henderson."

There are a few enthusiastic chants of "You're just a fat granny shagger" directed towards you know who, but my editorial head kicks in as I ponder at the looseness and ambiguity of the phrasing, which implies that it could be the granny/grannies who are fat rather than the 'once a blue, always a Manc' shagger in question.

But it's the removal of Salah in the second half that turns on the toxic tide. Or rather, Everton's goal in retrospect. To be fair, it wasn't a case of hindsight after the later equaliser setback, there was widespread mystification and criticism of Salah's removal as it happened.

Then the penalty. And the invective and the blame game begins. Dejan Lovren is brainless, he's got to go, how many more times?

"Fuck off Klopp" comes an unprovoked yell from my right.

"Want to know why we've just drawn against the worst team we've ever seen here. There's the reason, right there," says one pointing towards Klopp.

"Why?" I ask.

He turns on me, eyes flashing. "Why? Fucking *why?* It's fucking obvious isn't it you knobhead? Takes off your best player so we can sit back and defend a 1-0 lead. And leaves two of our best players on the bench for the derby, he hasn't got a clue that fella."

I wonder why he is equating taking off Salah with an attempt to go defensive. Unless removing your best attacker is automatically a defensive move, regardless of who you bring on to replace him.

Maybe he's resting him for Wednesday, but I've already been ripped apart for that suggestion.

"Your support is fucking shit" sing Everton's fans as the game draws to a close.

"Your fucking team is" I yell back.

Afterwards we agree that poor decision-making by three of ours has been the reason for not beating this abysmal, abject Everton. Sadio Mané for not passing when through on goal just before half-time. Lovren for making any kind of challenge in the box when the ball was heading away from goal and from danger. And finally Klopp, for his initial team selection and for his substitution of Salah.

It's almost a football cliché that if you fail to take your chances and add to your lead when you're 1-0 up in a game you're dominating, you'll end up paying for it. The fact that you've been second best (and in Everton's case downright dismal) but are still only 1-0 down serves to give the losing side encouragement as the game wears on, and inevitably starts jitters in the opposition. We come back to Mané's poor/selfish/inept moment pre-half-time.

As well as team selection, rotation and (outmoded concept alert …) 'not knowing his best team', there's also criticism of Klopp for changing formations from one game to the next.

"And if he doesn't, presumably he gets accused of having no Plan B?" I ask, seemingly forever cast in the role of Devil's Advocate. Cue the return of the hydra!

I can take it.

Bob overhears someone say there was contact with Lovren and Dominic Calvert-Lewin, and he adds that contact *is* allowed in football, it's a contact sport, don't be saying 'there was contact' as though that confirms it should have been a penalty. He's up for a debate today is Bob, though to be fair he had his works' Christmas do last night and may be a touch delicate!

There's one thing we do agree on though – the Blues might be superficially chipper just now – after all when you are incapable of generating your own pleasure all that is left is to try to deny your enemy of some of theirs – but we'd rather stick with the red hand we've been dealt, thanks very much. We think our future looks a good deal brighter than theirs if today's performance is any measure, we actually enjoy watching us play whereas Goodison will be empty watching that shite every week, and we'd rather have our manager than theirs. That we were only leading 1-0 was incredibly kind to Everton if largely our own fault, and the match ridiculously one-sided.

"They have nothing to look forward to, no joy, no life" says one friend.

Back to Lime Street, there's an information board with plenty of cancellations and delays on it, but mostly for trains heading south to or through the Midlands. My train to Manchester is okay and on time. Back at Victoria, the final connection, my train towards Leeds, is also on time. The weather has not affected my four train journeys or the match going ahead.

There are Man Utd fans everywhere at Victoria, including many waiting to get on my Leeds-bound train. They come from Rochdale, Halifax, Bradford, all over the place. I hear some talking and they seem agreed that they were second best today, and that the 2-1 scoreline flattered Utd (I couldn't help wondering whether they'd have been so candid if they'd known a Liverpool supporter was listening!). "They were 4-0 better than us today, and I'm sick of Mourinho's excuses afterwards." says one .

Music to my ears, after some of the stuff they've heard today from our own today.

West Bromwich Albion (H), December 13th, 2017
Nari Singh

Whatsapp message conversation:

"Mine says over an hour left still … yours?"

"Yep same. This is bollocks, I hate Liverpool Football Club's ticketing system. Every year, this crap, I've been logged on since 6am with hundreds of different browsers on all the devices I can get my hands on!"

Okay, I only have two devices, but, as we know, getting tickets to watch LFC is quite an ordeal. Last season, my LFC right hand man (Craig) and I managed to get five tickets, we thought it'd let us in to the early queue system for the following season, but the cut off was eight games. I think they just make it up as they go along.

So when Hemal posted on TTT of two tickets going for WBA, a mid-week game, I pounced on them like I was in Asda on Black Friday. They're in the Kop too, I've never had the opportunity to sit there, so, I can't wait.

Given it's an 8pm Wednesday kick-off, Craig and I decide it's best if we stay the night in Liverpool. The trains back might be a nightmare (and it always means we have to leave around 85 mins to ensure we get a cab, and I hate leaving early), so driving is the only option. Doing a late night drive back to London is horrible, I've done it once before for a late kick-off and vowed I'll never do it again.

Booking.com – Radisson Blu – Xmas offer – 2 twins – Booked. *Yes.* Sorted.

We both run our own businesses and look after our kids around work (the new-age Dad, don't you know?), so taking the day off takes a bit of planning. Craig is East London, I'm West, so he heads to mine and we set off up the M40 around midday. All clear until the M6, then stop-start, the traditional accident, rubbernecking and commuter in rush hour traffic conspire against us. We see a van with a Van Dijk Express logo go past us, unfortunately we couldn't see if the big man himself was in the driving seat, trying to force his transfer up north all on his own!

After checking in on how business and family is (all of five minutes), the conversation is mostly about Liverpool matters, the Everton game, penalty decision, and how managers can get away with zero criticism for instructing their goalkeepers to kick to touch all game, yet the progressive football playing ones (Klopp in this case) get criticised for "disrespecting" the derby. Surely that should be placed at Sam Allardyce's door?

I find a podcast I've been meaning to listen to from *5Live* about Kenny Dalglish, we play it through the car Bluetooth, discussing the King's unselfishness as a player and his selfless qualities as a human being for everything he's given to Liverpool. We agree with Kenny's thoughts on Klopp having been moulded for the manager's job and how badly the club got it wrong when appointing Roy Hodgson – the guy who recently told the media he hoped Christian Benteke's penalty miss didn't cost them at the end of the season, as if that's the one and only thing that will decide whether Palace get relegated. Nice one Hodgson, good to see you getting the excuses in early.

Craig is a passionate Red; his roots are in Liverpool having been born there. I on the other hand was born in Birmingham, to Sikh parents who had come over to England to work and build a "better" future for their family. Although there were some tough times in the sixties, seventies and eighties, I was largely unaware of the struggles at the time, having been born in 1981.

There was no history or link to Liverpool Football Club whatsoever in the family, but growing up in England, football was my sport and thankfully the Reds were my team. I can vaguely remember the 1990 semi-final purely because we lived close to Villa Park, and I could hear the crowd when a goal was scored, so I would rush outside to my back garden and jump up and down. I'd like to think I was an okay player, Barnes and Fowler being my favourite players growing up because I share the magic that's in the left foot. Mo Salah is the latest in a short list of fantastic left-footed players.

I feel the electricity of the football club running through my veins, charging my body with passion, dreams and romance, and feel this giant is slowly waking up, year by year. I feel the club is sewn into my DNA somehow, in a way I cannot succinctly describe without sounding like a loony!

We get to Radisson Blu around 6.30pm, park up, check in and drop our bags off in the room. (Tip: when booking the hotel we had put down the trip was for "business", so at the check-in desk we were given complimentary breakfast, not sure it'll work in all hotels, but it's worth trying for a free brekky!).

Back down to the lobby, we meet a fellow Red who is Norwegian and been here with his daughter, Belinda, since Monday, having done the Anfield tour on Tuesday. It's her first game so hoping she brings us some good luck. We all decide to share a cab, and it just so happens the driver is Egyptian. Yep, he's absolutely mad about Salah. I fasten my seatbelt in the back and hold on tightly to the door rest, hoping he concentrates on the road rather than constantly looking back at us to explain how important Mo is. I had read earlier in the day Mo had been taken off against Everton because he may have been feeling his hamstring, so we deduce that he may not play, which prompts the driver to turn around, his face in shock, saying "No Salah? Who will score the goals?" in genuine disbelief. We remind him that, although he's in rich scoring vein, there are others in the team that can also score goals. (Little did we know at that point that the whole team would forget where the goal was a few hours later.)

We get dropped off by the big car park at Walton Breck Road. The Norwegian fan insists on paying for the journey after I offer my fiver to go halves. It's very kind of him, we shake hands and wish each other good luck for the game.

Walking up from Walton Breck Road, we see a New Balance sign in the distance, something we've not seen before. The closer we get, the more we see – the new club shop! It's absolutely huge, two floors of morning wear, evening wear, smart wear, casual wear, kits, training tops, wallets, briefcases and on and on. It's a nightclub with clothes, the music thundering through the hi-tech speakers (I hate shops like that, I can't think, my head hurts, makes me want to get out quickly). I've had my eye on a training top as I really like the deep red colour of this season's kit, which I buy, then get out of there as quickly as possible. But it's really impressive, spacious and long overdue.

We check out some previous Liverpool vs West Brom games on the big screen on our way to the Kop. In we go after a quick pat down by security, Craig and I momentarily relive the horrific experience of our previous pat down: at the German-Swiss border when going to Basel for the Europa League Final a couple of seasons back. It was horrible – escorted to a secluded area by around 10 heavily armed men, being searched, quizzed, car searched and then being let go, an experience I'd love to forget. Thankfully we can joke about it now, but at the time, it took us about an hour to get our heart rates back to acceptable levels.

Our seats are towards the back of the Kop and we're surprised how good the view is. No one is sitting, which is great, as I tend to watch all the games standing anyway. There's good vocal support here. I've sat in the Kenny Dalglish and Main Stand before, and it's hit and miss with singing. I meet a fellow Sikh named "JD", with a bigger, much more grey looking beard than mine who seems well connected.

After a chat with him and his friends, we realise that he's one of the main guys who starts the chants. A huge booming voice nearly sends me all the way back down to the bottom of the Kop, I'm sure you could hear him halfway down the M6. We hear songs we've never heard, some of which were really weird. For example, one went: "We don't carry bottles, we don't carry lead, we carry hatchets to bury in your head". Very disturbing. Another was "Scouser Tommy" – I listen intently, trying to understand the words. What I didn't understand was why it was sung so much, only a handful of people knew it, and it's not very catchy. I heard and learnt the new front four chant, which mines The Jam's, *That's Entertainment*: Sadio Mané, Philippe Coutinho, Mo Salah and Bobby Firmino, *That's Entertainment, That's Entertainment*". Not that original, but better than the "Gini Wijnaldum" chant, which I'm not a massive fan of, I must say.

There was a lot of frustration in the front of the Kop with Loris Karius not releasing the ball quick enough, when, a lot of the time passing lanes were blocked off by West Brom, a clear tactic. Around the 34th minute, when a quick release failed and he released it short (I think to Ragnar Klavan), the crowd were annoyed – he looked back and shook his head as if to say to the crowd "just stop with the jeering and support the team". I felt for him, it must be so difficult to play in such conditions, you know yourself you're trying to release the ball quickly without having 20,000 people on at you.

The game finished and we were disappointed, but there were a few people around us trying to remain positive, "two away games coming up, maybe that'll suit the lads a bit better". I agree.

We finally get out of the ground and start walking down Walton Breck Road in search of a cab. The heavens open and unleash hailstones, "It feels like I'm being shot in the face, Craig" I say. "Well it's more shots than we had all game" he replies, we both have a chuckle.

84

We get back to the hotel with a very sore and broken voice, order some uninspiring room service (it's after 11pm and the chef's gone home – how considerate) and out like a light.

Mark Cohen, December 19th, 2017

Something occurred to me today that was at once so blindingly obvious and yet so utterly bizarre that I could barely process it.

A Manchester United fan I know was discussing football matters and made the throwaway comment that it was fairly obvious they'd finish second and that Liverpool would be battling away with the Burnley's of this world for 6th and 7th as our defence is 'so shit'.

He didn't say it with any particular mean spirit, and he is not a banter merchant, he just really saw things this simply.

I joined the conversation at that minute and said to him that whilst United possess a strong squad on paper, their underlying numbers were poor at both ends of the pitch, and that if I was a betting man, I'd actually place Liverpool a point either side of them come May.

He was incredulous and he laughed, again not aggressively I must stress, but more like 'wow' another simple 'Scouser'.

(A quick tangent: here in South Africa, you are humorously referred to as a 'Scouser' if you support Liverpool, this might seem trite but is in fact a fascinating discussion in of itself and one of the reasons Liverpool Football Club remains the last great community club – the inexorable link with the city from which the club hails. I mean, could you ever see a Chinese Manchester United fan being called a Mancunian? Anyway, that discussion is for another day).

The lad – he held up an open hand to me, as if imploring me to see sense. 'Liverpool aren't playing the same sport as us, Mark." He said, "We have scored more goals and our defence is the best in Europe, you have Lovren and Mignolet ... you have a manager that doesn't even pick his best team for the derby, and he has been found out for not having a plan B long ago anyway ...."

I looked at these lads having their discussion, and I saw that to a man, I appeared the idiot, it was me who was clueless and a dreamer, and it was they who were the parents spoiling Christmas by telling me Santa didn't exist.

I could see they were humoured by me, and I almost never speak to lads like these about football, but I asked them if anybody had ever heard of 'expected goals'.

They said no.

I asked them if they thought it was possible to train a team to play two entirely different ways, to a near perfect level and if it is impossible, should a manager rather work on his overall ethos and make that better and better, so essentially improving his plan A?

The main lad retorted that Klopp's plan A had been found out at Dortmund and he was 'almost' relegated.

I asked if there were 10 teams in the Bundesliga.

He asked why.

I said there must be, because three go down and Dortmund finished 7th that year from a standing start. So, narrowly avoiding relegation then?

He didn't get it.

I asked him if he understood perfect storms, or 'black swan' events, and they all stared blankly.

I asked them if they tracked any running averages, as if they did, they'd see an alarming pattern where United's expected goal difference is continually shrinking whilst Liverpool's is now one of the highest in Europe.

I asked them if they realised that Liverpool have massively outscored United since the third month of the season and the gap is widening.

I asked them if they'd be surprised to end outside the top four this season as their form is being propped up by one truly world class performer, sitting between the sticks.

They actually laughed.

"We are second, and if City slip up, we'll capitalise, and all this with their unprecedented spending!"

I asked if they realised for all intents and purposes that theirs and City's squads have been built with the same kind of overall expenditure.

I asked if they understood the pressure their team and manager are under due to the overwhelming expectations placed on them because of their size and spending.

I asked if they could see the team is becoming more and more defensive as the season wears on and that these were all signs of a pressure overload.

The main lad chuckled and said something about being in a crisis in 2nd.

He had a point, I laughed with him and left it at that. You see, every single footballing idea that I carry forward in my adult iteration as a lifelong fan of Liverpool and football in general, I have from TTT.

I don't know if Paul meant it when he started this thing, but it has changed mine, and I am sure thousands of other people's basic understanding of the game.

The depth in which I now view every single game is far beyond what I used to and I feel enlightened by the information which I have learned to use, all via this genius of a website. I will now religiously check the expected goals, not just our games, but dozens of games a week, just to see what really happened beyond the score line.

That will come in tandem with a five or six times a day reading of TTT to see what the brains are saying, not just the paid-for brains, but the comments too, like-minded lads and lasses putting their minds to work.

It is no longer enough for me if Liverpool win, we need to have won the vital stats. It's like having a defibrillator restart your heart. Yes, you are breathing today, but it would be better if your vitals were constantly strong, rather than having needed the jolt.

I take enormous solace from dropped points in great performances, just as I take wins with humility when we do them lucky, as I now know the difference. What Paul says in this piece is too true, in that, by using these tools we can see, with our own eyes, how large the improvement under Klopp is and that, regardless of a few results, we are on the right track if we continue to perform this way.

The Manchester fan today said to me that Liverpool and United are now playing a different sport. That was hyperbole.

What is reality is that that lad and I are now watching a different one.

Transfer Window Opens

Paul Tomkins, December 27th, 2017

Two days late – if not several months late – Virgil Van Dijk is a Christmas present to us all the same. The saga that became an epic in the summer, popped up with a stunning conclusion almost unexpectedly a few days *before* the latest transfer window even opens. Happy New Year, Reds!

I said in the summer that I can't think of a more ideal Liverpool player. The fee may seem enormous, but is only a world-record for a defender when ignoring inflation; Rio Ferdinand cost more for both Leeds and Man United, for starters, when applying our Transfer Price Index football inflation. (Ferdinand's move to Man United for what now equals over £150m, in 2018 money.)

However, van Dijk is of a similar pedigree to Ferdinand: quick, tall and skilful; cultured, but able to defend, and a goal threat at the other end, too (more so than Ferdinand, who got just seven league goals in 300+ games at United). And van Dijk, at 26, is at the age where centre-backs really start to blossom. There just aren't that many centre-backs who have all those attributes, and the way Liverpool play – while not as open as people seem to think (because any time a team attacks against Liverpool it seems to be labelled a cock-up, as if no one ever attacks anyone else in any other games) – does leave some gaps; there are no parked buses, à la Jose Mourinho. With Naby Keita pre-signed too, 2018 promises to be a hugely exciting time, *as if the Reds breaking club goalscoring records* wasn't already exciting enough.

The more business Liverpool do under Jürgen Klopp and Michael Edwards, the more sense it all makes. Every player seems perfectly scouted and ideally suited, and fits the profile of having pace, energy, commitment and quality, with their peak years (theoretically) ahead of them. Players want to play for Klopp, and £30m signings can look like £100m signings. There are no Rickie Lamberts, Christian Bentekes or Mario Balotellis to be seen, who just don't fit the style.

It would be wrong to expect van Dijk to solve all the defensive issues, and he arrives with a ton of expectation and pressure, but his aerial ability would perhaps offer Klopp the chance to give Loris Karius another try, and that in turn could speed up the Reds' play.

It would help on set-pieces at both ends. Indeed, van Dijk is the type to actually take direct free-kicks, scoring a fair few in his career. But his aerial ability is clear to see. (Klopp also inherited a generally small team, with lots of little players, and I spent his first season saying how adding height had to be a priority. Liverpool were almost always smaller than any given opponents, and my look into the data of aerial success rates showed that the taller a player was, the more he was likely to win the ball in the air; diminishing this idea plenty of fans seem to have that being small and able to jump would compensate. Organisation at set-pieces can help, but tall players *who can also jump well* are the best at dealing with crosses and high-balls into the box.)

It's just a shame Man City are so exceptional right now, but by next season they might have the title-defence dip. Liverpool look about as qualified to challenge as I can recall, although much will depend on the mood of the players if Coutinho goes.

Comment by Graeme Riley, December 29th, 2017

Since 1-4 v Spurs, Liverpool's Premier League goal difference is +25. Over 11 successive games, this is only the 11th season since 1904 it has been achieved, and only 3rd since 1988 (May 2009, April 2014). First time since 1980 with +23 or more in successive seasons after 20 matches.

Last seven games (since Stoke) Liverpool average 3.5 goals per game – first time since 1986-87 this has been achieved over sa even-game run and only 6th season since 1900.

Also the last six away games have seen Liverpool score 22 goals for an average of 3.66 per game. The only time in the club's history this was higher was the six games ending with the 5-1 at Brighton this season. Only twice before have we achieved 3.5 over six away games – 1895-96 and 1960-61.

Leicester City (H), December 30th, 2017
Chris Rowland

Amidst the loss of awareness of date and time that comes with what we call the festive period, I almost overlook the fact that this is that rarest of things, a Saturday 3pm kick-off!

Trains pre-booked, I have inadvertently clicked 'e-ticket' for my journey to and from Manchester, a first for me, so there's already a frisson of the unknown. Will my not-so-smart phone deliver come the day? Will Northern Rail's app work better than their trains do? Am I app-'appy? Will the battery last long enough? Will I end up having to pay twice because it all doesn't work? Too much tension ….

All goes smoothly until I saunter across Manchester Victoria to Platform three for the Lime Street train. This is the fast, no-stopping one, the Transpennine Express from Newcastle, rather than the local Northern Rail stopper that stops at everyone's house between Manchester Victoria and Liverpool. Unfortunately, there seem to be an unusually large number of people waiting, including more Liverpool supporters than I've ever seen at Manchester for this train, a fair number of them obviously non-British, judging by the international babble of languages.

The train arrives and is only three carriages long. After five minutes in which huge crowds seek to squeeze on at each door, it's apparent they can't all fit on. At least 100 are left behind, and for all those who got on at Manchester, it's cattle class standing from here on. To add to the general miasma, the toilet is out of order and a crying child in a pushchair has obviously soiled itself. There is widespread anger, and widespread derision of the announcement that "Transpennine Express apologise for customers' inconvenience, this was supposed to be a six-carriage train but only three turned up at Newcastle. This is due to a technical issue".

So where are these other three carriages? They're quite large, you can't really miss them! And what technical issue? Surely you just hook a carriage onto the one in front? More like a planning and logistics cock-up. Luckily it only takes half an hour of misery before the train staggers into Lime Street, only ten minutes late. Meanwhile Transpennine Express's Facebook and Twitter accounts are bombarded with damning condemnatory photos and comments about their shameful ineptitude and poor service, and reminding them that rail prices are rising in January while their service level definitely isn't. Rant over.

I meet with the Midlands contingent, which today includes a Leicester fan, the father-in-law of one of ours, bedecked in blue and white bobble hat, scarf etc., and we walk to today's meeting, as organised by one of the Liverpool lot, which is the Shipping News in Slater Street. We the move onto the Lime Kilns, one of the better Wetherspoon's for beer choice and quality, and the excellent Head of Steam. I get handed my card for today and my ticket for Burnley on Monday, with the accompanying news that nobody else is going as they can't trust themselves to be in any state to do so after New Year's Eve! So it's just me … I'll do what I can, leave it to me boys!

There seems to be nobody putting a negative slant on the Virgil van Dijk deal – quite the opposite, a declaration of intent and that's what you have to pay these days for elite players.

As we go to get two taxis to the ground, the Leicester fan injects the day's first unsavoury element by saying "no hurry, I'm happy to miss all that pre-match *You'll Never Walk Alone* shit."

We only say nothing because of the awkward position this puts his son-in-law in. It's a pity he doesn't appear to feel the same constraint.

Last week I pondered on the site whether the seismic impact of the game-changing van Dijk deal and the talk of Leon Goretzka signing would have any impact on the atmosphere. For a good part of the match it seemed not, though it did catch fire a few times in the second half.

Nobody thinks Emre Can and James Milner is working as centre midfield pairing, and the two seem to be vying for worst performance of the day, once Joël Matip's Mogadon mistake has set the tone. Sadio Mané's not much better, though all three improve as the game progresses. There is widespread criticism for Jürgen Klopp's use of subs, most would have made changes at half-time and certainly long before he finally does. But when his methods result in a victory it's hard to say he was wrong.

In the first half we feel every little thing is going their way, every bounce, every deflection, every marginal decision. And Mo Salah keeps missing chances. There's a definite change of mood in the Kop concourse at half-time, a defiance and determination set in. 'Right, enough of this' says someone as they turned to return to their seat, 'let's turn this around'. And behold, we did.

Back in Liverpool's cask beer mecca, the Dispensary, we agree this hard fought win was more use to us than another 4-0 spanking of the opposition. It showed that we can come from behind and do enough to get the three points.

Then the Leicester fan arrives and says "you were lucky today weren't you?"

"Yeah, lucky we were only playing you," I reply. "And you were lucky Salah didn't get five on his own."

"I couldn't believe how shit the atmosphere was" he went on. "How can so many people make such little noise?"

"Oh we make a noise when there's a big game but not for no-marks like you," says one.

"Coz we're not as full of shit as you," says another. Top sparring.

"Has Gerrard won the league, has he fuck?" he carries on.

"The Champions League, yes," I reply. "Plus being a better player than you've ever had in the entire history of your club."

I don't care about his son-in-law any more, if he's going to come out swinging blows like this he's going to get both barrels. If you can't take it, don't give it.

He starts discussing with his son-in-law what they're having to eat when they get home. "You'll be having the tripe won't you?" chips in another of our group. It's sparky alright.

Back at Lime Street, the Transpennine Express is again standing room only, though I manage to get the seat I reserved, even though they've removed all the reservations due to passenger numbers. Just think about that – you book in advance and reserve a seat, but that system won't work if they remove it before the journey. And what would happen if Liverpool sold 20% more tickets for a match than there are available seats? How has this come to be accepted?

An American woman and her family entourage forced to stand complains loudly that they have reserved seats. She's wearing a lanyard with 'LFC Boardroom' on it. It turns out they're from California and this is their first ever 'soccer' match, and they have enjoyed it. I explain the joys of British train travel and reassure her that she hasn't entered a third world country – though that may be a matter for debate. She tells me that they rarely if ever use public transport and they go everywhere by car, which does not make me faint with surprise. Apparently they live just 20 minutes' drive from their baseball ground, they drive to it and watch the first half then drive home and watch the second on TV! Imagine that! Like me they're only going as far as Manchester so have only half an hour's standing to endure.

Back at Manchester Victoria, my heart sinks as I see the train home has only two carriages. That's the main service between Manchester and Leeds, two of the north's major cities, and passing through big towns like Rochdale, Halifax and Bradford. Two carriages. Again I manage to get a seat, but many don't.

A few Man Utd fans have made it back from their 17:30 kick-off at Old Trafford, and are bemoaning the six points dropped in three successive draws. They're not happy with Marcus Rashford, Paul Pogba, Henrikh Mkhitaryan, and most definitely Jose Mourinho.

This rounds the day off on a pleasing note.

December's Results

02.12.2017 – (A) Brighton & Hove Albion 5 – 1
06.12.2017 – (H) Spartak Moscow 7 – 0
10.12.2017 – (H) Everton 1 – 1
13.12.2017 – (H) West Bromwich Albion 0 – 0
17.12.2017 – (A) Bournemouth 4 – 0
22.12.2017 – (A) Arsenal 3 – 3
26.12.2017 – (H) Swansea City 5 – 0
30.12.2017 – (H) Leicester City 2 – 1

Burnley (A), January 1st, 2018
Chris Rowland

Now here's a first – and not just 'of January'! Due to circumstances beyond my control, I'm going to Burnley on my own!

What I didn't know when I asked for a ticket from the guy in Liverpool who looks after such matters, back in mid-December, is that they would all later decide to give the match a *swerve*, as they say in Liverpool. The problem being that date, January 1st. It seems nobody is confident of their ability to be back home from New Year's Eve in time to leave it again for the match. But our group needs to keep its away allocation up, so anyone who uses one is helping. I'm practically doing us a favour by going to the match.

So it's just me. I can't recall ever going to a Liverpool game on my own, since the late 1960s when I first went to a match. Burnley, I should explain, is only 12 miles or so from where I live, so it's a local game for me, and unlike on Boxing Day there are trains running. Burnley Manchester Road is first stop.

Around where I live, Burnley is the biggest supported team. I know plenty of their fans who will be going, and a few had already offered to give me a lift. But I turned them down because I'll go on the train, meet the others at a pub by Manchester Road station and proceed from there. Except now there are no others. I only learn this on December 27th. I'll need to pick up my ticket on Saturday at the Leicester match, I'm told, rather than having it handed to me on the day at Burnley, as there'll be nobody to do the handing!

Also, I feel two matches in three days is taxing my reserves – financial and domestic, as well as energy! I'd better check whether the heating's on in the dog house I'll be spending some time in ….

It's weird, being on my own. I wander down the street from the station and into the Ministry of Ale, where we normally meet – except today I'm not meeting anyone. I get chatting to a couple of Reds and we discuss the prospects without three of the Fab Four starting. We agree it will need to be a different sort of win if we are to succeed, a battling one not relying on the creativity and goals of Philippe Coutinho, Roberto Firmino and above all, Mo Salah. The latter will be out for up to two weeks they say, which means he'll miss the derby in the FA Cup. They are fixated on the derby. No weakened team there, thanks very much.

I walk down Manchester Road into town – it all seems very subdued and low-key, all the shops shut and quite a few boarded up, slate-grey sky now 100% where it had been partly blue earlier. I try to find Burnley's most renowned cask beer pub, the Bridge Bier Huis, and my memory serves me well. I have a pint in there and at about 1:15pm decide to walk up towards the ground. I'll have a pint in the cricket ground (home of Burnley Cricket Club and England's Jimmy Anderson!), unless I happen to stumble across something called the KSC100 Club – the Knights of St. Columba! – which is in the 2018 CAMRA Good Beer Guide and is near the ground. Some Burnley fans I know from the pub where I watch the matches at home said they often go there.

As I leave the Bridge Bier Huis I see the weather has changed, which is a euphemism for rodding down. I walk along the main road towards the ground, through the driving rain. I get drenched, jeans sodden from thigh downwards. I suddenly see a sign saying KSC100 Club, and a 'Home fans only' sign attached to it. I ignore it, as several Reds have, pay 20p to enter and register as a guest, get a pint of a local beer by the Reedley Hallows brewery and watch the last 20 minutes of the Brighton-Bournemouth game on TV as I gently steam by a radiator.

Back out into the rain and into the ground. The facilities – for food, drink and toilets – are quaint, but not in a good way. The area beneath the stadium is crammed to the point of being unhealthy (like travelling with Transpennine Express, I thought – no, leave it, let it go).

To my seat, and I'm right behind the goal and only about 20 seats from the home supporters in that end. And what a bunch of in-bred tossers they turn out to be. 'We are the Long Side, Burnley' they chant robotically for an unbroken ten minutes. It must take a special mindset to be able to do that without feeling a bit self-consciously moronic.

"Fuck *alllll*, you're gonna win fuck all" they sing.

"Fuck all, you've never won fuck all" comes the reply. Not technically true of course, they have won the league and beat us in the 1914 FA Cup Final, just before World War One broke out! You can prove the past but not the future, of course, so their chant is a mere prediction, with no way of confirming or denying it.

As for the game, it's hard to know which is worst, the weather, the Burnley fans or the referee. We agree Adam Lallana has been impressive, and Dejan Lovren too, despite the repeated criticism of one about him passing back to Simon Mignolet – "that's it back to the keeper that's all you ever fuckin' do lad". I point out that there was an onus on the other players to make runs to create a pass for him, but none did, they were all marked up by Burnley's assiduous determination to keep getting in the fucking way, so he had no option but to pass it back.

At half-time I meet an old mate who runs a Midlands-based supporters' club, and stop for a quick catch-up. He knows I'm on my own today, he had a call from the guy in Liverpool who does our tickets to ask whether his club wanted a few more!

We've known each other for years, he always meets us at half-time at Anfield, pint in hand, for a chat.

It's so packed down there behind the scenes, people travelling in opposite directions to go to the toilets or get a pint or something to eat, that it starts to feel almost dangerous. Someone ahead is getting vexed and pushing, someone else responds angrily, there's some swaying and surging – not nice at all, especially for any kids in there amongst it. There's only one way in and out of the toilets and it's barely two people wide, so it's soon blocked, which means people can't get out to let others in, which leads to gridlock and more frustration. That queue starts to impact on the food queue, and so it goes. Premier League eh? I'm relieved to get back to my seat, with all its relative surfeit of space.

The second-half sees the Reds kicking towards us. Sadio Mané's goal leads to delirium and brings "you only sing when you're winning" from the massed morons of Lancashire. When we reply, they then take us back to the early 1980s with "You what? You what? You what you what you what?"

A Scouser next to me makes eye contact with them and just shakes his head in despair at them. "Time you got home to shag yer daughters you inbred wankers" he yells. The police eye him up and shout a warning to shut up – I guess it's easier to get tough with one individual than a whole group of fans. They sing "you're just a shit Theo Walcott" as Alex Oxlade-Chamberlain prepares to take a corner in front of them. "You're just a shit Blackburn Rovers" comes a very audible lone Scouse voice. There's a chorus of abuse from the Burnley fans in earshot at the mention of their hated local rivals.

Burnley's late equaliser is a hammer blow, and brings the inevitable "you're not singing anymore" from their gloating fans.

And then that delicious late winner right in front of us, Ragnar Klavan poking home at close range from Lovren's header. As the team huddles in ecstatic celebration before us, mirrored by the leaping, air-punching Reds fans in front of them, and the air fills thick with red pyro smoke, our response of "you're not singing anymore" feels as sweet as the goal itself. *That's* how you to win a game! "I fucking hope Klavan was offside" says a jubilant Scouser. "It would make it even sweeter."

We file out into the night with "Show them the way to go home" echoing around the fast-emptying stadium, thousands of fingers jabbing triumphantly at the departing home fans. "They're only half a football team, compared to the boys in red."

The streets outside the ground are again thick with smoke, and ahead red flares pierce the blackness and Stygian gloom of a Pennine night on January 1st, belching their acrid scent into the air. All around it's Liverpool song. It's quite a scene. *This* is what you go the match for, being part of all this. I'm taken along with it, a heady brew as we go singing down the street.

Mercifully the sheeting rain that fell for most of the match has relented, and I walk the 20 minutes back to the Ministry of Ale for a last pint before my train. There are Scousers singing in there too, including a Raggy Klavan song no less. There's a constant stream of sirens from the direction of town, there's been a bit of trouble says a Burnley fan. "There was against Tottenham as well" he adds. What's the common factor there then, I wonder. A crusty old Burnley curmudgeon (tautology?) rants on about an offside winner and Liverpool time-wasting, and you get booked for that if you do it at Anfield. I can't let that go: "Bloody hell mate, if people got booked for time-wasting at Anfield we'd be playing against five men most weeks. Including your shower."

With that, I'm out of there and walk 100 yards to the station for my train home and a curry to round off the festive season.

I'll be watching *Match of the Day* tomorrow night though, and listening out for the expected narrative that plucky little Burnley were robbed by a very uncreative Liverpool, as though any side missing Salah, Coutinho and Firmino would be unaffected by it.

Oh, and I've finally dried out! (In a rain-soaked sense, not the clinic sense!)

Paul Tomkins, January 1st, 2018

At worst, Roberto Firmino is international class, but world-class is apt for him, too, when also considering his work-rate and assists. He is elite at those things.

Mo Salah has a world-class scoring rate for Egypt, and 19 goals for Roma last season was amazing. "Oh for a Liverpool player to score 19 goals in a season", I thought. To have 23 for Liverpool since August is off the charts.

There's a sense that Sadio Mané could be world-class too, but again, at worst he's a top international player. His form is patchy at the moment, but he's still doing some very good things.

Naby Keita is world-class in the making; the potential is clearly there. I thought Emre Can could be world-class one day, and that holds true, but losing him on a free would have been more than offset by acquiring Leon Goretzka, a younger, taller, free-scoring midfielder, who I had hoped would like the Germanic connection at Anfield, but seems to follow the boring path to Bayern Munich, where the league is theirs every season.

Normally I'd worry about new players failing to settle, and my old Tomkins Law hit-rate theory of only 40% of all transfers clearly succeeding, but not a single first-team player signed since Klopp arrived has failed to settle and, indeed, improve under him. Marko Grujić arrived as a young squad player, and was always likely to need time, and Steven Caulker – on loan – was apparently bedevilled by a drink problem, and who was never used for that reason, and allowed to enter rehab. Otherwise, the new additions are all adding something.

Could Alex Oxlade-Chamberlain become world-class? It feels unlikely, but there's a ton of potential to unlock there, which we're seeing more of each game. He'll never be a world-class winger, but there's something about him in midfield that gives me a hope I didn't have after his early games. According to a Manchester City study (which sounds like it could have been composed by a certain ex-TTTer), around 80% of the quarter-finalists playing in the Champions League last season were playing first-team football at 17. Oxlade-Chamberlain fits that profile.

And to me, Virgil van Dijk most definitely is a world-class defender, his reputation hampered a little being in a struggling Southampton side and a Holland team that has lost its way. He's world-class in the air, on the deck, and with his pace, that twice saw him catch Sadio Mané last season in a sprint. He will also drive into midfield and score goals at both ends of the pitch; something Liverpool have lacked at the back since Martin Skrtel's departure, although alas, he used to score at *both* ends. (And Ragnar Klavan and Dejan Lovren have stepped up lately.)

Joe Gomez is a world-class defender *for his age*, especially as he missed 18 months of his late teens; all that development stalled, and yet here he is, simply outstanding at just 20, and a future star alongside van Dijk at centre-back, you feel, even if there's no rush to move him there, perhaps for another year, as he gains more experience and Trent Alexander-Arnold bulks up a bit to "fill out" his overall game at full-back. Gomez's one clear weakness was on display again – a bit of a delayed reaction to far-post danger – but otherwise he's pretty much the real deal already.

The pace of 'van Dijk' and Gomez, along with Alexander-Arnold and Alberto Moreno (or the impressive Andy Robertson) would give Liverpool the quickest back-line in the league. That would enable the Reds to defend higher up, and press even harder, which would be some prospect. It's not just van Dijk's defensive skills, but also how it enables the team shape to change.

Add the pace and energy of Keita in midfield to the pace and energy of the current front three, and Liverpool could continue to get ever closer to being unplayable; something we've seen in the last two months, and something Man City have achieved this season. (And Liverpool also now look capable to digging in and dogging it out.)

Losing Philippe Coutinho and Emre Can would be a big blow, but at least the Reds control the Coutinho situation; although player power may have its say.

Comment by Glasgow Red, January 5th, 2018

I'll tell you this for nowt. I'm fucking bored of the whole Philippe Coutinho situation already.

I have full faith in Klopp/FSG that whatever happens will be for the best and be part of the bigger plan.

Sell now and no incoming? Deal with it using the very good squad we already have. Sell now and some incoming? Better than above. Don't sell now and Phil goes on strike – see point 1. Don't sell now and Phil leads us to FA Cup, 2nd place and Champions League glory – rejoice.

I'm reading the oft-quoted book on here *The Subtle Art of Not Giving A Fuck* by Mark Manson. One of the biggest insights I've had from it (in fact it's so fucking profound), I'm now re-reading the book again, is this:

Rather than visualise and focus on the joy of the end goal and all its glory (i.e. League title, Champions League win, return to world dominance, etc.), you should focus on the actual level of pain you're prepared to endure in order to get to your chosen glory state.

I've probably not explained that very eloquently but hopefully you get the gist. The point is, if selling Phil now and getting no immediate replacement, finishing outside top 4, losing tonight and getting knocked out by Porto is the pain we need to endure in order to win the league in 2020 and Champions League the following year, would you accept it?

Exactly.

Now consider all the column inches and gigabytes being taken up with this Phil story. Consider the effect on us as supporters and then consider the effect on the players. It absolutely has to be affecting them at the moment.

As such, if I was in charge, I'd release a statement now saying that one way or another Phil Coutinho will not play for Liverpool at all in the month of January and that we have total faith in our squad to continue the wonderful journey we're on this season. Furthermore, no official from the club will be discussing anything to do with Phil Coutinho until such time as the club deems it suitable to talk about Phil Coutinho.

As you were.

Paul Tomkins, January 7th, 2018

For starters, there are 142,000,000 obvious reasons to sell Philippe Coutinho, although if a player wants out badly enough, there has to be some kind of compromise somewhere along the way. After a while, it becomes counterproductive to keep an unhappy player. From Day One, Jürgen Klopp has said he doesn't want players who don't want to be at Liverpool; just as he said the same at his previous clubs. You're either all in, or you can go … if the price is right, and if you can't convince the player to change his mind and commit to the cause.

Kevin Keegan, Graeme Souness and Ian Rush wanted to test themselves abroad between 1977 and 1987, and were allowed to do so, at a time when Liverpool were winning trophies and logically, it could be argued, needed to retain them to continue winning trophies. The fees were acceptable to Liverpool back then, the players got their wish, and everyone moved on, usually successfully. I don't see how that makes Liverpool a "selling club" now, but not back then? (Did Manchester United selling Cristiano Ronaldo make them a selling club?) The food chain, and footballers' ambitions, continue to regulate the market. Liverpool are a big fish. Barcelona are perhaps the biggest. We all know this; it's how the club got Virgil van Dijk from a smaller fish. It's how it works. And five years' service from an import seems a fair contribution to any club.

I don't *necessarily* think even a fee rising to £142m is enough to prise a key player away at a vital stage of the season, but if it buys a world-class goalkeeper and another outstanding attacker (and maybe another midfielder), then that's progress (if those players settle as expected). But is a £142m asset striking his way through January much use anyway? If he went on strike back in August, perhaps it was forgiven. If he's on strike again now, that might be a blow too far; too much disrespect to the club and his teammates. And this season, Liverpool have an excellent record without Coutinho, so it's not like losing the all-important Luis Suárez' although it doesn't help the Reds' chances in the Champions League on paper, unless new buys are free to play it (like van Dijk is). And the money must be reinvested.

I'd go so far as to say that the money has to be reinvested in the team this January, with replacements already lined up, or it could get nasty for those running the club. No panic buys must be made, but the club surely has a good idea of who it wants and who it can get.

The Fernando Torres money went straight back into the team, as did the Luis Suárez money, and thankfully the club has a more coherent buying strategy right now. Could Thomas Lemar be on his way? Will the Brazilian goalkeeper Alisson be sought?

It's been a hectic 24 hours, with the Roberto Firmino/Mason Holgate incident coming straight after the euphoria of a Virgil van Dijk winner, although I won't say too much on the controversy other than people have a right to make allegations if they feel they've been offended, but making allegations is not in itself proof. Maybe something was said; maybe nothing was said; maybe something was misheard. It was a melee, and you'd hope that the referee heard anything that was said. Whatever happened, I hope that proof is produced if Firmino is to be charged.

But for now, I'll focus on the impending departure of Coutinho.

I would imagine that outside of TTT the fanbase is melting down, although as noted at the start of this piece, it's the same situation as Liverpool signing van Dijk. You can't moan too much if you destabilise players at smaller clubs and then bigger clubs do the same to you, and in both cases, the fees received are huge. It's how the game works.

Coutinho is not going to a Premier League rival, and as also noted at the start, the club has always sold its best players, even when winning everything. The reason van Dijk is at Liverpool is because Jürgen Klopp met him in Blackpool, without Southampton knowing, and once he'd spoken to Klopp there was only one place he wanted to be. He didn't kiss the badge last night but he thumped the crest, as if to prove he got his wish.   I refuse to be downhearted about Coutinho leaving. You move on, welcome in new players, promote existing ones, and look to the future. Everyone has their price, and while Klopp said there is no price at the *wrong* time, this could be the right time, within reason, given it's not right at the end of the window. Barcelona left it too late in the summer, after all.

Liverpool's no.1 creative weapon has always been the work-rate and pressing from the front under Klopp, and a united squad is paramount to his ideas.

Paul Tomkins, January 7th, 2018

I delayed reading Raphael Honigstein's book *Klopp: Bring The Noise* until after the busy festive period was out the way. But I'd also been putting it off as I didn't want further confirmation of just how good the Liverpool manager is, almost for fear of getting even more depressed about those Reds who just don't get it. Part of me didn't want to invest more emotionally in the manager given how fractious the fanbase is about almost everything these days.

But all Liverpool fans *must* read this book. I don't know how you can support the club properly – or, at least, say anything about performances and what is being attempted – until you know exactly what he's all about. We've all read various interviews and soundbites, but nothing (in English, at least) goes this deep. It shows how Jürgen Klopp evolved Mainz, evolved Dortmund and is evolving Liverpool. (Alas, my sense is that our ultimate dreams may fall short due to arguably the greatest coach in the history of football – certainly of the past decade – following Klopp from Germany to the north-west of England and having the luxury of twice the budget and a better squad to start with … but Klopp is the next-best thing, and all Liverpool can do is look to be the best, on the budget the turnover allows.)

Honigstein's book helped me to understand why – when some managers who achieve success cannot then transfer that to a new club (but we still want that security blanket of their past successes) – Klopp has shown the ability to build something in each of his three jobs to date, even if the Liverpool project is perhaps only halfway complete (with both Mainz and Dortmund kicking into top gear around year three, and petering out only by year seven). It's a book that details Klopp's brilliance to a level many won't quite have been aware of. He is a *unifier*, a *uniter*. He has brought together all aspects of the club, for arguably the first time in decades. The subsequent loss of Philippe Coutinho does not change that.

The book also helps show how so many of his signings made at various clubs have bucked my old "Tomkins' Law" theory, where I worked out that only 40% of all signings clearly succeed and no more than 60% of *expensive* signings succeed: Klopp's attention to detail before signing a player, and his unwillingness to bend on his principles of what he wants – followed by his clear tactical ideas and wonderful man-management once the player arrives – means that when he signs someone it's not some speculative gamble. There is no 'throwing the mud at walls' of buying 10 players and seeing if five stick. Yes, signings can still fail, but very few of his seem to do so.

There are examples of Klopp meeting potential signings and those signings being ready to do anything for him. But there are also examples of strict questionnaires, asking a prospective buy about how hard he'd be prepared to run, whether he'd be happy scoring a few goals in games without putting in as much work; if they were the kind who didn't like to train too hard but would promise to give their all during matches. Anyone who wasn't 100% eager to work all week in training and all 90 minutes of game for the team was instantly dismissed. It was easy to see, while I was reading the book, why Virgil van Dijk would have shelved all interest in going anywhere else. Ex-Dortmund stars, like İlkay Gündoğan, seem in awe of the big German boss.

A lot of people used to claim that it was actually Michal Zorc who was behind Dortmund's success, and while he clearly did a great job when Klopp was there, it seems he did a less-great job before and after, if you judge a director of football on on-field successes. Klopp was the one who made it all work. It's clear in the book that Klopp is not just a motivator. He's an incredibly clever man, with immense emotional intelligence, stoicism, honesty, passion, compassion and humour, and a sharp tactical brain. Everyone Honigstein speaks to and quotes, in every walk of life (from players to owners to media people, to retired legends like Franz Beckenbauer) seem to be in awe of his character and intelligence. Some of Dortmund's players, after they'd faced the power of the Kop on a European night in 2016, were actually *pleased* for Klopp that Liverpool had won, in amongst their own devastation at throwing away the lead.

It shows Klopp as an obsessive winner, but less nasty about it than many who share that kind of passion. While Zeljko Buvač and Peter Krawietz are noted by Klopp as his "brain and his eyes", Klopp is incredibly smart; he is not simply the facade for their brilliance. He is the one who brings everyone together, from the owner and the director of football, to all the backroom staff. He empowers those around him, never belittles them.

Klopp is also shown as hugely phlegmatic, contrary to perceptions of him as just a fiery character. In truth, he's both fiery *and* phlegmatic, in that he is combustible but always quickly returns to being the bigger man, in all senses. He explodes, but then shows humility and apologises. He almost never bombs any player out completely, giving everyone second chances, even if it means that sometimes he obviously then chooses to sell them (if they're still not producing for him). But it's rare for anyone to be ostracised, sent to the "Coventry" of the youth team.

He makes the best of the hand he is dealt. At both his German clubs it was noted that he didn't complain about the limited budgets. He got on with it.

Klopp understands life; he appreciates that there are ups and downs, and that you can't bypass the pain. This is clear from the tales of his childhood and also his playing career. His early years as manager at Mainz were littered with near-misses: missing promotion first by a point, then, a year later, by a *single goal*. The third year they were promoted, for the first time in their history, to the top flight. After both of those first two seasons he bounced back, revved everyone up again, getting them to overperform against expectations.

This is utterly vital in sport. In another excellent book, Matthew Syed's *Bounce*, triple-jump star Jonathan Edwards talks about how his religious faith gave him the belief that good things would happen to him during competitions, something he lost once he lost his belief in God. (And that, looking back, Edwards sees it as folly, but a folly that supported his own mental toughness; he felt that God was on his side, as if God was spending His time looking out for English triple-jumpers.) Now, I'm an atheist, and I want to keep religion from TTT wherever possible, as it's so divisive (although I also believe that everyone has a right to their faith); and I don't want to say that it's purely Klopp's own faith gives him that kind of boundless belief. But Syed's book talks about how having unwavering self-belief is vital in sport as you always, *always* get knocked down, sooner or later, and often, repeatedly. If you can't bounce back, you're merely decorating the canvas.

Paul Tomkins, January 8th, 2018

The brilliant research professor Brené Brown nails a lot of our modern problems with her observation that "You can't selectively numb emotion."

In other words, if you try to numb fear, uncertainty, disappointment and sadness, then you automatically numb joy, spontaneity, hope, contentment, love. The process of numbing *numbs everything*. We put on suits of armour that weigh a ton, she says. And she is right.

Look on social media at many Liverpool accounts – and believe me, I try not to, these days – and the cynicism almost literally drips from the tweets and status updates. While the modern age requires some cynicism – there are some bad people out there, who will take you for a ride – cynicism is actually a key factor in what's making so many people unhappy. You can't enjoy any positives because you're worried about the negatives around the corner. You numb everything. (It's also why politics is now only about fear, I guess. We react far more strongly to negatives than positives, as I often discuss.)

Indeed, as I mentioned in my (roundabout) review of Raphael Honigstein's excellent book on Jürgen Klopp, it is Klopp's indomitable spirit – *his lack of cynicism* – that has driven him to so much success, along with his wisdom about life in general, which a lot of people could learn from. Klopp has had setbacks throughout his career, but he always wants to stay positive and think of ways to solve problems. That's why he's a proven winner and liked by almost everyone who has worked with him. Honigstein's book is a wonderful window into the Liverpool manager's myriad qualities, but it seems too many Liverpool fans are angry about absolutely *every-fucking-thing* to even appreciate what they have. I implore people to read it, to get an education.

Loss aversion means we fear loss more than we value gains, and that applies whether you're young or an "arl fella" from the Kop. So when Liverpool signed Virgil van Dijk, it seems people could not enjoy the addressing of a problem – a problem they themselves had harped on about as *absolutely the most vital thing necessary* – because they feared it meant selling Philippe Coutinho.

They were right, of course, but the two weren't necessarily connected; other than both players wanted to move up the ladder in their careers. This sense of cynicism is always going to be proved right, as these types of things will always happen. On the most beautiful day you can proclaim that it will rain soon, and then, four days later, if it rains, you are right. But van Dijk is *fucking ace* and wants to play for Liverpool.

Brené Brown calls this "foreboding joy", and it's killing us. It makes everything stressful. Something good happens and rather than being open to its joy, we worry about what will go wrong, or what it secretly means. Someone gives you a £50 note on a windy day, and you chide them with "what if it blows away?" Well, what if? Will the world end?

Let some joy in. Don't try to beat bad news to the punch. Stop being so cynical that you become the boring old know-it-all in the corner of the pub, whom no one dares sit near, as you drain the life out of everything. Life has let you down so you try to drag everyone down with you. There's no need to be excessively naïve and gullible either, and we all need warnings about pitfalls up ahead, but cynicism is so easy, such a predictable protective blanket. It's so teenage, so adolescent.

I probably read more about life, perceptions, heuristics, psychology and human interactions than I do about football these days, but all helps towards writing about football. (And I still read about football.)

Keeping everything is perspective is a constant challenge, but if you don't do that with your football analysis, then your football analysis can be worthless. Complain, for example, as an Everton fan, that your team is not winning the league, and that complaint won't be based in *reality*. Basing expectations on distant history is misleading, worthless. So it's a question of mixing football probabilities with how we perceive those odds, and what skews our thinking, whatever the subsequent results.

Comment by David Fitzgerald (AKA Madchenkliop), January 12th, 2018

This joyless tweet sums it up for me:

"Liverpool not having announced some sort of replacement for Coutinho yet is a real vibe killer. Genuinely can't fathom we're willing to gamble with these high stakes."

It's all about insurance. Some kind of projected future reality that has little basis on what's actually transpired this season. Why can't we enjoy the vibe from van Dijk's arrival? I just rewatched the match and found it extremely rousing stuff, along with Trent Alexander-Arnold and Alex Oxlade-Chamberlain's recent goals.

Philippe Coutinho has been marvellous when he's played, but we're over halfway through a season which could have been even better if he was entirely committed to the club. Who knows but were that the case maybe we would be within spitting distance of challenging City at the top. I don't personally think so, but the cold hard facts are that this is not a season we can win a Premier League title or the Champions League – especially with our main match-winners all wanting, as Coutinho has manifestly demonstrated by joining Barcelona when cup tied, to keep their powder dry for the main event of the World Cup.

Talent and pedigree are wonderful things, but they are nothing without motivation and commitment. I'm so glad Paul wrote his article on Honigstein's book, because it goes such a long way to explain how Jürgen Klopp works, and what I find most galling about the above tweet is it reveals such a wilful ignorance of what he's already shown us in his method and priorities when introducing players.

Having seen the progress made by Andy Robertson, Joe Gomez, Alexander-Arnold and Alberto Moreno, is it not exciting to see what Klopp can do with the other talented players at the club? Coutinho himself was high stakes at one point. Yes we're not buying in off-the-shelf superstars like the Manchester clubs and Chelsea, but do we really want to be just the same as them? What would be the point in having a unique manager like Klopp if we were to take that path? Surely the joy will be in seeing the next Coutinho emerge and having faith in Klopp's judgement that this can't be manufactured or rushed.

Personally, I can't imagine anything more thrilling than the ride we're already on.

Paul Tomkins, January 14th, 2018

Wow! City were owed a beating, after the game at the Etihad, where the best team in the history of English football (up to this point of a season), were given a helping hand by a decision that never seems to get given on any other occasion, as Sadio Mané was sent off in the first half for a high boot. But even without Philippe Coutinho – who wasn't missed today – and even without Virgil van Dijk (who possibly was), Liverpool ended the unbeaten run of a very special Manchester City side. The only downer was that it wasn't by a *bigger* margin. Jürgen Klopp extended his number of wins over Pep Guardiola to six, and that's testament to his qualities, while Liverpool are now unbeaten in 18-games (with 18 straight wins on "xG"); the club getting back towards the levels it was at from 2004-2009, when it was regularly tough to beat, and won more games than it failed to win.

The match, and perhaps the rest of the season, hinged on a blast from the past: Robbie Fowler at Old Trafford against Gary Neville, where 'God' almost gave a cry of "Get off!" to shove the United defender-cum-commentator (not to be confused with a cum commentator) off the ball before dinking over Peter Schmeichel. Roberto Firmino's goal was so similar that it reminded me of those old Baddiel and Skinner Fantasy Football sketches where they recreated famous goals, one of which even involved Fowler. (Others have obviously spotted the similarity too.) There was no need for that *other* Brazilian fella.

Liverpool actually did better without Coutinho in the calendar year of 2017 than when he played. And while with-and-without stats can be misleading, the £142m man missed some tough games and the Reds coped fine in his absence, still able to score lots of goals. Could it be whatever the little magician brought in quality was actually eclipsed by the greater work-rate and cohesion without him, with gegenpressing the ultimate creator Klopp says it is? Does the superstar carry a team, or does he hold them back; can others find themselves looking to those players a bit too much whenever they play, whereas without them, everyone has to take responsibility?

And today, every single Liverpool outfield player was off-the-charts-good, particularly unsung heroes like Andy Robertson, Alex Oxlade-Chamberlain, Dejan Lovren and Gini Wijnaldum. Which isn't to say that losing Coutinho is a good thing; I'm not trying to spin it – just that results were already better without him, and this only added to that perception.

Paul Tomkins, January 16th, 2018

…I now think Liverpool are capable of winning the Champions League this season, inasmuch as Porto and Liverpool did just over a decade ago, and Dortmund *almost* did in 2013. Why? Well, I think the Reds can beat anyone at Anfield, although perhaps an underdog will have more luck with a big 'shell' – parking the bus – than better teams that "come to play".

That doesn't mean Liverpool should be amongst the favourites – just that no big club likes facing a Jürgen Klopp team, and no big club wants to visit Anfield under the floodlights. This Liverpool side is better than the 2005 version, and the Reds beat Champions League-quality teams in 2016 to reach the Europa League Final. Klopp has European pedigree, if not yet a trophy to go with it. How many other managers have reached two European finals since 2013? Not many, I'd guess.

Comment by El Indio, January 19th, 2018

In the Greek epic of The Iliad there was one person who showed considerable intelligence and more understanding of the situation than anyone else.

A lot, in the modern world, is written about two others, Agamemnon and Achilles, yet both of them die upon their return to home.

Victorious Agamemnon gets betrayed by his partner out of lust while Achilles dies a hero amidst bravery. One dies on return, the other returns as a body.

But neither was more influential than Odysseus, who exhibits diplomacy and even man-management to unite different banners of Greek leadership towards inevitable sacking of Troy.

The Romans, understandably, called him the cruel or deceitful Ulysses (Odysseus is derived from Greek, while Ulysses is derived from Latin) because they couldn't stand his smarts and the humiliation he caused to their lineage when Troy was sacked. (For reference Prince Aeneas, who survives the Trojan War and sacking of the city, was thought to be an ancestor of Remus and Romulus – founders of modern Rome.)

However Odysseus does lose his way (ten years is a considerable time trying to get home after fighting a war for another ten years before it) as he intends to return home leading to an epic of his own. His travels and encounters with different people/Gods/monsters/other beings highlights his ability to find the solution for himself and his men regardless of seemingly worse odds for survival.

So what does it have to do with Jürgen Klopp? By no means is Klopp Odysseus reincarnate (or even his great grandchild) in the modern world but somehow his abilities and skill set doesn't differ much.

A lot of people take Klopp's IQ/EQ for granted since they either see a self-deprecating, happy character who doesn't mind dropping an F-bomb on live TV or an emotionally charged angry crackpot on the touchline.

Behind those glasses is a man who is exceptionally smart, understands the cause of things and reads the situation very well. He is also a leader in uniting different factions. Either through his written words, sideline actions, spoken words in the media or through his football.

He also brings about harmony to an institution that, despite its rich history, has had its share of madness on and off the pitch. It's not the harmony of an orchestra, it's more like melodic death metal which doesn't have guitar thrashing at the end. It's not perfect yet, as there is still more fine tuning of instruments required, but blimey, some of the days it's just an 11 out of 10 stage performance.

We have to admit, Liverpool Football Club does rule a bit of our lives. Values, honor, respect (even opponents), tradition and finally *You'll Never Walk Alone* – they all unite us across the world. We look forward to match days so as to drive away our daily struggles or fear of impending doom.

The 90 minutes matter.

It is worth revisiting that he had stated in his first interview of that it is his job to 'entertain' us. To make our lives better.

Today was one of those days.

Just like Odysseus, I hope the cunning Klopp (and Co.) will help us return to the promised land.

And I doubt it will take him 10 years.

Paul Tomkins, January 23rd, 2018
For the umpteenth time this season, Liverpool "won" 2-0 on xG (expected goals); although for the first time in months, the result was not in keeping with the chances. Liverpool did not play very well, but they limited Swansea to one quarter-chance (tucked gallingly into the corner) and had chances to score at least two goals, based on the quality of chances and the likelihood of them being converted. Had Swansea not scored early on they may have become more ambitious, but it's perhaps unlikely, as they seemed to set up for a 0-0, on a pitch destroyed by the downpour against Spurs and games of rugby that tear up its surface, against a Liverpool side that couldn't find a passing rhythm.

With irony, the losing goal came from the only Liverpool player to excel: Virgil van Dijk, who barely put a foot wrong, bar slicing the ball for a corner when it should have gone for a throw, which, of course, he himself then cleared, but only to some guy who sounds like he's from the 1940s (Alfie Mawson), who stuck it away.

Van Dijk defended and organised brilliantly for the other 89 minutes, and created great chances for Mo Salah and Bobby Firmino, who have 41 goals between them this season. Van Dijk is already a vocal leader, and in time it will reap dividends. But if your two players who have already scored more at this stage of a season than any single Liverpool player has managed in a full season since 2014 have off days, *c'est la vie*. If your opposing centre-back prods a ball into the corner with unsaveable accuracy, *c'est la vie*. Shit happens, and after 18 games unbeaten, you will not be immune to bad luck, even if it's just after beating Manchester City. Liverpool did not play well, but at the very least merited a point, if not all three, based on xG; the chances were there. It is the Reds' 19th straight victory on xG and hopefully, like Manchester City last season, Jürgen Klopp's men can build on making the scoreline reflect their xG/"both boxes" dominance.

Liverpool may have lacked the creativity of Philippe Coutinho, but the Reds – for all the wild shots from distance – did create two chances for Salah to score, and one for Firmino, and one for Danny Ings, and one for Sadio Mané (but his standing foot gave way on the crappy surface) as well as countless pinballs around their packed area, as they played 5-4-1 that at times became 9-0-1. And Coutinho would not have played even had he stayed. He would have been on strike or remained "injured" until the start of February, obviously.

If Liverpool decide not to replace him this window that's a worry, for obvious reasons, but equally, wasting the money on a compromise was what Liverpool refused to do with van Dijk and got their man six months later. Keeping Coutinho could have been counterproductive too, given how desperate he was (along with Nike, on his behalf) to play for Barcelona, in sunnier weather, in a more like-minded culture, and for tons and tons of their riches. This is a blip, after many blip-less months, and as Dan Kennett noted, Liverpool had a terrible January *with* Coutinho last year. And the Reds have broken down packed defences with and without him this season, and broke down Swansea enough to win last night.

As I said, shit happens.

Huddersfield Town (A), January 30th, 2018
Chris Rowland

When Huddersfield got promoted last May, I was delighted that there was a really local game for me to go to, just 15 miles and two train stops away. It's also a town with a legendary pubs and beer scene – what's not to like?

Then the fixtures come out in June and I find Huddersfield away is on a bloody Tuesday night in January! That picture in my head of how the day's going to be has to be hastily redrawn, my expectations revised downwards. And with the game due to finish about 21:50 and the last train 22:24, it's going to be very tight afterwards.

This week, having just lost to the bottom two in the Premier League, we've seen Daniel Sturridge and Ovie Ejaria move out on loan and had a near meltdown from our fans concerned about the transfer window. Then just as I'm about to set out I hear our world-record price for a centre-back might be missing through injury. There has been talk of fan protests tonight, of a growing "FSG out" (aka FS Gout) movement and even some mutterings about Jürgen Klopp's position. Careful what you wish for, folks! We really can't afford to lose to a third relegation-threatened side in a week, though of course that doesn't mean we can't.

All this is on my mind as I set out.

I have arranged to meet the only two of our usual flock who are going. There's one slight impediment to the smooth running of any arrangement. Their text tells me they'll be arriving at Stalybridge Station Buffet Bar at 1:30. It's on the main line from Manchester to Huddersfield.

For those who don't know, the Buffet Bar is one of the very few remaining Victorian station buffet bars, dating from 1885. It has retained the original marble-topped bar, the old 1st-class ladies waiting room and has a great range of beers. It's a great place to stop, albeit part of the weekend stag and hen circuit.

"We'll be the two pissed up twats" says the text. "Why don't you join us?"

Two reasons. I'm working, for one, and Stalybridge is 100% the wrong direction for someone who lives where I do and wants to go to Huddersfield.

But I have to meet them – one has my ticket. So we arrange to meet at the King's Head, one of two pubs attached to Huddersfield station.

I get the train and, via a change at Brighouse, 40 minutes later I'm in Huddersfield at just about 5pm. In the King's Head I meet the two 'drunken idiots' – except they're not. Drunken I mean! I didn't realise but they were staying in Huddersfield after the match and had been checking into their hotel, so only had one and a half hours start on me instead of three!

Apparently we've arranged to meet a group of diehard Liverpool supporters (about 40 of them!) at a pub called the Railway at Berry Brow, two train stops from Huddersfield. So after a tasty pint of Magic Rock Ringmaster I'm back on a train. We find the Railway, and the gathered masses, who have commandeered the jukebox and converted it to a Beatles-only playlist.

There was plenty of anti-FSG sentiment amongst them, they're just not investing enough in the club is the gist. On the end wall of the pub, the Sky Sports counter announces that Riyad Mahrez has handed in a transfer request and Man City look likely to get him. That prompts more debate on the same subject. It's amazing how two people in the same situation – Reds fans, similar ages and socio-economic circumstances etc., broadly on a level – can see exact opposites in it.

"See, City lose Sane through injury for six weeks and do something about it, sign a replacement. Where's our replacement for Coutinho? The owners have got Klopp's hands behind his back just like Rafa's were with the cowboys."

(A lot of assumptions in there – that Mahrez is being signed as a replacement solely because of Sane's injury – Mahrez usually plays on the right and in-cutting, like Salah, whilst Sane is definitely left-sided – and indeed whether the deal has even been completed. Is Sky's counter always right?)

"Oh, you think that's okay do you – a team can spend £50-70m on someone just because of a six-week injury? Most people don't do that because they can't afford it, and I don't want us to be like that either."

I point out that the transfer isn't actually confirmed yet. Two more beers and we're back on the train towards town from this lonely outpost. Back at Huddersfield station we notice the 'Welcome to Huddersfield – Home of the Terriers' signage all over it, on each step edge, along the sides, in the subways. Outside the station in the impressive St George's Square a lone bagpiper in full kilt regalia is playing 'Flower of Scotland' next to a streetstand selling matchday paraphernalia. Burns Night having passed days earlier, I ponder at this.

We get a taxi to the match and he gets us so close we can almost reach the turnstiles. "Come on Abdul, Row G, seat 52 please, bloody half-a-job!" says Pete (he had told us his name was Abdul, it wasn't random racist stereotyping). I have never had a taxi get this close to a ground before. Then when we get out we realise it's completely the wrong end for the away supporters, so we circumnavigate the ground. When we get to our bit, there seems to be slow-moving chaos outside it. It seems the police are only letting ten fans at a time towards the turnstiles, then holding the rest back while they're searched and processed.

Once in, we see immediately that the low-key lack of atmosphere around the town definitely does not extend to inside the stadium, which is loud and boiling with noise and movement, almost all of it from the over-excited home supporters, who appear wired like kids on Christmas Eve. It certainly feels like it's a bigger occasion for them than for us. The end we're in is shared, and their part of it makes a loud and constant din, aided by a bloody continuous drum, which many wish to insert none too sensitively or scientifically into its owner's anal orifice long before the end of the game. It-never-bloody-stopped, even when they were 3-0 down.

"One-nil and you still won't sing" they sing.

"No we'll wait till we're four up like we should be against you!" yells a shrill Scouse voice.

"It's because we can never relax and enjoy it till we're four up, more like" mutters my mate Jon.

It wasn't a scintillating Reds' performance but it was a solid one, the sort that gets called 'professional', in a half complimentary, half critical sort of way.

Oh and there were no signs of any fan protests.

At 21:45, I have to make my move and walk back to the station for that 22:24 last train. I realise it's a longer way than I thought, that it's mostly uphill, and that just following the crowd on its way back into town does *not* lead you to the station. After asking half a dozen people where the bloody station's disappeared to, I finally find it, after some blokes in a trench in Northern Gas high-viz vests send me in entirely the wrong direction.

I make it with ten minutes to spare, then can't find platform six. Huddersfield station is a bit weird, platforms one and two are the same platform just further along, and six turns out to be an extension of Platform eight! Good to see them shunning the so-obvious conventional numbering sequence that has served mankind so well for centuries!

This is the Leeds train, and I have to get off at Halifax and wait 25 minutes for my train home – the last one. It's on time. My wife is waiting at my home station to give me a lift home, sparing another 25 minute uphill walk that I'm very keen to avoid.

Just before midnight, we are home. A successful sortie, all in all.

Comment by Brian Davis

Was there last night, and what you say about the atmosphere in the ground is spot on. And that bloody drum.

I do not understand the FSG issues that keep coming up. Looks to me like they are doing a pretty sensible job. Not sure either why Klopp gets so much stick – he is a top manager that we are lucky to have.

Why do we not splash the cash like City? Firstly, Klopp only buys players that he wants and is prepared to wait, and secondly, we do not have unlimited finances like City and Chelsea, nor are we happy to let debt spiral like Manchester United whilst we still have a stadium to complete.

Comment by Paddy Smith

Thanks Chris, I was there last night with my boys, I got corporate tickets through a company I use based in Huddersfield – great seats behind the home dugout, if you look closely you can see my red scarf on the telly! I thought the away end seemed quiet last night, although that bloody drum might just of drowned all our songs out?! When we scored the first there was a big shout of 'yesssss' from behind me, you can imagine my surprise as I looked round to see who it was and it was none other than King Kenny! Also got a nice pic with Gary Mac with my son so good night all round.

January's Results

01.01.2018 – (A) Burnley 2 – 1
05.01.2018 – (H) Everton 2 – 1
14.01.2018 – (H) Manchester City 4 – 3
22.01.2018 – (A) Swansea City 0 – 1
27.01.2018 – (H) West Bromwich Albion 2 – 3
30.01.2018 – (A) Huddersfield Town 3 – 0

Tottenham Hotspur (H), February 4th, 2018
Graham Gilby

I've got a ticket for Spurs at home thanks to "my mate Dave". It's not as Ali G as it sounds though. My mate Dave is actually an academic, a sociologist with a keen interest in class and culture. A Scouser who these days splits his time between London and Edinburgh. His career is going well and today I am the beneficiary. He's at a conference, and I've got his ticket.

I'm walking out the door and my flatmate is staring at me with a puzzled look on his face. "What are you wearing?"

I look down at myself – Puma tracksuit, fairly standard match going fare. Then I look again. It's navy blue and white! I look like the love-child of the Spurs' team doctor and a Spurs hooligan (NB: I am neither a medic nor a violent person). Shit! Dressed in navy blue and white, London accent*, I'm a Spurs fan to all intents and purposes!

But it's too late to change. I need to get the tube from East London to Euston and I don't have that much time. I decide I'll buy a scarf when I get to Liverpool, which I've been meaning to do for ages anyway. It'll keep me safe by adding a reassuring splash of red to my outfit and keep me warm – it's bloody cold.

I booked my train a few weeks ago and managed to buy a ticket I didn't think actually existed. I'd heard it talked about, but I'd never seen it with my own eyes. The unicorn of train travel: the first-class ticket that is cheaper than a standard-class ticket. I mean, it's not cheap, but it's a full £3 *cheaper* than standard-class. The only issue is that it leaves London at 1:05pm, getting into Lime St at 3:37pm. Kick-off is 4:30pm. There is no margin for error.

The first (but not the last!) disappointment of the day is the realisation that Virgin West Coast First Class is terrible! I know there is no booze on Sunday. I've prepared for that with some vodka in a plastic bottle. But I am looking forward to my free mixers! But when the trolley comes it turns out there are no cold drinks, only tea and coffee.

I know TTT doesn't really do politics, and I don't want to open a can of worms, but this might be the final nail in the coffin for privatised rail for me. I don't really mind if the trains are run by the public sector or the private sector. Whoever can make them run on time for the best price can have the job. I'm a pragmatist. But when 1st-class has been reduced to no booze, a dry BLT and no cold drinks, I start thinking we should tear up Richard Branson's contracts and take back control!

So I have to walk from coach J to C (oh the ignominy) to get to the buffet car. My eyes are drawn to the cans of San Pellegrino on display. They think they are better than all the other cans, with their funny little foil hats. But the branding has worked and I buy two. Over the next two hours I drink them both with about 300ml of vodka. I work out that's six-doubles. Do I have a problem?

I'm drunk in a happy, warm and excited way. The trains get in on time. I've booked an Airbnb a couple of minutes from Lime Street. I drop my stuff off and get in a taxi. Talksport is on the radio. The presenter is talking about Spurs' new ground, and how Daniel Levy wants it to double-up as an American Football stadium one-day. Clever bastard, I think. The cabbie and I start talking about it. He tells me how nobody cares about the fans anymore, about how crap the 7:45pm Saturday evening kick-off against West Brom was. I start thinking about how crazy globalisation is. About how forces out of any of our control are transforming people's lives in ways they can't and don't want to comprehend. "If you think a 7:45pm Saturday kick-off is bad, just wait until Uber introduces driverless cars to Liverpool", I think, but don't say. I really am quite pissed. I decide to stop thinking about globalisation and start thinking about football again.

I meet Andy at 'the Bakery', next to the Kop. He's got the tickets. Another sociologist. I do have friends who aren't sociologists. Although every sociologist I know is a Liverpool fan. Is there something in that or is it just a coincidence? Andy is a good guy who enjoys playing up to his misery persona when it comes to football. He hates Jordan Henderson. He's not playing that up, it's clearly genuine. He's bought me a steak pie and refuses to let me pay him back. I tell him I'm thrilled Hendo is playing, which I am. We head into the ground about 15 mins before kick-off.

We're in the Anfield Road stand – the only part of the ground I've never sat in before. It's not really where you want to be for atmosphere, but at least all four stands are now ticked off my list. We're close to the Spurs fans who are as noisy as ever. If they beat us it's going to be awful (they didn't, but it was!)

We're ten rows back, just to the left of the goal. It's a terrible place to watch football. But in around two hours, we'll have an absolutely perfect view of Mo Salah scoring one of the all-time great Anfield goals (I still don't really know how he did it).

I thought the atmosphere was decent throughout, even in the Annie Rd end. At one point the Salah song broke out in the Kop and made it all the way to us. I belt it out. Andy turns around to me with a sarcastic grin, "I didn't know they were practising that in North London hipster bars?". He's no more Scouse than me but he lives closer, hates London and loves to have a pop. At one point Hendo plays a perfect pass out to the left to Mané, I grab him by the shoulders and says "what a player!".

We sang the Salah song throughout and it was great. I think we've missed a really good player tune since the Fernando Torres song.

"Mo Salah, Mo Salah … running down the wing … Mo Salah, Salah, Salaaaaaaah … our Egyptian King!" It's a belter that everyone can get involved with. And boy does he deserve a song.

A couple of guys behind us moaned about everything – the main focus of their ire was Loris Karius's ponytail. Fair play – it's not great – but who gets properly pissed off about stuff like that?! How can you not just enjoy watching this team play? Get behind the boys? Why are so many people overcome with negativity? I start thinking about globalisation again for a second, but thankfully the game is too good to pull me into that quagmire for too long.

Afterwards, I walk back from the ground to the centre of town in a daze. I've never been to a match that ended quite like that. I chat to my brother on the phone, but the reception is crap. He says both penalties were contentious. First was probably offside, and possibly a dive. The second was also maybe a dive and missed by the ref, only to be given by an attention-seeking linesman. Jon Moss and the Linos – a terrible tribute band? They were terrible today, no doubt about that.

I'm hungry. I walk into an Italian restaurant in the centre of town and order a pizza and a beer. I gather my thoughts. What a match! Ridiculous. Breathless. Controversial. Probably just about a fair result? I don't know how to feel. I don't feel too angry or sad.

Expectations play a massive part in how I feel at the end of a football match. We were 1-0 up for about 80 minutes. But we were pushed back for most of the second half and I did feel like if that continued they would probably score. And when Harry Kane stepped up to take his first penalty, I was resigned to losing after leading for most of the match. Then after Mo scored his worldie I thought we had the three points. Then the second penalty. A proper rollercoaster.

I make my way back to my Airbnb and watch the highlights. Still don't really know how to feel. It's definitely two points lost, but it doesn't feel like a disaster. We're still two points ahead of them and still within touching distance of second place. We're in the last 16 of the Champions League. I've just watched probably the second and third best teams in the league, in a really strong year for English football, play a thrilling match. Not bad to support one of them. In the last 10 years we've frequently been the 5th, 6th or 7th best team in a weaker league, and never this good to watch.

I'm up early on Monday, and back on the train for work. I'm still mulling over the game, still feeling a bit confused and still singing the Salah song. In the end I settle on the old adage "football, the most important of all the not-important things". That always keeps it in perspective. Definitely not worth getting too worried about, not like globalisation.

*Not that it really needs explaining but I was born in Scotland, to Scottish parents. We're Raith Rovers fans. Kenny Dalglish was a God in our house and my Dad's 'English team' (remember when English people used to have a 'Scottish team'?) was Liverpool. I grew up in London but from before I can remember Liverpool were my team.

Without wanting to get the sociologists too excited, this has led to a lifetime of confusion about identity and belonging when it comes to football. My brother and I support three teams with great passion – LFC, Raith Rovers and Scotland (for our sins) – and yet we sound completely out of place at all of them!

Bazz

I've had several failed attempts at getting to Liverpool games over the years, including my first three attempts which all involved just getting there and unsuccessfully trying to luck a ticket from somewhere. At least by the later efforts, there was a free bed and a few familiar faces to see. The failed attempts at getting tickets have left a little scar and I tend not to want to take a risk anymore unless I'm sure I have one – which was a sweet deal for a while when a friend was a fitness coach with the under 18s – but now if I'm sure I have one, I will do my best to make it over from Ireland.

My cousin Domhnall introduced me to Liverpool when I was around six and started becoming interested in football. He lives in London and is moving back to Ireland soon so wanted to get to Anfield once more, as he might not have the opportunity for a while. He had a spare and gave me quite short notice to take it, but I definitely wanted it. Sunday afternoon kick-off is not doing me any favours and flights are at around €250 for the cheapest before the add-ons, so I choose the sail and rail at €85 return and take the Monday off work. I later discover I could fly to Birmingham for roughly the same price and a return train on top for around £30 but it'll have to wait for next time.

Saturday rolls in and my first attempt at self-sabotage is to press "dismiss" instead of "snooze" on the alarm at the horrible hour of 6:30. Luckily the missus had offered to drop me to the port and her alarm wakes me. We get there and the ferry is cancelled due to technical issues, so they move us to a competitor to get us there. That boat now leaves later so I sit in a waiting room for three hours with my bedroom almost visible through the early morning dew. I stick on the Kenny Dalglish documentary to fill the waiting time but the tablet stops working with 20 minutes left. Hopefully it's not an omen for the game.

After checking trains and rearranging meet-up times I get boarded and settle into a full breakfast – I deserve it – and a creamy pint of Guinness; it's only 11am but I feel like I bloody well deserve that too. I overhear someone talking about Alexis Sanchez and some clichés being floated about whose boots he isn't fit to lace and the headphones go on. Cat Power will see me through the next hour. We get to Holyhead and the later (and slightly slower) boat means we miss the connection by mere minutes and suddenly have just over an hour to kill. Anyone who has been to Holyhead will tell you there are better places to be for an hour.

Mick and Nicola (Mickola) who I will stay with collect me at the railway station and my journey to Liverpool is complete. We joke about how I could have made it to India after my extensive journey and settle into a pub for food and drinks with their friends. Nicola takes off early, and the two of us lads get to talking about the season. Mick has some issues with FSG and our differences seemingly come down mostly to political or social differences in how to look at the club's progression, and with the tiredness and the booze setting in, it seems the right time to call a close to that discussion and the evening.

We grab Domhnall at the station and go to collect Leroy who's got a season ticket, and trades his girlfriend's dog-minding for a lift to the games from Mick, and off we go to the ground to get some drinks in and soak it up. We meet Iain from TTT to collect a ticket for Mick (thanks again!), exchange a few hopes about the game's outcome, and we all split our separate ways. It turns out my ticket is corporate, a free one at that, and Domhnall and myself get some street food and a hefty fill of more pints and get to our seats.

At this point in my writing I stop to read Graham's My Day at the Match, and he sums up the rollercoaster and the feelings afterwards, and I debate whether or not to press Ctrl+A and delete the above. I decide against since I'm nearly finished anyway. Side-note: I also studied sociology at Uni, so maybe there is something in that you know, Graham. There is a good crowd around us in the stand. Though the atmosphere is a little subdued – a bit nervy even – folks are mostly positive and praising of the good things in the first half. We are near the Spurs fans but Jesus they have no songs. We sing our fair share and the early goal sets a cosy atmosphere.

On a game note, that goal-saving challenge from Virgil van Dijk was sweet, a cracking save from Loris Karius (though it was offside), and a performance from Dejan Lovren in one of those halves where he is Neo from the Matrix. I also found a greater appreciation for Mo Salah due to the off-the-ball work he does, that you don't see on TV. The second half isn't quite as smooth but there are positives to take. We're all massively disappointed leaving the game, but on the balance of play there is consensus that a draw wasn't too bad for us to take away (it's worth noting that the next morning I asked Mick if Spurs were ahead of us in the table now which shows how I had already forgotten that it wasn't a loss such is how it felt).

We quickly meet Iain to drop back the member card, drive Domhnall to the train, and head off for dinner and a few drinks to round off the weekend. Monday feels calmer than a normal Monday for me as I go for the full quota of modes of transport on the long route home: walk down for a coffee; train from Central Station to Chester; change to Holyhead; ferry to Dublin port; bus to Connolly Station; tram to Smithfield, drinks and taxi home. Is it Tuesday already? I can't wait for the next game.

Paul Tomkins, February 5th, 2018
The star of the show – the man trying to write the headlines, officials aside (and apart from his own wastefulness when setting up others) – was Mo Salah.

Salah is just sensational. It's wrong to say that he's a winger, as he's not – he's a wide-starting forward who roams infield. He can obviously be found in central positions quite a lot, often running from outside to inside. But he also does some wing-work. He tracks back, too, and often starts his attacking from the wing in his own half, running with the ball. He's not only quick but *quick and strong in tight spaces.* His second goal – a mini marvel – seemed to have won the game, and it felt beautiful, an almost underserved win right at the death. But it wasn't to be.

Still, 28 goals at the start of February, 21 of which are in the league, and with only one scored penalty and no direct free-kicks, is beyond belief. He hasn't run up his total with goals in the cups against weaker opposition (not that Liverpool have played anyone outside the Premier League this season...).

So it's clear that Liverpool did not sell its best player last month, as he's still very much at the club. And in a game where Virgil van Dijk (after no preseason) and Jordan Henderson (after injury) had seen two key players tire, Salah was still going strong at the end.

With the Reds now having played eight of the ten games against the Big Six (80% of those types of games within just 66% of the season), Liverpool should be able to get back to some flat-track bullying, which, in contrast to last season, has been behind the Reds being in the top four.

Paul Tomkins, February 12th, 2018
First of all, let's be clear: all managers buy players. No team is ever eleven youth graduates, unless perhaps it's an end of season game and the manager is trying to prove that, yes, he does blood the kids, *honestly.*

Jürgen Klopp is no different to most managers – he is not relying solely on what he inherited and what is bubbling up from the youth ranks. (Which, though hugely promising, is largely caught in that catch-22 of U23 football not being competitive enough and the need to therefore loan them out, at which point they disappear from your own squad, and cannot be coached in the way you'd ideally prefer.)

Indeed, the German has overseen a sea-change of personnel within two and a half years. But there hasn't been wild spending – it's been a few carefully scouted signings each window. It's been calculated, calm; not scattergun.

For those who want constant big-name, big-money buys, and the giddy rush of new signings – which becomes the semi-grown up version of Christmas and birthdays (once we start getting only socks and yet more socks) – it's not really been an era to deliver; indeed, last season's player of the year, Sadio Mané, was greeted with cries of "too expensive!", even though he wasn't *that* expensive, and "another from Southampton?!", while Mo Salah was seen by many as a "Chelsea reject", and more quibbling about the price ("He's not worth that much!").

The only seriously big buy has been Virgil van Dijk, a world-record for a defender, unless you take inflation into account (and note that, using our

Transfer Price Index football inflation, Rio Ferdinand cost £137m when he joined Manchester United – when he was a British record for any position. And that's based on inflation up to last season, so it would equate to even more now.)

The players bought since 2015 are going into the first-team and succeeding an odds-busting rate, at odds-busting prices; there isn't a "buy 10 and see what sticks" policy, which sometimes the Reds have had in the past, and other clubs – particularly Chelsea and Manchester City at their richest – have too. (Indeed, it's very common in the "squad era", in part because you need more players.) There isn't a "pay a fortune for the biggest names" approach at Liverpool.

The targeting of very specific players and not deviating from that is down to Jürgen Klopp's strong beliefs in mental qualities as well as footballing ability. No one who is flaky will get anywhere near a Melwood medical, let alone lean on the wall with a red scarf.

Liverpool – like Spurs before them – are quietly going about a kind of revolution, with joined-up thinking and patience put above short-term fixes. The short-term is still important in football, because it can obviously affect the long-term too (you can't sell all your players and promote a bunch of six-year-olds to the first team because in 15 years' time they should be pretty good, by which time you've been relegated down through eight divisions), but at both Spurs and Liverpool there is a culture of incessant hard work, on and off the pitch, and the time for a manager to wait six months for the right player rather than feel it's now or never.

Comment by Peter Verinder (RedPeter)

I am a Class 1 referee who retired from the game in 2006. The formal rules knowledge test, which is part of the Class 1 qualification, is based on FIFA's criteria and therefore consistent around the globe. I recall that the pass mark for this test was 70%. This allows a Class 1 referee to not know up to 30% of the rules and still pass.

The referees' association that I was part of had several FIFA referees and assistant referees within it and at our monthly meetings we would discuss rule issues and in-game scenarios. I was constantly amazed that so many of the referees, including Class 1, 2 and 3 referees, didn't really know some of the key rules or their correct application. Once qualified, many referees seem to adopt their own "journeyman" interpretations of particular rules.

I recall Harry Kewell getting sent off in a World Cup game for deliberate handball on the goal line when a shot bounced off his body with his arm tightly held against his body. The ball hit the top part of his arm just below his shoulder. After the game the assembled FIFA referees announced that the game referee had correctly interpreted the rule and deemed that Harry deliberately played at the ball. I still think this is nonsense under the actual rule for handball. However, at the same tournament an identical thing happened to a German player and the referee played on, clearly ruling that the same contact was not deliberate. How's that for consistency!

My point is, if the relatively simple handball rule cannot be correctly interpreted and applied by an assembled group of the world's top referees, what chance a proper interpretation of the more layered offside rule?

I chimed in a couple of times on here after the game to post what I know to be the correct interpretation of the rules and essentially agree with Keith Hackett's opinion of the application of that rule as it related to the Spurs game (regarding Harry Kane being offside). This part of the rule has not changed since I was an active referee and I applied the different aspects of the "gaining advantage while in a offside position" rule in my games. In one game I had to explain the rule to my match inspector when I disallowed a goal scored by an attacker, who was standing in an offside position when a ball was played, before scoring after the keeper parried a save straight to him.

I have always understood that the meaning of "deliberate" in the gaining advantage section of the offside law requires a player to be in control of the ball such that they have made a back pass or other intended play that is intercepted by the attacker. If the ball is deflected off a player who intends to clear ball with an opponent standing in an offside position to gain an advantage then the attacker is offside under the provisions of that aspect of the offside law. As Keith Hackett has stated, there is further reinforcement to this position in that the player standing in an offside position creates the advantage because he causes the opponent to play at a ball that he would otherwise not play.

Champions League Knockout Stages

Porto (A), February 14th, 2018.
"Grover"
When Liverpool were drawn against Porto in December, I saw it as a perfect opportunity to see my beloved Reds away in the Champions League, and to visit Portugal – both for the first time. I also have a friend who lives in Lisbon and had been meaning to visit for a while. I booked my flights in early January and then came the major hurdle of finding a ticket for the game. I put the feelers out and fortunately a friend of a friend could not make it, so sold me his ticket at face value – cheers Max!

I flew to Lisbon from the UK and spent a couple of days in that lovely city. It was good to see an old friend, Richard, and to spend time in a really interesting and beautiful city. I would recommend it to anyone to visit. It's a wonderful setting on the mouth of the Tagus and has great history, beautiful buildings, as well as good bars and restaurants.

I hired a car and headed north for the three hour uneventful journey to Porto. I didn't know anyone going to the game (Richard is not a football fan), but that was not an issue for me as I knew I would meet some like-minded Reds. I am a regular at Anfield as I am a priority member, but I don't go to many away games. I have been a Liverpool fan for over 30 years.

It was pouring with rain on arrival and reminded me of growing up in Ireland. Porto is also a nice city but I didn't get to see that much of it before the game. I checked in at my hotel and made my way to the stadium as the weather was so bad. I had been looking forward to having a few beers in the centre of town, but given the weather it was easier to head straight for the stadium. I bumped into a few Reds at the shopping mall next to the stadium. They were the UK, but not Scousers. There are lots of Porto fans around of course and we have a bit of banter (in the real sense of the word) with them. We had some food and beers and made our way into the stadium.

The Estadio do Dragão is a decent stadium but it wasn't quite full, probably due to the horrible weather. Many of the lower tier seats are not under cover. Luckily the away fans section is in the upper tier and under the roof.

We all stand together in the away section, as nobody is in their designated seats. The police are very much present but in the background, which is great. Nothing to report on that score, thankfully. One thing that annoyed me slightly was there was mesh netting in front of our section for the whole game and this somehow made me feel more removed from the players on the pitch. I have no idea why it was there.

When they played the Champions League music before kick-off, the hairs on the back of my neck stood up. It is fantastic to be back in the knockout stages after nine years and feels like it's where we belong.

The 3,500 Liverpool fans are in fine voice throughout the game and thankfully we have plenty to sing about. Mo Salah's song is the most sung, but "Oh Mané Mané" is sung over and over by the end, with everyone shaking their hips and their scarves.

Some of the oldies are the best though:

"Bring on yer Internazionale, bring on yer Roma by the score. Barcelona, Real Madrid, who the fuck you trying to kid, coz Liverpool are the team that we adore."

It's such a good European ditty and makes me nostalgic for the days before the Brexit vote. The performance on the pitch is outstanding and we are all in heaven, hugging those around us after each goal. Sadio Mané's hat-trick (in the 5-0 win) was considered by all to be very significant for the remainder of the season.

We give the boys a great reception at the end and they all come over to acknowledge the travelling fans. Klopp gets the biggest roar of the lot. We have to stay in the stadium for 20 minutes after the final whistle, but we don't mind as we are dry and it is still chucking it down outside.

We have a few more beers and some food and a post-match debrief, before I head back to my hotel to catch up on all the reaction on the internet and to watch the goals on LFC TV. It has been a superb day and I am so thankful to be a long-time fan of this great club and to have Jürgen Klopp as our manager.

Paul Tomkins, February 15th, 2018

"Porto are no mugs" was the message before the game in the media. Afterwards, "they can't have been that good", as Liverpool won 5-0. The truth is somewhere in between: a good side, from a good league, were torn apart by a fast-thinking, fast-running forward line, that bamboozled the living daylights out of the home team. Portugal seems to have lost some playing and managerial talent in the last few years, having overtaken Italy in the rankings not too long ago, and England has benefited.

Liverpool are the 9th-richest club in Europe, but only the 5th-richest in England, and not guaranteed participation in the grand competition – as six clubs fight to snap up four spots, with only Man City getting a consistent run of qualification lately. Everyone else has been in and out, which makes it harder to have a consistently good European pedigree, and all that extra cash.

So domestically the Reds can still appear a bit "also ran", which misses the point that the top six has bubbled up even further towards the top, albeit with City bubbling towards a new league points record, and with Arsenal finally dropping properly below expectations despite some formidable attacking talents before and after the January transfer window. Arsenal are miles ahead (nine points) of the team in 7th, but miles behind Liverpool (nine points). Even though everyone else has bought some very good players with all the new TV money, the top six are in a league of their own.

The progress made by Klopp – which I think is marked – is masked somewhat by this overall improvement, and it's worth pondering where the Reds would be without him. People still talk about his win % only matching Brendan Rodgers' (52%), but Klopp's is improving over time, whereas Rodgers' stats were mainly down to one amazing season (out of Europe), after which came 15 months of stagnation and deterioration; and the half-baked squad he left for Klopp did not help.

The German's achievement, so far, is to keep Liverpool in the middle of this upwardly-mobile top five – while a team as talented as Arsenal starts to lose touch – whilst simultaneously rampaging across Europe. So Liverpool have to be considered one of the best sides on the continent right now. Spurs, too, have proven themselves in the competition, despite being unable to win, say, a League Cup, and only currently being 5th in the Premier League. Arsenal may be racking up the devalued trophies these days (and fair play to them, in a way), but it is Spurs who have been outclassing Real Madrid, Juventus and Dortmund, and Spurs who people take seriously right now, not Arsenal. It is Arsenal who people see as underperforming, even though they are winning a few pots.

And it is Liverpool who are racking up Champions League scoring records; and, including the tough qualifying round, have won six, drawn three and lost none in Europe this season. For 18 months, Brendan Rodgers had Liverpool playing some great football domestically (but *mostly* in an amazing six months from December 2013 to May 2014), before the wheels came off during an increasingly dire 15 months that followed, but vitally, the Reds were only ever duffers in Europe under his guidance. Klopp, without spending crazy money – indeed, he has chosen to keep the Coutinho powder dry until the summer – has made the Reds more consistent in the league over these past two seasons (with all the added Champions League games this time around), but also beat some strong teams on the way to the Europa League final in his first campaign, with half a squad that didn't suit his style. To suggest the two managers are equals is insane.

This feels less like a flash-in-the-pan, but a building of something special, and that building work is not yet even complete. New players will join in the summer, and many key members of the squad are still young and improving; while a key new addition like Virgil van Dijk – imperious these past two games – will improve with understanding and a loss of rustiness after missing so much football in the past year. Van Dijk's pace isn't quite there yet, but even without hitting top speed he oozes quality.

Comment by Tony Mckenna, February 16th, 2018

The mention of Leicester's title win gets me thinking again. Whilst their style was not aesthetically pleasing I often wonder was it also a strength? Once the Barcelona way of playing took hold in the football consciousness, you knew it was a phenomena upon hearing about the passing acumen of the likes of Swansea and Southampton. Everyone was doing it. So, what Leicester did was actually to be different; in as much as they were away from the crowd.

Lest we forget, the long ball approach – as anathema as it is to us at Liverpool – is often very effective. It can even be successful for an extended period as evidenced with Graham Taylor's Watford, rising up the divisions with astonishing celerity. Though, to be fair, Taylor had also incorporated an aggressive pressing approach, and were not as dour as the long-ball Wimbledon team. That said, the latter also enjoyed a sustained successful period of sorts.

The issue of teams trying to emulate Barcelona overlooked the fact that they had Lionel Messi, Xavi and Andrés Iniesta. You can play the guitar but you could never say you are going to play it the way Eric Clapton does. So, when everyone was inadvertently attempting to do a Clapton, Leicester were content to rely on three-chord, Status Quo, technique. (Apologies to any Quo fans.) But it gave them an edge, because they were different. And, facing up to it, they were bloody awkward to play against at times.

I do like to think that Liverpool can win the title under Jürgen Klopp. Whilst we are not blessed, or cursed even, with a sugar daddy benefactor, it is the element of teamwork that figures; where Liverpool are different and do have a possible edge. Klopp's relationship with his players, for instance, is second to none. Certainly wholly different to the one that Jose Mourinho has with his cohorts, and somewhat different to that of the soon to be departed Antonio Conte, who rather thinks he does not have the players he wants anyhow. And Mauricio Pochettino is off to Madrid, is he not?

Arsène Wenger is on increasingly borrowed time and … well, okay that leaves Pep Guardiola. But Pep did not win the title last year, so City can under-perform another time; much in the same way that the top six faltered and left a door open which let the Foxes in. Plus, we showed that we can exceed City in a one to one game.

Teamwork, however, is key. It is also another reason why the #KloppOut brigade need to *shut the fuck up*, because it attacks the very essence of what could possibly be our edge: it is the longevity of relationships that cements a winning team. Malcolm Gladwell pointed out that the best orchestras are those where the playing personnel have stuck together for a long time. It is rehearsal, after rehearsal, that obviates the weaknesses and accentuates the strengths. Gladwell also alluded to the 'overnight' success of the Beatles originating from the inordinate amount of hours spent playing in the Cavern and seedy Hamburg bars.

Okay, on the same point, we do have a potential problem: keeping our best players from the allure of apex predators; witness Fernando Torres, Luis Suárez and Philippe Coutinho. And Mo Salah? Nonetheless, if Klopp is permitted time to experiment, explore and exploit inefficiencies in other teams, then I do not rule out that Liverpool can eventually begin to retain top players. Especially if we do win a title and advance in the latter stages of the Champions League.

Whatever. You do not build effective teamwork by being on a manager's back. There are no Viagra quick fixes for under-performing entities. Rather it is hard work, commitment and dedication over time that attains eventual fruition. And we are already someway on that journey. As the article says: Klopp is *building* a team; not buying one.

Now this raises another point. Remember Angel Di Maria? Throw in a few other mentions and there we have Man United trying to buy a team. Doesn't always work, does it?

Paul Tomkins, February 17th 2018.
(Originally written as a guest post for the *Redmen TV* website.)
I like James Milner. There, I said it. I like Jordan Henderson too. They're not two of my favourite players (although I do have a definite soft spot for Henderson), and you wouldn't "pay to watch" either, assuming that people still pay to watch an individual (which, presumably, is only something the neutral does these days. You pay to watch your team, regardless, and few people go to see an individual – although you might if Lionel Messi was in town).

I liked Lucas Leiva too, in part because so many people were unfair to him, and because he stuck at it, and improved. He wasn't the best player (although he had become an excellent defensive midfielder under Kenny Dalglish – the Reds' player of the year at one point – before a serious injury sapped him of a yard of pace), but he was the opposite of flaky. These guys aren't the artists, nor the speedsters who have us off our seats. They don't rain down goals and yet more goals. But you need some glue in your team, even if it drives some spectators to sniffing the stuff.

Of course, if you would pay to watch certain players, you also need those who bolster that creativity; a few artistes to play the piano, the rest to carry it, as the old saying goes. Water carriers, you may call them – but remember, some carry the water carefully (like Henderson) and others spill it.

Henderson, in particular, gets a ludicrous amount of grief from fans, including with England, mostly because he's not someone else. With Liverpool you sense it's because he's not Steven Gerrard, and with England there's the bitterness of rival fans wanting their players selected ahead of him. He's the opposite of spectacular, but football isn't all about the spectacular.

The Liverpool captain is a clever short-passer, who often moves the ball quickly and can spot a longer pass, too. But he can't shoot very well, on average (his long-range shooting used to be better but he's lost his confidence; and only ever tends to side-foot, like Raheem Sterling – although Sterling is usually only two-yards out); and Henderson isn't supremely quick. People criticise the square passes but I think that's part of the mindset of keeping it ticking over. He has great stamina, and strength, and every Liverpool and England manager of the last few years has loved him. It's no coincidence. Jürgen Klopp has worked with some great midfielders, yet clearly rates Henderson.

Henderson is another of those players – like Emre Can – who played through injury and got the bird from the fans as a result. We want bravery, but when we can't see that bravery (as they don't have blood gushing from a wound), we react with anger. Again, unless they are limping around for 90 minutes, no one can see the pain the players are playing through, and managers obviously don't want to highlight those injuries too much in public, lest they invite reducers from the opposition.

(Of course, I also don't blame players who refuse to put their bodies on the line, because you'd rather they say that they can't run properly before the game than during it. And muscle injuries are often only made worse by playing on; they don't heal themselves during the match. That said, you can see why managers like those who make themselves available to play, no matter what.)

There's a lot that goes on at a football club that we cannot see. Indeed, we don't see much at all. We don't get proper insights into who has a good attitude during the week, who trains hard, who is early to Melwood and late to leave, who looks out for his teammates away from the pitch, who helps turn a group of players into a *team*. We don't get to see who is a slacker, a dickhead, a pain-in-the-arse in training; who disrespects the collective by being late, or mucking around at a time when seriousness is called for. We don't get to see who is more bothered about their pay-packet than working hard to improve. And we criticise a manager over his selections without knowing any of this.

Nor do we get to see tactical preparations, and therefore we don't know who is following instructions during a game and who is doing their own thing. We just get to see match-day. And we also get to see the in-form players at other clubs, on highlights clips and live broadcasts and YouTube showreels, and assume that we can solve all the problems by suggesting, on social media, which of them to buy.

We also get some media sound-bites from players and managers, to show us a glimpse behind the curtain, but it's mostly anodyne nonsense; platitudes and fluff. So we often don't get a particularly good insight; and even if the manager is eloquent and wants to talk about interesting things, he'll instead be asked about why his opposite number didn't shake his hand, or why so-and-so has been made captain, and which of the 73 players the club have been linked with that week are genuine targets. Nonsense, platitudes, fluff.

On *The Tomkins Times* lately I've been talking a lot about Raphael Honigstein's wonderful book on Jürgen Klopp, "*Bring The Noise*", and all the little details behind the manager's success in Germany. While I already suspected a lot of its contents, it reassuringly confirms the manager's attention to detail and his down-to-earth attitude. It's clear how all the major players and ex-players in Germany respect him, and see him as a unique talent. It shows how he built Borussia Dortmund up, from having zero money to spend, into double Bundesliga champions and Champions League finalists. A book like that can go into great detail in a way that even a good television interview or newspaper article cannot. It taught me a lot, and anything that teaches me something is always worth the time and effort (and I like to spend time sharing anything I learn).

I've also been discussing books like Angela Duckworth's "Grit" and Matthew Syed's "Bounce", which – amongst other aspects of success – build on the 10,000 hours rule (that it takes that long to be elite at something) covered by people like Malcolm Gladwell, as I continue to challenge my own long-held beliefs about natural talent. And books like those, which don't even mention Klopp (but do cover sports), are helping me to understand just how the Liverpool manager has had so much success in his career. Time, plus meaningful, testing training, and an impeccable attitude, means improvement.

I was myself described as a "natural footballer" before I hit my teens, including a gold award at an ex-pro's soccer school and call-ups for my county, but Super-8 footage of me kicking a ball around at the age of five shows I had no natural instincts whatsoever. But by the age of nine I was playing two years up for the school, in part as a couple of years earlier I started kicking about every night with kids of that age. Alas, I had little grit, and unlike now, was easily defeated by setbacks. And when I was the skinny little fancy-dan winger aged 13 up against kids built like boxers, in the 1980s minefield of bypassing the midfield (and on boggy pitches I barely had the strength to run across), I fell out of love with playing organised football. I had been a "natural", apparently, but I didn't work at it. Later on, once back in love with the game, I was scouted playing university football, but I still didn't have quite enough drive; still lacked sufficient grit. Whether or not my talent was ample enough, that talent didn't get me anywhere. I had a stint as a semi-pro in the mid-'90s, but by then my Liverpool season ticket had come through, and my health issues intensified.

Aside from any physical advantages, players become prodigies due to the work they put in at a younger age; and the earlier and harder they practice – and the more they are tested by good opposition and training that is not simply within their comfort zone – the quicker they will make the grade. Not everyone who puts in 10,000 hours of meaningful practice will make it to the top, but few who do go on to make it to the top will do so without it. (It might be 9,000 hours or 11,000 hours, or a combination of hours in two sports where there is some meaningful overlap, but the point stands. There is no overnight success.)

And yet when I hear managers saying that "this is where the hard work starts" after a youngster makes a promising debut, they are not wrong. Some players feel at that point that they've made it, and then they can ease off: goal achieved. But then they lose their advantage to players like James Milner, who can boast 750 career games, including several years at Man City and Liverpool, despite never being an *artiste*. The players who work hard, day after day, will tend to endure, injuries notwithstanding. They may be unhappy if they are not in the team, but they don't stink out the place with a bad attitude. If they are subbed off they may scowl, but they don't leave the stadium. If they are left out of the squad they work even harder, and don't put in a transfer request.

Milner himself was a prodigy of sorts, playing 100-or-so of those aforementioned career games with England youth teams of all ages, albeit a fair few of them as an overaged U21. He was strong for his age as a teen, and scored a crazy number of goals for England age-groups at that time, and debuted in the Premier League aged just 16. But I don't recall him being quick, or preternaturally gifted. You would never call him a "natural", but I'd guess that only 1% of all Premier League, La Liga, Serie A or Bundesliga players make their debut at such a young age in the top division of a major league.

Indeed, in an article I wrote on TTT last month I went through the entire Liverpool squad, to assess their youth pedigree – who broke through into a senior team first, who got a lot of international youth caps – in order to work out what the predicted paths for the players might have been. I had previously asked subscribers to the site to select the 10 players in the current squad they see as the most "natural" footballers at Liverpool (without – on purpose – defining what I meant by "natural"), and unsurprisingly Mo Salah, Roberto Firmino and Sadio Mané came out on top, with Virgil van Dijk not far behind. James Milner was near the bottom.

My point was in part about our perception of what a natural talent is.

If we see them as naturally gifted – and I think most people do – then why were Salah, Firmino and Mané such late-bloomers? They had little or no international youth experience, and were playing relative "backwater football" around the ages of 19/20, Salah in Switzerland, and Firmino and Mané in the second-tiers of Brazil and France. They moved to unfashionable European clubs – sometimes to two unfashionable European clubs – and only Salah got a move to a big club in a major European league in his early 20s; and that – at Chelsea – famously failed.

Similarly, Virgil van Dijk had virtually no youth football with Holland (just one cap before U21 level, and just three at U21 level) and was not a teenage breakthrough star. Only Celtic took a chance on him after a few years in Holland, and only Southampton took a chance on him after that, and even allowing for the later maturation of centre-backs, it's still taken a long time to reach the top. If all four are naturals, why weren't they successful earlier in their careers? And why are they suddenly so successful now?

Surely the answer is in no small part due to extreme hard work, allied to elite coaching. They have all overtaken players who would have been labelled far more gifted at a younger age; players who are now stacking shelves somewhere. Perhaps it's also about feeling settled at a club, or suiting its system, and all those other hard-to-judge details.

But how do players improve – or appear to improve – so radically? Last summer, before I'd finally had enough of Twitter, I was ridiculed for saying that Mo Salah had a world-class scoring record for a wide forward. And that was before he began to re-write the rulebook this season. People struggled to grasp the concept of an erstwhile Premier League flop being world-class at something. But his goal return in Italy was outstanding. To get 19 goals in a season, from out wide, for a team that wasn't running away the league, in a competition like Serie A, had to be world-class (which I'd say, loosely, is the top 5-10 global players in any position). Right now, Salah is probably no.1 in the world for the number of goals scored from a nominally wide position. I was careful not to call him a world-class *player* in the summer, but actually, I now would.

Yet people get locked into their beliefs, inflexible to changes and improvements. It's a bit like saying Salah isn't a "natural goalscorer", because he doesn't play as a no.9, where the "natural" scorers play. People want to bracket him within their own biases, where he cannot escape their established conclusions.

Even though he's not strictly a winger, why can't wide players be natural goalscorers? And why can't someone who seemed mediocre at 21 be outstanding at 25?

For starters, a lot of people assume that the talent is God-given, instinctive; "you can't teach it," ex-strikers will say. Except, you can. Clearly. Not to Sean Dundee, perhaps, but actually, with tons of meaningful practice (i.e. where your own limits are tested), anyone can improve at almost anything, if their physiology allows it.

Some phenomenal international youth strikers – such as Samed Yesil – have faded to relative obscurity, and the precocious Ryan Babel wasted most of his career; doing quite well lately, but aged 31, when his time is almost up. Meanwhile, someone like Salah – who, at 20, would have been seen as far inferior to Babel at the same age – scores more and more goals every season. Babel moaned about Rafa Benítez asking him to track back, whereas Mo Salah just gets on with it. He plays for the team.

The Egyptian scored some goals before joining Chelsea, in the Swiss league, but he wasn't ultra-prolific; however, his second season in Switzerland was more prolific than his first. This was after three seasons in his native Egypt, where in each season he scored more than the last. And his three seasons in Italy – before Liverpool snapped him up – saw him move from nine goals in 26 games (Fiorentina), to 15 in 42, to 19 in 41 with Roma. Are these not the hallmarks of improvement? (Yeah, but he's a Chelsea reject, right?)

Roberto Firmino is another who is "not a natural centre-forward/finisher", because when he arrived at Liverpool it was an attacking midfielder wanted by the committee but not by Brendan Rodgers (his choice was Christian Benteke, and the Reds ended up with both). Klopp replaced Rodgers, and Firmino became a false nine; and it would enrage pundits to see him dropping deep, or wandering out wide. "You're a no.9, get in the box!" they would shout in commentary, as if there is only one way to play football. "Not a natural finisher" they would add, if he got in the box and missed a chance.

Then many pundits warmed to him, for his work-rate and skill, but there was still a lot of sniffiness. "He'll never score enough goals". Indeed, one ex-Liverpool striker was still saying – a few weeks ago, no less, – that Liverpool still need a "proper number nine", which must be evidence of some kind of Tourette's from heading the ball too much. Firmino hit the 20-goal mark before mid-February.

But how? He's not a natural number nine. He's not a natural finisher. He's not a natural goalscorer. If he couldn't score goals for Liverpool aged 24, how can he do so aged 26? How can his goal return improve year on year at Liverpool, if he's not got the right "eye" or the right "instincts"? If it's all about God-given talent, Firmino was deemed near the back of the queue aged 19 and 20, and even – when it came to goals – aged 24 with Liverpool.

Liverpool's two main goalscorers this season already have 51 between them – including just two penalties – by mid-February, yet neither is a natural goalscorer in the eyes of ex-pros, nor were they naturals in terms of being teenage prodigies. (If they took better penalties they could have 54 goals between them.)

Well, could it just be that these things are not as defined as we like to believe?

I get annoyed when people use the saying "doing the same things over and over and expecting a different result is the definition of madness" when it comes to football, because that refers to scientific experiments; combine the same amount of the same two chemical elements in the same way under laboratory conditions and you'll get the same results. But football is not played under such conditions. What doesn't work one day can work another. And vice versa.

Take, say, Steven Gerrard and the art of taking penalties. For years he was utterly mediocre at them, missing some and scoring some. Then he became shit-hot at them, with practice and experience. So, if a manager picks a team that loses a game, then another game, you can't say that that team should never be picked again. For instance, I saw it said that Liverpool only won 7-0 in the group stage of the Champions League because Jordan

Henderson was missing. Yet the Reds won 5-0 against Porto with him present.

Providing that the team is young enough, it has the scope to improve, with understanding, and the individuals have the scope to improve, with experience, or just be in better form on another day. Very little is actually fixed at the same level.

This is the epitome of growth mindset vs fixed mindset, as outlined by the famous mindset psychologist Carol Dweck. People with a growth mindset believe they can improve and that nothing is fixed in terms of development, so they work hard and try to get better, and never stop working hard. Those with a fixed mindset think in more binary terms: that people are either good at something or not; they buy into the concept of God-given talent, the concept of the natural.

The trouble with a fixed mindset is that it stops you working harder – naturals don't need to practice, after all – and such minded people are more likely to give up when some kind of obstacle is faced. If they can't quickly overcome the obstacle, they will conclude, they therefore lack the talent. Steven Gerrard would have given up taking penalties before anyone knew he could become one of the best at them in the past 25 years of English football. Before that, he would have given up shooting altogether, as he only scored one goal in his first 50 Liverpool games. A good passer, you might have concluded, but not a goalscorer.

All of this happened to tie in precisely with Raphael Honigstein's book on Klopp, and the manager's obsession with unity, team-work and improving the players he has at his disposal. He doesn't ignore the transfer market – far from it – but he won't use it as the only tool, in the way that we, as fans (with no control over anything in a hands-on way), seem to act like transfers are the be-all and end-all.

And as someone who wrote the book on the clear links between spending and success (or at least, *a* book – *Pay As You Play: The True Price of Success in the Premier League Era* – and, more recently, an academic paper), I can also make clear that there will be outliers like Klopp's Dortmund, who blew away expectations; and there will be crazy spenders, who invest that money badly and suffer as a result (Manchester United in recent seasons have often been wasteful, and conflicted between buying good players and buying good marketing tools).

Liverpool cannot control what the Manchester clubs do, nor what those clubs spend, nor look to compete on the same level of outlay, given that one is backed by an oil-rich country and the other has been miles ahead of Liverpool commercially for two decades, and currently tops the world's rich-list. Liverpool need someone like Klopp, who will hang around for a long time, improving the players, uniting the dressing room, forging a distinct (but increasingly flexible) tactical style, and inspiring his charges.

A good 10-20 players have clearly improved since Klopp took charge of Liverpool in 2015, and some of them – like Kevin Stewart – were improved from a very low starting point, meaning that they were unlikely to be any better than 'good' players, but they could do a job for a few games and then bring in a few million quid. No one could have turned Vinnie Jones into Andrea Pirlo, after all. But under Klopp, "good" players are starting to be seen as "great". Very good players are getting better.

Mostly, the only ones to regress, injuries aside, are those with a slightly more lax attitude on the pitch and in training.

I decided years ago that I don't want the manager to pick the players I want to see, but the ones *he wants to do the job that he has set out*, with instructions to which I am not privy, based on form and fitness and attitude in training that I also don't get to see.

And actually, I love that Klopp – at a point where I'd sworn I never want to see Dejan Lovren in the team again – will then go and make Lovren captain for the next game. I think it's brilliant man-management, even if, over time, there should be fewer inconsistent players in the Reds' XI. (But overall, Lovren is getting better, I feel, with fewer bad games – but the match at Wembley against Spurs was a nightmare.) Sven Bender says of Klopp that at Dortmund he never made a player feel like he was dead to him – "on the contrary", he says, in Honigstein's book, "he always gave the player another chance if he was willing to take it."

Klopp will stick by his players whilst he has them, and try to get the most from them; but if necessary, he will move them on or edge them out. He would at times use Christian Benteke while he had him, but he also knew he wanted someone new the next season. That's a really good form of evolution. He gives players the chance to play themselves back into form, and doesn't damn anyone for having a nightmare. As long as their attitude is good (and so that counted out Mamadou Sakho), they can earn a reprieve. But it also sends a message of fairness across the whole squad.

As much as I've always had a fascination with those supposedly ultra-gifted kids – the *wunderkinds* – I've long-since documented my interest in the mysterious late-bloomer, too.

For instance, having looked at a lot of the top strikers in the world over the past two decades or so, there were a few who emerged as fully-formed teenage scorers, but many more who seemed to only hit their stride around the age of 22. And that's just the goalscorers. To my mind, slower players tend to blossom later (as pace is a good way to get into a team early), and centre-backs and goalkeepers often mature latest, due to the costly nature of their mistakes, which are often left to be made on someone else's pitch. But as the pressure on managers for instant results grows, players in other positions can see their chances limited, too.

Players like Jamie Carragher and Frank Lampard were not world-class teenagers. Jamie Vardy wasn't even a professional footballer at 24, and Ian

Wright – who was one hell of a striker in the '90s – was also a non-leaguer until well into his 20s. Harry Kane looked pretty hopeless at 21, and Alan Shearer only started scoring goals at 22 (having played in the top flight regularly since the age of 17), yet leads the way, by some distance, in the Premier League era for goals scored (and dull celebrations). Thierry Henry wasn't seen as a natural goalscorer, and Didier Drogba was in the French second-tier at 23. Luis Suárez was brought to Europe by a fairly low-key Dutch club before moving to Ajax.

The idea that there are a ton of Vardys just waiting to be spotted is wayward; but equally, the scope for improvement for any player must not be underestimated either, if they work hard and get elite coaching, and avoid debilitating injuries. If there aren't many Vardys around, there have to be a shed-load of potential Kanes (who don't then make the most of their talent).

What marks Kane out from many others, however, is his incessant work-rate on and off the pitch, and a manager who, like Klopp, has shown he can develop players. He keeps improving. He eschews alcohol all season long, and is in some ways boring, but he makes the most of his talent.

But some luck has to be involved, too; after all, Harry Redknapp was close to letting Gareth Bale leave Spurs for peanuts, and Kane was not cutting the mustard at Spurs at the age of 21 (after numerous unremarkable lower division loans), until things finally clicked. He is currently in his fifth straight year of improving goal returns. (So, don't assume that Dominic Solanke will copy Kane, but equally, don't assume that he can't.)

Like Kane, Bale was a standout player at international youth levels, but unlike Kane, Bale made an immediate impact in senior football, at Southampton, and quickly became a full international (whereas Kane looked too ordinary – not the quickest, not the most skilled, not the tallest). Bale had that searing pace. But after he moved to Spurs as a teenager, the Welshman had two very mediocre seasons and one decent one, at the age of 20/21. Although he started out at left-back, he scored five league goals in his first three seasons; then seven the next season; then nine; then ... twenty-one!

... Woah, where the hell did 21 come from? Well, he'd turned 23 just before the season began, so it's possible to see a massive leap at a point where most of us assume a player is already fully formed. Development is an ongoing process, especially with the will to keep improving.

One part of Honigstein's book that struck a real chord with me is the way Klopp and his assistants sounded out potential transfer targets. Klopp's verbal questionnaires to players he tried to sign when in Germany were fascinating, trying to weed out the selfish glory-hunters from the true team-players. (I assume he does similar at Liverpool, perhaps on the rollercoaster on Blackpool beach; anyone who doesn't dare get on with him, or who closes his eyes, is instantly discarded. Anyone who vomits is recommended to Everton ....)

Klopp didn't want anyone who would happily coast through training if they felt they would still deliver on match-day, because it might not be sustainable; but also, it sends the wrong message. To keep a fully-intense style of play, and to try and rely on ruthless dedication and never-say-die spirit, there needs to be that overriding ethos of effort. If some players are switching on and off in training then the whole vibe can be slacker. Peter Krawietz tells Honigstein that there is an informal but binding contract between all the players: everyone must do their share of the work and close down as demanded. First, because it doesn't work as well if only one man presses (it's easy to play around), and second, because everyone is equal. No one is too good to do his share.

Mo Salah tracks back, Sadio Mané tracks back, and the beauty of Roberto Firmino is that no one in midfield can slack off if the centre-forward is working like a dervish. A lazy no.9 might get you goals, but what do you lose without him also setting the tempo of the press? The striker has to set the tempo of the press and instantly destabilise the opposition's attempts to play out from the back, and then that triggers the rest to start pressing.

Last week, both Jonathan Wilson and Michael Cox wrote in the media about Liverpool's togetherness and work-rate against Porto, whilst lamenting the superstar, selfish nature of the Real Madrid and PSG 'super clash'. Incredibly, *every third Cristiano Ronaldo touch was a shot*. Neither of each of the two giants' main forwards exchanged a single pass with each other. Madrid still achieve success, of course, but it's somewhat soulless, built on spending fortunes on individual brilliance. (Even though the sight of him makes me feel nauseous, and for all his selfishness in games, Ronaldo is said to train to incredible levels, to stay at the top all this time. So, that's the secret of his success. But not only is Lionel Messi a better player, he does at least play for the team, too.)

With all this in mind, inbound transfers come with an additional risk, as they can burst the bubble of unity. Klopp probably works as hard as any other manager on maximising the sense of unity. So anyone new can potentially destabilise a vibe that has been built up since July, and in seasons before. They arrive in the middle of a flurry of competitive games, not with six weeks to prepare. They don't know the very specific tactics, either, and that can take time.

Of course, when Klopp does add players, it's because he knows they will fit in; the research, as mentioned, has been done. No dickheads need apply. It just means that he will put the squad as a whole first, and not disrupt things with panic buys. That's part of the reason why so many signings since he arrived have succeeded beyond expectations; a reversal of the fortunes seen under his predecessor, Brendan Rodgers, whose very bright start faded after players *he specifically chose to buy* flopped badly.

As much as I love an exciting inbound transfer, and as nervous or upset I can get over Liverpool selling a top player, there has to be some trust in a manager with a proven track record, especially as he knows all the finer details and hidden truths, and we don't. He was criticised for not compromising on Player B or Player C in the summer, but he knew van Dijk had given him his word (on the rollercoaster, one presumes), and Klopp had done likewise. Again, we don't get to see that, so we think he's insane, reckless. Well, hardly.

And if a player really wants to leave, then there comes a point where the harmony of the squad is more important there, too. And as talented as Philippe Coutinho is, a fully committed team may have its advantages. Indeed, Liverpool have arguably seen a better-balanced side since he was sold, although it remains early days. But without doubt, the Reds certainly haven't collapsed or struggled since he last played at the end of December. And for a player to effectively go on strike twice in the same season has to be considered a step too far in terms of trying to get everyone pulling in the same direction.

In Honigstein's book there is also a story from Klopp's playing career in the late 1990s, that highlights how a manager can get more than people expect from a group of players, and which also pokes holes in the talent myth. Mainz – then a tiny club – were marooned at the bottom of the 2nd tier of German football at the winter break. They had already been given a "0% chance" of escaping relegation by the magazine *Kicker*. It was then that their manager decided to switch from the traditional German sweeper system which came with man-marking in open play – which almost everyone still used – to zonally marking in open play (i.e. centre-backs don't follow their man all over the pitch but pass them on to the defender in that zone), hard pressing, and four at the back. The insurance policy of the sweeper behind two centre-backs was replaced with an extra body in midfield. The work off the ball was ramped up.

In a warm-up game before the season resumed, against the full-strength XI of the monied team that was set to be promoted and essentially replace them, Mainz were 6-0 up at half-time. They went on to win 32 points in the second half of the season, more than anyone else in the top two tiers of German football. Wolfgang Frank was the manager, and Jürgen Klopp was one of the two centre-backs. (Incidentally, Frank's two sons, Benjamin and Sebastian, now work as scouts for Liverpool, having consulted for Leicester City ahead of their crazy success in 2015/16.)

It's hard to make that kind of radical impact now – to be 6-0 up at half-time against a better team on paper, and to go from the worst side in the division to the best – given that everyone has access to similar knowledge, in the digital age. There aren't really any tactical shifts that can be so new and so devastating. But it shows that changing an approach – with the same level of "talent" – allied to training in a new way, can affect results; there was no need for them to spend their way out of danger, not that they had any money. It was Frank, inspired by Arrigo Sacchi, who in turn inspired Jürgen Klopp. Money still makes a difference if those blessed with it spend it wisely, and provide elite coaching and outstanding tactical wisdom. But Klopp, in particular, is one of those managers who can make a team more than the sum of its parts and compete at the top end of the table.

There is a lot more to a football team than we ever get to see.

West Ham United (H) February 24th, 2018
By Thomas Arthur

"She just said she wasn't in the mood because it was Tuesday. I mean, there's just no comeback to that."

Bloody hell it was cold. Seriously, this wasn't just "big coat" weather, it was "multiple-thermal-layer-with-an-extra-layer-just-for-safety-and-*then*-the-big coat" weather.

The older I get, the more layers I need. If I need *four* layers and a big coat when I'm 37 then how many am I going to need if I'm still going to the match when I'm 67? I hope thermal clothing technology increases in quality sufficiently in the next 30 years to warrant me not having to wear 16 layers by that time in my life. By the time I entered the ground today my thighs had seized up!

I should set more context here – readers usually expect that sort of thing. These diary entries are, hopefully, going to be mildly entertaining anecdotes of my car share journey to home matches. We have this routine which always includes a match prediction, standard, which I'll also revisit at the end of each article. If anyone wants to start a league table for our predictions then please, go ahead. I will say that in the five or six years I've been lucky enough to have a season ticket our predictions have been even less accurate than Mark Lawrenson's on a certain media website.

(For your information – I can guarantee that we will not have any celebrity guests to go up against – just to manage expectation.)

Now, usually when I arrive at the house I perform my standard polite two-knocks on the front door whilst simultaneously opening it and letting myself in anyway. This undermines the point of knocking but I'm stuck in a habit that I can't break now. What's a man to do!? This wasn't the case today though as I was running about ten minutes late. This is also quite common behaviour for me in all honesty, but I arrived to find the guys waiting in the car, ready to go. Trev panics you see, it's in his nature, so sitting in the car somehow helps him feel that the journey is underway.

Once *en route* (today taking the motorway as we're convinced it's currently the quicker and luckier route) we began our usual pre-match conversations. With the "how's things?" formalities out of the way things turned to a more 'revealing' chat this week; it appears Tuesdays are a "no bedroom gymnastics" night of the week. I mean if she turns around and says "not tonight love, it's Tuesday" what are you meant to do?

"How the hell are you meant to collect a stool sample? My first thought was to use an old takeaway tray."

Another common topic crops up again; are there any benefits to getting old? This theme has been going on for a couple of years now and, being the youngest of the group, I've got a lot of things coming that I am not looking forward to. Prostate, heart and stool checks – lovely. I'm almost certainly going to get arthritis in my knees, my hairline is starting to reverse whilst the remaining hair will undoubtedly turn a lovely snowy white. In short, we've yet to think of anything in life that improves with age.

Tattoos. I have a few myself but today the suggestion in the car was that people could use them for instructions rather than art. For example, if you're got a medical condition then have a tattoo about it. Or have a list of "likes and dislikes" as a tattoo. You could even have your strengths and weaknesses. Sometimes these points come up in the car and they're utterly ridiculous but so much so that you can't find any way to dismiss them. I remember once there was a theory that there has never been a top player who started his career bald. It's completely ludicrous but you can't disprove it, mainly because most men don't go bald till later in life so they're not likely to start their career 'naturally' bald (apparently a shaved head didn't count).

Back to football and we were all very pleasantly surprised with the Porto result. It means we've got a relatively easy second leg at home now which should have a crackin' atmosphere and get us all fired up for the Manchester United game at their place. Momentum can work wonders in football and another solid win against Porto could be just what's needed ahead of the tricky away trip.

Two players cropped up in our Porto chat; Sadio Mané and James Milner. Sadio because he finally looked like he'd shaken the shackles off with that third goal. If he produces more of those direct runs and early strikes, like last season and the start of this one, then it might be just what the team needs to keep the attacking line surprising the opposition for the rest of the season. Milner, or as we call him, Milnerinio, was pivotal in the Porto game and showed his true footballing genius by judging the angle of that shot to play for the rebound direct to Salah. There are not many players in world football who could judge that angle so perfectly.

As I'm sure most other fans do, our car share journey always includes an in-car score prediction. We're not allowed to change the predictions once out of the car and the in-car prediction is final.

Today's predictions take a familiar turn. Me? Well I'm going through a negative patch right now but I'm trying to get my "reality iced with a touch of optimism" mojo back. I'm predicting a big win; 4-0. Marko Arnautovic will likely cause us the odd problem but I don't see anyone else in their team who will cause us any difficulties, whereas our front three will be far too mobile for the likes of James Collins and Patrice Evra. We don't seem like we're ever going to miss now either, especially Bobby and Mo.

Barry, a sharp-witted piss-taker with more comebacks than the Reds between 2005 and 2007, is traditionally more negative. The cynic in him reckons that when we're under pressure or expectation to do well that's when the team freezes and so he goes for 0-0. He also thinks David Moyes will just park the bus and make it difficult for us.

Trev, the quiet one of the bunch, simply goes with a one goal victory for Liverpool. He's encyclopaedic in his memory of the Reds. Today's demonstration was a casual recollection of Raul Meireles' top goals for Liverpool, particularly his volley against Wolves. He agrees with Barry that we're susceptible to underperformance sometimes when it most matters, but he reckons Virgil van Dijk is going to help shake that out of us simply because he looks like a leader on the pitch. He's going 2-1.

Bob, the eldest and most-seasoned veteran of Anfield attendance, will never hear a bad word said about the club, the players or the manager (the single exception being Roy Hodgson). Typically jovial, he plumps for a home win, 3-0 with plenty of chances and their lot being absolutely woeful because, well, *it's a Moyes team.*

Arrival at Anfield is always the same for us. Out the car, walk up and past John's Supper Bar and the Arkles, crack some joke about the band in the fan zone being able to say they've played at Anfield, get tempted by the smell of chips. As we were leaving the car today the last song on the radio was *Roar* by Katy Perry which was then my ear worm for the next few hours. Trev also recognised an Eminem track when that was on too. I've no doubt that will validate Eminem's musical career to know that four blokes (three of whom are over 50) know his music and even know some of the lyrics.

(Slim Shady, mate – if you're ever in the area and need a lift to the match just give us a shout.)

I made my way up the Main Stand steps towards Gate V via a wishful glance into the VIP Entrance in the silly hope of one day bumping into a celeb like Daniel Craig. He was there once in the old Paddock (okay so technically he was in the *Directors' box*, but don't shoot me) and I'm sure I have a photo of him somewhere, slightly blurred because I was giggling like a child with over excitement at the fact that James frickin' Bond was sat mere metres away.

I always have a bag of sweets for half-time in my pocket too. Bob brings them for us, every match, without fail. This wonderfully caring, warm, friendly man still makes sure three grown men have something to keep us going at half-time. I often have a Scouse Pie before kick-off but there's always room for a midget gem or sports mix. It's when the Haribo comes out that it feels like a proper treat. Today was Aldi sports mix though. Seriously, I wholly recommend them. Plenty of taste, a good flavour variation between the different colours and just the right level of toughness to make chewing them a challenge but not so hard your jaw aches.

I had terrible wind during the match, and to be honest I didn't trust myself not to have an accident, so I basically worked the glutes by clenching for the best part of the ninety minutes. This somewhat detracted from my enjoyment of the match but I didn't want to be "that guy" who makes "that smell" and everyone is appalled by it but nobody wants to own up to it. We all experience "that smell" at least once per season.

Well, we were all very smug as we made our way back to the car, particularly me who probably snuck it with my 4-0 prediction. Bob went close as well but I simply argued my case louder as I predicted we'd score four and it's rare we predict that high and get it right. Our post-match analysis usually includes a man-of-the-match but today there were quite a few who played very, very well so it seemed daft to single out one player. For us, Milner, Andy Robertson, Roberto Firmino and Alex Oxlade-Chamberlain were the standout players for what they brought to the overall pattern of play. Van Dijk was excellent again, as was Salah, but it's Loris Karius that we reserve the extra bit of special praise for. Another couple of good saves, the one from the Arnautovic lob attempt in the first half was particularly good, just a shame we couldn't keep a clean sheet.

The drive home seemed quite short for me because I fell asleep (again, this is pretty standard behaviour for me) but whilst I was drifting in and out of consciousness I was aware of an ongoing discussion that I expect was part of the continued investigation into getting old....

"What is your prostate though, what does it do? Does anybody know?"

Tim O'Brien

From the time I moved to London from New York last November I knew it would not be long before I would have the opportunity to visit Anfield for the first time. My mate (and fellow TTT subscriber) Blake, from back in the US, expressed an interest in coming to visit and making our first pilgrimage together – it was great to go with my longtime close friend. We went for hospitality tickets since he had to book travel as well, and as long as we were going to have to pay a premium to secure tickets we figured it better for the money to go to the club than some dodgy website.

I took the train up Friday morning from London Euston to Liverpool Lime Street and he flew in from the US, via Dublin. We spent Friday wandering around the city, seeing the sights and popping into various pubs for a pint here and there. Thanks to a recommendation on here, we thoroughly enjoyed the Ship and Mitre.

We set out about 9am on Saturday and walked from our hotel near Albert Dock up to Anfield, enjoying the great views on a bright, clear day back down on the city from Everton Park. We arrived at Anfield and took it all in, doing laps around it, and having our picture taken with the Shankly statue. Then we visited the shop and bought our various mementos. After that, we walked through Stanley Park to have a look at that other stadium across the way and then made our way to The Village for our hospitality meal (pretty good!) and then had a pint in the Sandon before heading in to Anfield for the first time.

We sat in block 227 in the Upper Level of the Anfield Road end. No one warned us about the sun, which made an appearance about 30 minutes in and did not relent until full-time. No problem though, because we were at Anfield and a small thing like sun in our eyes wasn't going to stop us enjoying the experience. It was readily apparent that we were sat among fellow out-of-towners, with all the pre-match selfies and the like going on all around us.

Before long, the West Ham players were on the pitch, warming up in front of us. Then, suddenly, there they were, coming out of the tunnel, Mo and Bobby and Sadio and Klopp and the rest! We could hardly contain our excitement! We have both seen Liverpool play on preseason tours in the US but *This ... Was ... Different.*

Our proximity to the out-of-towners became even more apparent during *You'll Never Walk Alone,* as there were relatively few singing *all* the words around us. We held our scarves high and belted it out with gusto.

Almost in a blur, they were kicking off and almost as quickly there was Mo, about to score right in front of us at Anfield. But no, *the post.*

After about 10 minutes West Ham seemed to grow into the game for a while, and we could well have gone 1-0 down on the one Loris Karius tipped off the bar. From our vantage point we couldn't tell if he got a touch or not but later we would know he did. Soon Salah was taking a corner right in front of us – I felt I could have reached out and touched him, even from the upper level. He didn't beat the first man but we were able to get yet another corner almost immediately. Mo hit this second corner and Blake said, "That's better. Thaaat's better ... " and then pandemonium. Emre Can had scored! It was tough to see through all the traffic in front of goal but there it was, a memory that will last a lifetime.

After the first goal there were some great moments, seeing each of the front three score in their own unique way. Salah with the left footer on the ground into the corner, Firmino with the no-look goal, and Mané from a sublime cross from Andy Robertson with a great little chip and some karate kicks to celebrate. Usually when we have the lead I am willing the time to pass to secure the three points. Not this day. I wanted it to go on forever. Even the West Ham goal felt like a blip on a day that would surely be ours. I am always nervous but in the moment I couldn't be bothered with nervousness. Then it was over: Liverpool 4, West Ham 1. I snapped a photo of the scoreboard and we made our way out.

We had a nice walk back down to the city centre and a fun night (dinner and some more pubs) revelling in the victory and the experience. We took the ferry over to the Wirral on Sunday and on TV sadly saw Spurs steal a win at the end, then back to Liverpool to watch Man United-Chelsea and then Man City-Arsenal. After that we parted ways, Blake to the airport and me to the train. It was a great weekend with a great friend in a great city to see a great team.

I will end by saying the people of Liverpool were wonderful to us. Everywhere we went we were met by friendly, welcoming, genuine people who made a visitor feel at home in their city. It might be a while before Blake can make it back, but I am ready to start planning my next trip.

Comment by Blake

I am the aforementioned Blake in Tim's matchday post. I echo 100% how great the people of Liverpool treated us all weekend. Attending the game was amazing, of course, and experiencing such an emphatic win made the long trip more than worth it. But, Tim and I both thoroughly enjoyed exploring the city too and meeting some really proper folks.

That made it a truly memorable trip.

Now, it's time for the Reds to finish the run-out strong. I fly back to the States on Saturday, but I have the Newcastle game set to record so that as soon as I get back to my apartment, I can unwind from the travel with, hopefully, another dominant Reds win.

Comment by Kris Patterson

You know what, it's bloody lovely to read how much "out of towners" enjoy going to the games etc … I'm in the very fortunate position of: being about 45 mins away from Anfield; having a few good friends who offer tickets at a reasonable price; being able to afford to go!

I'll happily admit that I completely take it for granted that I go 5-10 times a season. I bloody love going, but you never forget seeing the inside of Anfield for the first time. Goosebumps all over …

Comment by Roger Lester

I sat in the Kenny Dalglish Stand near the front on halfway line, which was almost the same place as last time. What really struck me was the mood of those around me. Bearing in mind most were the same regulars there was very little moaning and when mistakes were made nothing much was said. A few were urging the back four players to pass forward quicker but on the whole it was a much more relaxed atmosphere than at earlier games.

And … there was singing, this was my fourth match this year in the King Kenny stand and the first time anyone around me had sang.

The match was, as reported, wonderful.

Paul Tomkins, February 24th, 2018

It's hard to get everything right in the same season. Since 2010, Liverpool have been very poor in the league, and average in Europe (first half of 2010/11); very good in the league but poor in the cups (early 2011); poor in the league but excellent in the domestic cups, whilst not competing in Europe (2011/12); mediocre in Europe and poor in the league (first half of 2012/13); poor in the cups but very good in the league (rest of 2012/13); sensational in the league but not even in Europe, and poor in the cups (2013/14); below par in the league, poor in Europe (Champions League and Europa League) but pretty good in the domestic cups (2014/15); and then poor in the league (2015/16) – at which point Jürgen Klopp turned up.

This is what Klopp walked into, and while his performance in the domestic cups has been mixed (a final in his first season, let's not forget, but then nothing at all after; albeit with only Premier League opposition faced this season – so no easy rounds), he has also taken the club to its first European final since 2007, and taken the Reds straight out of a Champions League group – as winners – for the first time since 2009. All this, whilst making clear and steady progress in the league, even if, as I always note, progress is not always linear. (A bad couple of weeks and the Reds could be 5th.)

Also, please note that during the travails of the past decade, the Reds haven't always faced the kind of opposition – teams *and* managers – that made life difficult the last time the Reds were part of a dominant quartet, 2004-2009. In the last decade Arsenal have fallen away from their levels of 10-15 years ago; Spurs had periods of mediocre management (Tim *Fucking* Sherwood!); Man United had the incompetent David Moyes and the boring Louis van Gaal; Man City had a period where the team got too old, and were managed by a good but unremarkable boss; and Chelsea stopped spending as much money when FFP was introduced over half a decade ago, and have flitted between managers both suited and ill-suited. Arguably, all of these teams (perhaps bar Arsenal) are really strong right now, and as between 2004-2009, this is reflected in Europe.

As good as 2013/14 was under Brendan Rodgers, at that time he was facing Moyes' collapsing Man United, Manuel Pellegrini's likeable but ageing Man City, an Arsenal that were neither winning trophies nor challenging for the league title, and a Spurs side managed by André Villas-Boas and then Sherwood for half a season. Rodgers deserves a ton of praise for how he got that team to play, but it was just one season, when the league as a whole wasn't as strong.

So if you want to compare Klopp to Rodgers – and people continue to – you need to remember such vital context. This is not to demean Rodgers, who is a good manager who still has time to improve, and who cannot be blamed for other English clubs making bad appointments at the time; but as with the weakness of the Scottish league, the Premier League at the time did not tell us about him in a *really testing* situation. Rodgers is currently winning a one-team league, and continuing to show nothing at all in Europe (with Europe the only route open to him to clearly *overachieve* at Celtic).

February's Results

04.02.2018 – (H) Tottenham Hotspur 2 – 2
11.02.2018 – (H) Southampton 2 – 0

14.02.2018 – (A) Porto 5 – 0
24.02.2018 – (H) West Ham United 4 – 1

Porto (H), March 6th, 2018.
Jennifer Thomas

First, the backstory. My partner comes from Liverpool and has supported LFC forever, so the rest of us had to follow. We moved around, finally settling in London – as far as anyone settles here – and so now all games are preceded either by long drives up the monstrous M6 or by rammed Virgin Pendolino. I tell you this so that you know and understand that I am not one of the tourists so despised by some hardcore supporters.

I was due to do a piece on the Newcastle game, got all ready including thermals and several layers, then checked the forecast again, and didn't go. Sat in said thermals and layers for half the day instead just to feel part of the experience.

I tried again for the Porto game. Motorways amazingly clear, so all went smoothly, which is unusual, especially if we come on the M6 with its 17-mile stretch of smart upgrading. Can anyone explain why they can't do it in shorter sections? It may be convenient for them to put all the cones out, but as it's not due to be finished until next year, it is neither convenient nor smart for the rest of us. In any case, in my experience of smart motorways, the information is out of date most of the time. No one believes the messages or takes any notice of them, especially the ones that warn of animals in the carriageway.

On the way we talk about the wonder that is Jürgen Klopp, and about Brexit of course. Long car journeys always mean that. Not quite sure why, because we just repeat the same arguments to each other and we agree about it all anyway, like picking a scab. Long time to rant all up the M6. We have the usual stash of Mars Bars and water.

We go via the food bank. As well as tins we take tampons and toothpaste. I don't tell you this so you think I am either noble or a braggart, but because it is appalling that this should be part of the match-day experience in 2018. To get to the food bank van we walk past the phalanx of young lads and lasses, all very glam, in the car park. They all wear black furry hats (very Kremlin-chic) and cheerily call, "Enjoy the game." I wish I could write it phonetically as it loses its charm when just flat on the page. Disappointingly, we don't get to hear the live bands that are usually outside at the start, and play cover versions. People are being frisked as they start to head towards the Anfield Road turnstiles. No water bottles allowed. Do they think we will chuck the bottles or just the tops on the pitch? It is a bugger as I have had a cough for weeks and carry water everywhere to try to control it. I stuff cough sweets in my jacket, together with hat, tissues, car keys, gloves, ticket, hair brush. This is done to avoid having a bag to be searched. So I am now gargantuan as my coat and pockets bulge. In the car park a little crowd is gathering around a car. This area used to have all the players and their cars. I remember Glen Johnson had a matt black beast of some sort with a personalised number plate. I have no idea who this one is. He seems to be cowering in a VW Golf.

I was invited to give a little of the female perspective and so now will tell you about the ladies' toilets. They have cunning little toilet-roll dispensers that are meant to allow you to have a couple of sheets that you pull ever so gently from the hole in the middle of a disc. What invariably happens is that the end gets stuck and so you have to hope that the nice lady in the cubicle next to you will shoot a friendly hand loaded with paper under the partition. I digress.

To the seats. Front row, Upper Kenny Dalglish, almost opposite the players' tunnel. Great views. The same neighbours most weeks. The cheery man across the aisle leaves early at half-time and at the end of the game, as he always does. Very odd, as he is animated and involved all the time that he is in his seat. In the row behind there are four guys who obviously work together and have somehow come by these tickets so they are having an evening out. They talk all the way through. They discuss how the software was all upgraded overnight, how good the golf was, how she – whoever *she* was – had been on an IV drip for two days. Everything but the game or the players. By half-time I had tried scowling but to no effect, so resorted to sticking tissue paper in my ears. They left early, to the delight of all those around.

In the Kop I was pleased to see someone had taken the trouble to handwrite a large notice declaring "Kelvin McKenzie. You are scum." The Porto fans took up their full allocation. A bit of a near cock-up when a minute's silence was announced for Davide Astori. It was announced in English but people seemed to think that silence meant applause so that when it was repeated in Portuguese you couldn't hear it with the sound of clapping. That is how I would explain that the silence was broken by a few Porto fans shouting and then being shouted at. Sensibly, the ref cut the silence short and we were off!

With a 5-0 lead from the first leg it was never going to be a blistering game, and from the team sheet, it was obvious Jürgen Klopp was being pragmatic, bearing in mind the upcoming Manchester United fixture. The first half saw a couple of chances from Sadio Mané and Dejan Lovren and some good, contained play from Jordan Henderson, Emre Can and James Milner in the middle. As the game progressed, the Porto fans were in fine voice, jumping, waving flags and chanting. They chant, not sing – and it is very loud. Porto didn't really threaten but seemed intent on avoiding an embarrassing defeat rather than winning the game. They are a technically skilful team, and their back four was an object lesson for Arsène Wenger.

Iker Casillas moved to the Kop End for the second half and as he took his place, he was warmly applauded by the entire stand. I note that he commented on how touched he was by this afterwards and said how unusual it is. It is unusual; it's been seen before at Anfield before. It is one of the things that makes the club special.

Mo Salah, Danny Ings and Ragnar Klavan came on as substitutes and the first two had a couple of attempts on goal. So not a show-stopper of a performance, but job done.

The highlight of any trip to Anfield is of course listening to *606* on the way home (that's meant to be irony, by the way). Robbie Savage, the Winnie the Pooh of punditry, but without the charm and eloquence, holds forth about anything and everything. That is on Saturdays of course, so we shall have to do without this evening.

Paul Tomkins, March 10th, 2018

Well, Man United fans – there's your man, Jose Mourinho, beating Liverpool with long-ball football that made 1980s' Wimbledon look like the Brazil side of 1970, and nine-man defences. Is that really what you want? Good, because you can keep it. The truth is that a team/squad that costs twice as much as Liverpool's couldn't even go head-to-head at football on their own ground, just hoofball.

You may not care now, in the aftermath of a victory, but *you booed your own manager* when he took off your only good attacker on the day – Marcus Rashford – and brought on yet another gormless giant, to make for what must be the tallest midfield of gormless giants *ever seen* in English football and perhaps the whole world, in the history of football (all three stand *six foot four*, no less).

Liverpool had 13 corners, to United's one. At Old Trafford. And United rode their luck on about half of them. Genius, or timid?

What a "tactical masterclass", hanging on for dear life despite a ton of expensive players, and stuffing the box with every available giant. Enjoy your tears of joy for they shall turn to tears of boredom; you're stuck with that miserable man and his grimly effective but utterly dismal football. You get the points today, sure, but you have to watch that dire football. Three points is a small price to pay to avoid that, in all honesty.

And the ref missed three penalties for Liverpool, two of which even Gary Neville called clear-cut, and in a fine display of homerism, Rashford didn't get booked for diving in on two occasions, kicking the ball away, and also for going into the crowd, which is an *automatic* booking. (Whether or not it's a fair rule, it should be applied 100% of the time. Same as when Bobby Firmino takes off his shirt. It's a booking.) Antonio Valencia only got a yellow for an outrageous kung-fu kick on Sadio Mané (oh the irony) – chest high; Alexis Sanchez was allowed to deliberately block quick free kicks, and the game was stopped as Smalling had a diddums on his leg. What a farce.

As much as I've hated VAR this season, I hate incompetent officials even more.

If Trent Alexander-Arnold's inexperience told in the first half, it was never more so than when getting up after being fouled by Rashford, instead of rolling around like Sanchez. The officials gave United everything.

Still no penalty in the Premier League since the opening day for Mo Salah, although in fairness, Neville only said he was fouled twice in the box in the first clear incident today; first tripped, then wrestled over. Yes, you can keep Salah quiet by hauling him over, although it's up to the officials to have the balls to give those calls.

Comment, March 16th, 2018 by Jeff Reed

The last time I missed watching Liverpool play a match in the Premier League was April 2015 because that was the day I drove to just outside Philadelphia to rescue Dallas the puppy. I watch every Liverpool match either on my 25 inch computer screen or my 55 inch big screen. Each and every game I see replays of offsides and yellow cards and red cards and goals and fouls and on and on. To me the broadcasters show replays, and it rarely interferes with the flow of the match.

Now, if I can see a clear offside or onside or anything else in this short time span, I see no reason why someone with today's technology sitting somewhere and getting the same feed I am watching could not arrive at the same conclusion. This being said, I am aware that sometimes video review may take longer when the person doing the video officiating has to look at multiple views but I would suggest that this is the exception not the rule.

I acknowledge that at times I have opinions that can be based on my gut and not on evidence. In the few matches in England where I have seen video reviews, I get the impression that the VAR official is searching and searching for something that will justify the call on the pitch and not looking for the correct call. To me this is why sometimes you get endless delays when there should be no real delay.

I grew up in the United States in an era when the three big spectator sports were horse racing, boxing, and baseball. Today, for all practical purposes, boxing and horse racing are dead as spectator sports, and baseball is no longer the pre-eminent sport it was 60 years ago, having been replaced by American football on both the college and professional levels, and basketball on both the college and professional levels. Baseball may be coming back but I need to emphasize the words coming back.

Football in England has changed beyond recognition from the sport I encountered in September 1965. At that time the number of professional players who made £100 a week was not large and the number who made, believe it or not, £200 a week was a dream for almost if not every player in the old First Division. In that era Bobby Charlton of Man United was the best English player of his generation and Sir Roger Hunt was the best English goalscorer of his generation. Neither of these men became millionaires from playing football and today if they were playing the game they surely would.

Money has changed football and for all practical purposes the money that has changed football comes from broadcasting matches. Broadcasters pay the vast sums into the game because they are making money – pure and simple. They are making money because people want to watch football on television all day on Saturday, a good part of Sunday and just about every evening in the week. If the NFL believed they needed to have video review more than 30 years ago it was because they feared they would lose public confidence in the results of games and if the public lost confidence in the results of games, viewership would decline, and if viewership declined the broadcasters would suddenly not put so much money into the game.

To me the problems with officiating that I see in just about every match I watch is the hidden crisis in English football, and a problem that the authorities simply either do not want to see or do not want to acknowledge and do something about. I believe that they do not see the harm they are doing to football and the fact that the gravy train of broadcast money can come to a halt and believe me it can. For example, I gave you the examples of boxing and horse racing in the United States. If football is not careful, the same could happen, and one of the nails in its coffin will be the refusal to see the problems in officiating.

Watford (H), March 18th, 2018
Paul Tomkins

For the last 15 years, due to chronic illness, I have tended to mostly only go to games in the autumn and spring, and miss the winter; indeed, I don't leave the house too much at all during the darker months. With an impaired immune system, the coldness can be crippling, and so yes, these days, I am a fair-weathered fan.

So when, in mid-February, the other two of our match-going trio of mates (dating back to season tickets together in the 1990s) suggested we all go to this one, I thought: yeah, my body can handle a warm spring game. Which, as a decision, proved about as perceptive as Abraham Lincoln thinking "this is a perfect night to go to the theatre and get a bite to eat afterwards".

Still, my decision definitely had the happier ending; there was no Mo Salah to lift Lincoln's spirits 152 years ago.

Since my divorce 15 years ago I have always had my son on Saturdays, and he's not into football, so that also stopped me going; but he's now 16, and recently got a Saturday job working outside. (Of course, I found out that morning that he didn't have to work that day due to the snow, so it would have been a rare chance to spend the day with him lately, but arrangements had been made.)

I try to make a few games each season, and have another lined up for April, but my previous match was with TTT stalwarts Andrew Beasley and Andrew Fanko back in August, for the 4-2 win over Hoffenheim. It feels a long time ago. I'm sure shirtsleeves were involved.

The old gang – Matt, Adie and I – haven't been together as a trio for a game in a couple of years (we are now dispersed about the country), and having travelled home and away with these guys for many years (including Rome, Barcelona, Athens, Istanbul and, er, Bolton) it's always a pleasure to join up again, and to make use of our old season ticket seats. I played football in West London with both in the mid-1990s, and it's great that we gravitated towards each other due to our red shirts and liverbirds in our very first training sessions. Adie's parents were from Liverpool, and Matt is from Chester. I'm the only one with no north-western lineage, although my dad did once do an impression of Ken Dodd (amongst others) on live TV on a talent show in 1976. (I don't think that qualifies me.)

I'm not well enough to drive to Liverpool and back in a day anymore, so Adie picks me up from Leicester – thankfully in his wife's Ford Focus and not his own Smart Car, which was, shall we say, an *experience* on a previous motorway journey to Anfield. (Great for small trips, less great when a lorry thunders past at 70mph. Although excellent for finding parking spaces nearer the ground.)

The forecast according to my phone is snow all day in Leicester, but no snow at all in Liverpool. I look on my phone and it's 8-degrees in Reykjavik, -1 in England. The snow that is already falling is light and breezy, so it seems it'll be doddle. It's cold outside, but never as cold as whenever we step outside our usual parking spot 20 minutes from the ground, and the wind whips in; which, every time we arrive there, I say, as a running joke, is the coldest place in England (it probably isn't, but it always feels like it).

On the way to the game I have a text exchange with a TTT subscriber over for Switzerland for the game, offering me a spare ticket that I thought Matt might want for his son, but Matt had already set off without him. And acclaimed American sports author Michael MacCambridge – a TTT subscriber who is over from the states for the game – wants to meet up if I get to the ground early enough, but it's a slow journey up, and there's not really time.

Walking uphill towards Walton Breck Road feels like scaling Everest, with the coldest wind and fine snow spitting in our faces. I'm already feeling unwell, and we're not even at the ground yet. I suddenly remember why I don't go very often anymore, although hours later I leave the ground feeling spoilt by what I saw. (Then, on the way home ... I remembered why I don't go very often.)

Adie and I had agreed to meet Matt in a café near the ground, but which café? He never specified. Once outside the ground, neither of our texts to him are getting beyond the frozen iMessage loops of "sending"; although Adie tells me he knows the guy who is due to put in new WiFi at Anfield. (It can't come soon enough.)

So we decided to go into the ground and instantly bumped into Matt by the turnstile. I didn't recognise him at first with a big woolly hat on and wrapped in a thick coat. In trying a modern-style handshake I knocked his phone out of his hand, and luckily it survived the fall.

Rather than take our seats once inside we get some hot drinks and huddle in a corner of the mezzanine of what was the Lower Centenary for all our years as regulars, but is now the Lower Kenny Dalglish (not to be confused with the great man's legs, which, as great as they are, are not suitable for huddling around; and anyway, I hear he tends to find it an invasion of his private space.)

Once in our seats Jonathan Hall from the Red And White Kop forum walks past as we all stand up to let him by – I can't have seen him in over a decade, and he doesn't recognise me with my glasses, my hat and my beard, and also there's the suspicion that he might be "well oiled" for this 5:30pm kick-off. I'm pretty sure he's slurring, but I can't hear much through my thick beanie. He used to sit one row in front of us for years (before our seats got moved), and back in 2001 I told him to try a new site I was involved with: RAWK. I recall a time a few years later when I was the regular columnist for the official Liverpool FC site but by then no longer going regularly, and there was talk by someone on RAWK that I was some dreadful fraud and I'd *never even been to a match* (which I used to get on other sites too); Hally was able to point out, quite bluntly, that I sat behind him every home game for many seasons. It was an interesting insight into how fake news – or *bullshit*, as it used to be known as – can spread.

For some reason I had it in my head all week that we were playing Norwich, as I mixed them up with Watford (again, purely in my head) due to the yellow kits. I'm obviously fully aware that Norwich haven't been in the Premier League for a while, but one of the more recent games that Adie, Matt and I had made it to together was early December 2013 (a rare winter outing for me, albeit warmer than this 'spring' game), against those yellow-shirted Canaries. So it kinda became a subconscious glitch.

Oh to have a player who could score four goals in a game like Luis Suárez, eh? Pah, those were the days.

I also have Norwich on my mind as Matt's aforementioned son is now at their academy, so we'd spent a good while before the game, with our hot drinks, discussing his progress, and talking about the more scandalous treatment of young kids by adult coaches; not the kind of awful paedophile scandals of Crewe or Man City all those years ago, but in not caring for the kids' mental wellbeing, in how they freeze them out or let them go, and depressingly, in how some teams are still full of six-foot 12-year-olds (one of the reasons I stopped playing organised football in the 1980s, despite having been a decent prospect, only resuming again aged 20 in the university leagues, before a stint as a semi-pro, which I may have mentioned once or twice before).

The game started under light snowfall, and the spray of fine snow fizzing from the ball as it rolled across the immaculately flat and whitened turf was an

147

oddly thrilling sight, revealing the bright green grass underneath. The forecast was wrong, and the Beast from the East was back, with whatever cutesy storm name they'd given it. (Storm Tinkerbell?) I tried to think back about when I went to games regularly, many during the winter, but struggled to recall one anywhere near as cold as this; almost -10 with the windchill, and it only feels colder still when sitting down for 90 minutes. The best I can come up with is being behind the goal at Aston Villa in the mid-'90s. (Games back then were much more likely to be called off, due to frozen pitches, I recall.)

Sitting in our seats, with the snowflakes rising on the icy wind, we needed some warming up. Some guy called Mo Salah (you may have heard of him?) obliged.

I'd been saying on this site in the previous game against Man United how Salah had to take at least one or two of those dribbles-before-shooting onto his right side, because he was being shown inside and then double-marked. Even if he fluffs them up, it keeps opponents guessing. Teams don't want him getting onto his left foot, but if he does, one can press him while another blocks his shooting angles, and it's much harder for him.

So when, with almost his very first touch against Watford, he squared up his man, who was 100% certain the little Egyptian was going to cut inside, it was like my prayers were answered; Salah flipped the ball onto his weaker right side – so effectively that the Watford man fell over in a heap. Then, Liverpool's no.11 only had to lash at it with his "swinger" to stand a decent chance of scoring. Which is exactly what he did; mimicking Lionel Messi's goal against Chelsea in midweek: hard and low with his weaker foot, right through the goalkeeper's legs or under his diving body. It wouldn't be the last Messi comparison of the evening, either.

I then spent a bit of time watching a lonely Loris Karius wandering up to the centre-circle, and doing sprints and jumps to keep warm, as the ball stayed up the other end of the pitch, but with Liverpool going nowhere. He then patted himself down, and did some stretches. There'd be no chance of a Watford player catching him cold. It was the kind of thing you don't really see on the TV, and showed a great attitude in keeping himself alert and lively.

Later in the half a wonderful move by Liverpool – Sadio Mané's incisive pass to Andy Robertson and his beautiful cross – led to Salah scoring his second right-foot goal of the night. Suddenly he was on a right-footed hat-trick, despite only supposedly having a left foot.

As against Man United, Mané was picking the ball up in deeper, central areas, and running at the opponents from there; but his passing was generally better last night, albeit punctuated with some weird touches and mishit through-balls. It looks to me like a deliberate new tactic, with Robertson becoming the left winger.

That said, it wasn't until we got home and watched *Match of the Day* that we realised how well Mané did – he had a great game, if you took out his umpteen mistakes, which could cloud you from the good he was doing;

although at the game I was at least able to see him deliberately find Salah in the box when his mate was on a hat-trick, and that became Mané's second assist of the night. It felt like Mané was looking to help his teammate get his third, and again, that was a heartwarming gesture in an age of selfish, egotistical players.

Jordan Henderson was also poor in possession for periods of the game, although was the only man brave enough to go with short sleeves and no gloves (he's from the North East, where everyone obviously goes topless all year round). One soused Scouse fella spent the entire first half shouting "he's shit, him!" and "Fuck off Henderson, you're shite", explaining to all around him that he's never, *ever* been any good; and then said nothing else all game. Not one positive word about *anything*, especially when Henderson lofted some lovely passes to the forwards.

The second half was a joy to behold, in terms of finishing. On the way out we all agreed that Watford didn't play that badly, and Liverpool weren't fully "at it"; yet it was a 5-0 demolition. Later I see the expected goals scores, and 2-0 seems about the average; and that seems generally fair (and recalls the winless run earlier in the season), but for Mo Salah's brilliance – the audaciousness of Bobby Firmino and the encouraging sharpness in the box of Danny (Danny) Ings, Danny (Danny) Ings.

In truth it probably felt like a 3-0 margin would have been the fairest reflection of the match, but as at Brighton and a few other places lately, the Reds had turned a 2-0 xG win into something that felt much bigger; redressing the balance from those drawn fixtures in the autumn.

There was also a big handball shout by the Kop, but we all know by now that Liverpool don't get penalties at Anfield, especially the Kop end, anymore.

"When was the last time we were at a game when a player scored four?" I ask Adie, by this time having shivered so much I had neck ache, earache and a headache, and brain freeze. He obviously says Luis Suárez vs Norwich. Of course! The yellow jerseys.

This means my four-goals-per-game ratio is pretty high lately. Going back further, I'm not sure I've missed a single four-goal haul since the days of Ian Rush in the 1980s, which was before my match-going time (while I wasn't at Anfield for Fowler's five against Fulham in the league in 1993, although I had been at Craven Cottage for his debut goal on a night of surreal lightning storms).

I saw Fowler score four vs Bolton, and a year later, against Middlesbrough, if memory serves; and was in the same seat for Michael Owen hitting four in a 5-1 victory over Nottingham Forest, circa 1999. They were all in the 1990s. Did any Liverpool player score four in a game in the noughties? Then came Suárez's four against those yellow-shirted whipping boys, Norwich (or maybe Watford).

For all competitions, Salah has now eclipsed Fernando Torres' best season, and Luis Suárez's best season. He's easily eclipsed the best seasons of

Daniel Sturridge and of Michael Owen. And he equalled Robbie Fowler's best total of 36, too.

All for a player who is nominally a winger, and all with just one of those 36 goals a penalty. With 28 in the league, he has equalled Fowler's best tally in the Premier League era, and is closing in on Suárez's 31 of 2013/14, which of course, included that quadruple against some team in yellow.

Salah looks set to eclipse everyone before the season is over, and is edging into peak-Ian Rush territory. Rushie's best league season was 32 goals, I believe?

Salah's third goal last night was one of those that will live long in the memory; crowded out by six defenders and the goalkeeper he jinked, dipped, turned and pivoted, and after possibly being knocked over, prodded the ball home whilst on the fall. It wasn't the cleanest of finishes, but such was the remarkable nature of even being able to get a shot away that the keeper was totally bamboozled. From where I was sat – right in line with it – I thought the chance had gone; the word "unlucky" forming in my throat, to exclaim about the loss of balance, before we were all on our feat, jumping for joy (or hobbling for joy, in my case).

I also have to say that the atmosphere was excellent all evening long, apart from a lull in the first half when the game had gone scrappy and people were being ejected from the Kop by the police (eliciting boos), and when Karius was able to run a keep-fit class near the halfway line. In some of my recent trips the songs rang out loud and proud for a few minutes until kick-off, then it went quiet; but here the songs continued, and the early goal helped.

In particularly, the droning, looping "Allez Allez Allez" song – a new one on me – kept the noise levels up, as it just winds around and around, complete with some continental style scarf waving too. I can see that being phenomenal against Man City in the first leg of the Champions League quarter-finals. This song seems vital, as Jürgen Klopp said early in his tenure that the crowd mustn't sing his name, but focus on the players; so there's no "Rafa, Rafael Rafael Benítez" or "R-R-R-Rafa Benítez"-type songs to keep the crowd vocal, and these days only a handful of players have individual songs that get sung anyway. So it needs new songs – or digging out old ones – to keep the place vibrant. This new one really fits the bill, as it goes on for ages.

It's also worth noting that, on a night colder than any Wednesday ever experienced in the history of Stoke since the last ice age, Liverpool's two Africans and their one Brazilian had no issues in the snow, which can't have been part of their formative educations in the sport; although in fairness, both teams sprinted off pretty sharpish at the end, as if to be out there for one second more was as painful as ice swimming in Norway.

It was also my first chance to see Virgil van Dijk in the flesh, and I was especially curious to see how quick he looked. But yet again, he never really had to break stride. He coasts through games, floating over the ground, heading it clear, passing to a colleague, tidying up like a Rolls Royce on kerbside cleaning duty.

At one point he found himself on the right wing and skinned the defender for pace, and that was the only time he had to really run; his reading of the game seems so good that he rarely has to get out of 2nd gear. He didn't play against City in the 4-3 victory in January, but he could make a big difference next month.

I also can't help but think that after missing the first half of 2017 with injury, then getting no preseason and only getting back into the Southampton team as October rolled around, he's nowhere near as fit as he can be – which is a frightening prospect for opposition strikers next season. The best players make it look easy, and he's in that bracket.

And in Joe Gomez and Andy Robertson, Liverpool have two more defenders who excel at defending; totally transforming the defence from having none when Trent Alexander-Arnold and Alberto Moreno were in the team, before van Dijk's arrival.

Alexander-Arnold will get better with age, of course, but right now is better going forward, rather than a defender. Gomez still has some issues with judging crosses without losing his man in the process, but like Robertson (*and* Alexander-Arnold), he has started to whip in a dangerous ball or two at the other end in every game he plays.

Robertson, meanwhile, is a revelation, as he is an overlapping full-back, but he rarely gets beaten by his man when he tracks back. Moreno was having a good season, but Robertson looks astonishingly good at both ends of the pitch. Liverpool's business this season has been tremendous, and Klopp continues to improve players, and clearly has them work on their weaknesses. It was great to see it all up close.

The walk back to the car was downhill, so that was a blessing. The drive home was in light snow, which grew increasingly heavy on the way back to Leicester. But by the time we hit the Midlands it was coming down thick and fast. The car skidded at Fosse Park in the whiteout but Adie pulled it back in time, and I asked if he steered into it – one of those counterintuitive things you are taught to do in theory, but who actually gets to go on a skid pan?

My personal stats for the day, via my Fitbit, were up there with Mo Salah's – covering more ground than usual, and breaking my flights-of-stairs personal best. Also, my SOPSFG (seeing one player score four goals) ratio gets better still.

Home at 11:15, the first thing to do is watch the recording of *Match of the Day*, in time-honoured tradition. It's in widescreen HD these days, but with Mo Salah a cross between Owen's pace and Fowler's skill, it seems that not a lot has changed since the 1990s after all.

Comment by SimplyRed, March 31st, 2018

What a relief. Today's win [at Crystal Palace] is massive. We overcame three things that normally work against us. First, I suspect going into the game most fans and players already assumed that we would win. We were playing a relegation-threatened team who lost four of their last five matches prior to playing us. And after the way we took Watford apart, surely a win against Palace would be highly expected. It almost felt like we only needed to turn up, play some decent football and go away with the three points.

That it turned out to be rather difficult, and yet we overcame it, is testament to the mental strength of this team. Second, we don't normally play well after the international break which seems to serve largely to disrupt the rhythm of the team, undoing the seamless understanding that was built up over weeks of playing together. And third, we probably have half an eye on the Champions League game against Man City. Being able to navigate past these challenges, let alone those contributed by the ref, speaks volumes about this team.

March's Results

03.03.2018 – (H) Newcastle United 2 – 0
06.03.2018 – (H) Porto 0 – 0
10.03.2018 – (A) Manchester United 1 – 2
17.03.2018 – (H) Watford 5 – 0
31.03.2018 – (A) Crystal Palace 2 – 1

Daniel Rhodes, April 2nd, 2018
Statistically speaking, this current Liverpool side are one of the most 'dominant' teams to have played together in the last decade – just behind Man City this season and Chelsea from 09/10. Not only that, but aside from Carlo Ancelotti's Chelsea, all the teams that are 'cut adrift' from the rest in terms of dominance – in a plotted visual [which can be seen on the website] are current sides: Man City, Liverpool and Spurs all have shown elite-level dominance of football matches rarely seen in the last decade. Not only that, but they are consistent with it, so it is likely to be sustainable over the upcoming years as well.

If this Liverpool side is so good then why hasn't it translated into points? As mentioned earlier, there were certainly problems last season and at times during this when the Reds concede 'big chances' all too often relative to the volume of shots conceded. However, even that has improved in recent months. Another crucial factor in my opinion is the quality of our goalkeepers' save percentage.

Under Jürgen Klopp we've never had a goalkeeper save even the average amount of shots compared to the rest of the league. Now of course the quality of chances has to be a factor in that, but even so, Man Utd have conceded more shots than Liverpool this season, and look at the over-performance of David de Gea. His performance is the best seen since 2009, and without it I'd be surprised if Jose Mourinho was still in a job; but that may be more wishful thinking on my part (or do we want him to stay?!). The Reds' keepers (Simon Mignolet mainly, and to a lesser extent Loris Karius) have consistently put in distinctly average numbers.

Finally, Klopp's Liverpool side are performing at a level that should be challenging for – and winning – the league title. It is reasonable to suggest that without this current Pep Guardiola-led Man City side Liverpool would have been challenging (with Spurs) for the hallowed Number Nineteen. Not only do the Reds have to get past the Citizens in the Champions League, but they are the target for the title. And it is a challenge, because all of City's underlying figures are at a level never before seen in terms of dominance, and on a par with Ancelotti's Chelsea in terms of shot volume and accuracy.

Perhaps crucially though, Liverpool have room for improvement. If Karius develops or another goalkeeper arrives we could expect a three to five point increase (or more if we get the De Gea outlier); add in the defensive improvement since Virgil van Dijk arrived – and then finally VAR (because the referees can *fuck the fuck off!*) – and those three things could be a trigger for the title. The final pieces in what is the most enjoyable Liverpool jigsaw of my lifetime.

Manchester City (H), April 4th, 2018
Glasgow Red

My youngest brother has been busy carving a nice career for himself in the murky world of corporate finance. So when the draw was made, I thought it was time to see just how big a hitter he was. "Pablo, use your influence and sort out some tickets for the City game." A few hours later he texted me saying "How much do you love me?". Very much, wee man. Very very much!

He then called that night to explain that there was a catch. The tickets were from his boss and they were an eye-watering £200 each. Turns out his gaffer has four season tickets for the Premier Lounge with primo seats in the upper KD just to the right of halfway line. As I suspiciously moved into the kitchen to be out of Mrs Glasgow Red's earshot, I said take all four as middle brother Ric and my Dad would gladly take the other two. I figured, worst case scenario, I'd need to cover their tickets if they balked at the price, but in my head the sensible chimp's financial concerns were already being drowned out by bad chimp loudly humming the Champions League theme tune. After some tense negotiation with Ricardo ("200 fucking quid?") my Dad ("200 quid *and* I need to drive?") and the missus ("I'll just add this to the list") we were all set.

So, Wednesday lunchtime and with my dad impatiently beeping outside, I kiss my girls goodbye, and proceed to remove the last three bottles of Corona left over from my youngest's birthday party at the weekend. Wifey asks me if I'm ever going to grow up, stating that I'll be having plenty tonight and there's no need to make an arse of myself on the way down as well. I reluctantly take her advice which proves sage.

No sooner are we on the motorway than Ric says he forgot his specs and we need to turn back as the game is just a blur without them he tells me. More on this later.

An easy drive down gets us to the extremely convenient Stanley Park car park and the wee man's taxi from Lime Street drops him off literally at the same time as we park. We take in the atmosphere with the fans waiting for the bus with their red smoke bombs and it's buzzing … and it's only 5 o'clock! Didn't find out until after the game what happened with the Man City bus and I wondered whether that affected them in any way? It couldn't have helped.

The entrance to the lounge area is all airport style security and glam girls putting wristbands on you. I'm not really sure what to expect as I'm a hospitality virgin but it's pretty relaxed and they even have prawns, but not in sandwich form! Proceed to get right on it and lambast the lads at their excessively slow drinking pace that sees me take an early one pint lead almost straight away.

Time flies by as the Guinness goes down nicely and we're in our seats about 10 minutes before kick-off.

As a Celtic fan as well, I'm in the very fortunate position of supporting the two teams with best atmospheres for big games. Supporters of other teams and some pundits go on about the cliché of the atmosphere at Anfield and Celtic Park on a big Euro night under the lights but it's a cliché for a reason. I've witnessed enough of these occasions over the years to understand just how much the atmosphere helps create an aura of invincibility. There's no other grounds with the same level of intensity and it can only raise your game if you're the home team and strike fear into the opposition, even if they'll never admit to that.

Last night was one of these occasions. After a pretty good start City were pretty much blown away with some death-thrash-metal football (copyright Mr P. Tomkins). They simply couldn't live with us in that first half and if you'd just landed on Earth from some distant planet you'd have called us a blatant liar when we told you that the team running away with league and setting all sorts of records was wearing blue.

When Mo scored, Dad lost his glasses in the bedlam. We found them quickly but in the carnage that was the celebrations for the 3rd, Ric lost his too, and he didn't get them back until the start of the 2nd half!

When we're on it to that level, there are very few teams that can handle us. Assuming we get through, it will be very interesting to see how Barcelona/Bayern Munich/Real Madrid cope with it. Of course, there's every possibility that we could lose heavily at their place in the first leg meaning the 2nd leg will not be anything like last night.

But if we're playing at home first or are still in the tie going into the 2nd leg at Anfield, whoever of Europe's big three have the misfortune to be drawn against us should look the fuck out 'cos they will not know what's hit them.

Overall, an amazing occasion, which was everything and more than what I expected. Sharing it with my Dad and brothers made it all the more special. I think I'll still be humming *Allez Allez Allez* right up until 12:29 on Saturday at this rate.

"Grover"

I usually don't go to European games as I live in the Midlands and midweek games are difficult to get to without taking time off work. However this week a season-ticket holder I know from way back could not make the game and offered me his ticket and I couldn't believe my luck. He said that he had chosen me as he knew I would make a lot of noise! I am a priority member, so do get to most league games at Anfield, but this was a relatively new experience for me.

I drove up to Anfield after lunch, after taking a half day from work and met up with some mates outside the Arkles pub at 5:45pm. It was bedlam there – flares going off and everyone singing loudly. When the buses arrived we couldn't even see them because of the flares, but could hear the animosity and knew City's bus was first.

I did not see anyone throw anything at the bus, but it obviously happened and afterwards I couldn't understand why there was so many broken bottles on the street. We sang and cheered when we assumed the Liverpool bus passed by and then made our way to the stadium.

A huge group of us walked along Arkles Road singing *Allez, Allez, Allez* and a number of residents on the street were standing in their doorways singing along. It was a wonderful moment of camaraderie and we were all feeling very optimistic that this was going to be a top night. How right we were!

I was not sitting with any of my mates, who had tickets in the Kop. I was in the Lower Kenny, close to the Kop, and it was a great seat. We were not interested in wasting time outside the stadium, so after grabbing a quick bite to eat from one of the vans outside the Kop, we parted ways and headed for our seats to start building the atmosphere before the game.

City players got booed when they came out to warm up and the Liverpool players got the loudest cheer I have ever heard for the warm-up. The Kop was already singing half an hour before kick-off and everyone was in a great mood.

George Sephton, the PA at Anfield, played all the right songs to get us going but to be honest they weren't needed at all. The Kop sang its own songs over the noise from the PA. *You'll Never Walk Alone* was sung with great gusto by everyone and I have never seen so many scarves held aloft at once, in each of the stands. When the Champions League music played, the hairs stood up on the back of my neck and we were ready to go. Watching all those amazing flags waving on the Kop made me so proud. I really admire the time and effort of those who make flags put in and it makes for a wonderful spectacle. The synergy is amazing. There was one which had "We conquered all of Europe" on it, made especially following the development of the *Allez, Allez, Allez* song which is only a few weeks old, but has now become part of the folklore.

City obviously won the toss and decided they would make us play into the Kop first half. What a mistake that was! Pep Guardiola got most things wrong on the night and Jürgen Klopp, the LFC players and the fans got most things right.

We stood for the whole match in the Lower Kenny. I have not seen that before as usually it is a bit sedate in there. Not last night. As each goal went in, we all just jumped around and hugged each other. There was absolutely no negativity at all from anyone and the whole experience was just a joy to be a part of.

Trent Alexander-Arnold got amazing support from us when he was playing in front of us in the second half. He didn't put a foot wrong for the whole match and after hearing him on *The Anfield Wrap* this week, I was just so chuffed for him. He is a lad of immense character and has a strong mentality, as well as being a very talented footballer. He is a credit to his family and LFC. Each and every LFC player did their bit though. I have never seen us defend as well as a unit as in that second half. I remember looking at the clock and it showed we were only in the 59th minute. I thought it was going to be an excruciating half hour but we weathered the storm for about another five minutes and then the whole stadium felt as if we were not going to concede.

Nobody left early. Everyone stayed behind to show their appreciation for the efforts of the team at the final whistle. The players and Klopp all showed their gratitude for the support and *Allez, Allez, Allez* was belted out again as the players left the pitch. I exchanged handshakes and high-fives with those around me and I was exhausted, hoarse but exhilarated as I made my way out of Anfield. All the Whatsapp messages started coming through from friends (for those who haven't been, there is very poor phone coverage in Anfield) and I was angry to hear that the Man City bus had been attacked. It put a slight dampener on my mood. I had a quick post-mortem with my mates out on Walton Breck Road and then had to head back down south. I soaked up all the reaction on podcasts and radio in the car and got home at 1.15am. I then was too buzzed to sleep, so enjoyed the goals on BT Sport (I had recorded the match). Needless to say, it was an unforgettable day and one I feel so fortunate to have experienced.

AnfieldIron

It's been a long journey from a packet of crisps in the Boys Pen, to chicken and celeriac ballotine, in one of the glass-fronted hospitality suites in the new stand. From a bunch of scallies trying to relieve me of my rattle, scarf and rosette, to a host of pretty young ladies, dressed as Scouse Cossacks, addressing me as Sir.

The match day experience has certainly changed over the years.

I awoke with butterflies, a fluttering nervousness, that would grow as the day progressed.

Adorned in my lucky "pants and tings," I set off for my brother's house, on the edge of Liverpool, to rendezvous with my brother-in-law and nephew. Driving in, we turned the corner on to Priory Road and heard the first strains of *Allez Allez Allez*, from the crowd gathered outside the Arkles.

Along with the hairs on the back of my neck, the butterflies raised their game.

Then a short walk from our priority parking place, (ooh, *get you*), to the Main Stand and the ascent to our lofty hospitality suite. After being met with a glass of Prosecco and a smile as wide and white as Bobby Firmino's, we made our way to our table. Set beautifully with sparkling cutlery and glassware, it was the ice bucket full of ale, in the middle of the table, that really caught my eye. Much needed, we made short work of what was there and ordered a few more. After a truly delicious meal, we made our way to our padded, yes, *padded* seats.

Next year sees the 60th anniversary of my first game at Anfield. In that time I've experienced hundreds of renditions of *You'll Never Walk Alone*. Rarely has one moved me as much as the one last night. Absolutely magnificent, with every corner of the ground giving everything they had. That small section of City fans now know how special European nights at Anfield really are.

With the Champions League tune blasting out, and kick-off moments away, those pesky butterflies had now morphed into squadrons of B52s performing loop-de-loops in my innards.

Everyone will have seen the game and read the details by now, so no need for me to comment on that, other than to say I saw things in this match that filled me full of hope for the next few years.

After the game, a few more beers were consumed before making our way back to my brother's place. The brother-in-law made his way home and the nephew went, exhausted, to bed. My brother, being a head steward in the Main Stand, arrived home an hour later. We sat and shared a few bottles of Bud into the early hours and dreamed of what songs we could be singing come the end of the season.

The hospitality suite was a wonderful experience. The view from my padded, yes, *padded* seat was the best I've ever had at Anfield. Yet, every few minutes, my eyes would drift to the right, to my spiritual home, The Kop. To a spot just above and to the left of the crossbar, which for many years, was my spec. I'd have swapped all the hospitality suite had to offer for a chance to stand there last night.

There's just no accounting for taste, is there?

Paul Tomkins, April 4th, 2018

A *proper* top manager. That's what it looks like. Proper ideas, proper philosophy, proper charisma. Manchester City clearly have more quality in a squad that costs almost twice as much, and already had much more winning experience, but while they undoubtedly have a world-class manager, so do Liverpool. Make no mistake. And Liverpool have the Kop, too. City are deservedly winning the league, but since October Liverpool have clicked into top gear, even with injuries and the departure of Philippe Coutinho.

Why? Jürgen Klopp.

I love it when teams think they know what European nights at Anfield are like based on the league games, and maybe adding 5% in their heads. *You haven't got a fucking clue!* Perhaps if Anfield could be like this every week the Reds might have won a league or two since 1990, but it's wrong to expect such passion and fervour on a consistent basis; like wishing it was Christmas every day, it would become meaningless. I was going to say that the Kop keep it in reserve, for the big nights, but the whole *stadium* does; and as I noted after being at the Watford game, the *Allez Allez Allez* song gives the place a constant hum and buzz. (The booing of every City touch was good for the buzz too.) Anfield on a European night is no myth

In March 2005 I wrote a piece for *Football365* on how Liverpool, as rank outsiders, could win the Champions League. Juventus could be beaten, I felt, and if Chelsea were drawn in the semis, Liverpool could do to them what Chelsea did to the 'Invincible' Arsenal the year before: gatecrash their party. Arsenal in 2004 and Chelsea in 2005 found that being by far the best team in the league is not enough when it comes to European games against English opposition. My hunch was that City could be in for the same, although in 2005 the Reds had the 2nd leg against Chelsea at Anfield. Still, Liverpool could still give City a hell of a fright in the first match.

After a slightly shaky start, Liverpool *attacked the living shit* out of City in the first half, and then showed in the second half that the manager knows how to organise a defence. It was a fantastic rearguard action; all the more remarkable considering that Mo Salah went off injured (giving City a boost and harming the Reds' attacking options), to join Emre Can, Adam Lallana, Joël Matip, Joe Gomez and Ragnar Klavan on the treatment table.

With all the context (players out, Salah going off, City being a sensational team in top form), I think it was one of the best all-round displays I've ever seen from a Liverpool side.

First of all, Trent Alexander-Arnold: sensational! One of the best games I've seen a young full-back ever have, reminiscent of Rob Jones snuffing out

Ryan Giggs on the Liverpool man's debut at Old Trafford in 1991, having joined the club three days earlier.

Dejan Lovren and Virgil van Dijk – colossuses! *Collosi?* Well, this was the Colosseum! All it needed was a thumbs-up from Klopp.

Andy Robertson! Perpetual motion, all swinging arms and gyrating hips, up and down the flank like a locomotive powered by nuclear energy. *Andy Andy Andy Andy Robertson!*

James Milner and Jordan Henderson – they both surely left the field without socks, as they'd worked them off. Milner's best game for Liverpool by a country mile (or a country 26 miles, as it seemed). He was *everywhere*, clattering into Kevin de Bruyne every time the Belgian got the ball in the first half. He snuffed the life out of him.

Alex Oxlade-Chamberlain! *Whooomf!* A sensational first-half, but alas, the second half showed that he really isn't a winger anymore. But that first half! What a strike, and another sensational turn should have been capped off by playing Firmino in for a shot, but he delayed the pass. Still, he looks sensational in the big games. He needs to work on his impact in lower-tempo games, but he is one of the best players I've ever seen when it comes to acceleration (even if his control isn't always as devastating, although it was in the first-half tonight). His pace off-the-mark is incredible.

Mo Salah – please let it be a minor twinge! It would be such a shame if the season unfolds and he misses out. His sharpness in the box in lashing home his 38th goal of the season set the ball rolling, after a strangely nervous start by the Reds. Once that went in then City knew they were in a game.

Roberto Firmino – not his best game on the ball, but the way he reacted to prod it to Salah for the opener was classic Firmino. You are never safe in possession when he is around.

Sadio Mané – a sensational first-half before running out of steam, like most of his team-mates. He is edging closer to 20 goals, and his all-round play, while inconsistent and infuriating at times, can be off the charts when he gets it right.

And the subs came on and ran around, adding some energy; Gini Wijnaldum also adding a bit of composure.

The introduction of Dominic Solanke brought the game back in Liverpool's favour, I felt; suddenly City had to deal with him charging about and Liverpool could hit long balls over the top for him. City still dominated the possession but after Solanke came on it felt like they were never going to break through.

Oh, and I forgot Loris Karius – did he even touch the ball?

This wasn't just Liverpool blitzing City, but it wasn't anywhere near the Reds' best 18 in the squad. Yes, City were missing Sergio Agüero, but they clearly had a far stronger bench.

But here's the kicker. With inflation, Man City's £XI this season (the average cost of the XI in all league games adjusted for Transfer Price Index

159

inflation) is £551m; Liverpool's is less than half, at £242m – the 5th costliest side in the Premier League. (Man United's £XI is also over £500m, and Spurs are now over £200m; Chelsea are at £354m.) Klopp is overachieving based on budget (to be 3rd in the league whilst having a chance of making the Champions League semis is incredible), but this summer there will definitely be more spending; the money already earmarked for Naby Keita (or Baby Keith according to autocorrect), and the Coutinho cash, if the right players can be found (i.e. the club won't blow it on timewasters). That can help close the gap. (As an aside, City's *squad*, after inflation, costs £888m, nearly twice what Liverpool's does, and Man United are getting close to £1billion, at £920m.)

However, there's one more really incredible fact that bodes well for the coming seasons.

And that fact is that, with average ages compiled by Graeme (Riley) – taken to perfect accuracy of the exact day (so, say, 25 years seven months and 13 days) – *Liverpool have the youngest side in the top division, at 24.3.* Man City are almost a whole year older, at 25.11, and 25 is the youngest any Premier League champion has previously been (Chelsea in 2004/05).

I believe this is the youngest ever Liverpool side in the Premier League era, and therefore, possibly the Reds' youngest of all time, given how teams (it seems) never used to be so young. The average for the entire Premier League this season is 26.0, and the oldest team, West Brom, are 27.9. (This is no country for old men; *taxi*...)

These Liverpool players will all be a year older next season, and so the average should rise to c.25.3. But hang on, if Emre Can goes, or if Naby Keita usurps Jordan Henderson or James Milner, then the average comes down again.

Everton (A), April 7th, 2018.
Ken Cooper

"Everton away mate, do you want me to try and get a ticket?"

Fuck Yeah!

"You've got a ticket but can you take my lad, James?"

Think I can manage that, yes. Tickets are secured.

It's been a while since my last Goodison visit as a 19-year-old pimply student, in 1985. The best two teams in the land. Unbelievably we were three-up at half-time and joyous. Everton then got two second half goals and I was almost in tears as we missed chance after chance to put the game to bed but just held on for the win. Would this game offer the same level of drama?

As it's a 12:30 kick-off my internal debate starts – get a train from Crewe or drive the 45 miles up the M6? Over the last few years the train has won hands down as it takes under 40 minutes. Too many car journeys crawling past Knutsford and the Thelwall viaduct have put me off 3pm kick-offs for years. However this is an early start so I leave at 9am and fly up the motorway, as most of the good folk of Cheshire enjoy a Saturday morning lie-in and leave the road relatively clear.

Liam is a Scouser through and through, and says it's okay to park up near his house. He goes to many aways and all at home, but couldn't put his hands on a ticket today. I immediately feel guilty – an out-of-towner using two scarce Liverpool away spots. On arrival I notice it's residents-only parking and am assured by Liam they've only come around once in two years and that they never bother when Everton are at home as it's less of an issue.

It's tipping down but Liam drives us to *Gorgy Porgies* for breakfast. Great scran – very reasonably priced, and opposite the Kop. We debate what actually matters today and come to an agreement that no injuries, the top players rested and having a go are top of that list, and a draw with a scratch 11 is more than acceptable.

James and I leave the café and stroll through Stanley Park towards Goodison, which neither of us have done before. We arrive pretty soaked but not to worry. I know where we are going and lead James to the Park End.

No sign of our entrance number 57 though, so we double back and bump into LFC stewards who show us where we should be going. It's in a different stand. Who would have thought anything would change in 33 years?

Going inside is like travelling back in time. Exposed iron beams thickly painted in royal blue lead upstairs to a stand with wooden floorboards. The roof is low and there's even a stanchion restricting the view ... but I like it. It brings back memories. I tell James that the atmosphere could be fantastic in such an old-style stadium.

We receive news of the teams. I'm always the glass-half-empty man and suggest we will struggle to score. The pitch is so sodden that the ball isn't zipping across the surface and Sam Allardyce is such a negative manager – it points to a low-scoring afternoon. I like a bet but acknowledge I lose money (like most gamblers), so place a restricted but cheeky fiver on nil-nil at 10/1 on my phone.

The game commences.

So much for the drama of '85 and the atmosphere associated with it.

At half-time James and I believed we were easily the better team and wondered how the home fans felt about not even trying to beat this depleted team from across the park. Eventually after 75 minutes Big Sam decided to push his team forward and look for a win. The pessimist inside surfaces quickly and I'm convinced another bet is doomed as Everton attack. The final whistle just like in '85 brings enormous relief. We stroll back quietly with 40,000 subdued home supporters.

No parking fine either – bonus. Ticket, food and fuel paid for with the winnings, and a point away under difficult circumstances, so a good day all round.

Paul Tomkins, April 7th, 2018

Derbies are essentially all about dick-swinging. The bigger picture must always come before local pride, even if the latter feels intense in the moment, and in the days after. Winning wars is always more important than winning *battles*, and it's easy to get bogged down in battles.

In this one, Liverpool had a player starting his first league game for two-and-a-half years, and another his first for almost a year; plus a youngster making only his fifth Premier League start, and a centre-back at left-back after an injury to the left-back in the warm-up, on the back of a massive game on Wednesday. Liverpool played an intense match less than three days earlier, and aside from a late period when the Reds' legs went, there was only one team playing any football. Everton, at home, were mostly a shambles. Wayne Rooney played like a man who'd had too many beers and walked into a lamppost.

The truth is, derbies often mean more to the side with nothing else to play for; just as worrying about petty local differences is usually confined to those with nothing else in their lives. If this was Everton's "cup final", then Liverpool are three (difficult) games away from playing in the most meaningful cup final in European club football. (And even if Liverpool don't reach that final, they at least got themselves in with a shout.)

While we all rejoiced at thumping Everton 4-0 a couple of seasons ago, the fact was that Everton had a cup semi-final a few days later. Of course, Liverpool were in the Europa League semis at the time too, but it was eight days away, rather than three. Everton's minds were clearly on a rare shot at something meaningful.

As such, history paints it as a hollow victory, as sweet as it tasted at the time. It didn't alter anything; Everton's season petered out after losing to Man United in that semi and Liverpool finished 13 points ahead, having reached two cup finals. So maybe derbies are more like junk food: they feel great at the time, but often do you no good.

Paul Tomkins, April 9th, 2018

I can't help but feel it could be hard for the Reds to be brave at the Etihad tomorrow, as Liverpool go there with a comfort blanket – the cushion of a three-goal lead – that could feel horrible if yanked away.

Liverpool have got themselves into a great position to progress, but it's only a *position*, with 90 minutes to play. City essentially have nothing to lose, and while Liverpool are capable of getting a result, you should always be wary of great sides with nothing to lose.

Paris St Germain also provide a stark reminder that even a 4-0 home leg victory might not be enough against a top side at their place; and while Man City aren't at Barcelona's uniquely high level of experience, they could benefit in the way Barcelona did at home from a goal after three minutes, an own goal, two penalties and two goals in added time. (Or from a sending off for a high boot, for instance.)

So I don't want to dampen spirits – just make sure everyone is at ease with the possible prospect of City turning it around – maybe by skill, maybe by luck – and that it won't necessarily be due to any glaring Liverpool deficiencies.

I think it's why managers are always so keen to lower expectations – to remove the pressure, and to make any subsequent failure less of a body blow – but a good manager will only look to tamp down expectations rather than try to drag them to such a low level that, say, losing 2-0 at Goodison Park is utopia (copyright Roy Hodgson, 2010).

Perhaps counterintuitively, my hopes are raised slightly by the fact that Liverpool have already lost 5-0 at City (albeit with 10 men), and so there should be no excuse for complacency. I don't think you'd ever get that from Jürgen Klopp anyway. Ahead of the game he recounted his own near-miraculous turnaround from his time in Germany.

Paul Tomkins, April 10th, 2018

To be honest, I thought Liverpool would struggle tonight, and in fairness the first half confirmed my worst fears. Liverpool got lucky with the disallowed Man City "offside" goal, but I thought on City's early, early goal that Raheem Sterling had clearly barged into Virgil van Dijk's chest at the moment the Dutchman had only one leg on the floor (as he was kicking the ball). That said, having moaned about English refs all season, given Liverpool's historically bad run with penalties awarded and conceded (the worst in its entire 126-year history when compared against goals scored and goals conceded), this ref was a bit of a law unto himself.

But for Liverpool to beat Man City 5-1 over two legs, *winning both games?* And deservedly so? That's a mauling. Liverpool have beaten City for the third time in 2018, and it's only April. And make no mistake – this is a *great* Man City side. It's even more remarkable after City scored within two minutes.

Liverpool were 10th when Jürgen Klopp was appointed two-and-a-half years ago, and while there's no way he took charge of only the 10th-best team or squad in England, the entire previous season had been a washout too.

The Reds had finished 6th, with 62 points but a scarcely believable +4 goal difference. Right now the Reds have a goal difference that is *ten times* better, and are already on 67 points, despite a much greater number of Champions League games than in the abortive group stage failure of 2014/15. And Liverpool have the youngest average age of any Premier League team this season, at just over 24.

Klopp took a struggling, marooned, one-paced team to two cup finals, including navigating a series of Europa League draws that were tougher than anything Bayern Munich have faced in this season's Champions League knockout rounds. At the same time Klopp took the Reds a couple of places up the league table, even whilst potentially sacrificing points by focusing on big European games. When he arrived, after eight games, the Reds had a negative goal difference, to go with the measly +4 of the entire previous season. In Brendan Rodgers' final 46 league games the cumulative goal difference was +2. That is clearly mid-table performance.

In his first full season Klopp had very few cup games, and steered the Reds to 4th with 76 points (a tally the Reds had only previously hit five times in the Premier League era) and a goal difference of +36. An improvement of 14 points and +32 goals can be put into context by noting that a drop of 14 points would have been close to a relegation battle; so while 14 points doesn't seem a massive amount, it's quite a lot when assuming that even some of the worst Premier League sides can often expect 40 points in a season. Even Manchester City's miraculous improvement this season may only be worth 14 points.

It's also worth reminding ourselves, one more time, how Liverpool had to fend off the overtures of Barcelona for Philippe Coutinho last summer (which the Reds rebuffed), before the player finally insisted – at the second time of asking – that he be sold. It didn't derail the start of the season but it didn't help. And it didn't derail the second half of the season. It did leave one less player to call upon, and a great one at that; but Virgil van Dijk was always likely to be even more important, and there's a bigger transfer budget this summer as a result of Coutinho's exit. Liverpool tried twice to get Naby Keita and at least we can look forward to his arrival in a couple of months.

As I've said a few times lately, my hunch is that from now on no one important to the club's progress will be sold. It's just a hunch, and not connected to any inside track from the club. It's hard to say anything with 100% certainty about football. But I feel like the Barcelona thing was not out of the blue, and had been in the background for two or three years. It was no surprise.

But Emre Can aside, everyone is under a long contract, and I don't think they will hurry to follow Coutinho's lead. For starters, Virgil van Dijk turned down the chance to go to City and *chose* Liverpool; and like Mo Salah, he has just arrived. I don't think clubs like Real Madrid or Barcelona would be prepared to pay whatever Liverpool's "crazy, not for sale" price would be on the marvellous Egyptian. He'll be 26 in the summer, and isn't as marketable as a Brazilian, and they seem to care about those things, especially with the Nike connections. (But here's a deal: Madrid can have Mo in return for letting us win the Champions League this year!)

If anything, Liverpool's mounting injury crisis has struck during a busy time for the third season running, but I think a lot of teams will rack up absentees during hectic schedules. All clubs will have periods – maybe just through bad luck, irrespective of fixture clog – where a number of players will be out at once.

Liverpool's squad has looked big enough all season, in terms of the XIs never getting paper-thin, but season-ending injuries in similar positions can take their toll on anyone. What would Manchester City have done, for example, had both Sergio Agüero and Gabriel Jesus been struck down for months at the same time? Would City be anywhere near as good with Kevin de Bruyne and David Silva both out for three or four months?

A key point was that the Liverpool squad looked fine *at the time*. The loans of the U23 midfielders – essential to their development if not getting in the match-day 18 at Liverpool – meant a gap in terms of seniority and experience when it came to filling the bench against Everton. But it's good for the lads who made the bench, and it's helping Marko Grujić and Harry Wilson to be playing competitive football in front of crowds of 20,000-30,000. Along with Ovie Ejaria, they are too good for Liverpool's U23s, who were walking the league until the best players were loaned out.

Nathaniel Clyne's return has been timely, and I was overjoyed to see Danny Ings play in a Champions League quarter-final. For sheer determination he deserves that. Ben Woodburn made the bench, and there's just so much youthful vitality about this side. And some *cojones*, too.

The character cannot be underestimated, especially on a night when Barcelona screwed up the exact same mission, albeit in a home/away reversal. That shows how tricky such games can be, but Liverpool stuck at it and fully deserved to progress. City fell away badly after the break and the Reds pounced.

Yes, Liverpool rode their luck, with the offside goal, and with a penalty shout for Raheem Sterling in the first leg.

But I think this scoreline will send shockwaves around the world, and perhaps make Philippe Coutinho offer up a wry smile. He'll get his league title in Spain – as good as wrapped up before he arrived – and he'll have some great seasons there, I'm sure; but the Reds have gone from strength to strength since he left.

Jürgen Klopp, his staff, the players and everyone running the club needs to take credit for outstripping expectations this season. To be just two games away from another Champions League final seemed unthinkable at the start of the season, or even halfway through.

And while I hope the Reds face Roma, right now we have to just enjoy this incredible, thrilling ride. No one will want to face Liverpool, that's for sure. Nothing has been won as yet, but the journey is often the best part.

Comment by David Fitzgerald, April 10th, 2018
Just watching Virgil van Dijk at the press conference and admiring how calm and unflappable with a twinkle in his eye, he is like an on-field version of Jürgen. Well, in fact, action wise he is much cooler than Klopp, but in terms of eloquence and making the right calls he is a chip off the old block. I know he was never a replacement for Coutinho, but seeing what we have – before

and after the January window – is a stark contrast in terms of whole team profile. From Phil's mercurial unpredictability to Virgil's galvanising presence. And I know a presser is 90% bullshit, but I was just imagining Coutinho in that press conference instead of big Virg; he would have had a communications aide nursing him through against the blinking cameras and daft questions. At the end of it LFC would be left with an atmosphere of vulnerability instead of the calm exuded by van Dijk which can spread to the whole team.

With the strong likelihood of Gini Wijnaldum playing the No 6 role, I'm also massively encouraged that his countryman is just behind him shouting instructions (in Dutch?). From that Everton showing, Wijnaldum has the potential to bring some attacking flair to the role as well as giving us a few heart attacks. It just might suit the game requirements, making us a little more unpredictable than with Jordan Henderson, and likely to spring surprise attacks. Also Wij's speed and quick feet could be useful against the tricky City players. He's not so good at picking out long range passes but is good at getting it to someone who can – like van Dijk. I think they can form a good partnership.

It was noticeable how Everton targeted our right flank in those nasty last 10 minutes and City will undoubtedly do the same. Henderson was definitely tiring at that time, as was Clyne with Lovren being left exposed. We need the leadership there. Fortunately, both Trent Alexander-Arnold and Andy Robertson have been rested, and looks like Alberto Moreno might be available as sub. I think, once again, their energy will be crucial. It's surely good that Leroy Sané has not been rested.

Daniel Rhodes, April 12th, 2018
There have been many accusations levelled against this Liverpool team over the past twelve months, particularly in relation to the defensive set-up and ability to prevent big chances. It's still difficult to believe the Reds only conceded once in this tie, and even that was questionable.

Crucially though, when assessing this Liverpool team I'm struggling to find a weakness anymore. If a team sits deep, the Reds can break them down with patient possession and still create quality chances. If a team comes at Liverpool and leaves any space the Reds can destroy them on the break. If they try and pass it out from defence, Klopp's men press them into oblivion. If they go long the Reds have centre-backs who can dominate in the air. The side has hugely improved on the amount of defensive errors they are making. They have improved on set pieces, at both ends. With a fully fit squad Klopp has got options off the bench. Plus, a goalkeeper making saves at crucial times.

Andrew Beasley, April 12th, 2018

When Loris Karius plays, Liverpool allow roughly half as much xG on target, and save roughly twice of much of it compared to when Simon Mignolet is in goal.

We must be careful before jumping to conclusions. Mignolet played at Manchester City, and his figures took a beating there which they didn't deserve. Without that match, his 'xG on Target Faced Per Game' drops to 0.50 per match; in small samples, one game facing the best side around with 10 men for an hour can really dent the figures. But it's equally fair to note Mignolet actually made some high-value saves in that match, and so by excluding it his xG Save percentage drops to 24.6%.

Things get really interesting when we compare Liverpool's keepers against the rest of the top six. I don't have a breakdown by goalkeeper for other clubs, but as every no.1 has played at least 30 of their 32 games, it will do for a simple comparison.

It would be wrong to get too excited about a 14-game sample, but this shows Karius in a very strong light. I wasn't planning to look at last season, but this inspired me to research Karius' figures from 2016/17. It won't surprise you to hear it wasn't as good as this season, but his xG Save % of 49.7 would still rank well on the table, and it was almost 15% better than Mignolet's efforts.

It therefore made sense to look up Karius' last two seasons at Mainz as well.

And it's not even a competition; Karius is streets ahead. The better save percentage is obviously key, but interestingly, the 'xG faced per game' figure is lower too. Any online debate about the German's improved performance in recent months always involves the name Virgil van Dijk. Yet the £75m Dutchman has only played in nine of Karius' 24 league games for Liverpool, so while the figures with van Dijk *are* better, they only represent around a third of Liverpool's current custodian's matches in the Premier League.

Bournemouth (H), April 14th, 2018
Andrew Beasley

As with any day out, when travelling a long way to attend a football match it's important to pack supplies for your trip.
Sandwich. Crisps. Apple. Water. Pasta. Rice.

Pasta and rice? How are you going to cook that on a coach? Well, *I* wasn't, but they were essential ingredients of my trip to Liverpool to watch their match with Bournemouth.

I travelled to the match with LFC London, as I have done in the past. A condition of getting a spot on their coach is that you bring items for them to donate to the food bank near Anfield. Who can argue with the following message, which is part of the email confirming your place on the coach?

"I think it is very important for us to join hands together again and help the people who are struggling big-time in their daily life. It is unacceptable for a city like Liverpool to have such levels of poverty. We go to games and spend a huge amount of money on beers, food and other stuff, it would be good to save some spending and support the food bank collections."

Amen to that. I boarded the coach at Euston station, and within about 15 minutes I'm greeted by the first poignant sight of the day. As the coach heads out of London along the Westway, we pass the Grenfell tower block.

A burnt-out monument to a tragic event, my mind can't help but also think of Hillsborough, as the match I'm *en route* to takes place the day before the anniversary of that horrendous day in 1989. Neil Atkinson of *The Anfield Wrap* recently penned a superb article for *The New Statesman* on the parallels between the two tragedies, and how little has been learned in the intervening years.

I'm sat to a nice chap called Chris on the coach, but I spend the majority of the match in my own world catching up on podcasts. Anyone who has travelled from the south to Liverpool for a match knows that traffic problems are a given, and that's before the city hosts the Grand National on the same day, as it does this year.

Ah, but the National. It's in my blood. A relative of mine was once the winning jockey. I'm not a close follower of horse racing, but when you back the winner you tend to remember. Papillon, Amberleigh House, Numbersixvalverde ... I can now add Tiger Roll to my list of successful picks.

My reasoning for choosing that particular horse was very scientific; *The Guardian* had it in their list of four horses who could win, and I like Tiger Rolls. #Cheesy. They also held a sweepstake on the coach, and people around me congratulated my luck in randomly pulling out one of the favourites. It fell at the first fence.

Despite my fears regarding the traffic, it's the smoothest journey up I've ever had. Well, apart from burning my mouth on a coffee from a service station, but I'd probably take that in exchange for not getting stuck on the motorway.

Upon arriving at the far side of Stanley Park, I head across it, past Anfield and to The Sandon pub. There I meet up with my friend Will, his brother, and Daniel Rhodes of this parish. I am immediately suspicious of their empty glasses which greet my arrival ... it looks like the first round is on me.

Dan and I head to the ground early, as we've been kindly given Centenary Club tickets by Paul Tomkins, also of this parish, strangely enough. After a pint, a carvery meal, and some words from John Wark (to the whole room, not just to Dan and me), we find our seats.

You'll have all seen the game – an easy 3-0 win – so I won't comment on it much, except to say that Liverpool's movement is a joy to watch live. The front three seem constantly looking to switch places and drag defenders around, and it's marvellous to see it unencumbered, as I usually am by the television cameras following the ball. Alex Oxlade-Chamberlain was my man of the match, with Trent Alexander-Arnold and Jordan Henderson not far behind.

After the match I headed straight back to the coach as per my instructions, and we set off. As much as the journey was fine, it was still another four hours when you just want to get home! I hadn't exhausted my podcast supply, but with an hour or so to go I decide to take a break from words and listen to some music.

The final track I hear as we head back along the Westway to our journey's starting and end point is a 14 minute jazz instrumental called 'Truth' by Kamasi Washington. I'm struck by several truths as I listen to it and my day at the match draws to a close.

It's true that I've had a great day out. It's also true that Liverpool are a very good footballing side, who can beat a decent enough Premier League team with minimal fuss these days.

But it's also true that the powers that be in this country should be ashamed of Hillsborough, Grenfell, and the fact that people are reliant on food banks in the nation with the ninth highest GDP in the world. My day at the match was more thought provoking than I would have expected.

Daniel Rhodes

Having been unable to get to a game all season for various reasons, it was a pleasure to be given the chance to see Jürgen's Army only days after their exhilarating victory over Manchester City in the Champions League quarter-final.

My journey from North Wales involves three trains (and a taxi) to Anfield – and as it's been pissing it down with rain since October 2017, it was a relief (and shock) when the sun came out on Saturday morning – albeit without the actual *heat* bit, as it was still fairly Baltic.

Deganwy is the starting point for the first train. It's one of the more picturesque railway stations I'm going to encounter on my to trip to Liverpool, outdoing Rhyl and Flint by some distance.

I get to Llandudno Junction around 10am (after the arduous four-minute journey from Deganwy), deciding it would be far more sensible to set off early and not get stuck in any potential problems surrounding all the extra folk travelling to Liverpool because of the Grand National.

As mentioned above by 'Beez', it's crucial to sort out any supplies for the potential journey – except it seems Andrew is far more forward-thinking than me with his pasta … and rice. On the other hand, because of the medication I'm on, I rarely have any appetite, so my bag's contents include: one electronic tablet, two prescribed tablets, the latest edition of Private Eye, a phone charger, a packet of Jakemans' cough sweets, and my notebook.

Most of it doesn't get used or read as I'm engrossed in a podcast – recommended by Paul T – called *West Cork* (only available on *Audible*). It's thirteen episodes long, and is superbly produced, written and delivered. It relates to an unsolved murder in Ireland in 1996, although spoilers from me though …

To my absolute horror, the first person I notice on the platform is a (I assume Liverpool) fan wearing the dreaded half-and-half scarf. To compound the issue – it's Liverpool *and Man City*. The mind boggles. Each to their own scarf of course.

The train from Llandudno Junction to Chester is fairly quiet, and there don't appear to be many obvious football or horse racing fans in my carriage. I get through episodes six and seven of the *West Cork* podcast before getting off in Chester and making my way to Platform 7B for the train to Liverpool Lime Street. I say 'make my way', because I can hardly get on the platform for various multi-coloured hats, skin-tight suits, floral dresses and clip-clop shoes and boots. Had you just landed on Earth – you'd think *what on Earth?* Looks like I've timed my journey to coincide with the racegoers, brilliant. As the train pulls up, and the official starter prepares to begin the Grand Train Dash National, we all cram into the carriages. How I got a seat I'll never know.

It's around midday when I get to Lime Street, and my first point of call is the adjoining North Western Pub which is a jumped-up Wetherspoons – but serves some good beer.

Having still not eaten, maybe starting the day with a pint of Brooklyn isn't the most sensible thing to do – but hey ho, it's full of hearty goodness, and they had a plug socket so I could charge my phone which seems to last 17 minutes before requiring a full charge these days. Again, it's jam-packed to the rafters with budding John McCriricks all sure they have the winning ticket in the National. Two things catch my eye though: first is the one-armed waitress, bringing food and drinks to punters with more balance and poise than Mo Salah through on goal; far be it from me to assume that carrying hot food and drinks requires two arms, and coming from a clumsy klutz like myself, it is a marvel to watch. Then there's the equally marvellous punter who orders a full English breakfast – and to my absolute horror – *eats the whole fucking lot with his hands*. First off he goes with the sausages, which of course is acceptable to a point, no mess, just pick it up and devour it. Then the bacon, again, who needs a knife and fork and you can strip chunks off each slice; but how he pulled off the beans, fried eggs and tomatoes I'll never quite comprehend. I decide I've been in this establishment far too long, and may never recover from the events I've just witnessed.

The next stop, before making my way up to Anfield, is a recommendation I'm sure Chris (Rowland) has made before on these pages, and that is Doctor Duncans which is about a five minute walk from Lime Street Station. After plumping for a Samuel Adams, the second American beer of the day, the barman said "it's £5.30, is that okay?".

170

Now, at time I just nodded. But in hindsight, maybe he was offering the opportunity for me to say "well, not really, I'd rather pay £3.30, is that okay?". Maybe this is some new ritual we go through – or, most likely, many have taken exception to this level of pricing before – and to be honest, I can't recall paying more than five pound for a pint very often, so this has to be one to savour.

You would have thought, for that price, I'd get a bloody Samuel Adams *glass* as well, but no ….

The pub itself has a funky and winding setup, with lots of different areas, and as I wander about I find this grandiose-looking room. If you're going to pay five pound for a pint, then this is the kind of room to drink it in, fit for kings. It's quiet, and the perfect setting to listen to the next episode of the podcast, and play some chess on the tablet. Incredibly, it takes me just over an hour to finish this pint! Won two games of blitz, after initially losing my first three.

At this point I check this site's Twitter account and notice Paul Joyce says Big Jürg picked out Thunder and Roses (66-1) in the sweepstake. That's my first pick (£2 on the nose), as well as four others to take my total spend to a tenner.

Now's the time to make my way up to Anfield, and I usually get a taxi from Lime Street – however on this occasion, as I'm walking back to the station, a fella asks if I'm going to the ground, and do I want to jump in this minibus for two quid (rather than £10+ on my own). What a stupid question, of course I do! Even better is the driver, whose clearly been doing this for years and reels off a host of stories to keep us amused, including that he'd managed to get tickets for the second leg against Man City from some regulars of his who travel over from Norway a few times a season. Except, they were with the home fans! His punchline: "I had to learn Norwegian very quickly."

When I first arrive, it's time for some food (around 1pm), so I get a burger from one of the food stands close to the club shop – before a brief visit to the Hillsborough memorial.

The Albert is my final stop before Beez arrives.

Earlier we saw the half-and-half scarves, but this place is like a mecca of scarf memorabilia and history.

It is incredible every time I go in there, and on this occasion it is much quieter than usual with room to breathe, unlike thirty minutes before kick-off when there's barely even standing-room only.

In here I find out Chelsea came from behind to beat Southampton 3-2. I'm hopeful Saints go down, so the premium we pay for players is reduced somewhat.

A message comes through from Beez that's he going to arrive soon, so I make my way to The Sandon and speak to Will and his brother about Charlie Adam being taller than Steven Gerrard. Now there's a factoid you don't come across everyday. We all time the drinking of our beer to coincide with Andrew's arrival.

The Centenary Club is plush, and the food and drink exquisite. A real treat. And yet, none of it compares to seeing Mo Salah in the flesh for the first time, and the incredible movement of our football team. As touched on by Beez, the intertwined nature of footballing cogs pulling and pushing in different – drilled – directions is a joy to behold. When one player does one thing, the rest react accordingly.

Liverpool lead through Mané, and at half-time we have a pre-prepared pint – or not, as there's a bit of an issue sorting it out! Because mine arrived a little later than planned, Beez finishes his and makes his way back to his seat – and I check my messages on my phone while finishing the beer. Unfortunately there's one from my dad saying my mum had been taken into hospital with breathing difficulties. I try to ring, but the phone service is shocking inside Anfield. So I make my way back to Beez to let him know I'll have to go outside to get some more information and find a spot to use my mobile.

It takes about half an hour to get through and there's no need for me to go back to Halifax.

I hear the screams for Salah's goal from outside, but decide to make my way back to Liverpool rather than go back into the ground. In fact, having seen him in the flesh for the first time, I must now be the only Liverpool fan on the planet who has seen him play live and not seen him score.

As it happens, tiger bread (and rolls) are also a favourite of mine. And Tiger Rolls happened to be one of my other picks. Bonus.

I tried five taxi firms outside the ground, with no luck, so set off walking back to Liverpool city centre. Thankfully, there is a taxi waiting about half a mile outside Anfield, and he agrees to take me to the station for what turns out to be an uneventful journey home with a podcast, no half-and-half scarves, and a burning desire see Mo Salah score.

Paul Tomkins, April 15th, 2018

I don't think I've ever quite seen a game like yesterday's against Bournemouth, in the way a midfield ran with the ball at pace on the counterattack and had five or six options ahead of him. In particular, Alex Oxlade-Chamberlain played like a man possessed.

The stamina and pace of this Liverpool side is incredible, and yet even the Reds' worst footballers are actually *really good footballers*. Andy Robertson was supposed to be a decent all-rounder, but he now looks a *sensational* all-rounder; his footballing skills on a par with his terrier-like defending, where he rarely gets beaten for pace or desire or due to bad positioning (although any full-back who has to attack will leave spaces in behind). At right-back, Trent Alexander-Arnold – after a difficult couple of games – has shown that the all-round skills that marked him out as a central midfielder are more effective as an attacking full-back.

Oxlade-Chamberlain can still at times have a first touch that goes further than an Ederson goal-kick, but can also turn on a sixpence and accelerate faster than a Maserati fitted with an jet-fighter's engine. His passing can be surprisingly exquisite, but his main flaw – at times – is trying to be too quick at what he does. That said, he has created goals and chances by dribbles with the ball tightly under control (even if his balance can look a little off), and also just by turning on the afterburners. So doing things so quickly – while the opposition are out of shape – is a key component of what he offers. We praise footballers who can slow the game down, but there's an art to speeding it up too.

This goes back to my analysis of last season, in that it seemed to me that Jürgen Klopp wanted a whole team of midfielders; or rather, that everyone plays one position deeper than was considered their optimal one (while the forwards are versatile, too). So, for example, Oxlade-Chamberlain was considered a winger, even though he preferred midfield. So he brings the skills of a winger to the midfield, while Alexander-Arnold and James Milner have both been moved from midfielders to full-back, before Milner tired of the idea.

Gini Wijnaldum played a key role last season in midfield, having arrived largely as a no.10. This season he's even played in a back three (at Brighton). Joël Matip is a centre-back who had also played in midfield in Germany.

And at the back, Virgil van Dijk is better on the ball than most central midfielders, and Klopp's beloved Roberto Firmino was of course an attacking midfielder, who was asked to play like an attacking midfielder from the nominal starting berth of a no.9. Liverpool's two wide-men – who share 57 goals between them at this stage – are not line-huggers who can only kick the ball and run; they are wonderful technicians who are happy infield as well. They pop up everywhere. That only works if you find the right players.

Good, positive teams have players who are comfortable in any part of the pitch – the old Total Football edict; but unlike, say, some of the recently exported Dutch iterations of their old masterful way, there needs to be pace and stamina too. In the last couple of years, Dutch-led teams have looked slow and ponderous (Louis van Gaal's Man United, Ronald Koeman's Everton and briefly, Frank de Boer's Crystal Palace), over-passing and boring the public, judging by their own supporters' reactions. Klopp's style – much like Pep Guardiola's – is a mix of the old Ajax mastery with fearsome pressing; Klopp a leader of Germany's gegenpressing style that adds something new to the old ideas, with a soupçon of Arrigo Sacchi's back-four work.

Comment by Tony McKenna, April 19th, 2018

I would like to go back a week, to the 2nd-leg at Manchester City. I had already posted about Roberto Firmino nicking the ball off Kyle Walker's toes in the first game, to deliver an assist for Mo Salah's goal at Anfield. Here,

Firmino manifests such concerted determination, and perseverance, for a ball that most players would have relinquished. It represents an edge. It is something different. It is majestic.

But let us look at Firmino's goal at the Etihad. Sure enough, a long ball is delivered up field, by Loris Karius, into City's half. Firmino contests the ball, during an aerial duel, with a City player. Both fail to make a significant connection. However, each player's subsequent action, and the differences therein, is so key in terms of mentality and application, I am out of breath just typing this. (Regrettably, I don't know how to post videos to enable a visual cue, but will do my best with the written word).

Immediately, Firmino turns to position in an area where the ball has landed. He begins to close the space. His City counterpart is lazily non-committal; criminally so. The situation deteriorates for the home team.

A defender – Nicolas Otamendi – now has Firmino bearing down upon him. The pressure impacts upon his decision making. His colleague, who originally duelled for the long ball from Karius, woefully fails to make the angle to facilitate a passing option. A shocking omission!

Caught in the headlights, the City defender becomes prey, and Firmino the predator. The latter seizes the opportunity, forcing an error, and he scores. A goal without a true assist, if you will, since a City player has not touched the ball, following the kick from Karius.

I am convinced that this style of play is an example of the intentional tactics that Klopp instils into his players: an edge gleaned by instructing players of how to apply themselves off the ball. Here, possession is not the be all and end all; but rather not having the ball, is a beginning. What a fucking wonderful different way of approach!

There is no shame in a long ball when played this way. Conscious endeavour, and application, can profit from randomness; creating opportunity. No one does it the way we do.

West Bromwich Albion (A), April 21st, 2018
Jonathan Davies

"Oi Jono, I've got four tickets for the West Brom game, mate; knobhead let me down after I got the tickets, y'am fancy coming?"

Hell yes, how many and how much?

Two days and £98 later the tickets arrive, West Brom v Liverpool, five days before my 41st birthday. My wife pays for an early birthday treat and my boys get to watch their new hero for the first time; the Egyptian King Mo Salah, and my Mrs gets to swoon over Jürgy.

My last game was Rubin Kazan, October 2015. Living in Mid-Wales and not part of any supporters group, getting tickets isn't always easy, it's always been easier getting midweek European games than weekend league fixtures – usually as my mate lends me his season ticket. My last Premier League game was a 2-1 win over Blackburn in October 2010 – the week the club were saved by NESV. If I remember correctly, Martin Skrtel played at right-back and the legendary Paul Konchesky left-back – whatever happened to him….

This is also my first game watching Liverpool as an away fan, and have a slight nervousness about it as I don't really know what to expect – I have no idea where we park or what the atmosphere will be like. Luckily Bob is an LFC-supporting Brummie, so knows the area well.

Text from Bob on the Friday night, "Meet ya at Ikea, 10:30am mate".

Having not been to a game for some time and never been to an away game, I have no routine, no lucky pants (I chose some red ones), not so familiar with the newer songs (You Tube…) I'm all a fluster! So I chill out by looking through *Facebook* and have a listen to the "new" version of Nothing Compares 2U by Prince, two years since his death. What a voice. We all listen to Prince over breakfast and the boys ask for a "quick game on Fortnite" – their new obsession. I then iron my Liverpool hoody – got to look the part. The boys wear their away kits, the oldest is in the old black one, the youngest wears the bright green. Both looking the part and singing the Salah song whilst playing their game.

My Mrs sorts out a packed lunch (game moved to the earlier kickoff meant a change of plans, we were meant to stop at the Cricketers pub (Bob's recommendation) after the match, which was originally planned for Sunday. Whilst she does that I'm stressing about the playlist for the journey. I settle on Chris Cornell live album (give it a listen, just him and his acoustic guitar – wow), the new Vaccines album and the new Jack White album.

Seventy miles, 1hr 30mins drive, we are sitting in the Ikea car park at Wednesbury when we get another text from Bob – "change of plan mate, we're in Burger King, decided against Ikea brekkie". Five mins later we are in Burger King, first thing Bob says is – "Y'am brave son" as he looks at me with my Liverpool shirt on – "We're with the Baggies fans mate". For fuck's sake, Bob, *you could have warned me earlier.* Luckily I have a red jumper in the car to cover my shirt. Now the pre-match tension levels are even higher. What do I do when we score? Do I sing the songs with our fans?

We follow Bob from Wednesbury to West Brom and find a decent parking spot, just a five-minute walk from the ground, £5 – bargain. We walk to the ground, perfect weather, sun is shining and the pre-match atmosphere is pretty decent around the ground. I get a photo of Albion legend Tony "Bomber" Brown, seemed like the right thing to do, something a "Baggy" would do. Allegedly Bomber was a decent player, real tough nut, sad to say I that until today, I had never heard of him.

We get to our turnstiles and the steward sees one of the youngsters with us (there are 16 of us all together) in his Liverpool shirt, the steward tells us he needs to cover his shirt as he can't let him in the home support wearing the shirt! Fair enough.

Luckily we are right next to the Liverpool fans, so my boys can hear the songs we had been practicing all the way up. Great view, we are about 15 rows back and can watch the Liverpool warm up. All three keepers were there warming up together, and watching it got me thinking how weird it must be being a back-up keeper. Plenty of crosses delivered under pressure from coaches. Loris Karius looks bigger than I expected and my Mrs now has a new favourite player with his wonderful flowing locks… Virgil van Dijk is also a big lad, quite a presence. Alex Oxlade-Chamberlain is the only player to come across and have photos with the fans; my oldest goes to the front and gets a smile and wave from Ox which made his day, although Ox gets a look from Željko Buvač for taking a break from the warm-up. Jürgen Klopp spends 15-20 mins staring down the opposition – love it. I would love to know his thoughts as he stands there almost motionless. Delighted to hear Salah is starting, was worried he may be rested for Tuesday's game.

The game starts and *boom!* Danny Ings' goal, couldn't be more delighted – daren't show it though, so squeezed my youngest tightly as he was sat on my knee. His first league goal since 2015, what a feeling for the lad, looked a decent, instinctive finish. Good work initially from Sadio Mané.

West Brom looked poor and rarely offered any football. The biggest threat was from Matt Phillips, the boy can deliver a corner. This looked a game we could win by four or five. West Brom were happy for us to have the ball, so many passes between our centre-backs with no pressing whatsoever from WBA early on. The times they upped their energy and put us under pressure on the ball, they caused us some problems. Salah looks a nightmare to play against, strong, bloody quick and never gives up. Virgil looks a boss at the back, organising and composed – brilliant signing. Ingsy should have grabbed a second before the break, should have chipped the keeper. Liverpool cruising this game, WBA offering very little. Fans booing every decision the ref makes against their team of thugs, they must be watching a different game to me – I boo occasionally just to fit in. Don't want my true colours to be exposed.

Half-time, take my boys to the toilet, decide against getting one of their famous spicy pies – it is a long journey home after all.

Second half, ref must have left his glasses in the changing room. It can be the only explanation for missing the rugby tackle on Ings – what the fuck was he thinking?! Seriously!? What explanation could he really come up with to deny us a penalty there?! Of course the Baggies fans are up in arms about this one, Ings must have dived. Minutes later Ings is fouled again and this time punched by Ahmed Hegazi (have to be honest I didn't see it until I watched *Match of the Day*) – once again the fans boo as Liverpool get a decision from the "foocking biased coont ref", so says the Baggy behind me.

Liverpool still cruising. I'm really impressed by James Milner, he's everywhere although you can see the Reds miss Ox's urgency in the middle. Be interesting to see how we line up next season with Ox & Keita. Ox made a difference when he came on, albeit in an advanced position. Delighted to see Bobby Firmino come on too, instantly you could see the difference he made. Delighted for Ings, but there really is no comparison between the two. Then the Mo-ment (sorry) arrives, Mo grabs his goal. Never in doubt after he was put through brilliantly by Ox after some initial good work from Bobby.

I was expecting WBA to change things up after this point and bring on Hal Robson-Kanu and go even more direct, but in fairness they bought on another decent crosser in Oliver Burke and bought Jonny Evans on at the back – Evans reception was a weird one, *both* set of fans seemed to boo him. "I'd have bit me own hand off for that £20m for that coont" says the man behind me. Seems his own fans aren't happy with him showing loyalty and staying.

Ten minutes to go and they get one back, seemed to be a scrappy one from the corner, similar from our first. The only way WBA were gonna score was from a corner or set piece. We still looked in total control of the game then give away a soft free-kick (*foocking biased coont ref...*) before the seemingly inevitable happened. From my seat it looked a bloody good header from Rondon, looking back on MOTD, Karius does look to be in no-man's land, and maybe Dejan Lovren could have done better. Credit where it's due, great delivery from the free kick and well executed header. Obviously I was *delighted* with the equaliser – I deserve an award for my acting today. Turns out there were some other Liverpool fans amongst us, they got thrown out for celebrating Liverpool's second in amongst us Baggies. Inciting violence, allegedly.

I thought Joe Gomez struggled at times (although Sky rated him 8/10), he will need to bulk up if he is going to be a long term option at CB. Alberto Moreno was awful, spent half the game appealing for offside – put your fucking arm down boy; obviously rusty and looked to be lacking confidence. Ragnar Klavan is a decent 4th choice centre-back; thought he did well first half, not so well second. Virgil is a beast, really leads by example. Would have liked to have seen more of Bobby, looked good for his cameo.

Man of the match – I guess you all know by now who. Mr Attwell, WBA. How we drew with that game I don't know, but as Klopp said after the game, it will mean nothing to them at the end of the season.

Right on cue, after letting slip a two goal lead, the bloody rain starts, so luckily our walk is a relatively short one. Slightly congested as we stroll from the stadium. During the walk back Bob tells me he was in Leppings Lane end at Hillsborough and that his mate pulled him out by his shirt and potentially saved his life. I've known Bob for a few years now – we've been on various coaching courses together, and his son plays in the same team as my oldest. First time he'd told me about this fact. Really makes you think....

Back in the car, the Mrs reminds me it's Record Store Day, and she will buy me an album if we find a record store on the way home. We stop at Shrewsbury town centre, 30 miles from home. Have a look around the stores for some bargains and find the Manic Street Preachers' new album (special Edition too) – birthday present No.2 for me. We listen to Jack White acoustic album on the way home, both boys fast asleep after their busy day. Both delighted to see Salah, but disappointed with the result. We get home around 5pm, just in time for the boys to play some more Fortnite, still singing "We got Salah…"

Genuinely gutted we dropped points, WBA were *really* shit, and we were cruising for the majority of the game. Top four should be safe, however there is now a little more riding on the Chelsea game.

Roma (H), April 26th, 2018
Nari Singh
Friday 13th April: The Semi Final Draw.

God the build up is *awful,* isn't it! The announcement came, Liverpool vs Roma. It was daddy day care, so my son wanted to know what I was watching on the iPad and why it wasn't Paw-Patrol.

That evening, I got a call from my Liverpool-supporting buddy Craig, asking me what I thought about the draw. I found it strange him calling, because he never calls me – but we got talking about the draw, and then he interrupted me, unable to contain his excitement: "I've got two tickets to the game, brother, we're going to Anfield to see the Reds!" I was in a bit of shock, as I had thought there was no chance that was going to happen; we tried getting some hospitality tickets for the Man City game but all were taken immediately after the quarter-final draw. "You up for it, yeah?" Just then, time stopped as my brain worked furiously: My wife and I bought and moved into a new house in January, it needed serious updating and renovating. The work was going to start on the 16th, and would probably last for 3-4 weeks. We'd have no access to a home, we'd most likely have to stay in a hotel and I'd be doing some of the work too, whilst ensuring my son was being looked after. To top it off, my wife had a work conference on Monday 23rd and Tuesday 24th finishing at 6.30pm so I'd need to look after our son on those days. "*Yes!*Absolutely, I'm in!" I said, whilst having no idea how it was all going to work in practice, but with these things, if it's something you love dearly, you'll make it work, somehow!

The following days, my brain was constantly on the go thinking about how I'd get to the game. I'm of the mindset that if you've got a problem, and let it whirl around in your head for a few days, solutions will come; they may not be the best solution, but they'll come (this approach has served me well in some very difficult times). I asked some close friends if they'd look after my son until 6.30pm but they were all busy. I felt like a terrible dad, trying to palm off my son to anyone who'd have him so I could be selfish and get to the game. I was resigned to let the ticket go, because my son had to come first, but then my wife and I decided we'd put him into Nursery until 6.30pm and she'd try and leave her conference earlier to pick him up. I felt bad to leave him in there for so long, but it was a one off, and that's the only way I'd be able to go. Sorted.

My mind has been on my house for the last 10 days so I've had no chance to think about the game, I've not even been on TTT to check in on the debates, which I've missed terribly. I've been waking up at 6am, trying to hack this fucking annoying woodchip wallpaper off (whilst having a burning desire to find the previous owner and unleash my rage after questioning his state of mind in choosing the strongest glue in the world to cover the whole house in this monstrosity!) I barely ate, and was going to a friend's to shower and to have some dinner, sleeping at 1am. On top of that my sister gets married on the 5th of May and being Sikh there are a few weekends of build-up functions which were organised in our family home in Birmingham – I was exhausted. Then, towards the end of last week, I woke in a panic around 2am because I hadn't booked a train ticket. I didn't want to do the drive this time because I was under a lot of stress, and had been driving loads, plus the thought of a four-hour journey from London up the M6 filled me with dread. I grabbed my laptop and as I feared, tickets were no less than the price of an "around the world" plane ticket – we all know how these tickets get hiked up for games, but I had no choice. Train booked, staying overnight in Warrington so I don't have to worry about getting the last train back to London.

The day came round quickly – son dropped off to nursery, checked in with the builders to see how they were getting on, all seemed okay. Now I could finally concentrate on the game, and the excitement finally started kicking in. I grabbed the train in to Central London to meet my wife to exchange car keys, and then headed to Euston. I was running late for my train, so flagged a cab. The taxi driver was an Arsenal fan, turns out – he plays veterans' football and his goalie is Rhian Brewster's dad! We got onto that topic as I was talking about Arsène Wenger's strong history of blooding in youngsters, which he's still doing to this current day. Liverpool moved the whole family up north so that Rhian could settle in, so the cabbie was complaining the team had no goalkeeper for a while! Got to Euston, quick takeaway from Leon, on the train, and I was off to Warrington to drop off my bag, meet Craig and then head on to Liverpool. (Craig used to live in London too, and we'd travel up together, but recently, his wife, who is Irish, found a good job in Dublin, so the whole family relocated. He flew into Manchester Airport on the Monday.)

Got into Liverpool around 5pm, about an hour later than planned as some trains from Warrington were cancelled. Once in Liverpool there were no taxis arriving to pick people up, so we decided to grab a stadium coach instead. Unfortunately we missed the arrival of the team bus, which we really wanted to see. Craig had opted for the lowest available hospitality tickets, at a very cheap £260! Unfortunately this is modern day football, it's just so expensive. Even a normal Premier League match will easily set me back £100 for the ticket and travel, and that's without food taken into account. But with the final being in Kiev, I didn't feel like I wanted to go there. I had been to Basel for the Europa League final, which was good, and having travelled around Europe a lot, I felt safe, but Ukraine isn't well known for their hospitality towards football supporters, so I was happy to spend the money to go to one European match in this current campaign. We had to pick up our ticket at The Village next to the Sandon pub. You do get a complimentary drink and hot food, though I can't say it blew me away. The food was … meh, and there were around four people there, so we had a quick bite to eat and made our way to the ground. The petrol station on Walton Breck Road just by the ground was taken over by youths, some of who were sat on top of the pumps chanting *Allez Allez Allez*, and were very quickly surrounded by police officers in horses. As we were walking to the ground we had to pass the away section, a few bottles were being hurled in our direction, with some being thrown back in theirs. I said to Craig that I was protected with my turban, but he'd better get inside quickly. (On a serious note, we found out after the game that a Liverpool supporter was in critical condition after an attack – so sad to hear. We later found out that he's from a town called Dunboyne, which is about 10 mins from where Craig has moved to – our thoughts and prayers go out to him and his family at this time.)

We got to our seats just before 7pm, the stadium was in good voice, there was a really positive atmosphere around us, everyone seemed excited. We were in the Anfield Road end, upper tier, with a decent view of the pitch, so we were happy. I've never been to a European night at Anfield in the Champions League, so for me, the noise was off the scale, *You'll Never Walk Alone* seemed like it went on for ages! I can't comment on how it compared to Chelsea in 2005 and the recent Man City game, but for me, it was spine-tingling stuff, it blew me away. When Mo Salah scored, everyone around us was hugging and shouting; I really love it when the whole stadium embraces each other, strangers, all with their own unique experience, coming together to celebrate a moment, it's such a fantastic feeling. For the second goal, the guys behind me were enthusiastically pushing and pulling me in joy, and I nearly lost my footing! After the 3rd goal, I actually couldn't jump and cheer anymore, as I was exhausted – I was just in awe at what we were witnessing, grinning from ear to ear. I felt like sobbing! (For the record I didn't!)

The mood was slightly deflated after their two goals when the Reds had been 5-0 ahead, but still, to score five goals in a Champions League semi-final is just incredible. I cannot see how they stop us from scoring in Rome.

We stayed after the final whistle for a little bit, took some selfies and then headed back to the hospitality area, where we caught some *BT Sport* highlights whilst eating prawn sandwiches.

There was an edginess outside after the match, lots of groups of men hanging around in clusters, looking very menacing, so Craig and I decided we get out of there ASAP (though we hadn't at this point found out about the barbaric attack). We hopped on the stadium bus to the city centre; everyone was still singing so the atmosphere was good. Hopped on the last train to Manchester Piccadilly, Warrington was the penultimate stop, and the train seemed like it was travelling at 5mph. We were stood in the aisle, one guy was who was sitting by us started throwing up all on himself, on his phone and on the seat. He then fell back to sleep. I wonder what he remembers from the game?! Surely that can't be worth it, right? The sight of him made me feel quite faint, and I nearly passed out, until I was offered a seat and some water by a very nice man. Having been stood the whole game and the amount of emotional energy invested, plus the singing, I think something had to give.

Got back to our room around midnight, lights out at 1am after a post-match debrief. I had an early train booked back to London so I was awake within a few hours, with the "Mo Salah" song ringing round my head. I grabbed some breakfast and jumped on the train, with a feeling of happiness and joy, but also sadness at my experience coming to an end and having to be reunited with that *fucking woodchip wallpaper!*

Come on red men, let's get Klopp's face permanently on a flag for next season eh?!

Torbjørn Eriksen
To give you a broader background of my day at the match, I must begin the report on Saturday in Oslo. Liverpool at West Brom on TV early afternoon, and then late night concert with The Waterboys, Mike Scott of course being my second Scottish hero of the 1980s (after Kenny Dalglish), and providing the soundtrack for my journey to Anfield. (Edit: My pedantic, proofreading travelmate points out that Alan Hansen was a Scot as well.)

I did my regular match-day routine of waking up, spending the waiting hours by reading the TTT preview and all the insightful comments, and then head off to my local pub to meet my mates.

On any given LFC matchday I guess there are at least 30 pubs in Oslo crowded with mental Liverpool-fans. In a country of five million people, around 40,000 are members of Liverpool Supporters Club Norway – the largest branch outside of England, Ireland included.

Most Norwegians in fact have stronger allegiance to an English club than to their local club. There is actually such a thing as Blyth Spartans FC Norway, with two souls and counting. The reason is that our public (and at that time the only) broadcaster started showing a weekly English game in 1969, and this became the only entertainment for us who grew up with black and white TV in Norway during the 1970s. In the analytical spirit of this forum, I also offer an auxiliary hypothesis: namely the general quality of Norwegian football. We have John Arne Riise and Ole Gunnar Solskjær, but our proudest and only claim to fame is beating England in 1981. (Provoking the legendary commentator's rant: "Lord Nelson! Lord Beaverbrook! Sir Winston Churchill! Sir Anthony Eden! Clement Attlee! Henry Cooper! Lady Diana! Maggie

Thatcher – can you hear me, Maggie Thatcher! Your boys took one hell of a beating!")

To underline just how far the passion can go: the unofficial archbishop of the Norwegian branch moved to Anfield Road when he was 18, married and named his first born daughter "TIA". I've also heard about a Norwegian with a dog called "Biscan" (The Norwegian word for nice dog is "bisken".) Then we have a friend of mine who is 47 and has visited Anfield 47 times. He is by no means rich, but not married either.

The word "Scouse" probably originates from the Norwegian national dish "lapskaus", a stew spread by Norwegian sailors in the 19th century. At least, that's what we Norwegian Kopites tell each other.

At the concert the strangest thing happened. In what must have been a first at a Waterboys gig, the crowd did not yell and demand "Red Army Blues". At the time I took this as a very good omen.

On Monday "I packed my bags, Brushed my cap, Walked out into the world", and boarded the original SAS. This being a midweek match, the passengers were a good mix of 1/3-baldish Tomkins, 1/3 greyish Eriksens and the last third a blend of both. Then we did what Norwegians who meet abroad do: look at each other, start drinking (Carlsberg, as a matter of principle) and then a little talking when it is time to disembark.

Travelling from Norway, unfortunately we often must endure an hour at Manchester airport. Then again, our ethos is not to spend a single penny in that city. I hit the ATM, and managed to escape Manchester with a negative net spend of 200 bucks.

The transport to Liverpool from the airport is either by train or with a Liverpool-based cab. At the Norwegian LFC forum a lot of people are able to provide a cell number for "Mike", "Harry" or "Jack", who in addition to being good drivers and nice company, also, without exception, happen to be Steven Gerrard's best friend from school.

I installed myself in an excellent AirBnb in Ropewalks, by far my favourite part of Liverpool, and went out for a couple of pints while waiting for my friend on a later flight. The night out was great fun, but the city centre was surprisingly devoid of fans. Almost as if the good people of Liverpool also study, work and have families!

On Tuesday we arrived at Anfield five hours before the game started. As many visitors do, we started with a brief, quiet moment at the Hillsborough Memorial. The 96 may not have sisters, fathers or cousins in Norway, but we are still family.

Which leads me to a reflection on foreign fans going to the matches, and I guess a worry expressed to me on TTT by Allen Baynes in asking me to sing *You'll Never Walk Alone* instead of pulling out the iPhone. I really know what you mean. All the honest Norwegian fans I know are acutely aware of the two main downsides of Liverpool FC being a global community: inflated ticket prices and diluted atmosphere. Not much we can do about prices except support expansion and a fair price policy. But we really have to do our utmost to contribute to the ceremony "when in Rome". Speaking of that city, I see our relationship a bit like the relationship between Rome and the wider Catholic Church. We foreigners respect the Scousers as *primus inter pares* and lucky inhabitants of the holy city, but you should acknowledge back and cherish that Liverpool FC has universal appeal. After all, you don't want to be Blyth Spartans.

After paying our respect at the memorial, we sought shelter from the rain at the club's founding site, The Sandon. A few pints and then off to receive our heroes at the intersection of Anfield Road and Arkles Road. For fully 90 minutes *thousands* of us sing our hearts out in pouring rain and dense red smoke. *Bring on your Internazionale, The Fields of Anfield Road, Allez Allez Allez* and even a few rounds of the Luis Garcia song for good measure. I guess very few of us saw the coaches arriving, but it probably happened since suddenly the crowd started moving towards the stadium.

You all saw the game, so I don't need to give you my analysis. I had been to Anfield three times before, but never on a European night. The sight of the banners, the singing, a truly electric atmosphere. I believe that the whole stadium were standing for 90 minutes.

Five-two. What a match, what a result.

Simon Wiseman

10,250: That's how many miles it is from Brisbane, Australia to Liverpool.

57.5: That's how many times you poor buggers down London way would need to travel from London to Liverpool to get the same mileage.

46: The number of years since my lovely Nan gave me that football annual and I have been following Liverpool FC. It seems that as I have got older my passion for the club has intensified, I can't explain it, just like I can't explain the reason why a crazy person decides to make such a trip for a football match.

Actually this is not the whole truth. I had originally been planning on visiting my ailing father on Gozo, Malta, around this time, and then stopping back in Kuwait to see my Mum for a couple of days on the way home, or preferably offering her a couple of days in Dubai.

10: The number of years which my lovely wife trails behind my love of Liverpool FC. Between the first and second leg of the quarter-finals I mention the possibility that as I am going to see my Dad, maybe, if we get through, perhaps I might try and see one of the semi-final games, if I can get tickets which would be unlikely. She asks if I am seeking her approval. I gently but respectfully ask if I need it? Of course not she answers, and tells me I must go if I can get tickets and I remember why I reluctantly married her, and just how lucky I got.

7: The number of flights I will have taken by the time I return home next week after the second leg. "Did I mention I was planning one game or two? Sorry babe, you must have misunderstood."

22.40: The time I leave Brisbane on Friday.

787: The Boeing Dreamliner that I wanted to experience because I'm still a kid like that and a bit of a flying geek. But it's on Etihad, instead of my usual choice of Emirates or Singapore Airlines. Why did I do that? Plain stupidity. Quite clearly they are investing most of their dirty money in that lot up the road, it's certainly not going to their hospitality or inflight experience.

6: Hours. Hang on, what the fuck?! I have to sit in Rome for *six hours* before I can get a flight to Gatwick? But it's not so bad after all, as I can sit and watch the game against West Brom, on my iPad, on a stream. It's not great – it's 2-0 and I am made up with Danny Ings scoring, but it crashes late on and so I head to the departure gate, and board only to see it's 2-2. Is this a bad omen, am I bringing bad juju for the team?

48: Hours from Brisbane to Tunbridge Wells, Kent. I arrive at Mum's late on Saturday night (it's Sunday morning to me actually). She is well, albeit very shocked and delighted, as she is not expecting me at all. It's a surprise. The surprise quickly backfires as I realise the house is in complete renovation mode, a building site, for her imminent return to the UK. I'll be on the floor tonight. "Oh, and can I pop next door as I've got no butter and can't even offer you toast and Bovril!" With a hearty supper of toast in me I surprisingly manage nearly six hours' sleep.

England turns on its best for Sunday, a sunny, warm, magnificent April day and we meet some old friends for lunch at a familiar pub, in the pub garden. It's wonderful. I love England on these days, it's glorious and reminds me of summers past when I was a regular visitor and not living back on the other side of the world.

15.00: The time on Tuesday in arrive in Liverpool. I had planned originally to arrive Monday night or early Tuesday so I could spend some time touring the city, taking in some sights again, soaking up some atmosphere, having lunch and coffees in locals. It's three in the afternoon and guess what, it's pissing down, so after a 30 minute wait for a cab at Lime Street I decide to head to Anfield. I don my warm and waterproof ski jacket (note to self – blue jacket, must get a red one soon!).

I walk under the Paisley Gates and I look up and around. I'm giddy, I feel a little light-headed right now, I can't quite believe I'm here, but it's raining so I head to the Megastore and support the club with a few purchases for the family to take home.

02540: This is the number of the plaque that I have been given instructions to seek out and photograph by my friend Adrian. Adrian also lives in Brisbane but is also of this parish, "Queenslander" and I met him through TTT. Despite originally hailing from New South Wales, what we would refer to as a 'cockroach; in Brisbane, he is a top bloke and we have shared some enjoyable time over the last couple of years since we met to see Liverpool in Sydney last year,

96: I head up to find the Hillsborough Memorial, and I seek a little shelter from the rain. I chastise myself for this, here of all places. I'm sure any one of those 96 and probably all of them would gladly stand in the rain outside Anfield on a European night – and so I step back into it.

I head downstairs looking for "NickM" of this parish; apparently he looks like a drowned rat, easy to spot then in a sea of drowned rats. He is wearing the orange kit, which I have to say I'm quite keen on. Certainly without it we would never have found each other, as my red beanie with tiny words *LFC Sydney 2017* was a pathetic effort for recognition. Eureka it's Nick, we chat and talk about the team, the game, bit of this and bit of that and we start heading to the stadium. It's great to meet another TTTer and put a face to a post that I can relate to. As we walk a bit of action seems to be occurring on the streets, we tut and question the idiots running to the problem, in the opposite direction to the stadium. But it's all good and I head off to the Anfield Road end. Thank you Nick, great to meet you.

I'm in my seat, if I'm honest it's not everything I had hoped it would be. Nick had warned me, but you see I've been a bit spoilt over the years with some of the sporting events I've attended. But honestly … I didn't care, I could have been in the toilet and been happy. I'm at Anfield for a European Cup semi-final – it just doesn't get much better than this. It's filling fast as kick-off approaches. I wasn't nervous, almost serene, not cocky but somehow confident. I was just very very happy. I didn't film *You'll Never Walk Alone* Allen, but I did sing it, shout it maybe. *Allez Allez Allez* rings out and finally we are underway.

20 or so: Those first 20 minutes are ok, we haven't hit our blitzkrieg button but I feel we are sounding them out. Roma look like they are settling in, they hit the bar —shit, what happened there?! I am gutted when Alex Oxlade-Chamberlain is injured, I am a fan, but the impact of Gini Wijnaldum in my opinion is instant and significant.

Sadio Mané has a couple of good chances but doesn't take them; clearly he is not held in the same regard as Mo Salah at this point and I sense those around me are disappointed with him. I'm not, I see the work rate and the chaos he is causing. It was good to be behind the goal for a change, as opposed to side on with the TV; it's so much better for getting a feel of movement on the pitch.

187 bpm at 35': The first is not a good figure and is a heart rate measurement. The second is the time on the clock that causes the first. Roberto Firmino plays an easy ball to Salah, but instinctively I know this is different, Salah is standing in an ocean of space. He strikes it and I watch despite all those standing in front of me as it sails. Momentarily I lose the ball but it hits the underside of the bar in the corner and bounces in. There is an explosion, it's ballistic alright. I am standing on my seat bashing the roof of

the stand with both hands, people around me are banging the rear wall of the stand. People jumping, stamping the floor, hugging, high-fiving, waving red scarves, yelling at each other's faces. A wall of sound hits my ears but my brain just can't understand it. I can't explain how I feel. But what I can feel is my heart. It is pounding like crazy, like *real* crazy, like it wants to jump out of my chest. I look at my wrist and I realise it's not good.

9: The months that I am post-open heart surgery for an aortic valve replacement, and a rate of 187 is not what my surgeon would be too happy about. Funnily enough I'm not that thrilled myself, it's why I'm supposed to take a pill in the morning and evening. Damn I've just realised I didn't take it this morning. You know what, fuck it, I am deliriously happy, if I'm going, this is a good way to go ….

I keep my focus on the game and the second goal doesn't have the same effect, by now my heart rate is under control around 120; not bad for standing still, a bit like the Roma team who seem totally shellshocked and using the same principle to defend. I try to breathe deeply and slowly, but I'm feeling fine. No, I am feeling great.

Mané finally scores the third, and those around me turn to acknowledge my wisdom in asking, earlier in the game, that he be cut some slack.

5: We score five, it's like a dream on steroids, pinch me please, is it real? I have travelled halfway round the globe for this, what if I hadn't come? The stadium is rocking, it's glowing with pride.

2: The number of goals we disappointingly let in after scoring five, and give the conquered Romans a sniff of a resurrection in their home city next week.

Paul Tomkins, April 25th, 2018

The future of football. A young Liverpool side, average age 24.3 – the youngest in the Premier League. Fast. *Super-fast*; Jürgen Klopp's wonderful *blitzkriegs* with beauty. Lightning war on steroids, thunderbolt football on fast forward. Flawed, yes; it's "all inclusive football", as Klopp said afterwards – warts and all. But after a nervous start and with a tired and ragged final ten minutes, the Reds still scored five, and could – perhaps *should* – have scored ten.

It was hard to recall anything like it; indeed, 23 years since a team last scored five in a Champions League semi-final. Liverpool were fulminating. To quote one of the Renaissance poets, "thunderbolts and lightning, very very frightening."

First the cynics said Maribor, who'd never conceded more than four in Europe, weren't very good when the Reds scored seven at their place. Maybe. Then they said Spartak Moscow, with a decent pedigree, were rubbish too – when the Reds scored seven again. Then Porto weren't very good, *apparently*, when shipping five at home to the Reds in the first leg. Of course, Man City weren't seen as too shabby at all, but the Reds got five against them on aggregate. Roma had already beaten Chelsea and Barcelona this season by three-goal margins, so it appears they're not too bad either. Yet they could do nothing against the tidal waves of attacks; tsunamis that broke over their defence, again and again.

And yet I felt strangely despondent last night after the concession of those late goals. It felt like Liverpool had lost by a three-goal margin, not won by one. Next week will now be a much tenser affair, but the odds of progress are still listed as 94%, on one analytics site, in Liverpool's favour; although as mentioned, Roma *can* beat good teams 3-0.

At 5-0 the tie was done and dusted. Liverpool were in the Champions League final. At 5-2 there's the hope from Roma that lightning can strike twice (albeit less likely in the face of Liverpool's lightning war than Barcelona's passivity and nonchalance), and that the Italians might reproduce their second consecutive turnaround from a three goal away deficit.

But Liverpool can also now go into the game with a sense of respect for Roma's own fast play, and no temptation to coast through the game. Roma can attack wonderfully well, but can they defend against the pace of Liverpool on the break, something an ageing Barcelona side could not offer?

Part of my disappointment was also the slight staining on what was, after a shaky start, one of the greatest attacking performances I have ever seen. To use yet another metaphor, it was as if Liverpool painted the Sistine Chapel, and Roma threw a couple of tubs of paint against the walls.

Roma contributed to their own downfall with an Andre Villas-Boas-style high line, but the runs Liverpool were making were sensational, while the touches and turns of the front three were sublime. Had Sadio Mané not had such a bad day in front of goal he might have bagged a hat-trick – although he still got one – as the Reds' terrific trident bagged all five goals, to take them to 88 for the season. For a player who "doesn't score enough goals", 27 for Roberto Firmino in 2017/18 puts him just one away from Michael Owen's best-ever season.

The Reds now have 128 goals for the season, which surpasses the 127 scored in Gérard Houllier's treble season, which was 63 games to the current season's 51. (That season also included games against Roma; I was lucky enough to be at the Stadio Olimpico in 2001, to see Owen score twice, although less lucky to be pelted by things from the home crowd. As in 1984, Liverpool fans were stabbed that day, and last night two Roma fans – as part of a group armed with belts and hammers – were arrested for attempted murder after ambushing a 53-year-old Liverpool fan outside the ground. They have some vile "ultras".)

The record for most goals in a season for an English team in the Champions League was already broken by Klopp's team. The Reds broke the record of 32 set by Manchester United in the 2002-03 Champions League campaign after the two goals scored at Manchester City, to take them to 33.

Five more last night makes 38. And from the 51 games in all competitions, 21 clean sheets is not so bad for a team that supposedly cannot defend.

Comment by Mark Cohen, April 27th, 2018

I usually never comment straight after or during a game for fears that my emotions shall dictate the nature of my words instead of my brain.

I am breaking from this usual tradition as, in reading the excellent comments from the game here, I note a dash of nervousness, a hint of bittersweet concern and a touch of disappointment.

Let me say this: that was one of the greatest European displays ever. Not by Liverpool. By *anyone*.

That Roma woke up and scored twice (one incredibly dubious, sigh) should not detract from the performance Liverpool have just produced.

Think about this: It's a Champions League Semi Final, the first for every player on our side. We already have a young team so you can imagine the nerves. As we, more than most, have suffered from the 'fallen giants' tag, the return to this stage is particularly fear-inducing, as the spectre of failure and missed chances waits at the door for all of our players, fans, owners, everyone. This could be a cataclysmic game for us, and we know it.

It is also, vitally, a generationally huge match for Roma. This is important because, following their utterly brilliant and miraculous victory over Barcelona in a tie they dominated from start to finish, they must have felt a sense of destiny. There is no doubt in my mind that this was the club's biggest match in 34 years.

Against this backdrop of extraordinary focus and desire from both teams prior to this game, for one of them to be 5-0 up on 70 minutes beggars belief. Truly.

Just how brilliant were we? Just how brilliant were we!

Well, I suppose the best way to think it about it, is that, at 5-0, the score seemed slightly flattering for Roma.

It is impossible to fully explain just how superb you have to be to demoralize a team playing their own generational match at the same time you are. It doesn't happen.

If it was a boxing fight, they'd have stopped at the end of the first round, just after Salah's goal as it was clear then, Roma were on the ropes, punch drunk.

Others, the media most keenly, have quickly snapped up the obvious clickbait narrative – Liverpool have given Roma hope because the Italians have done it to Barcelona already in the previous round but this comparison is skin deep only.

Having watched the two quarter-final legs in full, Barca were atrocious in both. The 4-1 scoreline in the first a horrible trick of the Gods, two own goals, some Roma misses and a late Luis Suárez goal giving the Catalans a lead they didn't deserve.

Having failed to heed the warning call, Barca arrived in Rome for the second leg believing the 4-1 first leg result reflected their superiority and failed to offer a single bit of bite until about the 85th minute when already 3-0 down and out on away goals.

Their complacency was so large throughout the tie that they opened the old Istanbul possibility, where a team is so much better than its opponents that it cannot maintain a focus against such an outclassed counterpart so it drops off and falls below professional standards and allows its middling, but still capable adversaries the opportunity to show its skills – they are professionals too remember.

Liverpool will not, and have not, suffered from such complacency. There is no doubt in my mind that the two late goals Roma scored will likely leave them beaten more heavily over the tie than if the game had ended 5-0. This is because had it done so, Liverpool would have pitched up and done a good job on killing the game in Rome, with their hosts offering similar solidity to avoid embarrassment on their own patch – a bit similar to Porto's pointless draw at Anfield when already knocked out.

Next week is now different. Roma's fans will push for them to perform another miracle like Barca, but this time the issue is this:

With Barca they deserved the result and believed in their ability to cause the Catalans drama. They knew the 4–1 was not a fair reflection and felt an early goal might get them a lifeline.

Tonight at Anfield, when both teams were playing at full tilt in this generational game, Liverpool led 3-0, and it should have been more. When Roma were demoralised, Liverpool added a 4th and 5th. Only when the Reds took their foot off the gas, removing Salah and changing the nature of our outball from one of speed and precision to a more clumsy one, did Roma hit back.

In other words, the final shot of Edin Džeko lying prostrate on the ground at the full time whistle is instructive: it tells me that regardless of what fans and media might want, the Roma players know that Liverpool are unstoppable when they play at full tilt and that the gig is up.

The two goals were nice for their fans in that they gave the scoreline a respectability it didn't warrant but there is more blood to come next week, and Džeko knows it. The players know it, and the belief to turn it around just won't be there because as I said at the beginning, this was one of the greatest European performances of all time.

Roma are outclassed by Jürgen Klopp's Liverpool and they now need to turn it around and win by three clear goals in seven days against a team vastly superior to them in almost every way?

Far from next week being nervy, we are going to smack them.

Stoke City (H), April 28th, 2018
Andrew Fanko

When my brother Martyn and I step outside at 7:45 on Saturday morning, there is a nip in the air that is more suggestive of early February than the final few days of April. I've definitely been to games in t-shirt and shorts at this time of year, but today we are both wrapped up in plenty of layers.

We are driving up from my house in Market Harborough (on the border between Leicestershire and Northamptonshire in the East Midlands). It's a really straightforward drive (A14, M6, M62) and one I've made countless times, but for Martyn this is a first ever trip to Liverpool, let alone Anfield. He is visiting from Columbus, Ohio, where has lived for 20 years with his wife and an ever-expanding brood. My love affair with the Reds stretches back as long as I can remember. For Martyn, the Reds have become a huge part of his life over the last three or four years. In the US, there is no restriction on broadcasting rights so he is able to watch every single game live (including the increasingly rare Saturday 3 o'clock kick-offs), and he has been eagerly anticipating this day for months. As we set off, I can't help but think of my first ever match, the infamous 0-1 defeat to Barnsley in 1997, when Karl-Heinz Riedle missed a hatful of chances and Ashley Ward scuffed a winner at the Kop End. I am reasonably confident my brother's first experience will be a happier one.

With the rain driving down relentlessly as we approach the bottom of the M6, we start to ponder the day's game. After hearing that Sadio Mané is unlikely to feature, we reckon Ings will slot in to the front three alongside Roberto Firmino and Mo Salah (both of whom were pulled early against Roma), and we also surmise that Dejan Lovren and Andy Robertson are unlikely to start and will be replaced by Ragnar Klavan and Alberto Moreno. I reckon Nathaniel Clyne or Joe Gomez will come in for Trent Alexander-Arnold, and I have a hunch that Ben Woodburn will replace James Milner in view of the vice-captain's advancing years and the crucial role he is likely to play in midweek in Rome. We briefly discuss whether Jürgen Klopp will tinker with the formation but decide that on balance he probably won't; after all, I can count on the fingers of one hand the number of games we have started in the last year with anything other than some kind of version of his tried-and-trusted 4-3-3.

All of a sudden, Martyn discovers that a filling he had done four years ago on a previous visit to the UK has fallen out, leaving a hole in one of his front teeth. He is worried that the jagged surface will chip and he won't be able to eat anything too hard or crispy. Don't worry, I tell him, there won't be anything on the menu of my usual pre-match chippy (Lucky Star on Walton Breck Road) to cause him too many problems. We decide there's no need to be down in the mouth, that he should grin and bear it and bite the bullet (well, perhaps not the latter).

As we listen to *The Anfield Wrap*, host Neil Atkinson is talking to a Swansea fan about how our respective sides can do each other a favour this weekend by beating Stoke and Chelsea. Neil reassures Guto (I think that's his name) that the Swans will manage to avoid relegation because they still have Stoke and Southampton to play at home, and both of them are abject, but the Welshman isn't convinced. He is certain, however, that Liverpool have absolutely nothing to worry about in terms of finishing top four; Chelsea haven't a prayer of catching us. I tell Martyn that this is a very typical discussion between two British football fans: far more pessimistic than an outside observer about your own team's abilities and prospects. It just isn't like that in the US, Martyn tells me. Americans tend to be hugely positive in their support of their team, and that is reflected inside the stadium, where each and every player is backed to the hilt and mistakes are met with roars of encouragement rather than groans and abuse.

The further north we get, the more pleasant the weather becomes, to the point where it is actually sunny and fairly mild as we park up in my usual spot on Lower Breck Road and begin the 10-to-15-minute walk to the ground.

We've arrived nice and early, so there's no queue at all in the chippy. We take our chips and eat them sitting on a wall outside the petrol station by The Sandon pub. As Martyn is enjoying this typically British pre-match tradition, an elderly Scouser approaches us waving a betting coupon and pointing to Fulham vs Sunderland (a game none of us is aware has actually already taken place the night before). "Ay, lads, are Fulham already in the Premier next season?" I tell him I don't think so but they're still in the mix for automatic promotion. "Ah right, can't be doing with that. Don't like it down there [London]; you never know where you are." I assure him that the Thames-side walk from the tube to Craven Cottage is actually quite pleasant. He looks slightly abashed as he hears my southern accent – "nothing personal, like" – and waves us a cheery goodbye.

Over the last 18 months or so, Martyn has been chatting to this guy called John while playing Words with Friends (older/more technophobic readers: this is basically online Scrabble). We have arranged to meet John in The Sandon for a quick drink before the game. It's still an hour until kick-off, so the pub isn't heaving, but there's a decent crowd in there and I ask Martyn how he will recognise this guy. Martyn is concerned because although he's seen a picture, John is middle-aged and bald and he has been struck during the first week of his visit by just how many English men are middle-aged and bald. It's not something I've ever thought of really (despite approaching both middle-age and baldness myself), but as we wander through the maze of rooms and corridors in The Sandon searching for John, I have to admit Martyn has a point. It's proper needle-in-a-haystack stuff. Eventually, after a few messages are exchanged, John and his friend arrive, and a pleasant discussion is had, interrupted by the team news confirming most of our earlier suspicions but definitely hinting at a formation change.

Before going through the turnstiles and soaking up the gradual build in atmosphere prior to kick-off, I take Martyn on a stroll around the ground, pointing out the many and various things that have changed in the 21 years I have been attending matches. My brother is suitably awestruck, particularly by the behemoth that is our new Main Stand.

We go inside, take the four escalators to the upper tier of the Main Stand and settle into our seats. There are some regular match-goers who get irritated by people who take pictures at the game because it adds to the sense of us being "just a ground full of tourists", as Stoke's fans would later remind us, but as something of an outsider myself (born and bred in the home counties) I've always been more forgiving and today particularly so. Martyn has travelled thousands of miles to cheer on his team and he is desperate to make the most out of what might be (although hopefully not) a once-in-a-lifetime experience. He will show his kids the video of the crowd singing *You'll Never Walk Alone*, and maybe that will inspire them to support Liverpool. That's a good thing, right? The more Reds in the world, the better.

I won't delve too deeply into the game itself, but there are a few things that really struck me: first, Salah's early miss was truly extraordinary and seemed to suck the life out of everybody, fans and players alike – such was the combination of the viewing angle and utter confidence in the Egyptian's ability, hundreds of people around me were genuinely still cheering and clapping as if we'd scored some twenty or thirty seconds after play had resumed with a goal-kick; second, I'm a big fan of a fluid formation, but whatever it was Jürgen was trying here, it simply didn't work for the vast majority of the game. The front three were interchanging, Trent was popping up all over the pitch and we seemed to permanently fluctuate between a back three and a back four – all fine in theory, but the team looked ponderous and bereft of ideas, and effective, penetrative movement. Minds were inevitably distracted by the huge opportunity that lies ahead on Wednesday night; third, Gomez's difficult start to the match might not have dragged on over the entire game had he received some of the US-style fan backing we had spoken about on the drive up. Frustration is understandable given how much we care, but it's surely blindingly obvious that the best way to help the team get the result we all want is to keep on encouraging any player who is having a hard time.

I had told Martyn earlier in the day that Paul had asked me to write one of these articles for the site and I would be focusing on his experiences as a first-time attendee, so he has been making mental notes throughout the day. On the long journey home, he articulates these thoughts into the following standout observations:

There is a real sense of community, both in terms of the rows of terraced houses, pubs and shops that surround the stadium, and the warmth and friendliness of the locals we have encountered.

The pubs themselves are something special. The memorabilia on the walls, the conversations, the general hubbub … it feels totally unique, not just to this country but to the city.

There is an overwhelming sense of history as you approach the stadium and realise that you are walking the same streets and probably feeling a similar sense of excitement as folk who did similarly 125 years ago.

Despite its relative modernity and size, the stadium itself seems to fit in as part of this community.

The Main Stand has been designed incredibly well in terms of aesthetics, access and functionality.

On walking up the stairs and glimpsing the pitch for the first time, it's all actually a bit smaller than you might imagine (this is exactly what I thought 21 years ago), but the feeling of finally being there is incredibly powerful.

Watching the game live is a far more collective and organic experience than watching at home on the TV. Being able to see and hear the reactions of all the players, the staff and the fans to every pass, tackle, shot and foul, you get an overwhelming sense of togetherness and there is a huge symbiosis between the crowd and the team.

Symbiosis is usually positive for both parties, but sometimes it can work the other way, and the Stoke game was one of those times. The crowd was flat and so was the team, or perhaps it was the other way round; it's the age-old question.

Down the years, opposing fans and players have mocked, derided or scoffed at both the physical presence of the "This is Anfield" sign that players and managers reach up and touch before they walk out, and also at everything that this notion represents: that Liverpool Football Club somehow has a monopoly on culture, history, tradition and alterity.

But for me, and now for my brother, there is and always will be something special about the place. The atmosphere, the people, the passion, the community, the sights, the sounds, the smells, all those things that Martyn felt and experienced as he fulfilled his dream of going to watch Liverpool play. It's all of this.

This is Anfield.

April's Results

04.04.2018 – (H) Manchester City 3 – 0
07.04.2018 – (A) Everton 0 – 0
10.04.2018 – (A) Manchester City 2 – 1
14.04.2018 – (H) Bournemouth 3 – 0
21.04.2018 – (A) West Bromwich Albion 2 – 2
24.04.2018 – (H) Roma 5 – 2
28.04.2018 – (H) Stoke City 0 – 0

Comment by David W, May 1st, 2018

As someone who is from Anfield, and still owns property near the stadium, I can tell you that newspaper article in question [from *The Guardian*] is churning some very loose stats and assumptions into a vague finger-pointing argument at LFC.

From the 1970s right through to the current decade, Liverpool was a city in decline. From a work perspective the city was a one-trick-pony, the docks. My grandfather was a stevedore, he and his gangs used to man-handle cargo off ships. The docks employed tens of thousands of people, and the industries that supported them tens of thousands more. The end of Imperial Preference saw the commercial traffic arriving at the port dwindle and containerisation put paid to it all. Two men can now do in a day what would have taken 30 men a week. Margaret Thatcher's policies of "just leaving it to fall" rubbed salt into the wounds – hence why she is so popular in these parts. Poverty in the city, and Anfield, is not the responsibility of Liverpool FC.

The housing stock around the ground is not fit for purpose. Most of it is Victorian era housing of the two-up-two-down style. No bathrooms or separate kitchens, a toilet in the yard was the only amenity. Many were "extended" in the '60s and '70s using the yard (3m x 2.5m) to build a small extension to accommodate a small bathroom and kitchen. From the '90s onwards people who had any choice didn't want to live in them – fleeing to "Barratt Boxes" in the outskirts and suburbs that even if cheap and nasty, offered some taste of 20th Century living and often a small garden too. I haven't had a tenant with a job in Anfield since 1995.

For as long as I can remember the club has bought houses near the stadium. It did so in order to build what is now the Kenny Dalglish Stand, and it had to do so with no assistance from the council. (That stand was delayed for many years as one family in one house refused to sell.)

At the turn of the century the council started working with club forming the Anfield Regeneration Project. This started before Tom Hicks and George Gillett took over the club, as there had been ambitions to redevelop or rebuild the stadium for a long time before they arrived. Their plans were hugely ambitious; they intended to basically buy up and knock everything down from the stadium to Sleepers Hill, so as well as the club, the council started to buy up houses and ultimately planned to use compulsory purchase orders to finish off the job. This effectively destroyed any market for these houses and created an area where nobody wanted to live, with houses that nobody wanted to live in.

The credit crunch of a decade ago put paid to the grand ambition of the scheme and the slashing of central government funding to councils buried it. The houses the club bought have been knocked down to make space for the stadium and the open spaces – with some areas handed over to housing associations for new builds. However, further afield the council was left with hundreds of "tinned up" empty properties that no one wanted, and no money to do anything with.

Things have started to improve recently. The council have improved some of the stock, some has been handed over to housing associations and some are being sold for £1. (You have to prove you have £25k in cash available to renovate the property, and there are time-based restrictions on re-selling.) With the death of 125% mortgages from Northern Rock and the fact that you have to be actually earning money to get a mortgage these days has made this an attractive offer for some, and for the first time since the '80s, owner-occupiers are returning to the area – which is always a good thing,

The poverty and decline of the Anfield and Walton areas are not the responsibility of Liverpool FC or Everton FC, they are part of systemic city-wide problems that started decades ago and the responsibilities for solving them lie with central and local governments, not football clubs. In the last decade, in my experience as a property owner in the area, the club has been forthright in its ambitions, keen to communicate, and looked to work with the council in partnership more so than it has ever done before.

Roma (A), May 1st, 2018
Allen Baynes

"We didn't win a raffle to get here", so Jordan Henderson had so rightly said. That demonstrated to me a) why he is captain and b) he/the team believe that we can do it. Not a shred of doubt, and neither did I have any before the City game. But, this is Roma. Like us they must be saying, hey we can win this.

I love European trips, this one started like so many at John Lennon Airport. The buzz of lads young and old, many old hands but many young ones too. A group of who I guessed to be sixth formers sat behind me on the plane and their conversation ranged from Archimedes to Astronomy and the speed of the expansion of the Universe. Highly enlightening and a sign of the times, this is what education does!

We, on the other hand, focused on guessing the price of a pint of Guinness in Geneva, our overnight stop. (For the record it was a few cents short of 10 Swiss Francs, about £7!)

So Mulligans' Bar, with its Irish-Manc barman, hosted our watching of the other semi-final, between Real Madrid and Bayern Munich. We managed a swift pre-match bite to eat and our waiter was an Egyptian – he nearly wet himself when he found out we were on our way to the match. He was a lovely lad, and we taught him the Salah song. Not just spectators but educators as well!

The big day, up at 4:30am and back to the airport in Geneva for a 6:40am flight to Rome. The airport shuttle driver saw us running to the bus, but sped past us. Happily that was the day's only mishap until we got to the ground. We found Rome to be very relaxed, the only hassle being that all the ticket machines at the airport station were broken. (I mention this because failed technology was a feature of the day.)

We couldn't get into our apartment, so went in search of sustenance. Every bar, of those that were open, was showing "no drinking outside", but we found a very quiet bar off the Via Corso. We were joined by two Danish lads who had travelled with no intention of going to the game, but were there just to savour the Liverpool FC atmosphere – it is "unique" in their opinion; they clearly love Liverpool, its humour, friendliness and the socio/political stance taken by many Redmen. Another reason to love these trips is because we always meet like-minded people from all over the world, all with a focus on fun, good football and a desire to be part of a great story, *our* story. A similar scenario has happened on all our trips over many, many years.

We decide at about 1pm we should go and find the location of other Reds. It was eerily quiet. We saw very few colours as I guess like us, they were being kept under wraps. The Trevi fountain was packed with tourists, but only a couple of banners. There were more Reds at the Spanish Steps but everyone was sat in cafés/restaurants in order to get a drink. There was a heavy police presence, but all very relaxed.

We moved on to the Piazza Popolo at about 2pm and secured a prime table facing the square, there were red scarves everywhere and the maître'd, Alfredo, welcomed us with real warmth. We were in: good table, friendly and efficient service and a regular supply of beer (sadly no Guinness). Great atmosphere building aided by that fabulous *Allez, Allez, Allez* song.

Soon the whole square was alive with sound of Liverpool Football Club. The police – who had kept their distance until now – lined up in a confrontational line facing our tables. We tried to get them to have selfies, no joy, we spoke to their commander, no joy, we sang the Beatles' *All You Need Is Love* to them, no joy. However, the wholly good natured atmosphere from the crowd, aided by Alfredo and his desire to be in every photo opportunity relaxed the police, and soon they were getting into photos as well. Scouse charm, eh?

After a few TV interviews, (I made it onto the BBC and Radio City apparently, happily with no lasting damage to what's left of my professional career!), it was off to the ground – 5pm! After walking through the Villa Borghese park (an ideal location to be ambushed by Roma fans), we arrived without incident and any evidence of police protection at the coach pick-up point. A pretty chaotic embarkation saw us waiting, packed like very hot sardines onto buses for 20 minutes before we moved. A stream of very vocal coaches then informed the Romans that we had conquered all of Europe and this was just another venue, albeit the scene of numerous conquests already. The Reds' Kop choir on wheels toured the lesser known parts of Rome to the bemusement of the locals before we reached Stadio Olimpico.

When we got to the stadium we encountered the usual pathetic UEFA-inspired disorganisation. It starts by ensuring that the fans, the paying customers, are treated like the last thing a football game needs. There were three single-person checkpoints, where you had tickets checked and a body search, with another body search two steps later. This took over 20 minutes to get through and then we got to the turnstiles for another long wait to find half the barcode readers were not working. You can imagine the sense of frustration, thank God for Scouse wit, and no one can take the piss like Scousers. Eventually we are in, and another three body searches, yes three – that is now *five* body searches. It is a long time since I have that many hands on my body in such a short space of time.

I have to say the stadium was better than expected, the atmosphere started to build and you will have all seen how electric it became. The Roma fans were mostly great, we had a few objects launched at us at the end, but the overwhelming response from Roma was just a lot of noise; orchestrated, but good.

The Redmen were soon bouncing and the game as you will have already seen went from easy to tense, to *oh fuck please no, it can't happen* and then back to *Allez, Allez, Allez.*

We are in the *final.*

We hugged, danced, booked flights to Kiev and worshipped with the players so ably led by Jordan Henderson. It was he who got the Sean Cox banner and led *You'll Never Walk Alone.* It quietened a bit and then the Meister appeared, sprinting to the fans to rapturous applause and general delirium. At that moment he took another step closer to the legend that is the great Bill Shankly, that moment will live with our fans through the years to come.

At just after midnight it was time to go; another chaotic coach journey, quieter but enlivened by some bizarre driving, we twice just missed the police car escorting us, and we finally spilled out into the quiet centre of Rome. We were guided to a bar by a new good friend from Drogheda: McQueen's, by the Vatican, and I was expecting a pint of Guinness in an Irish bar (after all it was named after Steve McQueen, the actor) and it was populated by Lazio fans who were as happy as us with the result. It closed at 2am, but we had enough time to teach them the Lucas song, with the ex-Liverpool stalwart now in their side. So, at 02.15am, we finally left, back to the apartment for 3am and then up at 5am and off to the airport to retrace our journey to John Lennon Airport, arriving back at 6pm.

What a brilliant couple of days. Rome learns again that we're not English, we're Scouse, and I think they loved it (well the Lazio fans did). No trouble, just fun football and another *final.*

Stephen (Leftfooter)

A big part of the attraction of being a freelancer is that it doesn't require much manoeuvring to set the wheels in motion when any event of interest pops up on the sporting calendar. Thus it was in December when a friend messaged me 'Liverpool playing three in a row at home, you coming over?' At the time I found myself mid-way through a cycling trip across the top of Italy and had no intention of taking a break. A no more than curious look at my flight app resulted in the bike being parked up and an unscheduled 10-day break to L4 ensued. A 7-0 goal-fest, a derby and a rather turgid affair against West Brom followed.

Thus it also was when the draw for the semi-final was made. At this stage, I was on the Adriatic coast and silently wishing for Roma solely for their proximity. Fortune's munificent visage shined upon me, inexpensive flights were booked from Corfu and once again, the wheels were set into motion.

The tragic events outside the ground involving Sean Cox, during the first leg, started to cause me genuine concern about my safety. Straight away I phoned the Rome Tourist Board and Stadio Olimpico local police and voiced those concerns in the strongest of terms. Their advice was both professional and helpful. It seemed the Italians were taking security concerns very seriously. Fast forward a few days and an intemperate story in *Il Tempo* predicted that 1,000 Liverpool hooligans were set to descend upon Rome for the return leg. My blood was boiling as an already-tricky situation had now just been needlessly inflamed. The article in the aforementioned rag included the name of the police spokesperson to whom the hooligan count was attributed. A quick search of social media turned up his contact details. I sent a remarkably restrained message (denuded of all profanity), laying out the recklessness of his words and the grave concern that I now felt for the safety of travelling Liverpool fans. He responded that evening and seemed genuinely distressed that his name had been used to create such a story and situation. His lengthy reply included his actual statement in full, which made no mention of any number of predicted hooligans, and moreover highlighted the threat that Roma's ultras posed to general security overall.

I was glad that I'd got in touch with all the parties involved, as I firmly believe that voicing your concerns in situations like these can at times have a real impact.

Arrangements finalised, bike dismounted, ferry taken and flight boarded. Once upon the plane, I found myself sitting beside a young Liverpool lad, whose passion for the club matched my own. An animated chat ensued. He didn't have a ticket but was hoping for the best. Security was a concern for him also.

On the day of the match, I'd decided I was going to take a spin out to the stadium early to check the lay of the land. Rented a bike from the bike sharing scheme and checked out a few sites including the Coliseum and Forum. A few Liverpool fans were there with what I thought was, a slightly provocative flag ... It read, 'No Wonder You Hate Us', and had five European Cups below. I cycled along the Tiber the whole way out to the stadium and was really enjoying the spin as Rome is such a fantastic city. Every corner you turn you come across something gobsmackingly impressive.

The police presence was evident even at midday, and I made sure that I found where the recommended bridge was to enter that evening. The stalls were set up selling scarves and shirts, but apart from the twin scarf, there was no Liverpool merchandise at all. Other interesting paraphernalia on display was the requisite 'Lazio Merde' sticker and a more interesting 'Odio Liverpool'. That one surprised me because I hadn't realised the level of resentment felt by their supporters towards us, going back to the '84 final.

I headed back into the city and cut through the Villa Borghese park. As I was puffing and panting up the hill I realised that all the buses to my right were the ones designated to ferry our supporters to the stadium. Ahead of them, there was a substantially armed police presence and swarms of media. I saw a couple of lightly-oiled Liverpool supporters sauntering on down to the buses with a bag of cans apiece and a pint in hand! The police obviously told the geniuses to hand over the booze and the lads resisted in parting with their precious nectar. There was only ever going to be one winner and a three-second scuffle ensued where said geniuses were relieved of their refreshments. When this happened, the fucking media hacks kicked into action, cameras whirring, just dying for something to kickoff. It's a sad reflection on our society when people are willing a bout of bad behaviour in order to get a salacious story and cast us as louts and hooligans.

Throughout the day I'd been messaging my fellow TTTers, Swiss Red and Supastrika, to meet up. Eventually, we got it together and met up at Adrian's Hotel and from there got a taxi out to the stadium. Everyone was in good spirits but apprehensive at the same time, I think.

No sooner had we alighted from the taxi we were picked out as obvious foreigners by the police and shepherded aside. Both myself and Adrian were annoyed that our inherent sophistication didn't pass the Italian test; Simon, however, knew better!

To cut a long ordeal short, we spent a frustrating hour and a half getting corralled back and forth for our own safety by the combat-ready police. Finally we were piled onto another bus, at which point everyone started singing *Allez Allez Allez*. The bus then swung in a big arc and we popped up at the back of the stadium ... Whahey! Off we got. Then followed a not inconsiderable period of tedium which saw us alternately standing around, queuing up, being parsed through gates, and then finally submitting to series of searches before the Pearly Gates opened. The Champions League theme soundtracked our entrance. Told Simon we'd see him after the game as he was in a different section, and made our way to our seats.

Finally, in our seats ... *surrounded by Roma fans*. I was trying to think back to the last time I might've had to suppress squeals of joy or contain my emotions. The best I could muster was back in University sneaking into my girlfriend's bedroom in her parent's house ... and that didn't work out too well. I wished the guy next to me 'Buona Fortuna' and he shook my hand and smiled, so maybe we were going to be okay.

The atmosphere in the ground was wonderful. The flags on display in the Curva Sud were an impressive sight. Their hypnotic sway back and forth accompanied by the entire stadium belting out the Roma anthem was a delight to experience. The Roma fans had turned up in full voice and the din was almost deafening. Our fans were penned in just to my left and also made an impressive sight, occupying a section rising from pitchside to the cloisters.

Liverpool were attacking the goal furthest from us and got off to a bright enough start, not looking at all overawed. It was interesting to watch Loris Karius slowing the pace down at every opportunity, and then enduring the collective hiss of derision of 67,000 that followed. A few nice passing moves from Liverpool early on were reassuring. Roma seemed to have decided to dish out some agricultural treatment to their former hero, with Mo Salah repeatedly hacked down. Our travelling support was by now finding their voice, while Adrian and I had to contain ours. In the 8th minute, Radja Nainggolan's misplaced pass was snappily intercepted by Bobby Firmino and we were away, with Sadio Mané finishing confidently. Our support erupted, and myself and Swiss Red had to content ourselves with remaining in our seats with clenched fists of muted celebration. Outside of the Curva Sud, the atmosphere evaporated from the Roma fans but swelled in equal measure in the away end.

The game flowed nicely and although it was quite a distance away, it looked like Mané had a clear shout for a penalty when he seemed to have been manhandled by a defender. Throughout the first half Virgil van Dijk was the epitome of calm, an unalloyed pleasure to watch. What followed next played out right in front of us. A huge slice of luck for Roma as Dejan Lovren's clearance struck James Milner and rebounded straight into the net. At this stage, Swiss Red's nerves were getting the better of him but I was calm enough. It was a freak event and the lads would know that.

Stephan El Shaarawy did seem to be having a lot of joy down our left side, and impressed more than he ever had in Milan colors. His attempt to buy a penalty later in the half had me seething. Also of note was how comfortable Karius looked every time he came to claim the ball. Being both Irishmen, we wondered if he had taken some recent lessons in Gaelic Football, with his fielding reminiscent of some displays you might see in St. Tiernach's Park on Ulster Final Day.

I'd been thinking before the game that it's been a while since we've scored from a corner. Andy Robertson's foray down the left when he totally skinned their right-back set up a great chance for Mané. From the ensuing corner Gini Wijnaldum opportunistically got to the second ball, and his deft header saw the net ripple. Again the Liverpool fans erupted, and again Adrian and I beamed silent joy.

Remembering my very first Liverpool game, the 1990 Charity Shield in Wembley, I decided I did not, in fact, needs to use the facilities at half-time in Rome. On that occasion, I had asked my Man Utd supporting sister to purchase our tickets, as she was the only one I knew with a credit card. She duly did so, but in the Utd end … half-time was not a fun affair!

Swiss Red and I performed a quick post-mortem of the first half, and I learned that his default setting during matches is one of pessimistic anxiety! I was happy enough with the state of affairs and the prospect of watching our front three, wreaking havoc, up close in the second half was enough to soothe any nerves. Lovren's yellow was cause for concern, as we could ill afford to have him pick up another one late on. Either way, we were 2-1 up, away from home and they were extremely lucky to even have that one.

The second half was a mixture of periods of calm and franticness. Our front three just couldn't seem to connect the way they have done so successfully many times this season. Mané was having a great game though, and never shirked a challenge. At one stage he was hacked down by a lumbering ungulate, quite close to us, and I immediately jumped up and shouted 'For fuck's sake referee, what the fuck is that about!'. Adrian put his hand on my shoulder to remind me of our environs, but I was lucky as numerous Roma fans had jumped up at the same time claiming that Mané was, in fact, the culprit. I knew though, that Sadio was a man more sinned against than sinning.

Džeko's equalizer came directly from a breakdown of our attack when we were three on three. The ball broke upfield and Trent Alexander-Arnold was well beaten by the excellent El Shaarawy. His shot was deflected into Džeko's path and he duly dispensed it. Two-all!

The Roma crowd, by this stage, had perked right up and were now roaring ribald encouragement to their team. The next 30 mins or so were characterised by Roma piling on the pressure but without much joy. Looking at footage on Adrian's phone again, it seemed certain that Trent should have had a penalty awarded against him when his flailing arms blocked a point-blank shot. Liverpool's final pass let them down time and again. Salah for once was having an off game, with the Roma defenders doing a pretty robust job of marshalling him. Jordan Henderson and James Milner both put in significant tackles but it was, nonetheless, undeniable that we were tiring. I personally think this has been the case for the past few weeks but it is to be only to be expected, as we are now as a team down to sinew and bones. I remember looking at the clock in the 82nd minute and thinking "We're home". Nainggolan popped up four minutes later with a goal that was worthy of the stage he was playing on. Next, we couldn't see exactly why a penalty was given but on watching the replay later it was a ridiculous call. It didn't matter, ten seconds later and the final whistle blew. This time we didn't bother restraining ourselves, arms in the air … *Allez Allez Allez!*

The immediate aftermath saw the bulk of Roma supporters around us leave, and we could then spot the other Liverpool FC infiltrators. Smiles were exchanged, and clenched fists pumped. The scenes on the pitch were wonderful. Jordan's reaction when the final whistle went summed it up for me, pure joy. The team came over to our corner and celebrated with gusto. Someone asked if they could get the Sean Cox flag that was hanging over the railings and the lads draped it in front of them as a group and continued celebrating. It was a wonderful moment. I noticed then Hendo, Milner and Danny Ings were still pitchside after most of the team had went back in. I slipped past a lot of security and managed to get a decent photo of them whilst giving the boys the 'Thumbs Up'. Smiles all around.

Thoughts now turned to our exit strategy. One of my thoughts directly after the game was that Roma having beaten us might have quelled any bloodlust their ultras might have had if we'd hammered them. We spotted a bunch of corporate types and decided to follow them out as we figured we'd be safer together. We chanced our arm getting on their buses but were rebuffed. Adrian bought the last two scarves some guy was selling and we put them round our necks making sure that the Roma name was clearly visible. I asked a couple of Police about the safest place to get a Taxi and were directed towards a square not far from the bridge. It was pretty dark and I'll be honest, I was nervous enough at this stage. We passed three lads on a wall and one of them said 'Fuck Liverpool'. We didn't even look back. No taxis were to be had so I spotted a bus that said *Termini* on it that was full of Roma fans. There were some families with kids and everyone looked pretty chilled so we decided to chance it. A half hour later we were deposited centrally, with no sharp objects protruding.

Swiss Red and I bade farewell to Simon as he headed to the airport in a Taxi. We decided to find a watering hole where we could properly do a post-mortem of the game. A bar called "The Yellow" provided the venue, on the door we were asked to remove our game scarves for fear of any hassle. We got our drinks and settled down to pour over the night's events. We were that engrossed in conversation that it wasn't until an hour later did I realise I was surrounded by inebriated young nitwits ... no matter, we were in the Champions League Final!

I have to say that one of the big pleasures of the whole few days was meeting my fellow TTTers, Simon and Adrian. Simon told me about following the Reds in Australia and it reminded me of getting up at ungodly hours to watch us when I lived Stateside. He showed me some great pictures of the Liverpool Supporters' Club in Malta where he had just arrived from. They have an actual statute of Bill Shankly and miniature Shankly Gates outside the club, now that's dedication!

When myself and Adrian got in touch a couple of weeks back, I was surprised but delighted that I was chatting to a fellow countryman. Like myself, Adrian has lived the ex-pat existence for longer than we care to remember. While the world may be large, it can also be a very small place at times. Not only do we both hail from Patrick Kavanagh country, we both went to the same school, at the same bloody time! Chatting to Adrian throughout the evening was an absolute pleasure. His work in journalism sounded so interesting and fair play to him on becoming a published author. I hope he doesn't mind if I give his book, a biography on the band 'Faith No More', a shameless plug.

I'm now sitting on the rooftop deck of my base, cobbling this piece together. As I sip a cappuccino and breathe in the Eternal City, all thoughts turn to Kiev. The dreams and possibilities that lie ahead … Mamma Mia!

Champions League Final

Paul Tomkins, May 2nd, 2018

Before people get too pissy about Jürgen Klopp losing his last five cup finals – noted as soon as the Reds reach the Champions League final – consider the efforts to *get his teams there*. Liverpool were around 40-1 outsiders to win the Champions League in August, and his young side – average age of 24.3 (and with the midfield decimated by injuries, plus Philippe Coutinho jumping ship in January, and the assistant manager taking time away) – find themselves in the final. To even be in the final is a ridiculously good achievement. To have been in the semi-final was an unexpected wonder, when Man City were drawn in the hat in the quarters.

Klopp's previous finals with Liverpool were against Sevilla – older, wiser, used to winning the Europa League – and Manchester City, with their much more expensive squad and their greater winning nous (and even then, it was only decided by a shootout). To be reaching major finals is a huge step forward; and just as Spurs shouldn't be expected to reach finals or win titles on their budget (so the "Spursy" tag is misleading), Liverpool should not be expected to win the biggest honours with theirs – especially not with financial behemoths in their way. Klopp has now taken two rank outsiders to the biggest game in club football.

Klopp lost his previous Champions League final against the superpower of Bayern Munich, who had just announced that they'd poached his best player (the start of a trend), but he took *Borussia Dortmund* to the final; a fairly big club, but a club that was bankrupt when he arrived in 2008. Irrespective of how Liverpool do against Real Madrid's ageing but über-expensive and über-experienced and über-talented side in the final, this has been an absolute joy of a season. Just as he did in leading Dortmund to back-to-back league titles, Klopp has defied the odds. And there can be little doubt that he's a world-class manager.

After all, how many other managers in England have taken their team to a Europa League final and a Champions League final in the last three years; incidentally, Klopp's only two seasons in European competition? (In part because the team he inherited in his first season was mid-table at the time, and well outside the European places.) Other managers have had far more money, and not seen their star leave mid-season, but he has shaped a wonderful team from youngsters, rejects and, yes, one expensive centre-back.

And although it was a bizarre night in terms of the scoreline, with nailed-on penalties missed at both ends by the ref and a soft one given to Roma again (I may have to revisit my notion that continental refs are better; there have been five handball penalties in the entire Premier League season, to contrast how rare these decisions are), Liverpool broke the Champions League scoring record for goals by a single club in a single season. Klopp's men equalled it with Sadio Mané's goal, and beat it with Gini Wijnaldum's – the club's 46th of the campaign. *Forty-six!*

That's more than all the amazing Barcelona sides managed on their way to multiple glories, and Liverpool still haven't even played the final. When Klopp turned up, Liverpool were averaging a single goal a game in all competitions; now it's nearly 3.5 amidst Europe's elite. And the Reds have 130 goals in all competition, which I'm pretty sure is close to another club record, and again, with fewer games than in many seasons (and no games against third division teams you can whack in eight against.)

Imagine doing that with a Chelsea reject, a player bought from Southampton (to choruses of "Really?") and a Hoffenheim attacker who "doesn't score goals" and whom the previous manager didn't rate? Imagine doing it with a Sunderland lackey who apparently only passes sideways, and a boring old journeyman alongside him, and a Hull City full-back, and a teenage rookie on the other side, and with players like Gini Wijnaldum, who plenty of ex-players said they just didn't see what the fuss was about when he joined the Reds (but who I think is the most underrated player in world football)? Imagine doing that when backed into selling the club's "best" player and not rushing into replacing him?

It's nothing short of a miracle.

I expected a tough game with the home side having nothing to lose – and with so many comebacks this season – and Roma provided that, albeit in fits and starts. I hadn't realised just how physically imposing the Italian side was in the first game, but they have about half a dozen absolute brutes. They are like Stoke or West Brom, but with *footballers*.

Real Madrid won't pose this kind of threat. And Madrid don't have as much pace, either. There is no doubt that the Spaniards – even though hot favourites – will be nervous about facing the Reds' super-trident, and hopefully some more of Klopp's midfielders will return from injury in the next three-and-a-half weeks.

There were perhaps too many nervy moments from Trent Alexander-Arnold, Loris Karius and Dejan Lovren, but the first two did a lot right as well, as they develop as young players, and to cut him some slack, Lovren was superb in the vital City clashes that got the team to this point.

Thankfully Sadio Mané had the game of his life, and is coming into form at just the right time, after a stop-start season (albeit with almost 20 open-play goals). He took his goal beautifully, and even when he's erratic, he can still finish. He looks fresh, sharp, confident and the wonderful touch and swagger is back.

Mo Salah, by contrast, looked out of sorts back at his old club, the pressure perhaps getting to him a little. Roberto Firmino, fresh from his mightily-deserved new contract, worked hard, but it wasn't his best performance. And even though Salah was wasteful, his presence meant Roma had to keep extra men back. But hey, Salah and Firmino did the damage in the first leg, and the front three nabbed two each on aggregate.

Time and again Jordan Henderson and James Milner broke up play and sent the front three galloping forwards, but there was just a bit of sloppiness, particularly after the flying start.

Liverpool could have had more breakaway goals had the front three timed their passes better, or not been as greedy (and unusual sight this season) when going for shots even though crowded out. But it's nitpicking, on a night when jumping up and down and saying silly things is the only logical course of action. *Fuck yeah!*

Roma somehow clawed their way back into the game but it was too little too late, and the Reds fully deserved their place in yet another Champions League final. This club has *heritage*.

As underdogs, the Reds can go to Kiev and try and enjoy the game and then, who knows?

Chelsea (A), May 6th, 2018
Richard Thorp

Like many football fans these days I don't manage to get to too many games. I've only sat in the Kop once, and only seen three games at Anfield due to time/money/life constraints. I'll always remember the chill of singing *You'll*

Never Walk Alone for the first time on that cold February night before watching Dirk Kuyt nod in from a corner against Sparta Prague, to continue our somewhat less illustrious European campaign that year.

This game, however, would be quite different; I was to sit amongst the Enemy. *Again.*

It's rarely fun, sitting amongst the opposition, but often this is the only way I get to see the boys in action, and I really wanted to see *this* team in person; the football we've been playing this year has been awesome and hopefully the best is yet to come! This game might disappoint, with the always-present possibility that a (fairly understandable) Champions League hangover might rear its head. Conversely, it might be the opposite; we've made it to the final, and that should bring confidence!

The last visit to Stamford Bridge is a cherished memory, enjoying the stunned silence punctuated by anguished groans of Chelsea supporters just after Jordan Henderson sent that beautiful shot top corner to seal the win in September 2016. If this game was to bring anything similar I'd leave a happy man. This time, though, I'd be flying solo – no Chelsea-supporting girlfriend (yeah, I know, I know. It's tough; but she's worth it!) to lend me some camouflage.

As I get closer to the destination more football fans are in evidence, the trains getting busier with more and more blue shirted legions. Off the train and towards the station, I hear some chants, it's the away supporters making all the noise. *Allez Allez Allez* is being jubilantly sung, to very little reaction from the home lot. Police are keeping an eye, but also keeping their distance, everything fairly calm. I watched them longingly for a bit, wishing I could swap my ticket for one where I could join in with the songs.

It's a lovely hot day, stadium seems pretty full, and my seat is in the upper tier above the halfway line, a good view of the pitch and the cornerful of Liverpool fans. The warm-ups underway already, I get my first in-person glimpse of that front three together, hoping quietly to myself they'd have the energy for a good result.

Before the game there's a nice round of 'get well soon' applause for Alex Ferguson, observed by both sets of fans. The applause for Roy Bentley before the game is also impeccably observed by both sets of supporters. Good to see that there's some human togetherness that ignores tribal lines when these sorts of things happen.

They had what sounded like the boxing announcer in to do the team introductions, which was a little odd. Then, a very cringe-worthy moment at the end when he changes his usual "let's get ready ... " line to end with "for football!" Lots of embarrassed looks exchanged, time for the game.

For most of the first half the only real noise is coming from our corner, the home fans only seeming to show signs of life when complaining at the ref. Then their goal – looked like a bit of luck really with what looked like a deflected cross, bit of a pain considering we'd been in the ascendancy but it's certainly looking like a post-European performance already. Wasn't impressed with the ref, but then again neither were the people around me so there's that at least.

Half-time and we've had the better of play but are one down, Sadio Mané looks the man most likely to produce something, and Mo Salah, despite scaring the crap out of Rudiger a few times, looks a little out of sorts to me. Rudiger, however, was very lucky a couple of times that his last ditch attempts to keep out our Egyptian King didn't end up with him in behind.

Second half and there's a bit more noise from the Chelsea fans now they're in front, but still nothing much compared to our boys and girls, who are still keeping up the noise levels admirably. I'm doing my usual 'sit on my hands' routine, to stay undercover and not give myself away by reacting. To be fair it wasn't that difficult as there wasn't a great deal to react to.

The match grinds on, very stop-start, which was probably their game plan. Definitely suited them more than us, though we looked better when Jordan Henderson came on … a chance for a repeat of that goal, I hoped?

Alas it was not to be, a few more half chances but nothing really to speak of, and the game is over. I make my way out and begin to walk around the stadium. As I'm walking toward the station I see a group of away fans, still in fine voice, bouncing up and down. The amount of noise they were making you'd have thought we'd won!

Figured I'd join in for a bit before making my way home, which was nice. Good to let out a bit of the pent-up energy. Plenty of fans from both sides were videoing this standoff on their phones, and a few of their lot were trying to get past the police lines between the sets of fans to try to start something. Still the singing continued, a couple of pockets of the home fans trying to start up a chant in opposition but always drowned out by the *Allez*. Eventually someone broke through and started a small scuffle, which prompted the numerous coppers to fly in and pull people apart. Despite chants of "we shall not be moved" people were slowly moving towards the station, and I headed that way myself.

All in all not a terrible performance, and a nice enough day out; would have preferred a better result, of course, but with the superior goal difference top four is still in our hands.

Paul Tomkins, May 7th, 2018

As ever, some context is needed after a section of the Liverpool fan-base melts down, as it so predictably does, after any kind of setback. You'd think the Reds were having a bad season, to read social medial and below-the-line comments on certain websites.

How many English clubs have reached the Champions League final in the last seven seasons and also finished in the top four at the same time? None. Mostly because they haven't reached the Champions League final, of course. But when Chelsea did way back in 2012, they finished 6th, despite having the biggest squad in the country.

Does this give a hint of just how hard it is to be competitive on both fronts? Remember, this is a league with six strong teams: a Rich Three (Man City, Man United and Chelsea), and a poorer three, although Arsenal's turnover has been increasing dramatically since they've emerged from the financial difficulties of funding a new stadium (although maybe the Reds' European adventures can close the gap). It's a league where the financially poorer sides tend not to try and play with *style* (as they might in Spain or France), but with bruising physicality. Spain probably has the best players, but England is the toughest test. It's a brutal league. (Although the two most-brutish sides, Stoke and West Brom, are going down.)

How many of the last three Premier League champions have finished in the top four the season after, often when adding Europe to their schedule? *None.* Not Chelsea in 2015, nor Leicester in 2016, and Chelsea, from 2017, are still likely to finish only 5th in 2018. (And Liverpool's brief rise to 2nd – having come close to the title – in 2014 ended in a nosedive as soon as Europe was added to the schedule.) My hunch is that this is because the Premier League is getting ever-tougher, due to the intensity of the game here, and due to the fact that you can play a team of tiny ball-playing aesthetes one week (Man City), and then a team with an average height (and width) of 6'2" the next week – and with a desire to use that advantage. Germany has physical sides too, but they also play 10% fewer matches in the league. *La Liga* has 38 games like in England, but a less-physical style and also a winter break, as they have in the *Bundesliga*, too.

To finish in the top four – as Liverpool can if they beat Brighton at home, or if the other teams fail to win both their remaining games – *whilst also playing a full Champions League season* (with additional qualifiers against a top-four German side) is sensational. Liverpool were comfortably within the top four until they became the only English team left playing huge European matches, with a squad that has almost no Champions League experience, nor the depth that comes from being in the competition year after year, and/or from having shady oil money.

Within 12 months, Liverpool have gone from finishing 4th whilst having no European football, to a chance of finishing 3rd whilst having a chance of winning the Champions League.

Okay then: how many English clubs have reached the final in the Champions League era with a squad cost, £XI cost (average cost of all line-ups adjusted for TPI football inflation) and wage bill that ranks lower than 4th in the Premier League?

None, until Liverpool this season.

Indeed, I believe Liverpool are the first English team to reach the Champions League final – since it switched its name in 1991 – with a squad this relatively inexpensive, and a turnover so relatively low in the domestic rankings. Liverpool had the 4th biggest Premier League budget (£XI) in 2005, and Arsenal ranked 3rd in 2006. Liverpool then ranked 3rd themselves in 2007, as Arsenal's spending dipped with the new stadium costs. Manchester United ranked top for £XI in 1999, and were 2nd in 2008, 2009 and 2011. Chelsea ranked 1st in 2008 and again in 2012. Liverpool will end this Premier League season ranked 5th on the average cost of their XIs, adjusted for inflation.

So, relative to other English clubs, this is England's "cheapest" finalist since the days of the old European Cup; and, I'm purely guessing here, probably since Aston Villa in 1982, although I can't recall what their outlay was.

Compared to Roma, Liverpool are a big-money team; but compared to Manchester City and Real Madrid, Liverpool are not a big-money team. The Reds were 40-1 outsiders for the Champions League, in part because of the financial gulfs, and also because the club had no Champions League pedigree whatsoever this decade (with two group stages in the past 10 years, both ending in the Europa League).

This isn't even the side Jürgen Klopp inherited as recently as 2015. The team he inherited is largely gone now, edged to the fringes or sold and/or loaned out. The stars of the team he inherited were Philippe Coutinho and Daniel Sturridge, the latter the only source of goals. The team Klopp inherited was averaging a goal a game, and conceding as many.

Klopp – and the now-vindicated transfer team – have added Mo Salah, Sadio Mané, Virgil van Dijk, Andy Robertson, Gini Wijnaldum (the most underrated player in Europe) and Alex Oxlade-Chamberlain (plus the current no.1 keeper) since the summer of 2016, as well as promoting Trent Alexander-Arnold, and transforming the career of Roberto Firmino, whom Brendan Rodgers did not want and had no idea how to use (instead preferring Christian Benteke).

How many managers have taken two different outsiders to the Champions League final in the past 25 years? I'm guessing none. Borussia Dortmund were in a state of financial collapse when Klopp went there, and he took them to a final at Wembley against Bayern Munich, losing in the last minute, after Bayern destabilised their best player on the eve of the match. Liverpool had recovered from a state of near-financial collapse by 2015, but the club had to be totally overhauled by FSG to get the Reds out of the mess of 2010. Irrespective of winning or losing in Kiev, Klopp has reached three European finals in the past six seasons.

What other managers are posting those kinds of returns, even if, as underdogs, Liverpool and Dortmund had the odds stacked against them in those finals?

Until this season, how many teams had scored 46 goals in a single Champions League season? None. Liverpool are the first, achieved with three strikers who each cost less than Everton's record signing. Have a think back to the 40-1 outsiders Klopp was managing in August, and then the two drawn games to open the group stage, and try to think that the team you're watching will reach the final and break goalscoring records; despite losing Coutinho in January and only signing a centre-back in that window.

Prior to Liverpool this season, how many English clubs had reached a Champions League final with an average age below 25?

None.

Liverpool in 2005 were 26.1, and in 2007 were 26. Man United in 1999 were 26.5, then 26.7 in 2008, 27.1 in 2009 and 28.2 in 2011. Chelsea in 2008 were 27, and in 2012 were 27.5. Arsenal in 2006 were 26.1. (All ages are accurate to exact date of birth across 38 Premier League games, with the data via Graeme Riley's database. While the Champions League lineups by these same clubs may vary from those in the league, it obviously won't be by a huge deal, as it's largely the same group of players who play in both competitions.)

As you can see, Liverpool's 24.2 in the Premier League this season is getting on for *two years younger* than any of this league's finalists in the past 30 years, and possibly younger than any of this country's finalists before then, too. It's the youngest team in England's top division.

That said, Klopp's Dortmund were *younger still*. And perhaps *gegenpressing* requires youthful vim, and therefore a younger age is to be expected. But of course, you therefore lack the kind of experience and game management that older teams possess.

It's a trade-off. And that's life; that's reality. Anything good we want has to come with a trade-off: eat lots of lovely ice cream, get fat; spend money on one thing, and there's no money to spend on something else; go out somewhere, and we can't be in another place at the same time.

If a team puts in a ton of effort in one game, then no matter the fitness levels, something will be lost if they play another just days later. Energy is not infinite, even in elite athletes. The bigger the occasion the more emotional drain there'll be, too.

If you have a budget that's 5th in the Premier League, and a side that costs a mere fraction of Real Madrid's, you can't expect to buy all the top-end technical players who are already fully established and replete with the ultimate game-management skills, as those are the most expensive players to buy, and then keep (because of the wages). You need to find younger, hungrier players, and a different approach. Liverpool can't be like Real Madrid, and the hope is that Real Madrid can't be like Liverpool in terms of pace and energy, and maybe even hunger.

If you have to overcome the financial odds with extra effort, then it can work. But you also know that the team may get fatigued later on in the season; just as, with a squad of any size, the removal of several players weakens it. To say that Klopp's approach brings about injuries or leaves players knackered by the end of the season – making it sound like a folly – is to say that another approach, with the 5th-biggest budget, would be better.

The only other team overachieving in recent seasons is Spurs, and they have a young team (although Liverpool are now younger), and they have a similar approach. Arsenal have a bigger budget than both, but the once-beautiful football they played has largely gone, and the passing style no longer gets them above their financial ranking, but has them slumped below it. Should Spurs and Liverpool be copying Arsenal, who probably don't expend as much energy over the course of a season, and somehow manage to win a few games in the last month of the season? Of course not. If anything it's going to be the other way around.

Liverpool have just posted back-to-back 70+ points totals for the first time since 2009*, and reached two European finals in two and a half years under the German. Before Klopp turned up, the average number of points the Reds were racking up this decade was 62. The average number of European finals was *zero*.

While I think what happened at Arsenal with Arsène Wenger is in part due to his decline with age, as others moved ahead of him, I think it was also symptomatic of the bile and hatred that surrounds the modern impatient game, and which negatively affects the atmosphere, which negatively affects the players, whose struggles feed-back into the hate-brigade. I think that very smart men like Jürgen Klopp see this, and don't like where it's heading.

I'd like to see Klopp valued and cherished, and the fans fully trust him; he knew what the fans at Dortmund gave their team, but that was a few years ago, before the cycle of doom grew quicker and quicker. Too many (online) Liverpool fans have a false sense of superiority and entitlement, while those at the games can be blasé at times unless it's a huge occasion.

And yes, the game is changing, even within the space of a few years. Everyone wants success, and that success must be *beautiful* too. In many ways, Klopp is delivering this. Liverpool are great to watch and winning lots of games; but if they don't win every game, all hell breaks loose.

No one wants their team to be near the bottom of the league, but even when a club like Everton moves up the table, their fans are still unhappy. And I get that – if you don't like the football the manager brings, then it leaves you disconnected (and it costs ever more to watch football these days). It just seems that style is becoming increasingly more important, as is winning every single game possible.

It's an "I want it all, and I want it now" culture. It really is. I can feel the speed at which it has all changed, over the past decade or two. Everyone wants better football and more victories, and in the process everyone appears far less patient.

We also live in a culture of blame and ridicule. Mistakes are all part of the learning and developmental process for anyone working even at the elite level; you never stop learning, if you have an open mind. Yet to admit you are wrong, or to make a gaffe, leaves you open to the kind of pillory once reserved for criminals trapped in those wooden stocks in town squares, which was a kind of punishment genuinely retired for being too cruel. Now it's part of daily online and tabloid life. It's about humiliating the other guy.

Managers who demand no mistakes and publicly blame their own players can end up with fear-fed football: safe, unremarkable, possibly even dull. Managers like Pep Guardiola and Jürgen Klopp are so good for football as they don't play it safe.

Look at the ridicule Guardiola got in England last season for dismissing Joe Hart and wanting a fancy foreign footballing keeper, and how it all went wrong. City, he was told, just needed to boot it long a bit more often, be more British, cut out the passing at the back; less possession, more tackling. And *more Joe Hart*. Fuck that, he thought. And he was 100% right.

Stoke and West Brom – still with legions of giants in their squads – tried to move away from dull-but-effective football, and they look set to be relegated despite mid-table budgets (ranking 11th and 13th respectively). Burnley fans are probably delighted with their style during this honeymoon period, but as we saw with Stoke, that can wear off; it's the hedonic treadmill, where we get acclimatised to improvements. Clubs are always trying to move away from the "effective but limited" approaches of managers like Tony Pulis and Sam Allardyce; the former is obviously the most synonymous with the long-ball game, but the latter wasn't liked at West Ham or Newcastle, and now isn't at Everton, the three biggest clubs he has managed. So clearly there must be something to the disdain.

The trouble is, there's never gonna be enough "good football and good results" to go round. Not everyone can have good results; anyone who wins means someone else loses. And it's really hard to play really good football on a frequent basis, and even harder when everyone is being so critical all the time. So there's a constant sense of unease, which only makes playing good football harder. Then there's a churn of managers and players, and it's just chaos.

Which brings me back to Liverpool.

I realised I was getting too stressed about the fallout from other people going ballistic on social media to actually enjoy the prospect of the Champions League final. I obviously care deeply that the Reds win the final, but if they don't, it's no shame. I'll get over it. Madrid are a bigger, richer club, with far more experience in their team when it comes to winning. Equally, I feel that Liverpool can give them a good fight, and potentially upset them. But if not, *it's not the end of the world*. I wrote after the Watford game on match-day one, before deactivating my Twitter account, that it's not the end of the world, nor even the season. It was the failure to win the first game.

And here we are, nine months later, with one game to re-qualify for the Champions League, and one game to achieve greatness (which would ... re-qualify the Reds for the Champions League). But no, let's all pile in on a 20-year-old reserve striker (Dominic Solanke) who has played just 500 minutes of football, or moan about how needlessly hard Liverpool are making life for themselves, as if this season is all just a case of meeting run-of-the-mill expectations. No fans in world football have a right to some of the stuff Liverpool fans have enjoyed this season.

The first legs against Manchester City and Roma were two of the most thrillingly memorable games you can wish to see in your lifetime. Going 5-0 up against Roma in a Champions League semi-final was a once-in-a-generation type of moment; surreal, almost a dreamland.

Maybe Liverpool peaked then, and we'd all rather they peaked in Kiev. But boy, *what a peak*; and you can't pick and choose when you do so.

(To have not peaked in that first leg may have again meant no final. It's no good peaking on the 26th May if your season is over two weeks earlier. You can work towards peaking later in the season, but you can't time it to the day, and you can't stop players from doing their knee ligaments when perfectly fresh and in superb form. For all the criticism of Klopp and the squad size these past few days – I had several messages about the lunacy of loaning out Divock Origi and the ever-injured Sturridge, etc., before I once against deactivated my Twitter account – Alex Oxlade-Chamberlain, James Milner, Virgil van Dijk and Andy Robertson are/were benefiting from playing fewer games earlier on in the season, and Sadio Mané probably looks the freshest of the front three because he's played the fewest minutes. And Solanke is at the club because he's willing to fight for minutes, whereas both Origi and Sturridge wanted to be regular starters, particularly with the World Cup looming. If players don't want to be on the bench, and therefore look to move for game time, what can you do? Hold a gun to their heads?)

Liverpool have had a gruelling month, with a load of big games and little rest; and gruelling months can take it out of even the best squads. But there's a full week before Brighton at home, then two weeks to the Champions League final; plenty of time to refresh and team-bond at a training camp.

Remember, Liverpool have scored 130 goals this season and broken the Champions League record, with 46, *en route* to Kiev. These are remarkable times. Please, for god's sake, *savour it all.*

Real Madrid (Kiev), Champions League Final, 2018

Chris Rowland, May 25th, 2018

The first mention of Kiev comes after we've drawn but before we've played Man City in the quarter-final: "forty quid flight from Warsaw to Kiev, six of us in so far, are you up for it? If so I'll need the money at the match on Saturday", says Pete.

"Er yeah, Okay, count me in" I reply in a somewhat bewildered tone that fully reflected my feelings at that time. This felt not unlike throwing two twenty pound notes down the drain. After all, how realistic was it that we would get that far, even if we beat City? Many questions began crowding in.

What day is this flight, just so I know when we need to be in Warsaw by? And how do I get to Warsaw, and then home again?

It gives some indication of the sheer difference in scale trying to organise going to a Champions League final in a 'faraway exotic' location – let's use those euphemisms, UEFA.

During the following weeks we spent endless hours on internet research, before finally filling in the blanks after the 1st leg against Roma but before the 2nd, when it looked as though it was done. For me it was UK-Warsaw, Warsaw-Kiev, Kiev-Riga, Riga-East Midlands, a train home. We watched the prices soar as the days passed – what we had spent less than £300 on would now cost something approaching four figures. And that's before we touch on Kiev accommodation or match tickets.

'Ow much for a night's accommodation?

When the details about match ticket allocations and prices are revealed, there's a cartoon double-take. The two clubs are going to get somewhere shy of 17,000 each. For a designated stadium capacity of 63,000. The same old story: where the fuck do almost *half* the tickets go? And for Liverpool FC that is not even approaching enough. The club issues a statement explaining how it will allocate its tickets – only 10,400 to "general supporters".

Then we see the ticket prices – Category 1, £394 – with a restricted view option of £350-ish. You can really pay £350 for a restricted view? *Really?* Other categories are £280-something, £148 and not many at £61. The cheap seats.

Liverpool FC hold a ballot amongst season ticket holders – most of our gang get one, I miss out, and the ticket hunt begins. I ask the secretary of a Supporters' Club who we know whether they'll have any spares amongst their allocation, when they know it. He says he'll look out for me, but doesn't expect there to be a surfeit, quite the reverse. One of our group, Dave, has family and friends in the ballot, four options in all, so he'll probably get at least one extra, which is mine. Trouble is, *he doesn't*; he misses out on all four, the unluckiest man of them all. Instead of solving my problem, he's now added to it by joining the ranks of the unticketed. The mystery man, Mr X, who sometimes drives Pete to and from the match when the trains are in chaos, is a man with contacts. But neither his contacts nor his UEFA ticket ballot are successful.

There's a German phrase: *Torschlusspanik*, the panic of closing doors. It's used in the context of reducing options are you get older – career, travel, activities, moving house, all sorts. But it has other uses … as each day ticked past and the departure date grew nearer, with one door slamming in my face, the awful prospect of being the only one amongst us watching in a bar came to haunt not only my waking hours. Until, that is, a TTT subscriber emails me out of the blue and throws me a potential lifeline….

Meanwhile, the accommodation prices in Kiev you already know about. Row upon row of £thousands per night. Sometimes tens of thousands.

The prices were so extraordinarily high, we could only foresee a city full of empty hotel rooms. Almost nobody can afford £thousands per night, and even those who can would be reluctant to be ripped off quite so spectacularly. That's not a feeling anybody likes. It wasn't just the local hotels, it was the international chains were at it too. I wondered whether it's because they hold a completely false notion of Western affluence to imagine takers for rooms at those prices.

Desperate or not, you can't find thousands of pounds you don't have for a room.

Just to check, I entered some different dates – May 28th and 29th, after the final – and watched as £2,600 a night miraculously became £64.

We were one of many groups who had accommodation booked (about £30 per person per night) and had it cancelled when we tried to confirm it. Suddenly they had had a computer booking error. Translated, it meant they thought they could get a lot more for the rooms than we were paying, so pitched us out. We were far from the only ones. With flights and ticket prices also going crazy, and dire warnings about taxi rip offs and sky-high mobile phone charges, and no doubt beer and food prices rocketing, the whole place began to feel very unappealing, as if wholly in thrall to gangster-run mafia-style racketeering.

As an angry and indignant response to the accommodation rip off, Kiev natives even set up a website where they offered rooms in their house for free to counteract the poor image of their city that was being portrayed by its hoteliers. The Kyiv free couch site became a compulsory reference after the *Echo* ran a piece on it, picked up by the national media.

Our problem was there we were a group of seven – not so easy to accommodate on your couch, never mind the queue for the bathroom next morning!

Apart from the seven of us are doing this trip via Warsaw, there are others in our group doing it different ways. Three more, travelling by train, have five hours in Warsaw *en route* to Kiev, via Berlin, Cologne and Brussels, and will join us for those few hours on Thursday evening. Others are going via Prague, and others are doing their own thing entirely.

Another issue that required a project manager all of its own was currency. What we knew was we would need Polish zloty for Thursday and Friday, Euros for Riga and for changing into Ukrainian, and UK currency. You can't take Ukrainian currency in with you – except we managed to get hold of some from London; £50 worth, just enough to pay for immediate needs when arriving there towards midnight on Friday. The accommodation wanted paying in sterling. Or Euros. How much of each to take? What if I still need a ticket and manage to get one *en route* or in Kiev? What currency do I need to take for that, and how much? In the end we all have four different lots of currency in our wallets. Almost inevitably too much of B and not enough of C.

The sheer logistics of the whole operation cost me a lot of sleep, my mind buzzing in the early hours, always conjuring one more potential hiccup or worse. What happens if we all get separated after the game and I can't find the accommodation, when everything is written in Cyrillic? We don't know what to ask a taxi driver for. My passport and bag will be there, I can't get home without it.

For around five weeks, this issue has occupied maybe two or three hours a day on average, in phone calls amongst a dozen of us, in internet research on flights and accommodation, in match ticket hunting. Do I want £50 of Ukrainian currency getting from London? Do I want a final T-shirt from Liverpool while they're there picking up their match tickets (£8)? Do I want to check in early with Ryanair (£6)? Do I want to take my bag on as hand luggage (£6)? I try to keep a tally of (ever-rising) costs, of currencies, of our tour itinerary. It's a part-time job in its own right, only instead of being paid, you pay.

My wife is aghast at the notion that a football match might be considered justification for all this, accompanied by much eye-rolling as the phone rings again. "It just sounds like total hell" she observes in disbelief at the accommodation prices and all the other potential pitfalls I mention. "I'm just amazed you all think it's worth it."

At times, it almost isn't. *Almost.* UEFA's callous disregard for what it puts the fans through. The almost accepted rip-off of accommodation, travel, match tickets. I hate all that. But this is my club, in the biggest match of them all. I have to be there with them. I have to see the final chapter, the dénouement of such an epic voyage. And we might just have some fun along the way, amidst the mayhem.

On the Sunday before we travel, I learn that there's a new train table in operation from tomorrow which has surgically removed the only train I can get to get to Leeds-Bradford airport in time. Just to remove any lingering doubts, it's also a strike day on Northern Rail! I now need to source a taxi to take me to the airport which adds still more to the costs. Instead of less than a tenner for train and bus to the airport, the taxi's going to cost £43.

Just five days before match day and three days before I depart these shores, I finally get the news I've been waiting for – a match ticket is available for me! Better still, it's the cheap seats, £61 – I was budgeting for a possible £394. With that major worry aside and my final boarding pass printed, all I have to sort out now is getting to the airport on Thursday morning and a spot of packing.

It's nearly ready. Let's do this!

Thursday May 24th

The day finally arrives. The culmination of all that planning, arranging, booking and confirming, checking in, phone calls in and out, with those I'm travelling with and also those of our group who are going a different route. And three whose route will intersect with ours in Warsaw. In theory.

I'm up at 04:45, just time for a quick cup of tea and some toast, and check my packing for the umpteenth time – passport, match ticket, train ticket, a folder full of boarding passes, a handwritten time schedule to refer to, maps of Kiev metro, city centre and stadium, LFC official guidance ….

The taxi arrives at 05:45, on the dot. The driver is Pakistani – a Muslim, and thus on Ramadan. He talks of nothing but food for the length of the journey, in a slow, wistful way.

As we depart – the familiar streets of my home town very still on this sunny morning – it occurs to me that this familiarity is going to gradually give way to a seething cauldron of the unknown and exotic, the multiple flights to Warsaw to Kiev to Riga, the Cyrillic script, the massive crowds of people and the inferno of a Champions League final, the giant accommodation rip-off in Kiev, a quiet minor key overture to what will become a tempestuous symphony of crashing cymbals and cacophonous horns. A calm beginning to an epic venture.

That I've never been to Warsaw or Kiev before, or even Poland or Ukraine adds to the sense of adventure. I'd never been to Athens or Istanbul before but at least I had been to Greece and Turkey. I have however been to all previous European Cup finals, this being the eighth.

I'm starting this journey alone, and will remain so until Warsaw, when six others will descend from various UK airports. It's a one-hour taxi ride to the airport, where I grab a bacon roll and a cup of tea and buy a few goodies for the flight – newspaper, travel sweets to offset the problems I get with ear pressure when a place descends for landing. I'll be flying for four days out of the next five, so a large tin of Simpkins travel sweets goes into my rucksack.

Aboard the plane, a young Scouser sitting next to me tells me an unsettling story about Polish crooks dressing as police, demanding to look at your passport and money and disappearing with them.

Being a Ryanair flight, it lands at Warsaw Modlin, maybe 35km from Warsaw city, but it actually arrives early. "At least it's in the same country" jokes one of the Reds in the unfeasibly slow-moving queue at passport control.

I have agreed to do a little research on travel options into the city while I wait for Pete, who's due three hours later on the Stansted flight. It doesn't take me long. A bus for €35 and taking 45 minutes straight into the centre, or a 10-minute shuttle bus ride to Modlin station and a 40 minute train ride into Warsaw Centralna station for 19 euros. As the next bus isn't till 17:45, the train it shall be.

With time to kill, I order a grilled salmon with salad and a bottle of water, imagining it to be maybe the last chance to do something healthy until we get back on Monday.

Pete arrives, a little late, and we head off to the city centre via bus and train. Three more of the group, from Liverpool, flying from Manchester via Brussels, will join us at our hotel later, and Pete's son is due to arrive later still, at 9pm. Couldn't get off work, apparently.

We manage to find the Apple Inn Hotel – and it took some finding, you could not accuse it of being ostentatious, or even conspicuous. But inside it's quite impressive, better by far than what lies ahead, we imagine. The accommodation issue in Kiev is still far from resolved, we have the possibility of someone from the Free Kiev couch website meeting us at the airport and staying with him, and also a hostel near the ground. Neither arrangement seems either cast-iron or ideal.

We spend the night in Warsaw's impressive old town, Pete's son and one other arriving to complete our group of seven. Something to eat, a few beers, all reasonably civilised. But we know this is just the aperitif.

Friday May 25th

After a leisurely breakfast, we use the hotel's reception area to sort out my boarding passes for our Kiev-Riga flight. We wonder why selecting 'Uk' as the language keeps producing something Cyrillic, until the Polish girl on reception points out that here 'Uk' means Ukraine! The Ukrainian national carrier site appears to offer no English option, so she suggests we select Polish and she'll translate. My boarding pass printed off, we head off to a bar to meet three others of our group who have chosen the rail route, Jon because he won't fly, Andie (that's how he spells it) because after Basel where he had to watch the match on the TV, he decided not to book travel until he knew he had a ticket. by which time travel prices were off the radar. And Jon could use some company. Tunny must have just fancied the adventure. And the others – well, maybe they just fancied the idea of a train to London, Eurostar to Brussels, a night in Cologne, a night in Berlin, then this afternoon in Warsaw.

When they find us in a bar in town, we laugh out loud at the eyes that stare out from their frazzled faces, the look that the expression 'eyes like pissholes in the snow' was invented for. It's clear how they've spent their journey so far. After hugs and handshakes and mutual catch ups, I ask Andie if they've managed to get some beer on the train – because it sure looks like it!

"Oh yes Christopher, indeed we have", he says slowly and over-deliberately, eyes failing to appreciate the value of teamwork. It seems they had a triple-bagged black-bin-liner-full, which took all three of them to drag aboard their couchette compartment – and had needed to restock in Berlin!

Andie will be joining our group in Kiev for our second night there, after the match, sharing a room with me and being one of four of us who fly to Riga on Sunday, and back to East Midlands on Monday.

The train gang depart, and we head for Warsaw's main airport, Chopin, for our flight to Kiev. Fittingly, there's a piano in the airport, banged on tunelessly by a succession of infants but coaxed into perfection later by an accomplished player; a surreal backdrop to what we imagine lies ahead. Not least, we have had two more disturbing reports. Pete's son Graeme says there've been reports of a gang of black-clad masked thugs bursting into a Kiev restaurant on Wednesday night and attacking some Liverpool fans with iron bars. Blood everywhere, one in hospital. Could happen to anyone of us, anywhere. The difference is, by the time we arrive there'll be thousands more of us, strength in numbers and all that.

Then I got a text from the man I got my ticket from, warning of large numbers of really convincing fake tickets being in circulation. Never a good sign. Few of us will be actually using the seats as we'll all be standing up (Anfield's had 'safe standing' for years for European matches!). But these reports unsettle us.

By late on Friday evening we're landed at Kiev's Zhuliany airport, which is a lot nearer the city than the main one, Boryspils.

We exit and feel the warm night air. But there is no sign of Vadim, our Facebook angel, so our accommodation fears resurface. We return to the UEFA checkpoint inside to ask what we should expect to pay for a taxi into town. Meanwhile Graeme posts some uncomplimentary comments about our friend Vadim onto that website.

The first few taxi drivers do not get remotely close to that figure, exceeding it by 100% and upwards. We return into the airport to seek further advice. Ten minutes later, a seven-seater cab arrives, and takes us to the hostel we had been accepted by. When we see it, we turn pale. A shady entrance around which furtive figures flit. An entrance reminiscent of the Bronx, which turns out to be flattering when we see what's inside, several flights of concrete steps up. It's a brothel, a drug dealing centre, a home for migrant workers from Armenia, and a few Scousers who must have been desperate. "Just got to get pissed to stay here", slurs one, staggering into a dormitory-style vision of hell. The madam shows us where we might sleep. We decline at first sight of the fluid-encrusted bedding, and return to the street corner. "We're better than this" says Pete.

It's now approaching 1am. It's now match day. "We leave Kiev tomorrow!" observes Bob, laconically. But the problem that has been plaguing us for weeks remains unresolved. We're on a Kiev street corner with no ideas where to go or what to do. Luckily, the weather's fine and the night air warm.

Saturday May 26th
A series of conversations ensue. The first is with a man and his wife who are volunteers on that Free Kiev couch site. They offer one person a night for tomorrow evening. After a phone call, they say two of their friends can offer two people two nights, but they live five miles away in the opposite direction. We thank them but politely turn them down. We can't be strewn around the city in different places, in ones and twos. This has been our problem all along – too many of us, for most taxis and most accommodations. A group of

Scousers walk by and they start talking about our obvious plight – the trolley cases on the pavement tell the story eloquently enough. One says they're staying just down there – he points – by an illuminated pharmacy sign. He tells us the owner wants 750 US dollars a night for a room for two. Again, we decline.

By now it is 02:30, and we're still homeless, and running out of options. We are discussing what to do next when a woman comes up to us, in tears, and says in halting English that it breaks her heart to see us like this, it is not Ukrainian "not to be friendly towards visitors", that her whole country is shamed by the sight of seven people with nowhere to go because of the greed of some of the city's hoteliers. Then she says "I can take two persons for tonight." We are touched by her generosity; she shows us her house, 30 metres from our street corner, and decide she's genuine. Bob looks at his daughter and nods. "You two might as well go, leave us five lads to sort something out." The two girls go with the woman, and leave the five of us on the pavement.

Three-am. The street corner has become our own, and it's time it stopped. Not least because a few now need a toilet. We decide to go and find a bar and at least discuss it over a beer, maybe the bar will know someone, or have a spare room themselves. And at least we'll be off our street corner and indoors.

And that's when things started happening. First, within minutes of entering the bar – it's called Sunduk – a German called Igor, despite or perhaps because of being ferociously drunk, offers us two spaces on his floor. He lives in Kiev, five minutes' walk away. When we point out that there are five of us, he says "Okay, five then, it's okay."

So relieved are we, we include him in our round – he takes a whisky and Coke. At the bar, two older Germans are noisily doing the Ukrainian vodka thing, to which we are about to be introduced by Andrei, a young local business man. The ritual involves much whooping before downing an unfeasibly large measure in one, then chewing on a slice of orange that's left on top of the glass. We have one each, and see Andrei has immediately ordered replacements.

Then in a quiet-ish corner, Graeme suddenly announces "I think we've got somewhere". He has made good use of the pub's wi-fi and found a hotel that "is waiting for us" through Booking.com.

"Is it genuine?"

"Where is it?"

"How much?"

It turns out it's about six miles away, £50 per room per night (cheaper than the bloody hostel!), and looks great. But we've seen plenty of places where the images and reality have not been a good match.

We go straight to the bar and ask Andrei, who speaks English, if he can help us get a taxi to this place and ensure we don't get ripped off. "We have one more round of vodkas to celebrate" he says. We offer to pay, but he will have none of it. He and Graeme stand looking at their phones for a minute, then Andrei calls a taxi. "It will be about twenty minutes" he says, "but normally they won't take five people. Maybe I can talk to him."

Before the taxi arrives, no fewer than eight police suddenly single-file in, move quickly towards the bar, pounce, grab the noisy German under his arms and drag him out. Some hold the door open and act as back up in case the first four can't handle a drunken elderly man.

I ask Andrei what just happened. "Oh he was too drunk and noisy so he will sober up in a cell," he says nonchalantly. "So who grassed him up?" asks Pete, but Andrei doesn't understand the question.

We explain to Igor that we won't be taking him up on his kind offer and explain why. We felt almost like letting him down, but I guess he could live without five drunken strangers lying on his floor and occupying his bathroom.

When the taxi arrives, Andrei goes to speak to him. He comes back shaking his head. "Cost is 250, but he can only take four of you."

Can nothing be straightforward here?

After another discussion, the driver agrees to take two, then come back for the other three. It's about a 20-minute journey, so there and back will take 40 minutes. It is now 04:15. Pete and his son take first ride, we remain in the bar another 40 minutes. We're flagging now, and wonder whether we'll ever see the taxi, or Pete and Graeme for that matter, again. But he comes back, and at 05:15 we finally get to the hotel. And it's a stunning location, by the side of the river, with a marina, boats bobbing in the water, sun reflecting off the water – it's now daylight, and the sun is shining through a cloudless sky on this tranquil early morning calm. The waterside hotel consists of log cabins, with a balcony over the water where breakfast is served. Right by it, a family of ducklings are having bread thrown to them. Just a few hours after when we were looking in the hostel from hell – we called it a *hostile* – we have this.

"It's like going to bed in your own bed and waking up on Neptune," says Bob. It is indeed a world away from the squalor we'd seen earlier. We check in and before crashing out, I take a photo from my window at the scene outside. Stunning. And when we wake up, it will be match day proper.

By about 11am we are gathered outside on the patio for breakfast. Bob has spoken to his daughter who had stayed with the tearful woman, and it's clear they've been looked after. The woman and her husband, who speaks the better English, plied them with food and drink till 4am, before the husband excused them and stood to leave because he had to go to work – at 7am! They expressed their amazement, but he just said "No, it is the Ukrainian way. Hospitality comes first, vodka second!"

We waited for them to arrive by taxi, and told them they had a nice surprise coming. We find we're at an area called Hidropark, famous for its river beaches and riverside bars, cafes and restaurants. There are kayakers, water skiers, power boats, fishing boats, a never-ending procession of water-based activity. More importantly for us, the bridge over the river carries the Metro, and Hidropark stop is just five minutes' walk from the hotel, I look at my Metro map and see how handy that really is – right into the centre from there, three stops.

The two girls duly arrive, check in and get changed, we all have a quick beer then it's time – 2pm on match day. We set off in warm sunshine towards the Metro station, only to find it's closed. A local woman says this and the next one are closed. We can see trains running, but they are not stopping at the station. She says we will have to walk. We know the city centre is six or seven miles away, but we seem stuck for choices. It would take a while to get taxis, and there are no buses on this busy dual carriageway. So we start walking. Every other passing vehicle gives us a toot on the horn. We wave in acknowledgement, but inside we're worried about the length of walk in this weather and the time implications on our day. We have others to meet, Pete has two others' match tickets on him and Andie is supposed to be stopping in my room tonight, and back via Riga. We have to get there. What a bloody day for the Metro to be closed!

Then we find out that the reason for the Metro problems may have been a bomb scare. "Bloody Russians trying to spoil our day!" says Pete. We arrive at the bridge across the vast Dnipro river, marvelling at the gorgeous golden-domed buildings, church spires and ancient stone structures of monumental scale and general architectural brilliance all dotted against the green hillside backdrop beyond, glinting and gleaming in the sunshine. With the river in the foreground, it's a compelling sight. But we have other fish to fry. On the opposite side of the river there's another Metro station, also called Dnipro. And it's also closed.

By now we're hot and distinctly bothered – and it's still over three miles to the city centre.

"Okay troops, time for a beer break in this bar," says Bob, nodding to one outside the closed station. "Our world turned last night after we walked into a bar, let's see if it does again".

And it did.

While we're having our beer, a local saunters over to talk to us. Suddenly he's telling us about his time at the front line near Donetsk, fighting for Ukraine against the Russians, and showing photos on his phone of him and his paramilitary colleagues, bandannas on their heads, clutching machine guns, Ukraine flag in the background. "I only killed five fucking Russians", he tells us. "I need to get some more." Then he produces a huge knife.

"In Ukraine you need to protect yourself. Now, buy me a fucking beer."

"Er yes, alright" we whimper.

Then behind us the Metro station doors open. It's back. We finish our beers and have one more while the queue dissipates. By 3pm we're on a train heading for the centre, and the singing can begin. It's *Allez Allez Allez*, of course. Locals take pictures on their phones. Ten minutes later we're right in the centre, emerging from the deepest underground station I've ever seen and emerging into the sunshine right opposite the Champions League festival site. But we head for Taras Shevchenko Park, the designated Liverpool fan zone, ten minutes' walk away.

As we arrive at the fan park, things suddenly go very wrong. One group of five are some way ahead, Pete and I sauntering along behind. I assume they've gone into the park, but can't see them. They've all got red shirts on, but that's not going to help much. I turn round to Pete, and he's not there either. In seconds, I'm alone. I try to stay calm, walk through the fan park, see if I can spot them. Some hope. *Allez Allez Allez* is being belted out, the air is thick with red pyro, there are thousands here rather than hundreds. It's party central, but I'm not in party mood anymore.

When I emerge from the park, I feel desolate. Is that it now? It's just me from here on? If I can't find them again, I'll have to make my way towards the ground (15 minutes away), eat on my own, drink on my own, get back to the hotel on my own (we all took a card from the reception desk in our wallets to show a taxi driver the unpronounceable name and address) and wait for them there. Not how I foresaw the day at all.

I've got my match ticket, passport, money and phone. My ticket isn't by the others anyway so I was always on my own for that part, but not this. I decide to get something to eat, near the stadium bag drop, and seat myself for some sea bass, fried potatoes, salad and a small beer. Then I start texting. I get two replies. Pete's says "Everyone has fucked me off, I'm on my own, trying to meet Lloydy to give him his ticket. Bob's text says "Antwerpen pub, Pushkinskaya Street. Everybody here." Except Pete and me, I thought. Then another from Pete: "Palace Premier Hotel."

I text them both: "On my way. Don't fucking move!" I ask the police directions and get sent the wrong way a couple of times. Then Pete's next text arrives. "Bar Prorock, just along from the Palace Premier."

By this time I've found the Palace Premier. "Which way out of the hotel doors, left or right?" I ask. But then I see it, and I see Pete sitting outside with a massive beer in front of him "For fuck's sake am I glad to see you," I say. We fill in the details. Pete needed a landmark he could arrange to meet by to hand over the tickets, and the Palace Premier Hotel was it. "He's flown all the way from Canada this lad, I've got to get his ticket to him haven't I? I've known him since the 1970s."

While we wait, I text the others again and ask the address of their pub. Pushkinskaya Street, comes the reply – the same bloody street! Lloydy finds us, the ticket is handed over, there's a group hug and chat over a beer, then he has to go. We decide to finish our beer then find the others.

A large group of 20/30 Madrid fans is walking past, many shirtless, with Ronaldo/Rafael Nadal torsos, tattoos – they look a bit moody, and seem to be their ultras. Then there's yelling, the cry of *"puta, puta"* (which I believe is the Spanish word for what Sergio Ramos is), and suddenly they pile into our bar, punching and kicking, eyes ablaze. It seems one of ours has unfurled a Catalan flag and waved it at them. Liverpool's fans fight back. Pete is holding a giant empty beer glass in his hand. The whole thing lasts twenty seconds, then passes, but very unpleasant to be so close to. Time to leave and find the others. This time, it works, and by now all our group have assembled, the three from the train, seven more from elsewhere, now our seven. There are now *seventeen* of us.

By 8.15pm we make our move, and make our way through the crowds towards the checkpoints and beyond them the stadium. We arrange where to meet afterwards, and with an hour to kick-off I'm in my seat.

The Liverpool support inside is staggering, way bigger than I expected, surely 40,000-plus. It sweeps away to my right, high above and curving, and stretches well into Madrid's half of the stadium. It's a bobbing, broiling, seething morass of noise and passion. The *You'll Never Walk Alone* is remarkable, the sheer volume of noise amazing.

We'll skip the match details, which are covered elsewhere in the book; other than to say it didn't go well. Afterwards we meet as arranged, and in fairly subdued fashion end up back at Sunduk. We leave late and drunk, and once again it's light when we go to bed.

Sunday May 27th

This time I am woken by the sound of Andie having a shower, and wonder why he's up so early. I check my watch and see why – it's 1pm, and our delayed check out is at 2pm. After a shower, something to eat and arranging a taxi, we get ready to get to Boryspils Airport for our evening flight to Riga. The airport is a bloody long way out of Kiev, an hour by taxi.

At the airport we decide to pay €25 for the airport lounge, get ourselves something to eat and a free drink. "It would cost you that much for a burger and coke out there," says Andie, waving in the general direction of the concourse. We get our money's worth, including a couple of vodkas, before boarding for Riga.

The sky is so clear, from 35,000 feet we see land for the whole journey, the outline of rivers, trees – it's amazing. By 10.30pm we're down in Riga, and check into the SkyHigh Hotel at the airport. The bar is closed but there are beers in the vending machine, she tells us.

We hadn't planned to go into Riga centre but change our mind now, and order a taxi. I've been there before recently and know a few good places in the old town. It's getting light again when we get back – I must sleep in the dark again sometime!

Monday May 28th

Another day, another flight – next morning at Riga airport we get talking to two Madrid fans who live in Dublin. One says how amazing Liverpool's support was. "When they sang *You'll Never Walk Alone* the hairs stood up on my arms" he said. "It was so loud, I could not speak to him and he was next to me, he could not hear."

We wished them well and went our separate ways, us to East Midlands. Graeme has his car parked there, and drops me off at Derby station for my train to Leeds, then finally one from Leeds to home. By then I've had enough of travelling, I'm flagging, by brain over-stimulated by too many cultures, sights, languages, currencies and alcohol.

My wife picks me up at the station, and soon we're having something to eat and a bottle of wine on the sun-kissed patio. She asks "So, how did it go?"

I take a deep breath.

"Well …."

Jonathan Naylor

The road to Kiev started for me in August with the 2nd leg playoff versus Hoffenheim. With a 2-1 lead from the first leg, I went to the game anxious that we could suffer a season-deflating reverse and undo all the good work from the previous season.

In a familiar pattern of what was to come in Europe this season, Liverpool removed anxieties by racing into a 3-0 lead before briefly wobbling as Hoffenheim threatened to start a comeback.

The Hoffenheim game was my first European fixture since a 1-0 win over Bayer Leverkusen in the 2002 quarter-final. During the course of this season, I was at all the home fixtures from each round with the exception of Porto, where I was lucky enough to go to the away match instead. That's six wins and one draw, with a barely credible 29-6 aggregate score-line (for an average score slightly better than 4-1). In fact, for the five matches after the Seville home game, it's 23-2.

Not wanting to tempt fate (both in terms of Liverpool's progression and me getting a ticket), I hadn't thought about the logistics of attending the final. I was in the ballot with two entries and the odds didn't seem too promising. After an interminable wait on the day of the draw, I was lucky enough to get tickets from both entries. The euphoria quickly turned to slight panic as the scale of the task of getting to Kiev slowly dawned.

Kiev could arguably be the most difficult major city to reach in Europe. Apart from the distance, there are no major cities close by and a constrained airport with limited scheduled flights and a shortage of hotel accommodation. Even the plan of hiring a car in Warsaw was scuppered, as you can't take hire cars out the EU.

With a deep gulp, we booked a coach trip from the UK to Kiev via Warsaw. It was relatively cheap and didn't rely on making multiple connections. The accommodation issue in Kiev would be negated. It would be an experience. I booked a flight back from Warsaw to avoid doing the whole journey by road.

On the other hand … it's a long way to Kiev. The trip from London-Warsaw-Kiev-Warsaw is 2,000 miles. I had travelled further by coach in the early 1990s, when I took a Greyhound bus from San Francisco to Boston. And there wasn't even a Champions League final at the end of that trip.

On Thursday morning, I was waiting at a motorway service station for the coach to turn up. There were three other people waiting. They all seemed decent fellas, which reassured me a bit. After a while I tend to get claustrophobic in large groups, even if they are friends. In my younger days I had been on a few football-playing tours abroad, and much as they were great, I was always glad to have a bit of time on my own again at the end of the trip.

The coach was late (to be a recurring theme). When it turned up, I was pleasantly surprised that it looked reasonably comfortable. My friend was only joining in Warsaw, so for the first (and longest leg), I had two seats to myself.

After a 30 minutes stop at the motorway services, we were on our way! But not for long – we had left somebody behind. The coach turned back and a slightly sheepish passenger got back on.

Industrial quantities of alcohol were being consumed on the bus. I enjoy the odd drink but with a long journey in front of us, I had decided to stick to water. I was very much in the minority in this choice.

The rest of the bus could be roughly split into two groups. Those drinking more that I could have put away even in my prime, but still remaining relatively switched on, and easing off at times. The remainder were more hardened drinkers, keeping going with the persistence of a marathon runner clocking off the miles. They shuffled round in a slightly zombie like state, Ozzy Osbourne without the spark.

The coach got to Dover, just missing our ferry due to the time lost returning for the missing passenger. We crossed on the following ferry; quite a pleasant sailing, and the opportunity to have a meal before the long drive to Poland.

By this stage we are a little way behind schedule. We set off from Calais, with the first blast of *Allez Allez Allez* on the trip. We drove through France, Belgium, Netherlands, Germany and then eventually into Poland.

For the first part of this leg we had a run through of the songs from the Great Anfield Songbook. As well as the usual suspects, there were blasts from the past and songs I'd never heard before, including an epic ode to Gary McAllister.

I completed a read of my Sunday newspaper, listened to a few podcasts, and watched a film on an ancient Kindle Fire before settling down for a long sleep. I slept pretty well, to the surprise of those around me who wondered if I was still alive at one stage.

Breakfast on Friday morning was in Poland at a McDonalds looking out onto a lorry park. Despite the unpromising location, the food went down well, the sun was shining and I was feeling surprisingly fresh.

We continued towards Warsaw, and I started reading the Klopp biography by Raphael Honigstein (recommended by several TTTers). It's a good read and makes me even more optimistic for the future under Klopp. The recurring theme of narrow, unlucky failures at Mainz and Dortmund followed by great success in following years provided some comfort after the match.

We pull into Warsaw almost four hours late, around 2pm. We have ten hours in the city as the coach drivers take their mandated break. I wander into the old town, and have a beer and a bite to eat. It's a beautiful day, and the old town is stunning. There are large groups of Reds throughout the city. Various Liverpool songs float through the spring air. I can hear a succession of Liverpool songs from the top of the viewing platform looking out on the old town. The atmosphere is definitely building even though we are still 500 miles from Kiev. I'm starting to get very excited about the game.

I do feel a bit sorry for couple getting married in the town hall-type building 100 yards or so from a bar packed out with reds. While I might have been happy to get married with a soundtrack of *Fields of Anfield Road*, I suspect it wouldn't have been top of their list of accompanying music.

I've booked a cheap hotel in case I need to catch up on sleep. In the end I only sleep for an hour but enjoy getting a shower after 24 hours or so on the coach.

I meet up with my friend and we have a quick meal before going back to the bus. Around midnight (two hours later than scheduled due to late arrival into Warsaw), we are on our way to Kiev.

We have a second incident of someone being left behind at a stop, costing us another half an hour or so. In the early hours of the morning, we hit the Poland-Ukraine border. There is a massive queue of lorries and cars. Luckily, we can bypass much of the queue to join a much shorter line of football coaches. Nevertheless, it's a slow process. We get to the front of the line, and a Polish border official takes all the passports off the bus to scan them in the computer. After an hour and a half, we are cleared to go.

A brief surge of songs breaks out as we cross into Ukraine and start the final leg to Kiev. Except we aren't in Ukraine yet, just in the zone between the two countries. It turns out we have to go through the whole process again with the Ukrainian border guards.

Things start to get a bit tense as the clock ticks on. We realise that we won't be in Kiev until well into the afternoon, and the first thoughts start crossing our mind that we could be in danger of missing kick-off.

The situation is probably not helped by one of the drunker passengers spraying beer around the outside of the bus, then going to talk to border guards to "smooth the process" along. Other passengers strongly encourage him to return to the bus.

Eventually we are on our way again, having taken four hours to clear the border. Again, a brief surge of songs until we realise Ukrainian police are sending us into a service station. We wait another half hour and then we are on our way with six or so other coaches in a police escorted convoy. It is around 340 miles from the border to Kiev. We drive at a modest speed along the single-lane roads while the coach drivers complain about the slowness of the police car leading the procession. We do calculations of distance left compared to our average speed, and the consensus is we should be in around 4pm – tighter than we would like but still in plenty of time for the 21:45 kick-off.

We then stop at a service station so drivers can swap. There is a single toilet for six coach loads, while people stock up on further alcohol. We spend much longer here than I would like due to the queues at the shop and people prioritising booze over actually getting to Kiev in good time. Then we are on our way, the police car peels off and we are on our own again.

We make it to Kiev for 17:30. Having not eaten since yesterday evening, we quickly find a restaurant for a meal and a couple of beers. Then it's the short walk to the stadium, with no time to visit the fan park or the city centre.

The place is buzzing, with Reds far outnumbering the Real Madrid fans in the surrounding streets. It is quite a spectacle to see supporters from around the world joining together for the game. As we get into the stadium complex, we start to see the many banners and hear the songs. In an instant, the trip is worthwhile.

We chat to various other fans. Most are incredulous about our coach journey. Someone else who got a ballot ticket mentions they were able to fly to Lviv and get the night train to/from Kiev. I admit this sounds a much better option than the coach trip.

One side benefit of the worrying about getting to Kiev on time is that I haven't been worrying about the match. Now the nerves kick in as we go to our seats. I keep looking at the clock to see how long to kick-off.

The Liverpool section is bouncing, and I'm really enjoying my first European final. We seem to be much louder than the Madrid fans. I hope that if we don't win, we at least stay in the game for a while so that the atmosphere isn't killed dead early on.

After the usual UEFA opening ceremony nonsense, the game kicks off. I've not seen any of the match on TV yet, so others will have much better perspectives. However, beforehand I felt there were many more ways that Madrid could win compared to Liverpool. This proves to be the case. Failure to be more incisive while we were on top in the first 30 minutes, the loss of Mo Salah, two massive goalkeeping errors and a wonder strike from Gareth Bale made this a bridge too far. Nevertheless, I was proud of the team and our support.

The coach out of Kiev was understandably subdued. We didn't leave until around 2:30am as the drivers need to complete their rest period (due to late arrival). While we were waiting, some luggage got stolen from the luggage hold, to add insult to injury.

The journey back was a bit fraught. There were tensions as, on clearing the Ukrainian side of the border, some passengers went AWOL to the duty free shop. While they were rounded up, three coaches pulled ahead of us in the queue for the Polish border formalities. As we got further and further behind schedule, people started to worry about their flights from Warsaw or for those remaining on the coach, whether they would be back in time for work on Tuesday.

Despite the loss of our position in the queue, the border crossing was quicker than on the way out. We got to the outskirts of Warsaw in reasonably good time. Then the coach driver pulled onto the side of the road, having taken exception to a comment from a passenger. He then wandered off telling us to sort our own way back to the UK. I signed up to Uber and was downloading the app in case we needed to finish our journey to Warsaw by cab.

Ten minutes later a police van turned up and the driver reappeared. It is not clear what was going on but we then had a police escort into the centre of Warsaw.

At Warsaw, I was very glad to be off the coach before a fully blown *Lord of the Flies*-type scenario developed. We got in a taxi to the airport. The driver took one look at our Liverpool gear, apologised for his lack of English then said "Fucking Ramos". Driving at great speed, he then proceeded to show us clips on his phone of the Salah wrestling move and the elbow to Karius.

At the airport, I said goodbye to my friend who was travelling back on a different flight. I then spent the best value £20 of my life to access a business lounge and have a shower. Feeling human again, I grab some souvenirs for the children then fly home. I'm back at the house just before midnight on Sunday. The adventure is at an end.

Jennifer Thomas

Warning. This is likely to be a rambling post but here goes. Didn't sleep for two nights as I was on two red-eye flights to get to Kiev and back. Shocking panic in the days beforehand but the organisation in Kiev was excellent and the stadium so easy to get to as it was in the middle of the city. On another matters, the food was shocking, the police and military had pretty much nothing to do but stand around in phalanxes looking suitably Slav as the fans were high-spirited but well-behaved. The flags and banners were tremendous around Shevchenko Square and at the stadium in comparison with the staged mosaics dished out on the Madrid seats and a huge Real Madrid banner just before the start – again probably staged. It was disappointing that the security people seemed to think Liverpoo FC fans posed more of a threat as they marshalled the LFC end with more bodies than the Real end.

As for the chanteuse with her skimpy outfit and fireworks and sparkly dancers (who looked like those silverfish you get in a damp bathroom) I just hoped it would be over soon and the game could start. Credit to Kiev for playing *You'll Never Walk Alone* before the start – not Gerry & The Pacemakers, I don't think, but still. The fans were in great voice.

Now the game. From the start I thought we were on top of things. There was pace and threat and the ball was in their half for most of the time. Then came the defining moment. I know Karius is getting the attention but the snap and focus just went when Ramos – proud possessor of 24 red cards up to the end of 2017 – brought Salah down. I don't believe that he meant to cause as much damage as he did – or do I? If it was a tactic, then it was a masterstroke because it caused disruption that we never really recovered from. To have only Adam Lallana, or possibly Dominic Solanke, was just not replacing like with like, apart from the gulf in quality. Loris Karius had a shocker, including the clout on the head by, who'd a thunk it, Ramos.

No-one collapsed but it was clear that Real were putting together some fine moves, gaining confidence as it went on. A moment that showed our problems was when Sadio Mané gave one of his lovely backheels in the box and Lallana just completely missed it. These moves are second nature between the front three.

By the end, no-one had surrendered. The back four and Mané were particularly good. All were still trying but the game was lost.

Complete silence on the flight home.

I feel desperately sorry for both Karius and Salah. I don't envy Jürgen Klopp his decision about Karius.

Paddy Smith

This story starts two years ago, sat in a bar in Basel after losing the Europa League final and, UEFA being UEFA, not nearly enough hotel rooms. I'm sat in a a bar with brothers, sons and nephews at 3am (having a good sing-song it must be said) when youngest son (12) throws up all the pop, crisps and junk food consumed in the last few hours all over our table. Three hours then waiting on a cold, wet train platform and I was determined to never let that happen again.

So, qualification secured for the knockout stages this year and we decided to book apartment in Kiev 'just in case' never expecting to get there, £800 for three nights sleeps eight, best bit of work done this year! Flights not so much but that was a jinx to far! Alarm set for 3.30am Friday morning and we're all set to go.

Nervous wait at the airport, and even as we're queuing to get on an older and worn airplane we're not 100% sure we're getting of the ground! But all goes well and we land in Kiev, through passport control and we enter arrivals more like film stars with TV crews and radio interviews being done as we walk through hundreds of people waiting to pick people up.

Pre-booked Taxi turns up and soon we're at the pre-booked apartment, it's almost as if we had a plan! Quick shower and we walk over to Shevchenko Square, it's 27 degrees. A round of 10 beers, four pizzas and some meat pies cost us £8! Loads of Reds already here, bumped into three or four lads I know already, great sing-song, in fact you can her *Allez Allez Allez* drifting all over the city.

Kiev is cool. I used to live in Moscow for three years so my Russian (which mostly resolved around ordering beer and getting taxis) comes in very handy! In the evening we move to the official UEFA fan park as the young-'uns want to see Hardwick who is apparently a dj, despite the corporate sell out we all have a good laugh and a load more beer, despite reports of trouble we see nothing but Reds everywhere having fun.

Saturday morning and we have a walk around town and Kiev is mobbed by Reds and one or two Madrid fans, we spend the afternoon at The Shevchenko fan park again, in the sun drinking beers and singing songs, fantastic atmosphere with every one in fine form. Get talking to Reds from all over the world, amazing tales of how they've got here. We start to wonder to the ground around 6pm, stopping for a couple of beers and again *Allez Allez Allez* drifting though the evening air.

Predictions range from 1-0 all the way up to my rather over-confident 5-0 which even now I think was possible if Salah stayed on the pitch! We get in to the ground about one and a half hours before kick-off and already it's packed, all red banners, flags and lots of singing. My boys want to be at the front behind the goal which is great, but due to the electronic advertising we can't see the goal line so have to watch any close goal action on the screen; for our goal it's only the reaction of the players that tell you we've equalised.

At the end almost every one stays behind to clap the team, feel heartbroken for Loris Karius and the rest of the boys but thought we never really played our game (after the Salah injury), back to the apartment and a few more beers, chat and mulling over the game and what might of been. I really think we're at the start of something special.

Sat at the airport now and we've had an amazing time, Kiev was brilliant and we've had so much fun, I guess we go again!

Paul Tomkins, May 26th 2018

I couldn't help but get a churning gut this week any time I even just thought about the final, with a sense of nerves that, I felt, should not be there. I don't recall being nervous about the finals in the (largely) pre-Twitter era of 2005 and 2007 (although being at those games maybe helped focus on the *experience*, rather than just the match). Back then, the world didn't have to end if you lost a big game. I was dreading Liverpool failing to overcome the mightiest team in modern European history, and yet all the pressure should have been on Real Madrid, with a wage bill so large they (scandalously) can't even afford to pay it.

It struck me that I was getting close to the dangerous psychological phenomenon of black-and-white thinking, even though I knew the bigger picture was far more broad. Black-and-white thinking narrows everything down to success or failure, win or lose – winner takes all – and while those things may feel true in the moment, things are rarely that clear-cut in life.

Indeed, football increasingly feels "must win", as if nothing exists afterwards other than the gaping chasm of a black hole where all your dreams are sucked in forever.

Maybe it's worse now as players are more likely to agitate for a move if everything isn't perfect – as the über-rich clubs hoover up the talent to protect their own position – and there will be calls for managers to be sacked within the space of a couple of bad results, when in the old days they could probably last a couple of bad *seasons* (if they had some credit in the bank). Everything feels on a knife-edge all the time. It never used to feel to me that so much was always riding on any given game. Even if *you* can keep your shit together, everyone else out there will seem to lose theirs.

Losing is simply *not winning*. But these days it feels like it comes with its own additional punishment, beyond disappointment; almost like a relegation playoff, or even losing a promotion playoff. In both those cases there's a clear punishment: relegation, or being forced to stay in the lower league. But here, there is no punishment; Liverpool are already in the competition again next season. Of course, we live in a punishment and blame society, where everyone has to pay for any kind of mistake, and so "heads must roll" if things aren't 100% perfect all of the time. (I wrote this paragraph before Loris Karius' nightmare in Kiev, but again, won't blame him.)

Remember two years ago, when Liverpool had to win the Europa League to qualifying for the Champions League, and had the double whammy when losing? Well, this was the Champions League final, and as just noted, Liverpool had already qualified via the league. This is a clear sign of progress, and the disaster that not being in the 2016/17 Champions League was painted as was, it transpired, just a minor inconvenience. This year, there was nothing to lose beyond not winning. There *is* a tomorrow.

The punishment, it seems – which doesn't relate to any on-field issues – is the *banter*, the snide, the mockery. Everton fans will be in their element, like gimpish spotty virgins laughing at their friend who just got dumped, or dolts who failed their GCSEs laughing at someone who failed their PhD. You don't get to laugh when you haven't even been close to that level of achievement, as you're only doubling-down on your own far greater personal failings. Yeah, Liverpool lost in Kiev. So, Everton fans, how was *your* season? Did you make any finals? Finish top four? Did you have exciting football, score lots of goals? How did all the money *you* spent work out for you?

But to me the truth is, as the ancient Stoic, Seneca, noted: "We suffer more in imagination than in reality." All week, my fear of losing was more powerful than the reality, which was hard to take, but not the end of the world.

Of course rival fans will revel in Liverpool losing, as you'd expect; I have no issue with that. And I don't choose to enter into banter with fans of other clubs when they struggle, and I steer clear of any when the Reds fall short in some way. But I think the utter mania of so many (online) Liverpool fans is that they are part of this very public banter exchange, and then it becomes far more personally devastating when the club loses a game, as they get to publicly humiliated on social media about it. And public disgrace is, to many, a punishment worse than death.

In some ways it feels now-or-never as there are fewer opportunities to spring surprises in football. Even since Istanbul, football has changed. The Premier League, bar one season (Leicester City in 2016), has had no outsiders in the top four since 2005. And the Champions League seems to be whittling down to the usual suspects of Real Madrid and Bayern Munich.

So what are Liverpool losing, beyond the game? There's perhaps the increased likelihood of Emre Can leaving, although as the Reds had qualified already for next year's competition, maybe that doesn't change anything. It seems he was likely to leave either way, although I still hope he stays. But even then, while it would be better to have him than to not have him (especially when no fee can be received), it's not like he was missed in the run-in. Liverpool's season didn't cave in when Emre Can got injured, even though it coincided with when Adam Lallana and Alex Oxlade-Chamberlain were also injured.

I think when the club is lacking direction from the top (such as the ownership fiasco of a decade ago), or has a manager who is not quite up to the task (as four years ago), losing key players can be devastating. But if the infrastructure is good, and the manager is proven to be world-class and still cutting edge, then these things are usually less terminal. Based on budget, Liverpool shouldn't be reaching Champions League finals. But Klopp elevates the Reds.

When Liverpool finished 2nd in 2009 it was with Rafa Benítez at war with owners who refused to back him in that summer's transfer market, as funds vanished. When the Reds finished 2nd in 2014 it was with the well-known internal war that John Henry mentioned this week, where Michael Edwards was having to "win battles" over transfers with the manager (who, while a good coach, was poor in the transfer market). The club was pulling in two different directions.

Only since Klopp has arrived has everyone been pulling in the same direction. So finishing 2nd in Europe is not likely to result in an implosion, while this season's equivalent of the key player sold in 2009 and 2014 departed in January, to no subsequent alarm.

In the moment when Philippe Coutinho was *set* to leave the club, it felt like a disaster; unthinkable, even to me, that the club would not replace him in January. It felt too risky. And as much as I have been able, over the years, to quote the examples of "best players" Kevin Keegan and Ian Rush leaving – only for the team to get better – it's hard to see past the fog of impending doom in the moment an important player insists he is leaving. It's like thinking that you can't live without your beloved in the maelstrom of a breakup; but in truth you do tend to live on without them. It may sting for a while, but life goes on.

In a way Coutinho was only actually missed in the final, when Salah went off injured, and that extra bit of quality was then absent; but no one can say the Reds would have got there with Coutinho in the ranks. The pace of Oxlade-Chamberlain was lost as well, to mean that, with Salah taken out, there was only really Mané providing that searing speed.

Even Luis Suarez leaving led fairly directly to Liverpool getting Jürgen Klopp, which in turn turned Roberto Firmino from a "flop" into a beloved icon, and precipitated the arrival of Mané, whom many didn't want before (an outcry over his signing), then with fans thinking the Reds couldn't live without him (when he went to the African Cup of Nations), and that rolled into the arrival of Mo Salah, a player we had no idea we were gonna love so much.

Of course, Liverpool did not *directly* swap Suarez for Klopp, but Brendan Rodgers' inability to get the team to score more than a pitiful supply of goals in the following one-and-a-third seasons after the Uruguayan's departure (which was ample time, with leeway granted after the superb 2013/14 campaign) meant that Klopp was sought out.

That fallow 15-month period enabled the club some thinking time to analyse what was needed and to go out and get the best. I honestly don't think there's a manager better suited to the job.

As such, and in part down to the very nature of Jürgen Klopp, October 2015 marked the starting point of true joined-up thinking by FSG. Until then they'd given the fans a beloved icon who no longer at the cutting-edge of coaching and management (but whose appointment was necessary to drag the club out of a morass), having inherited a team not even in the Champions League and near the foot of the Premier League with Roy Hodgson in charge; and then, when hoping to appoint a young manager with an older director of football, ended up with just the former, whose initial transfer business (ins and outs) was so alarming it resulted in the formation of the much-maligned transfer committee, as a compromise was sought.

And for a young manager who claimed to improve players and work with youngsters, Rodgers actually improved very few players and integrated almost no youngsters over a consistent period of time, but did get an almighty burst out of half-a-dozen players for a six-month spell from December 2013 to May 2014 (a spell with no Europe and virtually no cup distractions). With that fulminating half-year, and with the largely soporific 15 months that followed, Rodgers' very mixed bag (not least his terrible record in Europe and poor record in the transfer market when driving deals) left the impression of a good manager, but not a *great* one. The potential that saw him given the job was not an illusion, but he did not unify the club; indeed, it was cracking apart.

Klopp, by contrast, has yet to have a season in Europe with Liverpool where he wasn't taken the Reds to a final, and where league consistency has finally returned, given the club's first back-to-back 75-point league hauls in a decade, and only its second in the Premier League era. Klopp brought with him his experience of building a dynasty, as he essentially did at Dortmund, as well as winning experience in a major league. He brought with him a world-class record in *collaboration*. But the turnover and financial backing of the Rich Three is not easy to contend with. In the Champions League, the mega-wealth of Real Madrid and Bayern Munich is not easy to contend with.

It's therefore worth reflecting on what Liverpool have to look forward to, as even though this was an all-or-nothing end to the season, this does not signal the end of the 'Klopp project'. Far from it. This is just the start.

As such I thought it was worth recapping some of the points I've been making all season long, about the bigger picture – which would all remain true whether the Reds won or lost in Kiev.

Remember, Liverpool had perhaps their toughest-ever start to a season on paper (if you include the two games against the 3rd-best team in Germany, as well as early games against the rest of the Big Six in England); had its worst-ever season for penalties when comparing the balance of how many goals were scored to how many were won (versus how many penalties were given away to goals conceded); had a superstar go on strike in August and January, who eventually got himself off to Barcelona; lost its assistant manager on the eve of a Champions League semi-final, having also lost another first-team coach in January. (Pep Lijnders moving into management, aged 35, in Holland.) It's hardly been a campaign blessed with good fortune.

Again, contrast the way the club has responded to the departure of its most bankable asset to Barcelona in 2014 and 2018. The club is absolutely unified behind Klopp and work in tandem with him to identify players to buy.

Comment by Yassen

Some thoughts on Sergio Ramos' actions and Salah's injury from a martial arts viewpoint.

I have spent a few years practicing Aikido. If you are not familiar with this Martial Art it is all about falling to the ground. Almost every technique can end by being thrown to the ground and usually this is the case. So, in order to progress in Aikido you must learn to fall safely.

In a movie with Steven Segal or Aikido presentation on YouTube we will see people being thrown all over the place, falling really hard who do not sustain injuries. How is this possible?

There are two components in the art of falling. First, you learn for a year or two how to do it safely gradually increasing the risk.

Second – and this is what Ramos appeared to do deliberately to Mo Salah – is that your partner (the one who throws you in the technique) never ever interferes with your body during the fall. Most injuries in Aikido or Judo happen when during a fall your are not entirely released or when excessive force is applied at the later stages of the fall.

Ramos 1) did not release Salah body; 2) applied a force on it by landing on Mo. For these two actions he would have been expelled from an Aikido Dodjo.

Mixed Martial Arts analyst Robin tweeted a breakdown of Ramos' challenge, espousing the theory that it was totally intentional.

"Ramos initiates the step-across trip, creates the ledge which is the obstacle, he then applies rotational force on Salah, destabilising him and turning him."

"What is the key to this takedown? Well it's the grip on the forearm! That's the root of the control. The arm drag from wrist control and now let's put it all together."

"Wrist control to start, then hyper-extension on the elbow to force the body to follow and set the ledge to complete the trip, using the momentum created."

"It's a filthy outcome. All of Salah's weight and force come down on the radius and ulna, which are small bones. Huge impact... Nasty. Referees need to protect these athletes."

The European Judo Union also stated the fact that the technique employed by Ramos is actually banned in certain scenarios in their martial art.

Paul Tomkins, May 28th 2018
Two days on, and the dust has started to settle. The lingering sense is one of the game turning on a single incident, at which point Liverpool's odds of winning a sixth European Cup diminished. Several neutral football podcasts all noted a feeling of being cheated out of the final they had hoped to see.

By my quick calculations I believe Real Madrid's starting XI had no fewer than 31 previous Champions League Final appearances between them; and indeed, it was the exact same XI as last season's final.

By contrast, Liverpool had ... *zero.*

And while that doesn't *necessarily* mean a great deal – experience itself comes with no guarantees – it does show the difference in top-level nous; in knowing how to deal with situations. (And that's before getting onto World Cup and European Championship final experience.)

While Madrid's legs are clearly slowing a little, they were highly unlikely to be overcome by the occasion; and certainly the least likely to make rookie mistakes. If anyone had used up too much nervous energy before the match it was likely to be Liverpool, for whom, without question, this was the biggest game of every player's life. Nerves are natural, first time around.

The Reds' most experienced player in international terms was Mo Salah, and he was also the Reds' top scorer, main threat on the break and an elite creator. It was easy to guess that Sergio Ramos was always going to do his best to put him in hospital.

By contrast, Madrid's players had those 31 finals between them, plus Cristiano Ronaldo has played in a European Championship final, as had Sergio Ramos, who also has a World Cup winners' medal, along with Toni Kroos.

Madrid's average age was bang-on 29, to Liverpool's 25.8, a gap of over three years. I also saw a stat that Liverpool were the 2nd-youngest Champions League finalists, after Klopp's Dortmund (although I haven't been able to verify this). While Klopp's first great team wasn't able to be kept together, its key players went on to win German titles and a World Cup with Germany. They continued to grow as players as a result of that final.

In the end, the gulf in experience was just too big. Madrid's total international caps are more than twice as many as the Reds', at 799 vs 353, and that's not including bringing on Gareth Bale (with 70) as a sub.

The unfortunate Loris Karius has yet to play for Germany, and perhaps the occasion got to him. Performing at the highest level is about controlling nerves, and that often needs practice; or, alternatively, you can be very young and fearless, like Trent Alexander-Arnold (although even he had a spell of two or three games in the early spring where he could do no right, such as at Old Trafford, before turning it around).

Karius has my full sympathy, and while I think it could scar him for life, the bigger our mistakes, the more powerful they are to learn from. The flip side is that they can end up weighing too heavily; but rather than hate him, I have an extra respect for the way he fronted up to fans for his mistakes. At 24 he's not a kid, but he's still a young goalkeeper, with their statistical peak (in terms of their best save percentages based on historical data) between 28 and 30; and in terms of composure, probably later still, before, in their mid-30s, their agility and reaction times dim and they melt away.

Indeed, this wasn't even close to the youngest Liverpool XI this season, which has averaged at just 24.2 in the league; with James Milner and/or Gini Wijnaldum replacing either Emre Can or Alex Oxlade-Chamberlain to add greatly to the average for the final stages of the season.

If everyone had been fit, Liverpool's average age would have been perhaps 24-24.5. And yet, ironically, two of the Reds' most experienced players were absentees from the XI, and both are below the age of 25.

Both Can and 'Ox' are 24, but have over 250 appearances apiece for big clubs who play in the top European leagues (as well as including caps for their country). Oxlade-Chamberlain had also played almost 40 European games, more than any other Liverpool player bar the 86-game James Milner, the 66-game Salah (who was taken out of the game when Liverpool were on top) and the 47-game Wijnaldum. (Dejan Lovren also has 66 games, but mostly in the Europe League.)

By contrast, Andy Robertson – like Can and Ox, also 24 – has less than 100 games *in the top flight and international football combined*, and most of those were for Hull.

(Not that it tells with Robertson, but he is in the process of going from an excellent full-back into a world-class one. If he's this good after so few games, he should logically get better and better; unless he gets injured, which can happen, or he loses hunger, which you can tell is anathema to him. I can picture him aged 77, playing football with kids over the park, and chasing like the Road Runner. Meep meep!)

Otherwise, look through the Liverpool squad and all but a handful of players have played more than 32 or 33 games in Europe, with many having played 10-20.

For Madrid, their European experience almost exactly matches their international experience – 120 games in Europe for Ramos, 159 for Ronaldo, 100 for Modric, 112 for Benzema, 97 for Kroos, 89 for Marcelo; then 40-80 games apiece for Bale, Isco, Navas, Carvajal and Verane. Their least experienced European player is Casemiro, on 39. If Madrid's legs didn't give way, then their experience was absolutely mountainous.

But more than their experience as individual players, Madrid's experience as a *team* is incredible; indeed, it's absolutely phenomenal. The more a team plays together the better it should logically get, in terms of understanding each other's strengths, weaknesses and wavelengths, until it reaches the tipping point and age and injuries take a toll; the end of the cycle that hits all great teams if there isn't careful pruning.

I still can't decide about Zinedine Zidane as a coach *as he inherited their entire starting XI – and all three subs!* – and while he has to be a very good coach to achieve what he has, it's not necessarily symbolic of greatness. He took a well-oiled machine and it's still that exact-same well-oiled machine, only older and wiser. (This is no Bob Paisley building a side by snapping up young lower-league and Scottish unknowns and winning three European Cups.) By contrast, seven of Liverpool's XI arrived (or gained debuts) since Klopp took charge. Liverpool are not just a young team, but a *new* team.

Madrid are probably right at that tipping point now, about to teeter over into the melt zone – but just about at the pinnacle of the sport. In a year's time the same players will be an average of 30 years old, and few teams remain elite at such an age. There's almost no way the same XI could play the final for a fourth year in a row, while the luck (or medical magic) to have the same XI two years in a row is freakish on its own.

For now they can play on autopilot. Their age means that they could not easily handle Mo Salah and Sadio Mané, but once they cheated Salah out of the final it was easier – they only had one flank to deal with. (And Liverpool could only bring on the mid-paced Adam Lallana, with Oxlade-Chamberlain crocked.)

A couple of years ago I wrote about how long Liverpool teams had been together, with players at the club for varying periods of time; as a way of pointing out how fresh the "project" was. If you look at Liverpool's best team in the Premier League era – 2008/09 (86 league points and Champions

League quarter-finalists) – it was based on a core of long-term players: Jamie Carragher with 12 years in the team, Steven Gerrard with 11, Sami Hyypia with 10, and then Xabi Alonso with five, and Pepe Reina with four. They were all key players that season, and all had time to work together as a unit, for years on end.

Others, like Dirk Kuyt, Fabio Aurelio, Yossi Benayoun and Daniel Agger, were in their third season at the club or in the team – which is longer than six of the Reds' finalists in Kiev. And for all Man City's brilliance this season, it revolved around the long-term core of David Silva, Sergio Agüero and Vincent Kompany; and even Kevin De Bruyne, Nicolás Otamendi and Raheem Sterling were in their third seasons at the club. Liverpool's key-core is far more recently assembled.

In stark contrast to Zinedine Zidane's side, the majority of this Liverpool team only arrived (or made their debut) at Liverpool in 2016 or later, with two more arriving in 2015. Astonishingly, only Jordan Henderson has done more than four years at the club out of the entire squad available for the final. The average time spent at Liverpool for the Reds' starting XI was just 2.4 years, compared to Real Madrid's 7.1.

And when converted to 2018 money (Graeme Riley has just updated the very latest figures for our Transfer Price Index football inflation project, and inflation this season has been greater than I originally anticipated), using Premier League inflation as a guide, *Madrid's starting XI cost over £1 billion*. When adding the total of players introduced from the bench it makes for an eye-watering £1.3billion; more than three times as much as Liverpool's players cost. Those 14 players include three bought from the Premier League, two of whom were for world record fees.

(As a note here, Spanish inflation may work differently, but it's likely to paint Madrid as even bigger spenders, as, *relative to the rest of Spain* – Barcelona aside – they spend infinitely more than their rivals, not least in the past few years when the duopoly gained the biggest possible slices of the TV deal. The three buys from the Premier League accounts for over half of that £1.3bn in 2018 money.)

For further context, the most expensive Man United £XI on record (from a few seasons ago) tops out at £819.5m, while this season was also the costliest £XI Man City have ever posted (so Pep Guardiola's brilliance also required some spending). Chelsea under Jose Mourinho remain the costliest side English football has ever seen, with consecutive £XIs of £916.1m and £1.07billion in the mid-'00s, and that gave him a c.£300m advantage over Man United at the time; now at Man United he has a £60m disadvantage to City, although United's *squad* is currently the costliest in England.

The Premier League's wealth is now spread – albeit not evenly – across six teams, with the Manchester clubs hogging most of the expensive talent, and where Chelsea (who clearly used to hog the most) still a fairly expensive side, ranked #3.

In Spain, it's just Real Madrid and Barca who can pay the big fees and wages; and in Germany, Bayern have a monopoly. To me, things are veering towards a European super league, as too many domestic leagues are closed shops. Bayern, Barca and Real Madrid feed off anyone who dares challenge them, and as such, cannot ever realistically finish outside the top four. How long before they field B teams in their domestic leagues and their best teams in some European format?

But most of Madrid's spending is fairly historical; their biggest buys in the current squad – ranging from £107.9m to £336.6m in 2018 money – are from 2005, 2009 (twice), 2012 and 2013. A big bulk of their spending is wrapped up in six elite players, now aged 26, 28, 30, 32, 32 and 33.

The time at the club that Real Madrid's players can boast is incredible, *but only because they are the apex predator of European football.* No one steals their players. The same applies to Bayern and Barca, although Barca made a mistake in not factoring vast inflation into Neymar's buyout clause, and were suckered by the dodgy money of PSG; another club buying success on credit and bending the financial rules. Players tend not to want to leave these clubs either, as they play the biggest wages and compete annually in the Champions League. In Italy, the talent flows up to Juventus; winning seven titles in a row as their richest club.

Juventus, Madrid and Bayern (and until recently, Barca) are seen as these paragons of "knowing how to win", as if it's some great quality to have, but in truth they just hoover up the best players and then are the only clubs that can afford to pay their wages. And they win. It's no accident. And that experience helps them win again, and again. Little changes, even when they swap managers. In England, even the top teams can drop out of the top four because there are six contenders. Man United can match the wages of the other über-clubs, but have struggled to nail down a top-four place in recent times.

So it's not just Madrid's age but also their time spent together as a team that marks them out as almost unbeatable foes in finals. It's almost unprecedented.

Again, by sharp contrast, Liverpool's back four (and goalkeeper) had only been together for few months. Of those five players, only Dejan Lovren was a regular in the side before this season, while van Dijk, Robertson and Alexander-Arnold weren't even in the team (beyond a game here or there in the case of the latter two) in December 2017. Defences improve with time spent together, as it's the most choreographed aspect of football; so time will benefit these players, if kept together.

And given the average age, the team as a *whole* should improve. It genuinely feels as if something very special is brewing, if the team can be kept together.

Finally, to quote the great man himself, singing along with fans just hours after the final: "We saw the European Cup; Madrid had all the fucking luck; We swear we'll keep on being cool; And bring it back to Liverpool".

May's Results

02.05.2018 – (A) Roma 2 – 4
06.05.2018 – (A) Chelsea 0 – 1
13.05.2018 – (H) Brighton & Hove Albion 4 – 0
26.05.2018 – (N) Real Madrid 1-3

Post-Season Review

Paul Tomkins, May 2018
Back in mid-May we at TTT Towers (which, essentially, is just all of us in our own homes spread across England, congregating on a *Slack* channel) sat down to pen some post-season analysis.

Most of this section is shaped around analysis of the key players, but to start with there's also a look at some of the truly bizarre statistical quirks of the campaign, which saw unprecedented levels of *quantifiable* bad luck. (Even the Champions League final hinged on the underhand injuring of Mo Salah and a missed elbow on Loris Karius, both by Sergio Ramos.)

Statistical Quirks in a Black Swan Season

Paul Tomkins, May 4th, 2018
Earlier in the season (and indeed, in this book) I discussed TTT subscriber Tim O'Brien's version of the American statistical model, the Ratings Percentage Index (RPI), to highlight how unreliable I suspected the league table of being in October (after Premier League match nine, aka PL9), when Liverpool sat 9th. RPI is calculated by looking at the form of the teams played, to add some context to unbalanced fixture lists.

At the time of writing, with two league games to go, the table should now be a more 'honest' reflection of quality and consistency. So, how did RPI compare?

Well, if you took the league table from PL9, you'll find eleven teams who, seven months later (PL36), currently sit within three positions of where they were in the actual league table in October, with an overall average of 3.9

places difference. However, when comparing Tim's RPI from PL9 against the actual league table after PL36, no fewer than 15 teams sit within three places, for an average of 2.9 places difference.

At the time of writing Liverpool have risen from 9th to 3rd in the actual table, having been 2nd in the RPI table after PL9. In October West Brom were 13th in the actual table, but 20th in the RPI version – so Tim's model perhaps foresaw trouble for the Baggies that maybe wasn't picked up on at the time by the wider football public. The model also said that Everton under Ronald Koeman should have been 7th, not 18th, based on the difficulty of opposition faced, and that the few points they gathered were in essence more "valuable". To see them rise to 8th is merely realigning with reality for a team that spent big over the summer, and nothing particularly miraculous from Sam Allardyce.

Indeed, in the past I have written extensively about predicting team performance when compared against financial outlay; working with Graeme Riley to create the Transfer Price Index in 2010, from which we devised the metric of the "£XI": the average cost of a club's line-ups across a league season, when adjusted for inflation.

With near-identical results to the league table from PL9, the £XI rankings for the season have eleven clubs finishing within three places of their ranking, for an average of 3.9 position difference. (So the headline figures are the same, but the finer details of the results vary slightly.) In other words the finances present a reasonable guess at the final table, as does the actual league table with three-quarters of the season to go. But the Ratings Percentage Index is more accurate than the £XI and the league table at PL9, as it was in 2016/17.

To test this, I went back and compared everything to the first league table of the season, which should logically be very random indeed – although not *totally* random. After one game, both Manchester clubs were in the top three; but so were Huddersfield. Spurs and Arsenal were in the top six, as expected, but West Brom were 8th. Liverpool were 9th, and Chelsea 14th. Overall there were still ten clubs within three places of their position 35 games later, so only one fewer than the RPI and £XI models; but the overall average was that clubs were within 4.8 places, compared to 3.9 places from PL9 and £XI, and against 2.9 places from RPI.

However, where the financial predictor of the £XI comes into its own is in the top half of the table. If you look only at the top 10 £XI rankings, then its predictive power improves to within 2.6 places of expectations, whereas PL9 remains much the same as it was, at 3.7; while the RPI gets better still, at 2.3 places different to the league table in early May.

Look at the top seven, however, and £XI becomes the best predictor of how things will look at the end of the season, compared against the league table after PL9 and the RPI model. The average disparity between the £XI and the league table falls to just 1.3, with RPI at 1.9 and PL9 at 2.7.

In other words, the richest clubs gravitate to the top.

This is probably because the financial gulfs at the top are so marked compared to the differences lower down the table. For example, Southampton's £XI, at £100m, is only 5% greater than Crystal Palace's, at £95m. These two are the 8th and 9th richest clubs in the country, based on the cost of their selections, and with such a little difference it's hard to say which should be finishing above the other. But the two Manchester clubs' financial advantage over Liverpool is over 200%; their £XIs costing more than twice Liverpool's. Meanwhile, the Manchester clubs' £XIs cost over five times the amount of Southampton's; so if, in a way, the Mancunian pair are twice as likely to finish above Liverpool based on their wealth, they are five times as likely to finish above Palace, and twenty times as likely to finish above bottom-ranked Huddersfield, whose £XI averages out at just £26m.

This (like any other model) can never take into account all the external or unpredictable factors, like luck, injuries, fallouts, inertia, and the number of cup games played, as discussed at the start of this book. Remember: if a club like Liverpool, Arsenal and Spurs plays 20 cup games in a season, then something will most likely be shaved off the league points tally (and the tougher the cup games, the more damage it will logically do). If a club like Huddersfield plays ten cup games, the same will happen. Even the Rich Three could lose ground in the league if playing a lot of cup matches, although it usually takes around 25 extra matches to make a marked difference.

Paul Tomkins, May 31st 2018

Now that the league season is over I can sum up my extensive penalty analysis, based on the following: 16 seasons' penalty data (all penalties won and scored in the Premier League, listed by club) for all clubs; Liverpool's own penalty luck/bad luck since 1892 (yes, *1892*), as well as the clear trends in the club's penalty fortunes in the Premier League era; and analysis of *why* every Premier League penalty (for all clubs) was given in the past two seasons of the Premier League, and for this season, who won it (individual player/club), and whether it was home or away.

I will also present a series of actual probabilities – based on historical precedents – for Liverpool getting the kind of confluence of decisions that dogged this past season. It genuinely is incredible.

In addition, I have examined this season's home/away metrics in terms of what I will call "attacking intent" in the Premier League, to highlight how, I feel, referees almost exclusively compensate and favour the home side (a clear cognitive or situational bias); and do so pretty much everywhere but at the stadium where there's this big myth of one particular stand "winning" its club penalties.

Of course, it is also admittedly a myth that may have some basis in (distant) historical truth, back when the Kop was 24,000-strong, at a time when Liverpool were the dominant force in English football (therefore you suspect more likely to win penalties), and also, in an age when the referee's concern of "pleasing" fans was obviously the gigantic mass of people within a ground – before cameras made the TV/internet audience of billions the most important people to please. I would assume that referees in the old days were perhaps too generous to Liverpool at home, but that doesn't mean they should try to now make two wrongs into a right.

A lot of what I cover here is about biases, and accusations of biases, and how that then alters the enforcement of rules and laws.

Being biased is worse in the eyes of onlookers than being incompetent. So referees are under enormous pressure in the digital age to *appear* unbiased. This, in turn, creates a bending-over-backwards bias.

For years, the police all over the world would think that anyone who admitted to a serious crime was guilty of that serious crime; yet 20% of all convicts who were later exonerated based on DNA evidence had initially (or repeatedly) confessed to the crime. (Which isn't to count those who cannot prove their innocence.) The perception was that you had to be guilty to say you did it; the reality is very different, and relates to all kinds of pressures put upon that individual. The police had a bias towards believing what they wanted to believe, and eased suspects into parroting that narrative; interviewees who were honest were told that, no, they were *dishonest*, over and over, for maybe 12 hours straight. Funnily enough, in the end, to get out of the room, they said they did it.

The decision-making of law enforcement officers over the decades has also been swayed by racial prejudices; and there's the dangerous preconception that a woman "invites" a sexual attack based on how she dresses; plus the nonsensical idea that homosexuals are more likely to be paedophiles. Remember, this is *decision-making*, often (but not always) by people trying to do the right thing. It's only the accumulation of data that shows anything counterintuitive. Because people always intuit what *feels* right, not what *is* right.

And the more I watch football, the more I see the cogs turning in a referee's mind as he considers "how it will look" or how it will play out. You can see it at least 50 times in every game, with the different application of the law in higher-pressure areas of the pitch.

It seems less and less about just looking at something and weighing up only that evidence in the moment. Not least because the moment comes and goes so quickly; the difficulty of "seeing" something has been outlined over the past 50 years in the groundbreaking work of Daniel Kahneman and Amos Tversky; but which still hasn't fully entered the global consciousness.

But also because there's the clear need to appease home fans (unless there's already a *perceived* bias towards that home), or the need to consider – consciously or subconsciously – whether the player is a "diver", and what the managers might say after the game, and so on. They often take the path of least resistance.

If a foul takes place on the line of the area you can bet that even though it's *technically* a penalty, they will award a free-kick one inch outside. It's politically expedient. If a player is fouled but carries on running, the path of least resistance is to ignore it. There were literally dozens of examples of Mo Salah trying to stay on his feet this season rather than go down; until at Chelsea away he just threw himself to the ground, and got booked.

What I found so remarkable about the recent Arsenal vs Atletico Madrid Europa League semi-final was how the referee saw both of Sime Vrsaljko's fouls within the first nine minutes as bookings. And yet why this amazement, given that both were *clear* bookings? It's precisely because refs spend all their time weighing up the politics, the appearances, and fudge the issues. To hell with it being a big game; just make the decisions that the offence dictates must be made, without worries of "ruining the game" or accusations of secretly being a fan of the club your decision benefited. If it's in the first minute, and it's a booking, then book the player.

If decisions are borderline, then fudging is understandable. Not all judgement calls are obviously black and white. But when they are blatant, and the ref still fudges it because it's early in the game, or it's at the Kop end, or it's in a derby, or it's a player who was once booked for diving (or is/isn't "that type of player"), then it's damaging the integrity of the game.

And the data this season suggests that a) foreign players are treated more harshly than British-raised ones in terms of winning penalties; b) home teams are favoured beyond fair limits by referees, except when it's Anfield; and c) most big clubs are actually given far fewer penalties than many smaller clubs, as if referees know that they cannot be seen to favour the big clubs. Once I was aware of this fact I noticed how many fans of smaller clubs said "big clubs get all the decisions"; but it's a fallacy, albeit one that probably drives a reverse bias.

With the exception of Man City, those big clubs – who obviously play the most attacking football – are getting far fewer of the penalty calls than the more defensive-minded minnows (whose British players win a high percentage of their calls; although indeed, as does Man City's Raheem Sterling, and as did Michael Owen and Steven Gerrard in Liverpool's history). And even then, Man City won fewer penalties than Crystal Palace.

Smaller clubs, with the exception of Man City, comprise the top seven penalty-winning teams this season – but Liverpool (who ranked 10th in terms of penalties won) come off worst overall from the Big Six by being the most harshly punished at the other end too; and of course, most often punished in front of the Kop.

Remember, Liverpool won zero Kop-end penalties this season in around 1,800 minutes' of Premier League football; Spurs won two in one 20-minute spell. And that's not to say Spurs' two weren't penalties – I think both were, based on the general application of the rules, albeit with the first following a ludicrous interpretation of the offside law. But more blatant incidents have not been given to Liverpool at the Kop end all season long, based on those same laws. By the final game of the season at Anfield, against Brighton, there were no fewer than three blatant penalties that occurred right in front of the referee, but as all were at the Kop end he just looked on, blankly, as if wondering how it would look to give a penalty as the Kop (rightly) demanded one. In the previous home game, against Stoke, there'd been another blatant handball at the Kop end, but again, the referee acted as if he didn't see it. If it were just three or four decisions, you could write it off. But it's well into double figures on the what-the-fuck scale.

Liverpool also had a legitimate goal disallowed at the Kop end late on in the game against West Brom because the ball accidentally brushed Dominic Solanke's hand; which, if the referees insist on penalising (and this one seemed to do so based only on West Brom's protests, given the delay), then you have to start giving far more *blatant* game-changing handballs as well, such as the stonewallers seen against Stoke and Brighton in successive games. It can be conclusively said – without doubt – that Solanke had to have known less about it because it deflected off his thigh, whereas the decisions that should have gone in Liverpool's favour were from right-sided crosses (not fast-moving shots) that travelled 30 yards in the air and connected with an oddly outstretched arm.

Then there was Mo Salah in on goal at the Kop end against Newcastle, and literally booted up in the air by Jamaal Lascelles, and nothing was given. It's hard to see a more blatant free-kick and red card, but the officials just acted like nothing happened. It was beyond odd.

Again, I can only conclude that referees are terrified of looking like they bow to the Kop's power (the power of which isn't even seen that frequently in the league these days), and visiting managers from within English football (Paul Lambert, Mark Hughes, David Moyes, *et al*) still mention it before and after almost every game. The narrative is clear: Liverpool will be given some dodgy penalties, because perhaps they were in 1979. The data says: Liverpool are given a ludicrously low number of penalties at Anfield.

Again, if you happen to support someone else and don't want to hear my rose-tinted sob stories on this issue, then I can't do anything about that; however, if you are Liverpool fans, then you need to cut Jürgen Klopp some slack based on what is, *definitively*, the worst season in the club's history for penalties won and conceded in comparison to goals scored and goals conceded. It's not so much a black swan as someone daubing the Liver bird in the darkest paint possible. Then there's my data - going back to 2002 – that shows that Liverpool clearly tend to win more penalties when they have a greater number of British attacking players in the side (forwards, wingers, attacking midfielders and overlapping full-backs), and then win fewer penalties when the players in those positions are foreign.

The cognitive biases of referees pops out of the data like a beacon, and shows trends that I think are worrying; human decisions where *prejudice* (and not necessarily *agendas*) play a part. The issue with just observing something in isolation is that it can seem sporadic; data draws everything together. Liverpool not getting a decision at the Kop end is just how it goes some days, until you analyse it and it happens *every* game. At a conservative estimate, the balance of bad decisions for/against Liverpool has cost the club 10-12 points.

If penalties are totally random, then why does the league average remain, season after season (including this season), at 2/3rds won by clubs at home? – even though the playing metrics (based on analysing every single Premier League game this season) in no way favour home teams by such a clear margin? Possession, shots, goals (*including* penalties!), touches in the opposition box are all between 51% and 57% in the home team's favour, with an average of 54% from all those metrics; yet the home penalty awards are 66% ... unless you're Liverpool, where it has dropped from that to-be-expected 66% in the 1990s to ... 41% over the past five seasons.

Yes, this also means that Liverpool therefore get a greater percentage of penalties away from home than anyone else. But there is no clear reason for referees to do that; there is not a provable away-team bias, after all, in the way that I can show that referees give c.10% more home penalties than the flow of the play and the balance of attacking would suggest is merited. The 'homer' bias is very much real, Anfield aside. (Weirdly, the richest three clubs get an even greater percentage of their penalties at home. Man City get 75%.)

The logical conclusion would be that Liverpool win a fair amount of penalties away, and an unfair number at home, given that there's no incentive for various referees to regularly be generous to an away team, as there's no myth about how Liverpool always win penalties at, er, Burnley.

Unless, of course, refs are consciously making up for not giving Liverpool decisions at Anfield, which could be true. And yet while that would mean I have no grounds to complain, it would also show that refs are kinda just making this shit up on the fly. They can't go around being purposefully stingy in half the games and purposefully generous in the other half, as that would be utterly ludicrous. And it ignores that, aside from Simon Mignolet not getting sent off at Stoke for a red-card offence, Liverpool haven't exactly seen much luck away from home, either; in the Man United game at Old Trafford, Gary Neville thought Liverpool should have had two, maybe three penalties. They got none. Sadio Mané was booked for diving at Crystal Palace even though he was booted on the ankle in the box. Danny Ings was bodychecked at West Brom by a player not following the path of the ball, just the path of the man. That said, Liverpool did win two penalties away, and only one at Anfield; so overall, the home gripes are the greatest.

My desire with all of this is to see referees give decisions on *merit*, not on whether someone has already been booked, or if they think foreign players are more likely to dive, or if they think Liverpool get too many penalties at home due to the Kop baying for blood (as if other terraces/stands *don't*). I'd happily stand against VAR, and its slowing down of play, if I thought refs were just making *human* errors, but prejudicial thinking is beyond the scope of what I find acceptable. Unfortunately, it's too highbrow for the average football discussion.

As Daniel Rhodes noted on TTT, after I asked him to look deeper into the referees' union's frequent claims about getting an unbelievable 98% of decisions correct (something that is clearly beyond human ability):

"As demonstrated in my own video analysis, it seems like the Professional Game Match Officials Limited (PGMOL) inflated their own figures by including literally every decision (active or not) taken by an official, even if they are 100% obvious what the decision is. For example, Player A kicks the ball out of play (uncontested). If you asked 100 random people off the street who kicked it out and which team get the throw-in, 100 people would confirm the correct decision. Crucially, the vast majority of decisions are like this, based on the PGMOL's parameters. However, once you dig down and present a panel of independent officials with a big enough sample of decisions, and break those down by difficulty, then you can see the results are very, very different.

"The open access studies found that only 36% of 'difficult' decisions were accurate, compared to the 94% of 'major' decisions claimed in the Premier League. Across the rest of the research accuracy figures ranged from 55% to 85%, and intuitively that feels to me more realistic."

In fairness, Liverpool won an insane amount of penalties (12) in 2013/14 (but of course, were insanely good going forward, scoring over 100 league goals); and yet 75% were awarded away. Liverpool's metrics are always better at home, whether the team is flying or crawling, attacking or counterattacking, but for years it is almost never reflected in home penalties; apart from in European competition, where a Liverpool penalty at Anfield arrives four times as frequently as a home penalty does in the league. Which is just bonkers.

I will give the referees some benefit of the doubt, and not evoke crazy conspiracy theories. But by almost every metric available, this has been the most remarkable season for Liverpool in terms of getting the rawest of deals from referees. Indeed, compared against all other 126 seasons in the club's history, this ranks the worst; so it's not even a case of saying that refs are against Liverpool (as the club has obviously had favourable seasons in the past), but that this season, either by luck or due to biases, referees have been wearing the kit of the black swan.

Of course, by stating something like this – even with data – you immediately lose all credibility, because only nutters rant about refs, but we have to address the cognitive biases and external pressures that referees consciously and subconsciously process in those moments before pointing to the spot (or ignoring what looks clear to everyone else). The application of the rules has drifted, to the point where most referees ignore certain offences, but others don't. It can't be a fair system with such a variation. It's not even about how common sense can kill consistency: there seems a totally varied application of the rules.

However, on a general trend, it seems that referees in England don't give handballs anymore. Last season three times as many handballs (18) were given as this season (six), while there were fewer penalties overall (78 to 106), with a fall of 26%. But a fall of 66% on handballs is *remarkable*. A handball penalty in the Premier League now arrives as rarely as one almost every two months. To get a handball now the opposition has to literally punch the ball ... unless it's one of those few occasions when they don't. It seems so arbitrary.

(As an aside here, Liverpool had the black swan rarity of conceding handball penalties in both games against Roma, and neither were remotely deliberate; although the one deliberate offence – the "hands in unnatural position" of Trent Alexander-Arnold – was not given against the Reds. Liverpool's luck in Europe with big calls certainly went against them in those two games, albeit after the Reds got one or two fortunate decisions against Man City in the quarter-finals. In Europe it has balanced out a bit better, but in the Premier League it certainly has not.)

The notion that the spectre of VAR – and the new anti-diving laws – have affected the referees seems logical; although penalty numbers do fluctuate from season to season, from over 100 some seasons to around 80 in others. However, this is the lowest number of penalties awarded in a league season in 13 years. And remember, the offside laws have been tweaked in that time to favour the attacker, so you'd expect more goalmouth action these days, given that attackers are less likely to be flagged offside before/when entering the box, and thus more penalties occur.

Of course, it's weird that Man United won two of the league's six handball decisions this season (33%, albeit on a small sample), both of which were at Old Trafford. That said, they can argue that they were only given one "foul" penalty; albeit while themselves only conceding a single penalty this season (but when there were *at least* two clear calls, according to Gary Neville in commentary during the Man United vs Liverpool game, and then soon after, the Ashley Young near-assault on Sergio Agüero in the Manchester derby). United only scored 68 goals as well – a relatively low amount compared with City and Liverpool – meaning that they were not a particularly elite attacking team, despite the talent.

My hunch (expressed on this site before Andrew Beasley found the penalty data for last season) was that referees have started making (or not making!) fewer decisions, and the data backs it up.

In the age of VAR, diving crackdowns and internet rage, it's easier for them to not give a decision (that is therefore still a *mistake*) than it is to make a conclusive call about something that is 99.9% certain. Non-calls are, as noted, still mistakes, but somehow not as "real" as giving calls. The penalty not given is somewhat fluffy, and can be put down to fan paranoia; the penalty given is something solid.

But actually, Liverpool's one VAR game was so different to every other Anfield (domestic) home game this season proved my point: the referee on the pitch was prepared to give Liverpool *nothing* against West Brom in the FA Cup, but the VAR official 200 miles away, in a quiet room, gave Liverpool a rare Anfield penalty (outside of European competition) and disallowed a WBA goal. It was the "luckiest" game of the season at Anfield in that respect – but it wasn't *luck* at all, because it was a referee unable to ignore the video evidence, forced to confront the hardest of evidence; no fudging was possible. Even after the VAR flagged it as a foul on Mo Salah, we saw footage of the referee having to see it played over and over, at least 10 times, because he could bring himself to give it.

Liverpool not being given (at least) two stonewall penalties against Man United at Old Trafford or two at home to Brighton (again, all four were nailed-on according to Gary Neville), or the one at West Brom when Danny Ings was taken out in the most blatant fashion imaginable, or the clear kick on Sadio Mané's ankle (before he flopped over) at Palace, or the handball by the Stoke defender in front of the Kop, or the way Jamaal Lascelles booted Mo Salah in the air when he was in on goal, are more nebulous than Liverpool being given seven penalties and Newcastle having a man sent off. Penalties not given are not officially recorded, so we have to search our memory banks for them. It's probably just Liverpool fans whining, as ever.

Of course, other clubs will have had clear penalties not given, too. But almost every other Premier League club either were awarded more penalties, or conceded fewer, than Liverpool. Yet Liverpool were the 2nd-best attacking side, and the 4th-best defensive side. Indeed, to score this many goals and have such a bad penalty "balance" is unheard of.

Since 2002/03, when the available data commences, 17 teams have scored 80+ goals in a Premier League season. (Six teams also did it between 1992 and 2002, but I only have the full penalty data for all clubs since 2002/03; and I certainly don't have the pre-Premier League data. But football did definitely exist.)

Those teams averaged 88.5 goals (a fraction more than Liverpool's 84 this season), and won an average of 7.5 penalties each per season.

None of those clubs won fewer than three in a season, and Arsenal in 2004/05 join Liverpool as the only other club awarded that rock-bottom figure of three. On the range of 3-12 penalties that each high-scoring team achieved, Liverpool this season rank as the joint-least-favoured team by referees. (If it was a tie-breaker, Liverpool would come off worst: three conceded by Arsenal in 2004/05, six by Liverpool this season.)

And of course, remember that some of these teams only scored 80+ goals *because of penalties*. If you remove the penalties *scored* (not the penalties won) from their totals – to give an indication of open-play scoring ability - you get just 12 teams to have scored 80+ goals without the aid of spot-kicks. This season's Liverpool are obviously one of them. The average number of penalties won by the remaining 12 also remains at 7.5, more than twice Liverpool's three in 2017/18.

And talking of penalties conceded, if you look at all those teams, none has also conceded six spot-kicks in a single season, apart from Liverpool this year. These 17 teams have an average of +4.3 in terms of penalty awards for/against, firmly in their favour. Out of the 17 teams, only Arsenal in 2009/10 (aside from this year's Liverpool) are in negative figures, at -2; while the Reds ended this campaign at -3.

Now, if this is not refereeing bias, then it shows that Liverpool had "black swan" luck. But there are just too many anomalies with how referees interpret events for the sport to be in any way fair and balanced.

To conclude this piece, here are some actual probabilities:

- 11.8% chance of scoring 80+ goals in the Premier League and getting only three penalties (since 2002).

- 5.9% chance of scoring 80+ goals in the Premier League and ending with a tally as bad as -3 in terms of penalties for/against. (Only one team has done that since 2002: Liverpool this season. So prior to this season, the likelihood was 0.0%)

- 0.6% chance of Liverpool Football Club getting so few penalties in relation to the number of goals scored *versus* penalties given away in relation to number of goals conceded. This is based on 126 years' worth of data.

- 10% likelihood of being awarded more penalties away from home than at home over a 5-year period.

Followed by some guesstimates:

- 1% chance of Liverpool winning fewer penalties at Anfield in a season than Spurs.

- 0.3% chance of Mo Salah winning zero Anfield penalties in the league, when considered in relation to the number of touches he had in the opposition box (27,567,553, give or take a touch or two) and the number of goals scored.

- 0.2% chance of Liverpool winning as many penalties at Anfield this season as Everton in relation to the number of touches in the box.

Combined chance of all these things happening: 0.001%....

Player Analysis

Mo Salah, by Paul Tomkins

PFA Footballer of the Year. Football Writers' Footballer of the Year. Premier League Footballer of the Year. Golden Boot winner, with a new record of 32 Premier League goals in a 38-game season, scored at a pro-rata rate better than Andy Cole and Alan Shearer managed when scoring 34 in 42 games in the 1990s.

Record-breaker, and Egyptian pharaoh – nay *demigod*.

But for all the goals, Mo Salah isn't a spree finisher – he's a *consistent contributor*. He is also not a regular penalty taker, although assumed that duty later in Liverpool's season; which was an unusually barren one for the Reds getting spot-kicks anyway. While all goals are in essence equal in the record books (the record books that tally up the totals and say nothing of their beauty and importance), there are cheap goals and there are valuable goals. If a player frequently only ever scores the final tap-in in low-key routs, then is he contributing as much as someone who keeps opening the scoring, or keeps equalising, or keeps notching the winner? Of course he isn't.

Indeed, what about scoring in *big* games? Salah did it, time and again, as I will go on to list.

It's not just the quantity of Salah's goal, but the *spread* of them, across so many games; against teams good and bad, and in games big and small. Of the 44 scored, 40 had a clear impact on the result, if we discount any goals scored beyond the establishment of a three-goal margin (and Liverpool had 4-0s, 5-0s and two even 7-0s). Not single one of them was scored against lower league teams or European part-timers.

Salah scored in 34 different games in the season, breaking Ian Rush's club record, and also broke the Premier League record with goals in 24 different games.

In preseason Salah looked like he could get goals; and indeed, it surprised Jürgen Klopp just how good a finisher his new buy was. Salah already seemed on the same wavelength as Philippe Coutinho, but a day before the opening game of the season at Watford, the Brazilian went on strike. Liverpool's most creative player had gone AWOL. Klopp and his colleagues were instantly plotting on ways to get Salah into more central positions from open play.

Salah scored the majority of his goals with his left-foot, but he is also a fine header of a ball, even if he's not going to win many aerial duels. He had a spurt of finishing with his right foot, just to show he could do that too; and indeed, his shot accuracy is better with his right-foot, but this has to be down to the "safer" types of shot taken with the old pros called their "swinger" (he didn't go for elaborate finishes on his weaker side and just concentrated on hitting the target.)

Forty-Four Goals

Salah opened his account with a tap-in – -or rather, a bundle-in – after Roberto Firmino lofted the ball over the goalkeeper. It turned out that the other Brazilian was more important to Liverpool, and that the act of pressing – -which Klopp always insisted could be a team's best creative weapon – -was the way forward. The deftness of Firmino's lob meant that Salah just had to get a foot onto the descending ball as it dropped close to the goal-line and he'd edge it into the net.

His second was equally simple – and he must have started to think that he just had to stand in the inside-left position and the ball would magic its way onto his foot; this time, Gini Wijnaldum's shot rebounded off the post and the Hoffenheim keeper was faced with what was essentially Mo Salah taking a penalty against him from six yards out. Salah looked offside, but the full-back on the other side was playing him on.

But it was Salah's third goal that showed he's not just a poacher; picking the ball up 25-yards from the halfway line – *in his own half* – -as, incredulously, Arsenal's Hector Bellerin tried to win a challenge as the Gunners' last man. It's hard to recall many other goals like this in the history of football above the under-7s age group. Salah entered into a sprint with the jet-heeled Bellerin, who was ten-yards behind by the time he knew what was happening, and as Sadio Mané, Emre Can and Francis Coquelin all tried to influence the play; a scene that was best summed up when some wag took footage filmed at pitch level and added the Benny Hill theme song. Salah slows up as he approaches Petr Cech but he's still well ahead of the chasing pack, and he slots a low finish into the corner.

At this stage of the season Salah was heavily favouring his left foot, and also missing a fair few good chances – -which, of course, most top strikers do from time to time. He got some luck against Sevilla, with a heavily-deflected strike from distance that probably wouldn't have troubled the keeper. But it's also fair to say that he hasn't relied on deflections, or taken a slew of penalties, to boost his tally. (And he certainly hasn't claimed any goals that rightfully belong to his teammates.)

The home draw against Burnley saw the first of what became more of a trademark goal later in the season – running from the inside-right channel across the face of the keeper to the inside-left channel, before firing back across goal. Even though Salah ends up in the position of a traditional left-winger, the inverted role allows a better body shape when shooting having run from the opposite flank than it would to the old days, when a left-footer played on the left. Cutting inside onto the stronger foot is the main advantage of the inverted role, but it's easier to strike back across the ball with the favoured foot – as Salah does here – -than to dribble infield from a left-sided starting position.

To run at goal with the ball on the outside foot means any curl when firing across the keeper – unless using the outside of the boot (more common these days but trickier) – takes the ball away; if the shot is to beat the keeper it will probably also curve wide of the far post. The only main options are to curl into the near post – as Salah did against Arsenal (but where the angle of the run was fairly straight) – or to blast it.

And by running across the goal – from one flank to the other – -there's always the option to shoot early, or to shoot centrally; meaning the keeper is never quite sure where and when the shot is coming from. Any faints to shoot can bamboozle not just the keeper but any lingering defenders. And at all times the ball is in a good position to get a shot away, right up until the point where the attacker goes too wide; but Salah seems to find some kind of dinked finish even if the angle looks too tight, and defenders – seeing the need to cover behind their keeper – are still left helpless on the line.

These are not the kinds of goals that someone like Ian Rush – the Reds' last 40-goal hero – used to score; although Rush developed his own unique lateral movement – from the full-back across to the centre-back, and then beyond – to develop a style of breaking the offside trap (he'd run across the back four, already on the move for when the through-ball was threaded his way). When he arrived, Salah was not considered a "natural goalscorer", even though his numbers were increasing in Italy.

Indeed, at Basel he had to stay behind and have finishing coaching. He got into double figures each time, but his pace was a big factor. But any notion that Salah is winging it (in the faking sense) can be dispelled by his international goals record: 33 in just 57 games, heading towards the World Cup. And while you get some oddly prolific internationals who are, at best, decent goalscorers domestically – to name Robbie Keane, Peter Crouch and Milan Baros from Liverpool's own 21st century history – it is surely a sign of world-class quality to get 30+ for your country by your mid-20s, and to land a 30+ league season in one of the world's top leagues; and to do so largely without penalties (he took two, missing the first), is extra-impressive. And all this after scoring 34 goals in Italy in just 83 games, while often stationed as a more traditional winger.

Next came a remarkable far-post header against Leicester, where he met Coutinho's deep cross almost on the touchline, but somehow managed to power a header past Kasper Schmeichel at his near post. He'd scored headed goals in preseason, but this was evidence of someone who – like Robbie Fowler in his pomp – could find special direction and power when rising to meet a ball, even if he wasn't going to win many aerial duels.

Then came too goals against Maribor in a 7-0 shellacking, the first where he found space behind the Slovenians' defence on the inside-right channel, and opens his body up for the simple left-foot curled finish – something he'd already tried several times in the season, but often found too little power and the shot too close to the keeper, having telegraphed where he would put it due to his body shape. His second of the night came as he and Firmino collided when trying to tap the ball into an empty net; the Egyptian getting the telling touch.

His 9th, away at Wembley and with Spurs in control of the match, was a run down the inside-right channel and a slightly scuffed right-footed shot that bounced in off the post due to its accuracy. It could have been the turning point in the match, but Spurs reasserted themselves and went on to win 4-1.

Maribor were the victims again as Salah reached double figures, glancing in a vicious Trent Alexander-Arnold cross. Number eleven came at West Ham, as he kept pace with Sadio Mané and, as Alex Oxlade-Chamberlain peeled to the left, Salah took the ball twelve yards out and as he had done against Arsenal, hoodwinked the keeper by tucking it neatly – -almost unnaturally – -into the near post; Joe Hart clearly spreading himself for the aforementioned open-body-and-curl-to-far-post finish. Salah's 2n goal that day was very Rush-like: far side of the area, taking a sublime touch to get the ball under control – and out of his feet – before lashing a low arrowing drive into the far corner.

Numbers 13 and 14 came against future team-mate Virgil van Dijk, whose rustiness after "doing a Coutinho" in the summer was clear to see; in addition to missing the whole second half of the previous season with injury. Coutinho himself was the creator of the first, with a lovely outside of the foot pass; and again, this was a Rush-like goal, with Salah moving across the centre-backs to stay onside and move into space, and hitting a first-time shot back across the advancing keeper. The second of the game was special: the first time he showcased the John Barnes-esque curler into the far corner from a wide angle outside the box.

Number 15 was his third goal against the Big Six, as Oxlade-Chamberlain cleverly nudged the ball into Salah's path, and the Egyptian took one touch to take it out of his path and, with Chelsea players closing in, slid it under Thibaut Courtois.

By the time Salah hit 15 it already felt like he'd scored all types of goals, but his 16th was a far-post volley at Stoke, where he rifled Sadio Mané's cross back with stunning accuracy and pace. Number 17 swiftly followed – and he'd only been on the pitch a few minutes, as a sub – as a partial recreation of that bizarre goal against Arsenal, although this time Stoke's Erik Pieters was only 30 yards from his own goal when he did a "Bellerin". Salah latched onto the poor touch, but showed his growing composure by allowing the keeper, Lee Grant, to blink first; slotting the ball alongside him to the far post as Grant anticipated the near-post finish produced against West Ham.

At this stage the only predictability about Salah's goals were that they would probably be left-footed, and that there'd be one in almost every game. And then, just when the opposition thought that at least they could keep him on his weaker right foot, the Egyptian scored his 18th of the season, against Spartak Moscow at home, in the second 7-0 drubbing handed out in the group stages of the Champions League. The ball fell onto his left-foot nine yards out, and as two of the Russian team's defenders slid in to block the inevitable left-foot shot, Salah dragged the ball onto his right – finding all kinds of time in melee – to shovel a shot into the roof of the net.

Number 19 was when the goals started to defy belief. It helped that it was against Everton, but the way he shrugged off the defender outside the box on the flank, pirouetted into the box with a drag-back, deceived the next defender with the Diego Maradona feint – looking like he will go to his own left side but dragging the ball almost unnaturally onto his right – was sensational. Even though he'd gone to the right of the last surviving defender – Salah had the time and space to strike the ball with his left-foot in a natural shape; and, without having to contort himself to use his preferred foot, curled a beauty into the far top-corner.

While he'd scored some excellent goals, he was now combining several aspects of his game to score *sensational* goals. The pace, skill and determination made him hard to stop in the box, although an apparent bias against foreign players (as suggested by my research with Graeme Riley this season) when it comes to being fouled in the box meant that illegal methods were resorted to, and at times successful, with no domestic penalties awarded by a referee on the pitch for fouls on Salah in the box since the opening game at Watford; the only other domestic penalty – against West Brom in the FA Cup – requiring the intervention of the Video Assistant Referee, to point out something Liverpool fans could see in almost every game.

Indeed, at this stage his 19 goals were all from open play; no direct free-kicks, and no penalties, having missed the only one he'd taken, as the Reds managed to harm their goal tallies by missing four by the midway point of the season; Firmino missing two and the penalty hero of last season, James Milner, failing as well.

The landmark of 20 was hit with another sensational goal, and more Maradonaesque magic. Picking the ball up outside the right-edge of Bournemouth's area, he deceived his marker by using his left foot to dribble the ball onto his right side. He would left the full-back for dead with his trademark acceleration, but the defender was grappling with the Liverpool no.11. With the angle too tight for a shot, and with the defender all over him, and with the ball on his right, Salah used his weaker foot to bring the ball inside, and just as Nathan Ake closed him down, he nipped the ball away and swung a low shot into the far corner.

And he wasn't even halfway through his scoring streak for the season. With the pace and height of Michael Owen, the heading ability of Robbie Fowler, the wing-play of John Barnes and the finishing of Ian Rush, Salah showcased skills from some of the club's best-ever attacking players, and – in terms of a single season output – eclipsed them all. Indeed, Salah had more assists than many of the top creative players in the country, to go with the goals. While he has yet to show longevity – something you cannot do after one year at a club – his peak is as good as anything we've seen.

While he has fewer similarities with the two best forwards the club has had in the past decade or so – Fernando Torres and Luis Suárez – he has eclipsed their best tallies for the club. Two years ago, the thought of Daniel Sturridge missing games left Reds nervous (if not surprised), but by the point Salah was hitting 20 goals for the season – mid-December – Sturridge was preparing to be loaned out, such was his superfluous nature with the all-round brilliance of Roberto Firmino, the mercurial Sadio Mané and the ruthless and versatile Salah.

Going back to Roger Hunt, the club has had an incredible lineage of goalscorers, with Ian Rush, in 1980, starting a trend that almost never seemed to abate: John Aldridge, John Barnes (albeit like Salah a nominal winger), Robbie Fowler, Michael Owen, Fernando Torres, Luis Suárez, Daniel Sturridge and, of course, Sean Dundee. (One of these kids was doing his own thing; one of these kids is not like the others. All the hail the Dundee, and his refusal to be stereotyped!)

Not even Christmas, and Salah was on a roll (something he learnt in Switzerland?). Arsenal were the victims again, for no.21; in the luminous orange kit and channeling his inner Johan Cruyff, Salah picked Firmino's pass up 40 yards from goal, jinked right and, when looking like he would jink to his left, took a shot instead; grazing off the knee of Shkodran Mustafi, for only his second deflected goal of the season. (Unlike the first, this may have been going in anyway.)

Next came Leicester at home, and a ball into Salah's feet 30 yards from goal allowed him to turn Harry McGuire – who was too tight, and frankly, all over him – and wriggle free; such a hold had McGuire had than when Salah skips away he has his red Lycra undershirt dangling over his hand, like some useless appendage. And for the third time in the season, Salah opened up his body to curl one into the far corner and purposefully dragged the shot to the near post, rocketing past a bemused Kasper Schmeichel. It's a skill that makes his finishing utterly unpredictable. If keepers ignore his body shape and anticipate the pulled shot at the near post then they may make an easy save;

but in doing so they just make the more natural finish – -the curler past them – -all the easier.

In football, if you can go either way you instantly put doubt into the mind of an opponent, and that split second's hesitancy is all a top player needs. The only game where Salah became too predictable was away at Manchester United, where, double-marked, he cut inside every time; although United players also used illegal tactics to stop him as well.

Number 23 was another weaving run – not across 50 yards of the pitch, but in the tighter spaces across the face of the area – as Salah, taking in an outrageous back-heel flick from Mané, evades a sliding tackle from Ben Chilwell, drops his shoulder to turn Daniel Amartey into a living statue, and yet again wallops a reverse shot under the goalkeeper. (Harry McGuire looks befuddled throughout the whole move.)

And okay, by 23 goals you'll have expected to see most types of finish from a player who – upon winning the PFA Player of the Year award a few months later – was called by one BBC Sport texter (presumably sent from a secure institution) as "one dimensional"; but no, no.24 came from fully 45 yards, as Manchester City's keeper Ederson came flying out to beat Mané to the ball and instead just whacked it to Salah. Salah takes a touch that takes the ball out of the centre-circle and lofts a curling shot that is so perfect it's well above Ederson's reach but drops precisely onto the goal-line, equidistant between the two posts. In other words, there was zero danger of it going over and zero danger of it going wide. (Afterwards, the ground staff should have checked to see if there was a sixpence on the spot.) If it was golf it would have been a hole in one, albeit where the ball lands straight in the hole without bouncing.

This was Salah's 5th goal in Big Six clashes, and in one of those – away at City – the Reds had played most of the match with ten men and, as a result, in retreat. (The only Big Six team he failed to score against was Manchester United, and so that's something to look forward to. It took Ian Rush 12 years, so hopefully he's quicker than that.)

Number 25 came courtesy of a bad touch by West Brom's fellow Egyptian, Ahmed Hegazi. Salah lashed home a low first-time shot.

Number 26 provided yet another type of goal – a penalty! Having missed his previous penalty – against Huddersfield at Anfield – Salah insisted on taking the spot-kick in the return fixture at the Kirklees Stadium, and sent the keeper the wrong way. This was in January, and would be the last penalty Liverpool won all season.

Number 27 came against Spurs at Anfield, latching onto a poor back-pass to almost repeat his goal at Wembley, and shoot low to the far post past Hugo Lloris. Number 28 – his 7th of the season against the Big Six – came later in the game, and looked to have stolen the Reds a dramatic win, shortly after Spurs equalised in a manic end to the match (the visitors winning two penalties in the process, and thus being awarded more league penalties at

Anfield this season than Liverpool. The second penalty, shortly after Salah's goal, enabled Spurs to snatch a draw at the death).

Perhaps the best of the lot, #28 saw Salah pick the ball up on the right of the area – as he had against Everton – and bamboozle several Spurs defenders to the point of them almost begging for mercy. He turned this way and that, as he accelerated away from four opponents; and as Lloris and Eric Dier closed in on him, scooped the ball over the keeper for a Suárezesque piece of improvisation, after a Suárezesque dribble in a tight space. Not even six months into the season, Salah was visibly improving; running the gamut of finishes, and as often as not creating his own shooting opportunities.

Salah's 29th came at Southampton, courtesy of a frankly pornographic half-back-heel, half laser-guided pass by Firmino, in one of the best one-twos you could ever wish to see. Salah's finish was first-time, and one of those where he opened up his body and ... shot as expected (but where shooting to the unexpected side had become half-expected).

Salah's 30th – away at Porto in the 5-0 drubbing – equalled his wonder-strikes against Everton and Spurs, and this was almost a goal deserving of its own unique category: the ball rebounding straight at him in that favoured inside-right channel after James Milner's shot flew off the post, and although Salah didn't know much about his first touch – the ball almost literally hit him – he then scooped the ball up on the volley, headed the ball past the keeper, then, at the precise moment the ball fell and kissed the ground, swept it into the net past the despairing dive of the last defender. As the ball hits the net Salah stops, as if he can control time itself.

Then came number 31, created by Oxlade-Chamberlain digging out a clever pass just as he's falling over, and Salah simply turns and reverses the shot into the far corner; arrowed through the defender's legs. At this point he was cruising.

Oxlade-Chamberlain, with a burst of pace and some fine awareness, created Salah's next, at home to Newcastle – the ball played to the Egyptian in space in the box, leading to a cool finish; albeit a bit scruffy compared to the previous 30, in that the keeper almost saved it with his leg.

Number 33, notched against Watford, drew Salah level with Suárez and Fernando Torres' best seasons in a Liverpool shirt. By the end of the game – Salah's one and only act of gluttony – the new Liverpool idol would be on 36 goals.

It began with another inside-right dribble, and having just failed to go on his outside at all against Man United, Miguel Britos was certain Salah was going to do the same again. But Salah jinked right, not left, and Britos' world seemed to collapse, along with his legs, as Liverpool's maestro left Britos and the covering defender for dead before rifling a low right-footed shot past the keeper. Even though Salah rarely strikes the ball with any great conviction on his right side, the times he takes the ball onto that side of his body only further confuse defenders.

Salah then added a simple tap-in – again with his right foot – from a sumptuous Andy Robertson cross; and while almost unmissable, the moving ball coming across the striker from the flank is often the hardest to deal with, at least in terms relative to how easy it looks. (When strikers miss open goals, it's often when taking a first-time finish from a ball from the flank, where too much contact or too little contact can take the ball away from goal, and where the greatest challenge is often to get set up for the finish with good footwork; any hesitation – especially when trying to read the bounce of the ball if it skips off the surface – and it can often end up with the wrong type of contact, or maybe a complete miss of the ball.)

Number 35 completed Salah's first-hat-trick for the club, and is another contender for his finest. In the snow of a mid-March blizzard (hardly African weather; I was freezing amidst the -8 windchill in my old season ticket seat in line with the area), he picked the ball up once again on the inside-right channel, albeit only a few yards away from the penalty spot. Four Watford defenders faced up to him, and just when they thought Salah was going to shoot for a right-footed hat-trick he turned sharply, leaving half the visiting team's defence in the Main Stand. As a sliding tackle came in, Salah somehow managed to take the ball away with a quick shift, but it was behind him – and he was off balance – when he decided to shoot. It made no sense; a wonderful piece of improvisation. He barely got any power, as it was impossible to get any backlift whatsoever, but the slow poke took it past the bemused Orestis Karnezis in the Hornets' goal.

His 4th of the evening was rifled in from close range after Danny Ings' shot was well saved by Karnezis. Salah's first goal glut was complete, and he got to keep the icy match ball.

Thirty-seven arrived at Crystal Palace; a late winner to kill the home side's spirited display. The ball was directed across goal from Robertson, and as ex-Red Mamadou Sakho vainly stretched to intercept, Salah just waited for the ball to arrive; slowing time as he had begun to do earlier in the season – like an assassin in a science fiction movie – with a touch and a finish as composed as you could ever wish to see.

The next goal – no.38 – was not too dissimilar, although the magnitude of the match was far greater. Roberto Firmino prodded the ball to Salah in Manchester City's six-yard box and, in front of the Kop, Salah again took a touch, dissolved time, and lashed the ball into the net. City's bright start in the Champions League quarter-final disintegrated, and the Reds piled in two more quick goals, to effectively kill the tie.

Of course, at their own ground, City could easily score three goals against anyone, so the tie certainly wasn't over; and when they scored after just two minutes, the comeback was on. But the Reds hung on, and in the second half Salah broke onto the loose ball in the area, skipping around the flailing Ederson, before cooly dinking the ball over the despairing Nicolas Otamendi on the goal-line. For someone with a clear passion and with the warmest of smiles, the Egyptian appears – at the vital moments – to have ice in his veins. Nine of his goals came against the Big Six.

Number 40 arrived at home to Bournemouth: a wonderful improvised header to loop Alexander-Arnold's arcing cross over a bemused goalkeeper; yet another type of goal from the Reds' no.11.

Number 41 for the season was also number 31 in the Premier League; equalling the record for the competition (since the rebranding in 1992) for a 38-game season, and including only one penalty. It came at West Brom, and was yet another run across the face of the goalkeeper before cooly lofting the ball into the net. If Salah had a trademark goal – amid myriad styles – then it felt like it was going to be kind he scored versus Arsenal in August; running from distance with the ball to beat the keeper in a one-on-one. But instead it's the clever run across the face of the goal, and the reverse shot – either past the keeper, or with the keeper already dummied and stranded – into the net just before the angle gets too wide.

In amongst Salah's impressive nine goals against the Big Six – almost a quarter of his goals – were two in the Champions League quarter-finals. By half-time of the first leg of the semi-final he'd already bagged two more. Cometh the hour, cometh the man; and yet Salah had come twice within 45 minutes. Anfield was in a state of utter delirium.

His 42nd was pure Barnes: positioned at the conjunction of lines on the right-side of the area, he seized the space and curled the ball into the top corner in the way that 'Digger' did so often in the late 1980s and early '90s (recall those goals against Everton and Aston Villa, albeit if memory serves, when Barnes was using his weaker right foot!). Barnes' goal in the fateful Mersey derby was important, but Salah's here was vital. He had already tried with one of his weaker efforts – too close to the keeper, who happened to be Alisson Becker, the Brazilian no.1 linked with a move to Anfield in the summer. But even standing on Boris Beckers' shoulders, and maybe with Ted Danson reprising his role in the sitcom Becker – standing on a ladder on the goal-line – they would not have stopped this goal.

Salah's 43rd was another ridiculous act of coolness and accuracy. It came from a lofty Virgil van Dijk clearance, with Salah cushioning the dropping ball with first-touch delicacy on the halfway line, into the path of Firmino. The Brazilian beat his man, albeit with a slightly fortunate ricochet, and Salah made a run off the ball, into the inside-right channel, as if he was going to go outside the left-back. His former teammate presumably expected him to continue that run, but instead he darted inside, into a traditional centre-forward's position; a movement made possible at Liverpool by Firmino's constant vacation of that space, in contrast to the Egyptian's role at Roma, which was to supply the centre-hogging Edin Dzeko.

Firmino rolled a beautifully weighted pass into Salah's path and, with Alisson sliding out to the edge of his area, Salah dinked it over him. What made it all the more aesthetically pleasing was the way Salah tickled it into the net; the ball trickling beyond the reach of the desperate defenders. His first goal of the night was recorded at 68mph, but this was audaciously just above the speed that a defender could run. It was almost disrespectfully arrogant, although he showed great class in refusing to celebrate. (In the second half he turned down chances for his hat-trick by setting up his teammates for goals. Some luxury, that.)

And then … nothing. At least, not for three games. *Three games!* Looking a little jaded, and possibly spooked – as well as being double-teamed in sapping heat – he struggled to make an impact in Rome, and at another previous club, Chelsea, in the penultimate game, with a glaring miss in the interim, at home to Stoke. He was in on goal early on, dinked the sprawling keeper in exactly the same way he had Roma's Alisson, but the ball somehow drifted harmlessly wide. It seemed to suck the life out of the stadium, and indeed, Salah himself. Liverpool drew, and then lost at Stamford Bridge, meaning no goals for the Egyptian and no wins in three games for the Reds.

But he wasn't finished. With Liverpool needing to avoid defeat on the final game of the season to qualify for next season's Champions League, the Reds were rampant at home against Brighton, with Salah opening the scoring. Dominic Solanke flicked a clever ball 'around the corner' (what corner?) to Salah, and he lashed a low shot right into the bottom corner. Boom! Goal number 44, and no longer did the Reds have to beat Real Madrid to qualify for 2018/19; although Chelsea lost 3-0 at Rafa Benítez's Chelsea (oh the sweet irony!), and Liverpool could have lost 15-0 to Brighton and still qualified.

And, it transpired, 44 was where it ended; Salah's Champions League final curtailed by some serious foul play. Even so, it was at least 24 goals more than most of us were expecting.…

Sadio Mané, by Andrew Beasley

If you're a fan of popular music, you will probably be familiar with the concept of the difficult second album. The theory goes that bands who have incredible success with their debut LP then struggle to replicate the quality of their first album with their sophomore effort. As the adage goes, you have your whole life to write your first record, but then just six months while touring and promoting to pen your second.

For me, the whole notion is a crock. Take a look back through music history, and you'll see that any band worth their salt gets better through time. If your first album is the best you ever manage, then you weren't very good after all. You just fluked your way to writing a handful of songs so good that people overlooked the filler on side two.

During the early months of 2017/18, it felt a little like Sadio Mané was apparently struggling with his difficult second album. The Senegalese international had enjoyed a stunning debut campaign for Liverpool, deservedly picking up the club's Player of the Year and Players' Player of the Year awards at the annual end of season shindig.

He directly contributed to 21 goals, by scoring 13, assisting seven, and winning a penalty (remember when Liverpool used to do that?). But for missing seven matches for the Africa Cup of Nations, and eight thanks to a late season injury, he'd have surely got close to 30 goal contributions.

So what went wrong this season? Nothing really; Mohamed Salah just went very, very *right*. Lest we forget, when the Egyptian was signed he was viewed by most Kopites as simply the pace for the side if Mané was absent. It seems crazy to say that after the absurdly strong season Salah has enjoyed, but that was certainly the prevailing view in August.

It's not even that Mané started the season particularly slowly. If you include winning the free-kick from which Trent Alexander-Arnold scored at Hoffenheim, Liverpool's number 19 directly contributed to a goal in each of the first five matches of the season.

However, it was game number six where the wheels came off. Or more accurately, Mané's boot went into Ederson's face. His luck wasn't helped by picking up an injury shortly after he returned from suspension either. In the two months between Liverpool's trips to the Etihad and London Stadiums, Mané started just three matches.

By this point, the Kop had a new darling. Never mind that Mané was contributing to goals as often as he had the year before, Salah was blowing him (and the rest of the Premier League) out of the water.

Not that numbers are everything, of course. Mané's football hasn't been as easy on the eye this season, and his decision making has often been poor in 2017/18. The wasted opportunity to put the Reds 2-0 up in the Merseyside derby at Anfield was probably the most memorable example, but it's far from the only one.

But then we should cut him some slack too. Having excelled on the right last season, he was moved to the left to accommodate Salah. Yes he's played there before, but not at Liverpool, and so it meant establishing relationships and link ups from scratch with players on the other side of the pitch.

With hindsight, we should've expected a drop off in his finishing too. In his first year at Liverpool, the former Saint scored eight of his 11 clear-cut chances, for a conversion rate of 73 percent. That's the highest rate of any Red to have attempted at least ten (excluding penalties) in the last seven seasons. Mané's conversion record of 50 percent across his two years on Merseyside is still very good, but a downturn after such an impressive start was always inevitable.

While he scored fewer in the league, his expected goals per 90 minutes increased, as did his expected assists. Mané's impressive Champions League campaign mustn't be forgotten either, and he was the only Liverpool player to score in both legs of the semi-final.

Perhaps the most interesting aspect of his 2017/18 campaign is how his role has changed within the team over time. Mané is perhaps the player who has flourished most since the departure of Phillipe Coutinho, and that's reflected in his statistics. The Senegalese star has almost become the team's number ten over the last few months.

A heat map of his chance creating locations from 2016/17 reveals a high proportion of them were on the right hand side of the penalty area. Yet the majority this season have been from central areas just outside the opposition's box.

Mané has become more creative in the absence of Coutinho too. He created at least three chances per match in 10 Premier League games in 2017/18, but only three of those were games in which the Reds' now departed Brazilian started. Assists are a flaky stat which can be very erratic, but five of Mané's seven in the league this year came in those 10 games.

It's a similar picture regarding his overall involvement too. Sadio attempted at least 40 passes ten times this season, but only once in a game where Coutinho started. Has Mané replaced him without Liverpool having to sign someone? It's too soon to make such a claim definitively, but right now it's not looking an entirely fanciful notion.

When all is said and done, the former Southampton man never went more than three starts in a row without either scoring or assisting a goal this season. If this was his difficult second album, it was definitely more *The Bends* than *The Second Coming*. I for one can't wait for 2018/19, as I reckon Mané might deliver a *Parallel Lines*, a *London Calling*, or perhaps even a *Forever Changes*.

Andrew Robertson, by Anthony Stanley

You've probably all had a look at the tweet. A few words typed on a phone screen as a sense of desperation and frustration descends with a tangible force. A couple of months after Kenny Dalglish had been sacked by a footballing giant, the other side of the sport's sphere was laid bare as Andy Robertson used the hashtag #needajob as he noted that 'life at his age is rubbish without money.' He was eighteen years of age and was about to sign for the Scottish Third Division side, Queens Park.

Less than six years later, 'Robbo' is about to play against Real Madrid in a Champions League Final, two weeks after scoring Liverpool's 84th and final league goal of the season. As rags to riches stories go, it's almost a trite cliché; not far removed from an absurdist '90s footballing flick starring Sean Bean. But this is, of course, real life, and Andy Robertson is living out his dreams in front of an adoring Anfield crowd.

And the left-back is absolutely *adored*. There's something about his astonishing story that just gets Kopite juices flowing. In an age of the superstar footballer, as far removed from the normal working Joe as can be imagined, here is a young man hewn from the working-class granite of Scotland, a lad who is absolutely determined to make the most of his opportunity, who has known the heartache of being dumped (by Celtic) and of relegation and is all the more thrilled with his current situation. And we have all jumped onboard with Robertson, have gloried with every tackle, every lung-busting run, and every fiery performance.

But this tale is made all the more remarkable by the fact that Robbo has arguably been the best left-back in the Premier League; certainly since Christmas. Originally it all looked rather odd. He wasn't exotic enough to please the masses; Hull not exactly a fashionable shopping place, the fee almost inconsequential. Robertson came in for his first Liverpool appearance at home to Burnley and seemed to do well enough. But there was a nagging doubt about his defensive nous, and some pondered that his habit of swinging a cross in at the earliest opportunity was not conducive to Klopp's footballing *modus operandi*. The Scot then vanished from first team football for a while as Alberto Moreno, who can count himself unfortunate to be the sole Liverpool victim once Robertson grabbed his chance, looked steady and fluid in the early months of the campaign. Klopp and his assistants, though, surely had a fair idea of the former Dundee United defender's capacity to learn, and one can imagine the training sessions as Robertson's footballing intelligence and ability to soak up instructions became more and more apparent. By the time he was thrust into consistent action, he was more than ready. Robertson has lit up the Premier League form a position that has long been a troubling one for the Reds and there is now genuine hope that he could be a custodian of the left-back berth for a number of years.

If there's any doubt that this kid fits Liverpool perfectly, that we haven't got an absolute bargain, and that his current skill-sets aren't perfect for Klopp's vision, just have a quick look at the Man City home game last January. Watch Robertson run, almost snarling in a frenzy, as he presses all the way to the City keeper. From *left-back*. That was probably the moment the defender truly arrived in Kopite's consciousness and he hasn't looked back since.

Trent Alexander-Arnold, by David Fitzgerald.

In some ways, I think the best way to evaluate how far Trent Alexander-Arnold has come over the course of this season is by looking at the two performances he has had in midfield in the recent games against Stoke and Chelsea. First and foremost it shows that Jürgen Klopp trusts and rates him. These were not throwaway games and the chances were that Liverpool's fortunes, both in creating and conceding chances, could be in the young man's hands (or hopefully feet!).

So how did he do? It's easy to remember his errors towards the end of the campaign – there was one in the Chelsea game where he lost the ball just in front of the area and I'm sure we all thought –'there's a goal'; it was reminiscent of the bad old days, but fortunately it didn't happen. There were also the uncharacteristic miscued crosses and shots. However, who remembers all the one touch passes and flicks that were good enough to open the door for attackers, but who weren't able to seize the opportunity?

I think what you have to remember with Trent is that virtually every match he's played – even the so called 'off days', for LFC there has been a lot of good stuff. He's been amazingly consistent and reliable. He's never disintegrated after an error and he always strikes a mature balance between enterprise and responsibility. What Pepijn Lijnders said about him at an early age was he has an incredibly capacity to listen and take onboard advice and instructions.

That's why one of the most memorable sub plots of this season was when he had the 'bad day' at Old Trafford; when he was targeted as the weak spot, (although they would have done the same with Joe Gomez); but then back he came with an incredible sequence of games, including his man of the match performance against City where his defensive shut out of Leroy Sané – as City almost obsessively sought him out – may well have made the difference for the Reds' progression in the Champions League.

Anyone can see he's talented – from his free kick at Hoffenheim to the fabulous passing that's been a vital component in the 11 matches this season where Klopp's men won by a three-or-more goal margin – but what is less obvious is the grit with which he tackles his own development. He never gets fazed. Being so young and inexperienced, he's always going to encounter new situations and make mistakes, but he always responds with renewed determination and application. Application to what the coaches are telling him and his belief in how he can contribute to the team.

And that's what it's all about for Alexander-Arnold; talk about LFC DNA, his celebration with the fans in Roma was well, fanatical! Personally, I hope he keeps honing the right-back role rather than moving to midfield. His skills, working in tandem with Andy Robertson on the opposite flank (and using the space Mo Salah vacates), are so complementary to the whole team shape. It's not so much that he wouldn't be marvellous in midfield given the chance to blossom there – it's more that we'll never find a better all-round right-back in my opinion – they are so rare.

But whatever happens position-wise, mark my words, there is so much more to come from him. As a youth-team player, he would romp the length of the pitch *á la* Ryan Giggs, and score spectacular goals on a regular basis. What we're seeing right now is him in the learning phase, where he's trying to cement his place and to some extent curb his natural flair. But just wait until he's done that and then allows himself more freedom to express his skill and eye for goal.

Roberto Firmino, by Daniel Rhodes

Clube de Regatas Brasil is where Roberto Firmino Barbosa de Oliveira was first spotted – in what must be the most appropriate and apt example of scouting in the history of football – *by a dentist*.

Many would later speculate Bobby Firmino was in fact created in a dungeon on the outskirts of Jürgen Klopp's hometown – with the help of

Victor Frankenstein – as the purpose-built, perfectly-suited, pristine-toothed, pressing machine that leads Liverpool's devastating attacking front three.

Klopp asked of Victor: "With my tactical system, I'll need someone who can tackle like Beckenbauer, work and run like a Volkswagen, but has the flair, intelligence and creativity of Pele, as well as the finishing ability of Muller. Yes, it sounds impossible, but we must try! Boom that machine!"

Of course it would be unfair to compare any part of Firmino's game to any of the above legends, because they're the peak, but when trying to genetically engineer human beings you need to aim for best. And in our no-look finishing forward we have the best in the business when considering all aspects of the game. He's the best all-round football player in the world. And until this season, barely anyone noticed. In fact, the general consensus was we should buy in a "proper number nine" to replace him.

Forwards are measured solely on their attacking productivity by the vast majority of fans, and rightly so because ultimately it's their job. In that sense, the 2017/18 season was quite extraordinary for Firmino – with 27 goals and 17 assists – or a goal involvement every 93 minutes. Only Mo Salah's all-time record breaking season (every 70 minutes) was better in Liverpool's squad.

Nevertheless, on *The Tomkins Times* we've had a subscription to the scouting software Wyscout for a couple of seasons and in preparation for this article I watched his "best bits". No filters, let them decide. No hardcore dance music to accompany it ... Four of the first five clips were defensive duels.

In the opening clip he wins the ball back on the centre circle against Chelsea and starts a counterattack; next he's on the edge of his own area against Man City and pokes the ball away just as Sterling is about to shoot; minutes later he gives De Bruyne a three yard headstart before chasing back and winning the ball cleanly as the Belgian approached the Reds' penalty box, starting another counterattack; finally, he dispossessed Otamendi – after prowling like a lion in the wild waiting for his prey to make one slight mistake – before tucking the ball away and feasting on knocking the Premier League 100-pointers out of the Champions League. Of course there was also the delightful control and perfectly-weighted throughball for Salah's second goal in the first leg against Roma at Anfield, as well as the poachers' tap-in – which had a hint of the no-looks about it – from a Salah dribble and cross; then there's the headed fifth goal, getting on the end of James Milner corner in front of Virgil van Dijk – no mean feat – and sending Anfield into Champions' League ecstasy.

There's so many moments to be described, so many presses, tackles, drag backs, no-looks, dribbles and flicks but across the season Klopp – a manager who always prefers to focus on the team – has had quite a bit to say about him, so in the spirit of Firmino's gnashers, the final word is straight from the horse's mouth:

"Roberto is a player who is always involved in all offensive and defensive action. He has a natural skill. He doesn't think too much, he's an instinct player. He can play in nearly all offensive positions. He has the physical ability to be in the centre and that's the toughest job physically as you are involved on both sides. When we are a bit deeper, he's involved. He always has a job to do.

"Roberto delivers, delivers and delivers. He doesn't score all the time, he is not always brilliant, but if he is not brilliant then he works like a horse. It's very important that you have this kind of stability there. But it's well deserved – everything. He's a fantastic football player.

"You see him in training and think 'what a work ethic, what an attitude', and he brings it on the pitch as well. He never rests. You have to pull him out, you have to tell him 'come on, stop, sit here, calm'.

"I hear in the stadium [Anfield] that people like him – good idea – but I have no real idea if anybody thinks he's not important or whatever. I'm not too interested, to be honest. I'm pretty sure if I give the players the opportunity to have a free choice in training [to] build teams by themselves Bobby is one of the first they would pick.

"[It's] nice to have him around – better to have him than in the other team. That's maybe the best thing you can say about a football player."

Afterword

By David Fitzgerald, May 31st, 2018
Do you ever wonder, are we all in denial? All the time?

Sports are the ultimate manifestation of a willing march over the edge of a cliff. Like lemmings we are bound to the belief that winning is all. We commit life-endangering exploits and risk depressive mental illnesses, all in the name of victory. We invest our whole beings into belief systems that are a) totally vulnerable to moments of random happening, b) repeatedly put us into situations where the odds are massively stacked against us and c) most perplexingly, accept the tag of losers even when we know the values we hold dear may have been cynically manipulated to alter the result.

I mean, given those circumstances, why do we care so much about the shitty result?

And then, when one in fifty times we get lucky, we take it as the green light to rinse away our tears and start all over again. It's fucking crazy! People say you are in denial if you can't accept a loss, but I suggest that the denial is most evident in the mindset where winning is all and losing equals less than nothing.

I wonder, is it because we have an innate chemical nature which needs to continually confirm who is the strongest? The most powerful? And it's only by continually hurling new contestants to compete against the behemoth (I've just watched a *Thor* movie!) that we can make sense of a world that rewards the most powerful.

The weird thing is not that this may be the true nature of the world, but that we are so committed to believing that this natural order can be upset! I mean, the plot of virtually every Hollywood movie revolves round this precept. And in football, we open ourselves to the most acute, potentially life-changing pain of loss in this extraordinary pursuit of strong feelings of euphoric victory. It truly is bizarre. It *is* the human condition, but I don't really see that that is a reason to benignly or even gleefully accept the way it is. I can see that there is truth in what Brené Brown says that there are greater rewards from opening yourself up emotionally, rather than being overly self-protective, but if anything, that makes the massive question mark about why emotional affect is so important to us even more nonsensical. We are too accepting of the shovel-loads of emotional shit that get thrown on us in the name of belief, in my opinion.

I'm writing this after Liverpool's Champions League defeat to Real Madrid and I'm really determined to catch my own emotional reaction before those feelings have subsided and the cooler analytical mind starts to make sense of what happened. I'm angry about what I *feel* is injustice. I don't *know* it, but it's impossible not to *feel* it. It's very hard to believe that the world's most successful defender didn't employ the dark arts to take our most influential star player out of the game. But there's that word again, 'believe'....

Mo Salah and Sadio Mané pray to Allah before the game, Jürgen Klopp and quite a few others have a word with God, and if the state of Dejan Lovren after the game was anything to go by, his belief system was well and truly crushed. Then there was Loris Karius, who was clearly focused on more

269

lofty notions when his brain farted twice or the magnificent Gareth Bale, expressing his belief in the Nietzschian superman. Not to mention the bat-crazy, self-obsessed Cristiano Ronaldo, who provided my favourite moment of the evening when the poor poppet's belief he deserved a goal was stymied.

And of course the fans get drunk on belief. Klopp's turned us from supporters into believers and the role that's played in our recent success has clearly been a crucial one.

So what is this thing we call *belief*? I'm reading this fascinating book by Antonio Damasio called *the Strange Order of Things*. He is basically a philosophical biologist/neuroscientist who has written a book in which he attempts to chart the origins and significance of *feelings* and the role they play in human culture and actions. He writes:

"Feelings contribute in three ways to the cultural process:

1. as motives… a) by prompting the detection and diagnosis of deficiencies and b) by indentifying desirable states worthy of creative effort.
2. as monitors of the success or failure of cultural instruments or practices.
3. as participants in the negotiation of adjustments required by the cultural process over time."

If that doesn't describe people's fascination with football matches and the vast majority of what we discuss on TTT, I don't know what does. Essentially football only exists as a mechanism for us to test our feelings and that can only be done by creating an *emotional imperative*. As far as I can see, that is what belief is – it's a reaching out of body and mind and soul and everything to test the waters and its nature is composed of feelings.

The emotional narrative of the match that I just watched was that our hero, Salah, was the living embodiment of a sizeable number of the world population's belief system for a seriously significant amount of time. His profile and demeanour was capturing people's imagination in a way that challenged categorisation. I'm tempted to say the phenomenon went beyond football, but I'm not sure that's really true, because football is, in Damasio's terminology, 'a cultural instrument'. It built up during the weeks leading into the game and in a dreamlike way it continued into the first part of the match. Liverpool were riding the wave. Then *bang!* The surge of feeling that swept through the stadium after his enforced departure was tangible and it clearly affected the players too. I don't think it's really possible to get past the enormity of what happened – it was the pivotal moment of the story. It doesn't even matter what happened afterwards, it was no longer a fair contest. It's fucking Greek tragedy of the highest order – Achilles dragging Hector in front of the walls of Troy.

For us Liverpool fans it's a total sickener, because, like the 2013/14 run-in, it was one of many nearly moments when we essentially failed to win because of some very harsh twists of well, what's the word? – *rubbishy things happening*. It's a familiar feeling. In fact, it's becoming so familiar that I'm seriously beginning to consider what I want out of this whole football following shebang.

The thing is, I don't feel inferior to Madrid. I just feel unluckier. And what's more, I don't respect them because they win by cheating, both financially and in some of their players' actions. But put through the prism of us (certainly anyone involved with LFC, but also the wider public) 'as participants in the *negotiation* of adjustments', maybe this great drama can edge us towards a better world. Of course the fairytale ending aspect of the narrative was exploded, but you can't say that the waters were not tested. Ramos's villainy now stands taller than any fictional baddie and his behaviour is there as a marker for what we might want to 'adjust'!

But you know what? I don't want to care anymore about winning old big ears! Or the Premier League, or any of it. What would be much better would be to become more sophisticated about what football *is*. The culture of celebrating winning trophies over all else is incredibly crude. I can't actually see anything that I don't like about our football team. They were brilliant tonight and they've fought like tigers all season.

The world is fixed – our emotions con us into feeling loss; that we should own something, deserve something before it's a reality, and I guess in football that's a good thing or we wouldn't be arsed to try really hard in the first place, but in many ways I'm glad the season has ended this way. I don't want to feel bitter and I want to enjoy my football, but not at the cost of being duped into a false belief that there is a level playing field out there. Real Madrid are a bunch of rich bastards who, just like Man City, win by having more resources. Full stop. Liverpool can't bring on Bale to win a game when our best player is scythed down. I don't want to feel 'Real' Madrid style, I want to feel reality and savour its subtleties.

The Karius errors were created by emotion and the emotional situation was created by Salah going off. (As well as the emotion of being elbowed in the head moments earlier.) It's all connected and we're all complicit in creating that situation. We're playing a game, but we're also playing a game with our emotions. Sometimes the intensity is kind of revolting and it's just not playful. It can be sad, but it doesn't need to be brutal and it's a good thing that we are trying to move away from that. It can be a very rough game and if it gets too rough (like it possibly did today) it's not fun anymore. Who knows, maybe the hype about Salah caused that extra hint of violence in a fearful Ramos?

Karius himself even played well, *generally* – it wasn't like he was weak and wobbly like Mignolet has been on occasion, giving them a sniff; his were complete mental aberrations in the context of his wider performance. I do think it's tough in that whereas Karim Benzema and Bale tried their luck because experience has taught them it's worth it, Karius, who is a relatively young keeper, was surprised because of his inexperience (and possibly also by a Ramos elbow). We all knew experience would probably count but this was pretty jammy. Obviously we want a keeper who doesn't have those kind of aberrations and there's no point in making excuses for him, in part because, like Joe Hart, he now has unwanted high profile baggage which is now even more likely to draw attention in big matches.

However, Liverpool under Klopp will seemingly always play in this high intensity way, so I think it's important to ascertain to what degree it was about experience or we may never end up with a keeper capable of learning from his mistakes.

Liverpool did enough to draw in my opinion, and two of their goals were freaks. I don't think I'm even going to allow myself to be disappointed. The world is what it is, and Liverpool FC is as fantastic as I ever remember it being. At times, back in the glory days, it was more like Real Madrid and to some extent people hated us with good reason because we were the unassailable, rich bastards!

This particular Liverpool team, under Klopp, with its emphasis on character, patience and loyalty, has a great set of values. There is real integrity there and it's a joy to watch them testing what is possible with that unique approach. There's so much more to life than mindless victory. I'm not saying I don't like winning or don't get euphoric, but I'm officially giving up on senseless domination.

Real Madrid, you can shove the cup up your royal arse!

TTT Benefactors

Adrian
Agnar Lavik
Aiden Halloran
Alan Raleigh
Alkesh Dudhaiya
Allan Høy-Simonsen
Andrew Argyle
Andrew Chow
Andy Coles
Anthony Partridge
Anthony Rodenhurst
Anton Black
Arun Butcher
Ashok Kelshiker
B Wright
Banerjee Saugato
Benjamin Cottle
Benji Howell
Bernd Schorr
Bijin Benesh
Boo Soon Yew
Brian Davis
Brian Dolphin
Chong Sze King
Chris Bracebridge
Chris Tang
Christine F Andrade
Christodoulos Christodoulakis
Christoph Tung
Christopher Bruno
Christopher Sewards
Claus Ulrich Dahlfelt
Damien Parsonage
Danielle Warren
David Evans
David Gilleece
David Miller
David O'Reilly
David Perkins
David Ryan
Deena Naidoo
Dennis Lindsey Laurie

Donald Rock
Eamonn Turbitt
Edward Robinson
Francis Tan
Gareth McMahon
Gary Fowler
Gary Wilson
George Ebbs
Gina Hoagland
Glenn Perris
Gøran Schytte
Greg Vinikoor
Guy Parr
Haluk Arpacioglu
Hong Kheng Tan
Ian Hopkinson
Ilan Shaw
Iyad Zahlan
J C Penton
J F Nolan
James Kelly
Jason Ball
Jason Inge Charles Rowe
Jason Ng
Jassim Jamal`
Jesper Marcussen
Joe Power
John Clarke
John Goldie
John Gordon
Jon Arnold
JonasIuul
Jonathan Bolton
Jonathan Sowler
Joseph Aung
Karapiah Tamilarasan
Kay Zat L
Kelley McDowell
Kinsley Ransom
Knudseth
Kostadin Galabov
Kris Barber

Laurent Sampers
Lee Hammond
Lee Smith
Leifur Geir Hafsteinsson
Leon Aghazarian
Leon Snoei
Li Guohao
Lim Fung Han
Lindsey Smith
Lodve Berre
Mike Begon
Michael E
M Hajialexandrou
M R Dancey
Marc Samuels
Marius Røstad
Mark Cohen
Mark Jeffcoat
Mark Jefferson
Mark Wise
Markus Topp
Marret Abraham
Martin Cooke
Martin McLaughlin
Matthew Beardmore
Michael Cheyne
Michael Fong
Michael Sum
Michael Thomas
Michael Williams
Mohammad Al Sager
Mohsin Meghji
Neil Gold
Neil O'Brien
Niall O'Harte
Nick Hall
Norman Hope
Omar Arnason
Panchapagesan Arjun
Patricia Jill Adamiecki
Paul McCormack
Paul Morgan
Paulus Adhisabda
Peter Barber

Peter Cooke
Peter Doyle
Peter J Robinson
Peter Short
Peter Verinder
Peter Vranich
Quinn Emmett
Richard Harrington
Robert Sangster
Rolf Hoel
Ronny Knutsen
Rupert Eve
Ryonadai
S Ramsey
Sacha Pettitt
Sam Henderson
Santhanakrishnan Periathiruvadi
Sergio Trevino
Sim William Teck Sin
Simon Barrington
Stephen Anderton
Stephen Capel
Stephen Rowland
Steve Lucy
Steve McCarthy
Stuart Lloyd
Suzanne Wiseman
T P Stringer
Thomas McCool
Tim Collins
Tom Nygaard
Torbjørn Eriksen
Tristan Wyse
Vidar Kjøpstad
Waleed Alsager
Wally Gowing
Waqas Kaiser
Western Ivey
Will Acworth
Yasser Zayni
Yau Choi Yeung

Printed in Great Britain
by Amazon